Several theories and conceptual frameworks in political science, legal scholarship, and sociology address issues of governmental authoritarianism, abuses of power, and corporate crime and professional deviance. The theory of societal constitutionalism offers social scientists an opportunity to isolate instances of social authoritarianism, which is defined as arbitrary exercises of collective power by private organizations and institutions within a modern civil society. The author argues that by distinguishing analytically between whether social order within any organization, institution, or sector of a society is based on actors' demonstrable social control or on their possible social integration a nation-state's susceptibility to social authoritarianism can be isolated empirically.

Bringing this distinction to the literature and to research, the theory developed in this book leads to a critical reappraisal of the findings of comparative politics and also the findings of the sociologies of law, professions, and organizations and occupations. Research findings in these fields that have hitherto appeared unrelated are now revealed both to explain historical shifts in a nation-state's direction of social change and to predict contemporary shifts. For instance, certain practices by physicians within hospitals, by chemists within corporations, and by lawyers before the bar may now be seen to reflect and contribute to shifts toward greater social control and susceptibility to social authoritarianism. The theory also provides the means to examine whether these practices can be found either historically or currently in particular nation-states, whether they are present, for example, in the United States or Japan as well as in traditionally authoritarian states such as the Soviet Union, Brazil, and Argentina. The author argues that the presence of social authoritarianism is independent of whether an economy is market-based or centrally controlled or of whether Western cultural traditions are institutionalized rather than Eastern or Third World traditions.

The Arnold and Caroline Rose Monograph Series
of the American Sociological Association

Theory of societal constitutionalism

See page 367 for other books in the ASA Rose Monograph Series.

Theory of societal constitutionalism

Foundations of a non-Marxist critical theory

David Sciulli

Department of Sociology
Texas A&M University

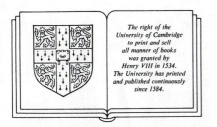

The right of the
University of Cambridge
to print and sell
all manner of books
was granted by
Henry VIII in 1534.
The University has printed
and published continuously
since 1584.

Cambridge University Press
Cambridge
New York   Port Chester   Melbourne   Sydney

Published by the Press Syndicate of the University of Cambridge
The Pitt Building, Trumpington Street, Cambridge CB2 1RP
40 West 20th Street, New York, NY 10011, USA
10 Stamford Road, Oakleigh, Melbourne 3166, Australia

First published 1992

Printed in the United States of America

Library of Congress Cataloging-in-Publication Data
Sciulli, David.
    Theory of societal constitutionalism : foundations of a non-
Marxist critical theory / David Sciulli.
        p.   cm. – (Arnold and Caroline Rose monograph series of the
American Sociological Association)
    ISBN 0–521–41040–1
    1. Political sociology.   2. Social control.   3. Authoritarianism.
I. Title.   II. Series.
JA76.S376   1992
306.2–dc20
                                                          91–15690
                                                              CIP

A catalog record for this book is available from the British Library

ISBN 0–521–41040–1 hardback

Contents

Chapter 1. Introduction: societal constitutionalism as critical
      theory   1
    1.1. Limits of comparative research   1
    1.2. Two issues of societal constitutionalism and an
      illustration   11
    1.3. Societal constitutionalism as critical theory   15
    1.4. Acknowledgement   17

Section I. Conceptual foundations of societal constitutionalism   **21**

Chapter 2. Social integration and social control: the importance
      of procedural normative restraints   23
    2.1. Social order and social control   23
    2.2. Social control in the literature   27
    2.3. Conceptual limitations in political sociology?   33
    2.4. Implications of the concept of social integration   37

Chapter 3. Liberalism and the Weberian Dilemma: from
      restraints on government to restraints on civil
      society   40
    3.1. Implications of rationalization: drift toward
      authoritarianism   41
    3.2. The Weberian Dilemma as negative liberalism   43
    3.3. Unmediated drift as "rationalization"   45
    3.4. Can the Weberian Dilemma be resolved?   46
    3.5. Illustration: "professional integrity" and limits of
      Weberian sociology   51

Chapter 4. Conceptual foundations of societal constitutionalism:
            from internal restraints on government to external
            restraints on drift   54
            4.1. Four analytical distinctions and four institutions
                 of restraint   54
            4.2. The importance of institutions of external
                 procedural restraint   56
            4.3. Four institutions of restraint: from liberalism to
                 societal constitutionalism   59
            4.4. Social integration: again, a preliminary definition 83

Section II. **Origins of the analytical distinctions and conceptual
             foundations: retracing steps taken by Habermas,
             Fuller, and Parsons**   **85**

Chapter 5. Societal constitutionalism's grounding against
            relativism: from Weber's legal positivism to
            Habermas's communication theory   87
            5.1. Taking stock and looking ahead   87
            5.2. Habermas's critique of Weber and later legal
                 positivism   90
            5.3. Habermas's alternative: communicative action or
                 procedural reason   96

Chapter 6. Societal constitutionalism's threshold in practice:
            from Fuller's legal theory to societal
            constitutionalism   107
            6.1. Procedural legality as irreducible threshold:
                 Fuller's contribution to the social sciences   109
            6.2. Three foundations of societal constitutionalism:
                 procedural grounding, procedural threshold,
                 and procedural formation   121

Chapter 7. Societal constitutionalism's organizational
            manifestation, I: voluntaristic action as a distinct
            concept   131
            7.1. The importance of voluntaristic action   131
            7.2. Parsons's point of departure: the normative or
                 nonrational   132
            7.3. The distinct concept of voluntaristic action   134
            7.4. Three meanings of voluntaristic action   144

Contents

Chapter 8. Societal constitutionalism's organizational
            manifestation, II: from voluntaristic action to
            collegial formations   150
            8.1. Again, the possibility of social integration   150
            8.2. The organizational expression of internal
                 procedural restraints   159
            8.3. The collegial form of organization   164
            8.4. Preliminary proposals for orienting empirical
                 research   171

Section III. **Implications of the analytical distinctions and
              conceptual foundations**   **181**

Chapter 9. Procedural institutionalization beyond the Western
            democracies: three bases of voluntaristic restraint   183
            9.1. Once again, the Weberian Dilemma   185
            9.2. Three bases of voluntaristic restraint   187
            9.3. Institutionalizing collegial formations as public
                 policy   205

Chapter 10. External restraints: prospects for reason and
             "tradition"   214
             10.1. Why Parsons and Weber distorted restraints   214
             10.2. Are restraints on drift intrinsically
                   unreasoned?   224
             10.3. Rethinking tradition: lived distinctiveness v.
                   transferable qualities   228
             10.4. Prospects for "tradition"   232

Chapter 11. Collegial formations as external procedural
             restraints: prospects for a public realm   242
             11.1. Speculations on collegial formations today:
                   two restraints not institutionalized   242
             11.2. Collegial formations today: institutionalized
                   restraint beyond left and right   254
             11.3. Unwitting beneficiaries of the collegial form   266

Notes   271
Bibliography   325
Name Index   349
Subject Index   355

1. Introduction: societal constitutionalism as critical theory

1.1. Limits of comparative research

1.1.1. A presupposition and a lacuna

Given the enormous diversity of conceptual frameworks, levels of analysis, and methodological techniques informing historical and comparative research, many studies may be found that are uncompromisingly critical of existing Western democracies. At one point, beginning in the early 1960s and extending through the 1970s, first prominent Latin American theorists and then American comparativists described basic institutions and practices of Western democracies as intrinsically repressive. They leveled specific criticisms at *dependencia,* or the impact that these institutions and practices were having, and had, on Latin America. Yet, their central thesis was much broader. They insisted that Western democracies perpetuate and exacerbate inequalities, cross-national and domestic alike, that are both unjustified and unnecessary.[1]

Admittedly, it is far more common today for social scientists to attribute particular social problems to structural or institutional defects of capitalism, or of the welfare state, or, ultimately, of modernity itself. Yet, this too "radicalizes" these problems. It suggests (but by no means demonstrates) that these problems are beyond the scope of possible liberal reform because they are reflections of Western institutions' structural defects. The *cumulative* effect of these studies is not much different, therefore, from that of the more strident *dependencia* school: Basic institutions and practices of existing Western democracies are portrayed as structurally, irreparably, defective. Interest group politics within the United States has been roundly criticized along these lines for now over three decades (chapter 4).[2] The professions have been increasingly criticized in this way since the late 1970s (e.g. Larson 1977; Collins 1979; Parkin 1979; Murphy 1988 for a review). Related criticisms of both social democracy and neocorporatism in Scandinavia and Western Europe continue rich traditions of radicalism (see Popenoe 1988 for an intriguing "reaction").[3]

Still, radical and critical social scientists in the postwar era share with

1

their most conservative and apologetic colleagues both a presupposition and a conceptual lacuna. The presupposition is that:

> The very particular political institutions and social practices that characterize existing Western democracies *exhaust* actors' possibilities anywhere in the world (a) for establishing a nonauthoritarian social order, and (b) for securing opportunities for social integration as opposed to social control.

This may be labeled the *presupposition of exhausted possibilities*.

The conceptual lacuna that comparativists also share ultimately prevents them from methodically questioning this presupposition let alone jettisoning it. This conceptual lacuna is:

> The failure to distinguish analytically between (a) a social order that rests to some extent on heterogeneous actors' and competing groups' *possible* social integration and (b) a social order that rests exclusively or to an increasing extent on their demonstrable social control.

This may be labeled the *lacuna of integrative possibilities*.

1.1.2. Conceptual limitations, collective prejudices

There is no available social or political theory, nor any available body of social science research, that can support a presupposition as grand as that of exhausted possibilities. It is a prejudice. Rather than being a scientific proposition, or a value-neutral empirical generalization, it is a strictly normative generalization, a comforting ideology. As a presupposition, it typically goes unseen, to say nothing of unargued, by those adopting it. More often than not, researchers today adopt it by default. Rather than embracing it directly or purposefully because they are convinced it is sound in itself, they adopt it indirectly or inadvertently because credible conceptual alternatives do not seem to be available.

What would a credible conceptual alternative to the presupposition of exhausted possibilities involve? It would provide concepts that can simultaneously (a) inform detailed empirical research, and (b) credibly claim grounding against normative relativism. This is a tall order for any social theory to fill. Consider, on the one hand, that Marx's concept of alienation claims grounding, as does Habermas's concept of communicative action. Yet, neither concept has informed *detailed* empirical research.[4] Consider, on the other hand, that social scientists today who are critical of mainstream research in political sociology and who also are critical of existing Western institutions and practices fail to point to *conceptual* (and epistemological) limitations within the presupposition of exhausted possibilities (e.g. Tilly 1983; Evans, Rueschemeyer, and Skocpol 1985).[5] They do not operate with concepts that can credibly claim grounding against the presupposition's normative relativism. Instead, they advance their sharpest criticisms of existing Western democracies by radicalizing the mainstream's relativism, and using the latter against it.

Charles Tilly's most theoretical work provides an excellent example (1984; also 1985). He refuses to be bothered with distinguishing legitimate from illegitimate uses of collective force *conceptually.* He insists instead that any such distinction is a mere label that is intrinsically normative, and ultimately ideological (also Black 1984).[6] In illustrating why this is so, he points out that the rise of existing Western democracies followed a path indistinguishable, in principle, from that of protection rackets. He explicitly insists that Western democracies secured control over their populations historically in much the same way that organized criminals today secure control over neighborhood shopkeepers. Existing institutions of Western democracy are no more "moral" or "legitimate" within Tilly's framework of concepts, therefore, than the organizations established by rational criminals. Tilly is confident, of course, that this is so iconoclastic that it establishes the value-neutrality of his research in the face of any and all charges of Europocentrism, including the presupposition of exhausted possibilities.

Yet, at a second glance, Tilly fails to provide any concepts that challenge the presupposition of exhausted possibilities in any way at all, let alone radically. His easy comparison to protection rackets ironically has quite the opposite effect: It secures the presupposition's status as an unseen, seemingly incontrovertible collective prejudice. Existing Western democracies may well have emerged in the manner of protection rackets, but how can Tilly rebut the facile reply that they happen to be the best protection rackets possible under modern conditions? Nothing in Tilly's writings suggests why this belief is false or even narrow-minded. Indeed, Tilly's (and others') failure to tackle the conceptual distinction between legitimate and illegitimate uses of collective force, or to develop typologies of nonliberal or nonmarket "democracy," is one reflection of his (and their) more basic failure: the failure to challenge the presupposition of exhausted possibilities directly with critical concepts that can credibly claim grounding.

Still, the elevation of the presupposition of exhausted possibilities to a collective prejudice began only in the first third of the twentieth century. Few of the classical social theorists of the mid-nineteenth and early twentieth century, for instance, operated with any such presupposition. Yet, these theorists, too, failed to distinguish social integration from social control, and, as a result, their works are clearly marked by the lacuna of integrative possibilities. If the presupposition of exhausted possibilities cannot be found in their works, and yet this lacuna can, then the former's elevation to a collective prejudice cannot be traced exclusively to this single factor. Its elevation must be a product of other factors distinctive to the early twentieth century. A second factor coming into play, beginning in the mid-1920s and early 1930s, was strictly practical rather than theoretical or conceptual: This was the international elevation of the "moral" status of Western democracies in the face of unambiguously authoritarian threats from left and right (Mann 1987).[7]

This moral elevation, in practice, continued into the immediate postwar years with the seemingly unrivaled, and unbounded, promise of the United States. In the context of a dangerously polarized cold war, the presupposition of exhausted possibilities was literally institutionalized within the social sciences by modernization theory, and then by other developmental theories. Whether viewed macrosociologically or microsociologically, "progress" appeared to be a linear process of maturation, one surprisingly amenable to instrumental and strategic assistance. Even more surprisingly, this process of maturation was portrayed as more immutable than contingent, and, for that matter, unaffected by old age (Huntington 1971 on modernization theory's optimism, and Luhmann 1990 on system immutability). The status of the presupposition of exhausted possibilities as a collective prejudice was simultaneously perpetuated conceptually by functionalists, including Parsons, Merton, and today Niklas Luhmann, and no less by "conflict theorists" in both Great Britain and the United States, including Rex and Giddens, and Coser and Collins.[8]

As America's promise of the immediate postwar years gave way to at best an uneven performance, second thoughts about the "moral" status and legitimacy of existing Western democracies were bound to increase. This began in particular in the mid-1960s, with violent resistance to the civil rights movement in the United States, early student and Vietnam protests internationally, and increasing violent crime and urban blight in the United States. It continued into the 1970s with the oil crisis and sustained recession across the West, and then through the 1980s with international economic and cultural competition within the West and seemingly insoluble problems of drugs, poverty, and displacement in the United States. Today, with processes of democratization and liberalization underway in Eastern Europe since the fall of 1989, second thoughts about the "moral" status of existing Western democracies can only accumulate. Without an "evil empire" available to conveniently guarantee Western democracies' "moral" status irrespective of everyday performance, how can they not?

Indeed, are East Europeans embracing Western political and economic forms today because they are convinced that the latter ensure a nonauthoritarian *social* order, and also enhance actors' possibilities for social integration within sectors, industries, and organizations of a modern civil society? As they zealously adopt Western political and economic forms, do East Europeans have in mind the permanently marginalized British working class or American underclass, or the increasing rigidity of stratification systems across the West generally, including Scandinavia? Have they considered how neocorporatist peak associations across Western Europe and Scandinavia have irreversibly altered these forms, in practice, and how pervasive corporate crime is across the West – even more so in Western Europe than in the United States (Braithwaite 1984: 32–7)? Or are East Europeans instead reacting, as best they can at the moment, to systemic pressures of international economic competition, the unrelenting harshness of everyday life across the former Eastern bloc, and the West's demonstrated capacity, whatever its faults, to keep government's boot off people's necks and both to encourage and sate middle class consumerism and possessive individualism? The issue, regardless, is whether the "moral" status of existing Western democracies can be expected to become more or less uncertain after the fall of 1989.[9]

1.1.3. Filling the lacuna: the distinct concept of social integration

As was the case at the turn of the century, the lacuna of integrative possibilities is once again becoming the sole factor preventing comparativists from exposing the presupposition of exhausted possibilities for what it has always been: a comforting collective prejudice or strictly normative generalization. This lacuna accounts for why this normative generalization implicitly informs the works of social scientists who are endeavoring to be critical of existing Western institutions and practices. It explains, for instance, why Latin American researchers such as Henrique Cardoso, or, say, Theotonio dos Santos further on the left, or Helio Jaguaribe and Guillermo O'Donnell further on the right, also have failed – like their American, European, and Scandinavian colleagues – to scrutinize and criticize the presupposition of exhausted possibilities. The conceptual frameworks currently available to comparativists contain the lacuna of integrative possibilities at their cores, and this shields the presupposition from methical challenges irrespective of mounting uncertainties, and an increasingly palpable sense of drift.

How did *this* state of affairs in comparative research come about? With rare exception (e.g. Philippe Schmitter's use of Tocqueville in 1971), the *most basic* ideal types and concepts underlying the theoretical frameworks available to comparativists today were derived, in one way or another, from the works of Marx, Durkheim and, particularly, Weber (chapter 3). It is startling, actually, how persistently theorists and researchers today resort to Weber's concepts of purposive-rational, value-rational, and substantively rational action (see table 8.1 for alternatives). The problem is that the lacuna of integrative possibilities riddles all three classic social theorists' works, and this lacuna has yet to be filled in the many works of their successors, including the works of the Frankfurt school, and both French and British structuralist Marxists; as well as the works of Parsonian functionalists, symbolic interactionists, rational-choice theorists, organization theorists, and both exchange theorists and network analysts. Because the social integration/social control distinction has never been a topic of debate within any of these theoretical traditions, the lacuna of integrative possibilities rests quite comfortably at the very base of all of the conceptual frameworks available to comparativists today.

One of the purposes of this volume is to fill the lacuna of integrative possibilities by distinguishing social integration from social control *conceptually*. This distinction is also demonstrated to meet both of the requirements of any radical critique of a normative generalization or collective prejudice: It can credibly claim grounding against normative relativism and inform detailed empirical research. Because it can credibly claim grounding, the concept of social integration poses an alternative not only to the relativism of Weberian ideal types but also to the sovereignty of actors' subjective interests at the center of rational choice theory (Coleman 1986, 1990; Hechter 1987). It also poses an alternative to normative generalizations regarding the supposedly consensual or coercive bases of social order, as well as to Tilly's relativism in refusing to distinguish legitimate from illegitimate uses of collective force. Because it is capable of informing falsifiable and ultimately operationalizable research, the concept of social integration also poses an alternative to critical concepts of neo-Marxism, including the concepts of alienation and communicative action.

For present purposes of introduction, the concept of social integration may be defined preliminarily in the following way:

> Heterogeneous actors' and competing groups' *possible* social integration within any sector, industry, organization, or organizational division of a modern civil society rests on whether they can, at the very least, recognize and understand *in common* the shared social duties being sanctioned there.[10]

Whenever the social duties being sanctioned within any complex social unit are incapable of being recognized and understood in common by the actors and groups affected, social scientists may conclude that their behavioral conformity – and the resulting "social order" – is *reducible* to their social control. At best, these actors and groups are being manipulated; at worst, they are being coerced. By contrast, whenever the social duties being sanctioned within any complex social unit are at least recognized and understood (even if not accepted) in common by the actors and groups affected, it is no longer legitimate for social scientists to assume or assert that their behavioral conformity – and the resulting "social order" – is *reducible* to their social control. Instead, it *may* rest *in some part* on their social integration.

The central purpose of this volume is to propose a social theory that allows social scientists to advance empirical research beyond the presupposition of exhausted possibilities in two significant respects.

First, it allows them to specify when social integration is a possibility, in practice, within any sector, industry, organization or organizational division of a modern civil society. With this, the lacuna of integrative possibilities is filled *conceptually*.

Second, it allows them to isolate such possibilities wherever they may be found, without presupposing from the outset that they are to be found exclusively within Western democracies. With this, the presupposition of exhausted possibilities is jettisoned *conceptually*.

Putting this advance differently, the social integration/social control distinction allows social scientists to monitor the following two developments, in practice, that escape the presupposition of exhausted possibilities. First, are any Western democracies maintaining their current political institutions and economic practices, even as manipulation, control, and coercion are increasing substantially within more and more sectors of their civil societies? Conversely, are selected nation-states of the former Eastern bloc and the Third World failing to adopt many of these institutions and practices, even as manipulation, control, and coercion are decreasing substantially within more and more sectors of their civil societies?

Each of these developments is a practicable rather than hypothetical possibility. Empirical evidence of each development is likely to be discovered in new primary research and also, ironically, to be found buried in the literature of comparative politics and comparative political sociology. If this is the case, then why state each development so provisionally? Why not turn immediately to concrete examples of each? Due to the lacuna of integrative possibilities, and then the presupposition of exhausted possibilities resting on it, comparative researchers have yet to convert even unambiguous evidence of either development into discrete accounts amenable to falsification. They instead interpret and present such evidence *on the basis of* the presupposition of exhausted possibilities. Thus, the literature obfuscates and mislabels research findings that already directly challenge the comforting collective prejudice; it will be shown in time that this is particularly evident in the literature of corporate crime.

In emphasizing the importance of the direction of *social* change within modern nation-states, the theory of societal constitutionalism subordinates the importance of focusing on forms of government in and of themselves. It also subordinates the importance that constitutional theorists and liberal theorists have in the past accorded to the division of powers, the interrelationship between a market economy and a liberal state, and even actors' "natural rights" and the sovereignty of their subjective interests. The theory of societal constitutionalism proposes instead that shifts in the direction of *social* change – shifts between heterogeneous actors' and competing groups' *possible* social integration and their demonstrable social control – hinge on whether a distinct *form* of organization is, respectively, present or absent within a civil society: the *collegial form*. The theory of societal constitutionalism does *not* propose that the presence of collegial formations within a civil society guarantees that heterogeneous actors and competing groups are integrated rather than controlled. It does propose, however, that the *absence* of collegial formations *does indeed guarantee* that actors' behavioral conformity within any complex social unit, and the social order that results, are both *reducible* to their social control.[11]

But what are collegial formations? And why is their presence so critical to the direction of social change? Answering these questions is a central task of this volume, and the concepts needed to do so are introduced in chapter 4 and fully presented in chapter 8. For now it suffices to say that the theory of societal constitutionalism offers a framework of analytical concepts that substitutes the social integration/social control distinction for normative generalizations regarding "democracy," "authoritarianism," or "social order."

What is wrong, for instance, with the democracy/authoritarianism distinction? "Authoritarianism" is defined residually, against the backdrop of the presupposition of exhausted possibilities.[12] It is ultimately defined by the absence of the particular political institutions and economic practices of existing Western democracies (e.g. Hall 1987, Mann 1987). The problem with this is the narrow-mindedness involved in elevating the latter to *the* standard of comparison, whether explicitly or implicitly. This is narrow-minded not only because (a) the presupposition is itself a normative generalization, (b) one side of the democracy/authoritarianism distinction is a mere residual category, and (c) the distinction itself is applicable only to forms of government rather than to sectors of a civil society. It is narrow-minded because it is not possible to apply the democracy/authoritarianism distinction to shifts in the direction of social change. Yet, is it self-evident that increases in control and social authoritarianism are restricted, in practice, to the civil societies of the Third World and former Eastern bloc? Is it self-evident that existing Western democracies are somehow intrinsically immune from social authoritarianism in every single sector, industry, organization, and organizational division of their civil societies? Exposing these issues to empirical study in itself challenges the presupposition of exhausted possibilities directly: It moves empirical research into areas of study obfuscated by this collective prejudice.

1.1.4. Can collective prejudice be attributed to researchers?

Even though empirical researchers today share the lacuna of integrative possibilities with both classical and contemporary social theorists, it is undeniable that substantive findings in the social sciences have accumulated over the years. We know far more about deviance, law, corporations, interest associations, political parties, classes, the stratification system, and functional, ethnic, and religious solidarities than the classics ever knew. Researchers' substantive findings not only routinely refute or significantly amend those of the classic theorist-researchers but also exceed the possible scope of application of the latter's concepts and ideal types (see Walker and Cohen 1985 on "scope statements"). The problem is that researchers today nonetheless continue to present their findings in terms of ideal types and concepts that, after all is said and done, remain derivatives of the classics' own. Because substantive findings have gone unmatched by advances in theory construction,[13] the numerous respects in which research today exceeds the scope of application of existing conceptual frameworks in comparative political sociology, and simultaneously calls into question the presupposition of exhausted possibilities, have yet to be appreciated.

Consider the organizations literature. Substantive findings here are routinely reported that exceed the scope of application of Weber's ideal type of bureaucracy. But too often these findings are left in a catch-all or residual category: the "nonbureaucratic." They are not placed into, and thereby illuminated by, positive categories attuned to their own richness and suggestiveness (Perrow 1979 is quite clear about this, but consider also e.g. Scott 1981/1987 and contributions in Zucker 1988). These findings are at times categorized more positively in terms of Weber's even more basic *concepts* of social action: the purposive-rational, the value-rational, and the substantively rational. Yet, as one example, John Meyer's characterization of organizations' "institutionalized environments" is literally hamstrung by such Weberian terminology (Meyer and Rowan 1977, Meyer and Scott 1983). Meyer is clearly reporting something of great significance when he refers to "rationalized institutional myths" within these environments. But the crude Weberian concepts he employs in presenting his findings hopelessly obfuscate what this might be (see chapter 8 for further discussion). In too many other instances as well, the classics' concepts turn out to be unnecessary crutches in the hands of remarkably skillful researchers.

To be sure, when stated bluntly and formally labeled, a great many comparativists, including Meyer and researchers in other specialties, would object strenuously to having the presupposition of exhausted possibilities attributed to their works. These comparativists include, as prominent candidates: Barrington Moore, Charles Tilly, and Theda Skocpol; Philippe Schmitter and Walter Korpi; and S.N. Eisenstadt, Reinhard Bendix, Seymour Martin Lipset, and Neil Smelser. Still, *none of these researchers can demonstrate that their works distinguish social integration from social control, either explicitly or implicitly.* And only on this conceptual basis can comparative study escape the presupposition of exhausted possibilities. For three interrelated reasons, it is fair to attribute this presupposition to their works as well as to those of many other researchers:

First, there is not a single ideal type of nonliberal "democracy" to be found in their works, nor in the literature of comparative political sociology and comparative politics generally.

The comparativists just noted do not explicitly close the door on the possibility of there being a nonliberal "democracy," of course. But by leaving the latter a residual category, they do so implicitly. This is a good example of how theory broadly orients research. Even the most richly documented empirical studies, supported by the most sophisticated methodological techniques, fail *ever* to yield the conclusion that a modern nation-state is closer to nonliberal democracy today than it was ten years ago, or twenty years ago. In short, the meaning or significance of any set of social events is tied inextricably to researchers' basic concepts and presuppositions (Alexander 1982a). Only alternative concepts at this basic level can possibly allow them to detect and then overcome distortions of meaning or significance, not additional empirical studies or methodological advances.[14]

It is fair to attribute the presupposition of exhausted possibilities to these researchers' works for two additional, related reasons:

Second, the social integration/social control distinction is collapsed in all of their works in particular and in the literature generally (Tilly 1984 is one particularly eloquent example). As noted above, it is also collapsed in the works of classical and contemporary social theorists.[15]

Third, as a result, an ideal type of heterogeneous actors' and competing groups' possible social integration within any unit of a modern civil society has never been applied to a nation-state that currently lacks most Western political institutions and economic practices, and that is unlikely ever to recapitulate all of them (whether, e.g., Brazil or the Soviet Union, Zaire or the People's Republic of China).

In short, the presupposition of exhausted possibilities does indeed inform: (a) how Moore, Skocpol, and Tilly (and e.g. Alapuro 1987) characterize the *direction* of revolutionary change, as well as the prospects for contemporary revolutions, (b) how Schmitter characterizes neocorporatist arrangements within Western Europe and Latin America, and also prospects for "societal" and "state" neocorporatism, and (c) how Walter Korpi and others (e.g. John Stephens, Gosta Esping-Anderson, Adam Przeworski, and Leo Panitch) characterize labor movements and social-democratic parties within Scandinavia, and also prospects for greater egalitarianism. What is ironic is that these comparativists and others have already published substantive findings that richly contradict the presupposition of exhausted possibilities. The conceptual limitations that these otherwise diverse researchers share literally prevent them, individually and collectively, from seeing their own findings in this light.

1.2. Two issues of societal constitutionalism and an illustration

This volume challenges the presupposition of exhausted possibilities at its roots. Rather than employing counterintuitive case studies and anecdotal illustrations drawn from the Third World or the former Eastern bloc, it challenges the presupposition at its own level. Still, as a point of departure in this endeavor, it is worthwhile to consider a hypothetical example for illustrative purposes. This example is referred to throughout this volume as the theory of societal constitutionalism is presented. In illustrating the first possibility noted earlier – the possibility of manipulation, control, and coercion increasing within a Western civil society – it is designed to shed light on why a new conceptual framework is needed in comparative research in order literally to "see the evidence."[16]

1.2.1. Illustrating the possibilities: a static example

A young chemist, William, is employed in one of a dozen or so large research divisions of a major pharmaceutical company. He presents his supervisor, Scott, with the most recent results of his laboratory analyses. Taking one look, Scott hands them back, saying: "Look, William, I gave you one set of compounds to test drawn from a much larger project. Hundreds of man-hours have been invested in this project already. Your results are not anywhere near the results that we need for your set of compounds. This could delay the entire project. Worse, it could reduce next year's budget for our division. Keep in mind that once this project comes on-line, no one is ever going to take it apart and retest its various sets of compounds in isolation. Not anyone in government, at the Federal Drug Administration. Not anyone in this firm. Not anyone in any competitor's firm. And, certainly, not any of your professors in the Chemistry Department of your Ivy League college. So, be a professional, William. Be a team player and bring me results we can use. There might even be a bonus in this for both of us."

As the young chemist walks away, his mind races with three very different considerations. One consideration is how methodical he was in the laboratory. Because this was his first important assignment, he not only tested his set of compounds the standard number of times, he doubled the number of tests. Moreover, he ran some tests at a laboratory station different from his own so that he could test "fresh," outside of the prejudice of familiar surroundings. He is convinced that it is not possible for him or any other chemist to run any legitimate test that would yield the results Scott is expecting. William's only consolation is that the compound he is testing is by no stretch of the imagination toxic or life-threatening. His greatest fear, however, is that this could change once it is brought into the larger project. This is not likely. But it is a possibility.

Walking to his laboratory station, William's second consideration is to appraise his options realistically:

> First, he could go to the manager of the division, Dr. Elston, and explain his situation. But Elston would immediately consult with Scott, and William would be accused of going over Scott's head. Elston may not know what is going on, of course, and may appreciate William's candor. But it might also be the case that it is Elston who is pressing Scott to get results.
>
> Second, William could discuss the situation informally with colleagues. But after a year and a half in the division, it is not clear to him who Scott's eyes and ears are among the chemists, and Scott seems always to know what is going on.
>
> Third, William could anonymously inform someone at the Federal Drug Administration or the American Chemical Society. But William doesn't know a single official in either organization. Even if he did, neither a governmental agency nor a professional association would take action against a major pharmaceutical company with a single incident in mind, based strictly on information provided by a single employee – even if the information is scrupulously documented. Worse, if the FDA got wind of this particular project, the firm's management would never believe that the tip had been anonymous. One or two other chemists in other research divisions also may be testing this compound, of course. But it may also be the case that William is the only person testing it. He will never know.
>
> Fourth, William could resign on principle: Scott is asking him to act unprofessionally, and William takes pride in his credentials and skills. But how will William's career look to prospective employers once he resigns from one of the better entry-level positions in the entire industry? Who could he approach to recommend him to another firm? His career literally could end right here with a hasty decision. His marriage could end as well. What is certain is that his status among his friends would plummet since they envy his position. What is also certain is that William has never been attracted to reformers, nor to their causes.

Even before taking his seat at his station, William knows precisely what his only "option" is: He will bring Scott the results that Scott is expecting. The third consideration now looms largest in his mind: What will Scott ask him to do next? What does it mean to be a professional chemist within a corporation? Does this sort of thing occur often across the firm's research divisions, or across the research divisions of the industry – or is this an anomaly?

William would clearly be instructed by John Braithwaite's study of corporate crime in the international pharmaceutical industry. Braithwaite found (1984: 109) that "data tampering is [so] commonplace" that a realistic stance by the Federal Drug Administration would be one of "*a priori* reservations about the validity of data supplied by industry." Moreover, Braithwaite reports (1984: 32–37) that American and European executives in the industry agree that the European industry is "even more corrupt" than the American.

1.2.2. Implications for both possibilities

William's situation is an illustration of a possible corporate crime. But more importantly for present purposes, it is designed to illustrate what would qualify as one bit of *empirical* evidence of an organization extending social control and contributing to social authoritarianism (see Braithwaite 1985 for a literature review).[17] It illustrates an arbitrary exercise of collective power within a Western civil society. To the extent that Scott is not acting in isolation but instead on the basis of management's explicit or implicit instructions, the corporation's collective power is being wielded arbitrarily. Arbitrary power is defined later in this volume in terms of a conceptually grounded *threshold* (chapter 6). The latter allows social scientists to specify when the *shared* social duties being sanctioned within any complex social unit are no longer capable, in principle, of being recognized and understood in common by heterogeneous actors and competing groups. For now, the central point of the illustration may simply be asserted, and left available for further elaboration as the theory of societal constitutionalism is presented: William's situation illustrates the problem of arbitrary exercises of collective power within a civil society. This problem goes beyond the issue of corporate crime to illustrate extensions of social control and increases in a nation-state's susceptibility to social authoritarianism.

This illustration is designed, actually, to raise issues that speak to *both* possibilities posed earlier in the form of questions. The first possibility, just noted, is that of increasing social authoritarianism within a Western democracy. Comparativists' concepts currently orient them to assume implicitly that the presence of Western political institutions and economic practices largely guarantees that, even though corporate crime may riddle certain industries, *increasing* social authoritarianism is either not a possibility or else is ultimately insignificant. Indeed, because many instances of outright social authoritarianism within Western civil societies are currently labeled corporate crimes, this distorts the significance of their impact on the direction of social change from the very outset. The presupposition of exhausted possibilities guarantees this distortion, after all, by conceptual default.

With this in mind, consider that the comparativists noted earlier whose works were said to illustrate the collective prejudice of the presupposition of exhausted possibilities might readily refute this charge by answering the following questions: If the issue of social authoritarianism is significant, and if comparativists' theoretical frameworks are left open conceptually to considering the empirical evidence as it stands rather than to prejudging it by casually accepting the label of corporate crime, then where might one find case studies that put the empirical evidence in this light? To the extent that corporate abuses of power are indeed increasing across Western civil societies, do none of these abuses challenge the presupposition of exhausted possibilities – albeit anecdotally rather than conceptually? Clearly, William may own property, vote, speak, assemble with others, and either worship as he prefers or read pornography (or, for that matter, racy criticisms of political and corporate leaders' public and private behavior). Moreover, the press and electronic media all around William are relatively "free" of government control. But does any of this somehow guarantee that William is any more integrated, or any less controlled, in *his* everyday life than his counterparts in Brazil, the Soviet Union, or France?

Moreover, is it really the case that the vast majority of professionals within Western civil societies never or seldom experience William's situation within their respective sites of employment? Or is it rather the case that such situations are only too typical today, and, if anything, are increasing both in their frequency and seriousness all across Western civil societies? Put differently, is the multiplication of such abuses intrinsically insignificant? Or does such a trend provide unambiguous evidence of the decay of the *social infrastructure* of a nonauthoritarian direction of social change under modern conditions?

One purpose of this volume is to demonstrate that these are empirical rather than speculative or ideological issues. Another purpose is to specify why comparativists' conceptual frameworks currently prevent them from seeing these issues in this way. Currently, even should the multiplication of abuses of power within a Western civil society reach the point where situations such as William's are literally pervasive – and this point might already have been reached, at least within selected sectors of selected Western civil societies (Clinard and Yeager 1980; Braithwaite 1985) – comparativists currently have no alternative *conceptually*. From the outset, they can only categorize *both* (a) the (possible) increasing number of such situations within Western civil societies as well as (b) the (possible) decreasing number of them within Third World or Eastern civil societies as equally insignificant.

Researchers often demonstrate, of course, that Western democracies are inegalitarian. For the United States in particular it is an easy matter to show that the gap of disposable income available to upper classes and both middle and lower classes is increasing rather than decreasing (Gans 1988). Researchers also often decry "status closure" or "credentialism" (Larson 1977; Collins 1979; Parkin 1979; Murphy 1988). Yet, these same researchers lack the conceptual apparatus necessary to *demonstrate* that even economically privileged actors within Western democracies are increasingly being manipulated and controlled. They clearly fail to demonstrate that this, more than any of the inequalities just noted, contributes directly to shifts in the direction of social change. It does so by undermining the social infrastructure of a nonauthoritarian direction of social change under modern conditions.[18]

The second possibility raised earlier in the form of a question is that of decreasing social authoritarianism within non-Western nation-states. Even more clearly here, comparativists lack the conceptual apparatus necessary to recognize and describe *prospects* for a nonauthoritarian direction of social change within nation-states that continue to resist adopting all of the political institutions and economic practices of existing Western democracies. Bringing the same example above to such a nation-state, but now *reversing* William's situation, would a multiplication of *restraints* on such abuses of collective power within a civil society not contribute in *some* way to a nonauthoritarian direction of social change? That is, if William and other professionals were protected from such encroachments – even as they could not vote or read popular exposés, and even as the electronic media in particular remained more monitored by state agencies than is currently the case in the West – would they be less controlled in significant ways in their daily lives than their counterparts in the West? Can restraints on abuses of collective power within a civil society be institutionalized, both in principle and in practice, quite irrespective of whether all of the political institutions and economic practices of existing Western democracies are also present within a nation-state?

1.3. Societal constitutionalism as critical theory

The multiplication of William's situation within a Western nation-state and the reduction of such situations within a non-Western nation-state are two sides of the same conceptual coin, of course. The theory of societal constitutionalism offers comparativists a critical yet decidedly non-Marxist framework of concepts with which to explore each side of this coin methodically. It is designed to specify those organizations and institutions that contribute to shifts in any modern nation-state's direction of social change. In this way, the theory broadens the scope of critical theory beyond Marxists' critique of ideology and class struggle, and beyond their penchant to apply critique rather exclusively to advanced capitalism. In truth, the theory of societal constitutionalism severs critique from the Marxist tradition altogether. It endeavors, on the one hand, to pinpoint when specific exercises of collective power within particular sectors of a civil society remain consistent with heterogeneous actors' and competing groups' *possible* social integration. It also endeavors, on the other hand, to pinpoint when specific exercises of collective power are manifestations of these actors' and groups' demonstrable social control.

The theory of societal constitutionalism rests in large part on a synthesis of concepts developed at different levels of analysis and for different purposes by Talcott Parsons, the Harvard sociologist; Lon Fuller, the Harvard legal theorist; and Jürgen Habermas, the German critical theorist. Parsons, Fuller, and Habermas are the most important postwar representatives of three quite different traditions of social theory, respectively: the functionalist tradition, the common law tradition, and the tradition of critical theory (as one significant strand of neo-Marxism).

In 1964, with the first edition of *The Morality of Law,* Fuller systematically formulated for the first time in the long tradition of common-law theory and practice the most fundamental, general principles underlying civil opposition to arbitrary government within Anglo-American countries. With these principles, he held that he had specified a threshold of procedural norms marking the most irreducible basis of the lawful/lawless distinction. But Fuller's principles are more generalizable than this, and more sociological. His procedural threshold specifies whether heterogeneous actors and competing groups can recognize and understand in common what the *shared* social duties are that are being sanctioned within any complex social unit, and not simply whether a nation-state's positive laws are lawful or not.

By the late 1960s, Habermas's work also took what he calls a "procedural turn." He developed a communication theory in an effort to specify when actors' mutual understandings of "speech acts" are either purposefully manipulated or inadvertently "distorted." Habermas proposes that an admittedly "unreal" or "counterfactual" ideal, that of actors' nondistorted and nonmanipulated mutual understanding or what he also calls "communicative action" and "procedural reason," replaces Marx's alternative conceptual grounding, the concept of alienation, as well as Weber's most critical concept, the concept of substantive rationality. Habermas is convinced that to charge social enterprises with alienating labor or with being substantively nonrational is unnecessarily vague and, ultimately, unnecessarily restricting. Whether his own standard of procedural reason is (a) grounded against normative relativism, (b) capable of supporting charges that are simultaneously sharper and broader, and (c) capable of informing detailed empirical research, are, however, all open questions (chapter 5). What is not problematic is that a standard of *procedural* reason can credibly *claim* conceptual grounding against the relativism of actors' subjective interests and normative beliefs whereas standards of *substantive* rationality cannot (including that underlying Bloom's entire 1987 polemic).

Habermas's communication theory was not available to Fuller, even as Fuller was familiar with, and at times referred to, the later Wittgenstein's treatment of language games. Even today, however, Habermas remains unaware of Fuller's work. The theory of societal constitutionalism demonstrates that their most important contributions may be readily synthesized, and that this synthesis neither distorts nor reifies either theorist's concepts (chapter 6). Aside from providing one of two conceptual foundations of the theory of societal constitutionalism, this first synthesis also yields two proposed contributions to social theory: First, it specifies how Fuller's procedural threshold brings Habermas's purported grounding of procedural reason to detailed empirical research, even as Habermas acknowledges he is unable to do this himself. Second, it specifies how Habermas's communication theory may ground Fuller's procedural threshold against normative relativism, even as Fuller was unable to do this himself.

The source of the other conceptual foundation of the theory of societal constitutionalism is the writings of Talcott Parsons, and in particular his early references to voluntaristic action (chapter 7), and then his later references to procedural institutions and what he at times called the collegial form of organization (chapter 8). Parsons's works are not addressed at great length in this volume, however, because in order properly to demonstrate his contribution to the theory of societal constitutionalism, it is necessary to introduce six quite fundamental reformulations into his most important theoretical contributions. This is accomplished in a separate volume dedicated exclusively to this task (Sciulli in preparation, a).

Rather than concluding this introduction with a chapter summary, the following may suffice for now: Basic analytical distinctions underlying the theory of societal constitutionalism are introduced in the next three chapters, and brief chapter summaries are provided after this, prospectively at the opening of chapter 5 and then retrospectively at the opening of chapter 11. The reader is forewarned that chapter 4 is one of the most difficult in the book. I encourage readers to bring criticisms to all of the chapters, but I ask for particular patience and care when reading this one.[19]

1.4. Acknowledgement

Social theorists are a curious lot, as are methodologists. For both, criticisms come to their lips more readily than breath itself. In my view this enriches collegiality within the academy in the only way that matters. Most sociology departments sense that it is a good thing to keep around at least one each of these curiosities, and on occasion to tolerate their criticisms. But the best departments appreciate that one of their strengths is that they have many more of these curiosities around, and that they are encouraged to do what comes naturally, however annoying this may be at times for everyone affected.

Over the past two or three years many colleagues have responded critically to chapters of this book in draft, or to the preliminary and partial arguments that appeared earlier in journals, or else to my own public or private presentations of the theory. I begin by thanking in particular Ira Cohen, Dean Gerstein, and Bernard Barber. I thank them not for doing what theorists do naturally but rather for doing it so skillfully and with such eloquence and helpfulness. To be questioned by any one of these three social theorists is to receive simultaneously a high honor and a humbling experience. To be questioned by all three independently is to feel prepared to meet any other audience, whether one of social theorists or, possibly, one of methodologists (to consider a worst case scenario).

At the same time, this book would never have been written, for a great variety of reasons, if Jeffrey Alexander had not revitalized the enterprise of social theory in the United States beginning in the early 1980s. I am personally convinced that only Jeff could have accomplished so much at that point in time. More than anyone else in the 1980s, he has made it easier for all of us – here and abroad – not only to seek but possibly to secure an audience in the United States. This is something that his critics would do well to acknowledge. It does not violate tenets of our curious lot for them to do so. At the same time, Jeff is not likely to agree with much of the argument presented below, even as many of these points of disagreement are fruits, albeit indirect, of his remarkable labors across the last decade. If social theory's audience is to continue to grow rather than to revert to its sorry state of the late-1970s, it may well be that open, rigorous, and specific disagreements are the only means we have to secure it.

There are two other colleagues without whose assistance this book would never have been written, but now I am referring in the most literal sense to my personal, material situation of the mid-1980s. Mayer Zald and then Russell Dynes each offered me a different kind of academic position at moments most dire. Anyone reading this now who considers this hyperbole is demonstrating handily that he or she did not know me then. Even now, with relative "affluence" staring me in the face, with its own special hazards, I suppose, I cannot forget what those moments were like. I have also learned a great deal from the following colleagues, several of whom have lambasted my work plenty in the curious manner of our shared lot: First and foremost, in Washington, D.C., Ruth Wallace, William D'Antonio, and John McCarthy. Among my former colleagues at the University of Delaware, Sally Bould and Gerald Turkel in particular. More generally, Harold Bershady, Frank Adler, Robert Antonio, Denes Nemedi, Birgitta

Nedelmann, Anna Wessely, Elzbieta Halas, Robert Merton, John Braithwaite, Paul Colomy, David Willer, Wendell Bell, Donald Levine, John R. Hall, Michael Hammond, Robert Marsh, David Jacobs, Michael Kennedy, Carl Klockars, Wallace Dynes, Scott McNall, Frank Lechner, John Meyer, Mark Mizruchi, Kurt Finsterbusch, Terence Russell, Sheldon Stryker, and R. Stephen Warner. I also received excellent comments and suggestions from an anonymous reviewer, from a second reviewer, Karol Soltan, from two anonymous members of the Rose Monograph Series Board, and from series editor Teresa Sullivan.

In addition, three graduate students at the University of Delaware were enormously helpful at various stages in this work's completion; they are William Lofquist, Patricia Jenkins, and in particular Pan Hao. Their contributions are exemplars of voluntaristic action in the sense that the latter is defined in this volume.

At home, my greatest debts are to Cynthia Sciulli, Julia and Emilia Fernandez, Oreste Sciulli, Michael Poli, Joseph Rutkowski, and Kathyrn Plesivac.

Conceptual foundations of societal constitutionalism

2. Social integration and social control: the importance of procedural normative restraints

2.1. Social order and social control

It is useful to begin by characterizing social order in positive terms rather than leaving it a residual category, whether as an antonym of entropy or randomness (Parsons 1937a: 752; 1968c; Alexander 1978, 1982a, 1987). Researchers may say that any social unit is ordered when members' behavior typically falls within *acknowledged ranges of acceptable behavior.* The latter is that entire set of behavior that other members typically acknowledge is acceptable rather than either exemplary or deviant (see Brennan and Buchanan 1985: 98–104; Ridgeway and Berger 1986 on expectation states theory). Indeed, this behavior is so unambiguously acceptable, that, if anything, the *questioning* of such behavior by any member of the group runs a greater risk of being labeled deviant (as, for example, nosey, intrusive, or prelusive) than the behavior questioned.

With this in mind, a staid religious congregation may be ordered at one moment in time, and then become disordered, as actors' behavior no longer meets members' acknowledged ranges of expectations regarding ritual, dress, or donations. Similarly, a criminal motorcycle gang may be just as ordered in its own way, and then become disordered, as actors' behavior fails to meet members' acknowledged ranges of expectations regarding, drug-running, tatooing, or fighting. Nudist camps or concentration camps may be ordered or disordered in their own ways (see Kaplan 1980 for an application to juveniles' behavior).

This view of social order is indeed positive rather than residual, and yet it is also disconcertingly relativist rather than critical. The point at the moment, however, is not to worry about the substantive activities to which any particular social unit may be dedicated. The point is that researchers may *legitimately* say that a social unit is "ordered" in the sense above irrespective of whether a social unit's substantive ends are virtuous or vicious.[1] This may be said even if manifest coercion (as in concentration camps) explains why a mass of actors conforms to a handful of power holders' expectations. This may also be said even if the actors involved are competing zealously over scarce material and symbolic resources.[2]

In short, the orderliness of any complex social unit cannot be said to rest on the absence of moments of manifest coercion, interest competition, and personal anxiety. Nor, for that matter, does it rest on the absence of moments of outright conflict. But it can be said to rest on the absence – however temporary – of unambiguous behavioral encroachments against its members' acknowledged ranges of expectations regarding acceptable behavior. This may be said irrespective of how distinctive or idiosyncratic these ranges might be in any given case. Correlatively, the antonym of social order is by no means entropy, randomness, or even competition and conflict; it is subjectively unacceptable behavior. When members of a congregation or a gang begin to encroach against acknowledged ranges of expectations, by no means are they necessarily acting randomly, entropically, or even conflictually. Their behavior is nonetheless subjectively unacceptable to other members, and thereby disorderly. At the same time, a congregation or a gang engaged in conflict with other social units, or else riddled internally by its own members' intense competition, may be well-ordered: Each actors' behavior may fall within members' acknowledged ranges of expectations (see note 2).

This strictly relativist definition of social order becomes more difficult to apply empirically, of course, when researchers move it to more macrosociological units such as social movements, complex organizations, or national institutions. And yet, evidence may readily be found of *heterogeneous* actors and *competing* groups endeavoring independently to restrict their behavior to what they independently perceive to be the ranges of expectations acknowledged (or institutionalized) within macrosociological units.[3]

Such acts of self-restriction may be attributed to one or both of two broad sets of mechanisms of social control. First, actors' self-restriction within a social unit may be attributed to their rational or strategic calculations of their own material and symbolic self-interests. These calculations may either be made individually by each actor or through networks and collectivities. They include calculations of how best to reduce or eliminate any possibility of immediate or eventual physical coercion, monetary loss, loss of prestige, or loss of future opportunities (Brennan and Buchanan 1985; Coleman 1986, 1988, 1990; and Hechter 1987 revolve around this set of mechanisms of social control). Second, actors' self-restriction within a social unit also may be attributed to some *prior* narrowing of their subjective interests. To attribute social order to a prior narrowing of actors' subjective interests, however, is to account for social order in terms of exercises of "coercion" that are now quite subtle, and yet palpable.

These more subtle self-restrictions may be traced to at least three sources. First, they may be traced to informal mechanisms of social control,[4] whether internalized or negotiated in local interactions, as is the case when actors endeavor to avoid shaming (Braithwaite 1989). Second, they may be traced to either institutional or systemic mechanisms of social control,[5] as is the case when actors defer to purportedly "objective" limitations on their access to material goods and services. Third, and the subtlest self-restrictions of all, they may be traced to cognitive obstacles that distort actors' understanding of what is being expected of them, including which of their own subjective interests are acceptable and which are not.[6] Actors misunderstand just what the scope of behavior actually being sanctioned within their social units is.[7]

When actors place unnecessary restrictions on their own behavior, a social unit's orderliness can no longer be reduced to any combination of informal, institutional, and systemic sanctions. Instead, social order is tied in some part to *cognitive* limitations, and these can be traced to two sources. On the one hand, actors may misunderstand which shared social duties are actually being sanctioned with a social unit at any given point in time (see chapters 3–5 on shared social duties). On the other hand, and more importantly, certain shared social duties may be intrinsically difficult for *heterogeneous* actors and *competing* groups to recognize and understand *in common*. This is the case, as examples, when the shared social duties are: (a) ambiguous in and of themselves, (b) inconsistent with those being sanctioned within the other social units to which these actors and groups also belong (whether family, or sites of employment, leisure, or worship), or, finally, (c) inadvertently (or purposefully) skewed to the advantage (or disadvantage) of certain sets of actors and groups.

It is not essential at this point to address how researchers can specify in comparative perspective when shared social duties are themselves intrinsically difficult for any set of heterogeneous actors and competing groups to recognize and understand in common. This is addressed in time (see chapter 6 on the "threshold of interpretability"). The point at the moment simply is to propose the possibility, in principle, that *heterogeneous* actors and *competing* groups within complex social units may restrict their own behavior unnecessarily as a result of either type of cognitive limitation. When actors experience cognitive limitations, moreover, none of the other mechanisms of social control comes into play at all. The *ranges* of expectations regarding acceptable behavior that they *believe* are acknowledged or institutionalized within a social unit are already narrower than the ones actually being sanctioned, whether informally, institutionally, or systemically. To the extent that this is the case, their self-restriction is more stultifying than any actor or observer can warrant as essential to maintaining social order.

This issue of unnecessary self-restriction is complicated, and also strictly sociological rather than social psychological. There is no good reason at this point to reduce its complexity prematurely in a rush to operationalize concepts. In the first place, actors' self-restrictions may not be purposeful products of power holders' actions. They may rather be inadvertent products of social change that happen to work to the benefit of power holders; after all, actors' formulation and articulation of challenges to their authority are being delimited from the outset. In the second place, it is precisely when they are experiencing cognitive limitations that even the most heterogeneous sets of actors and the most competitive sets of groups may well accept subjectively, by any number of inconsistent or unwarranted rationales, that their behavior is a product of their "free will" rather than of their social control. Actors may never believe for an instant that they are even modestly constrained or disadvantaged (Etzioni's 1961/1975 "compliance theory," for instance, takes such subjective beliefs at face value). Indeed, when all of the mechanisms of social control noted above are operating most effectively, surveys of actors' subjective beliefs are quite incapable of revealing the latent coercion, manipulation, and self-restriction that is involved (Dryzek 1988).[8]

Standing back from all of these possibilities, it may be said with confidence that power holders within any complex social unit – whether a revolutionary social movement or a capitalist corporation – either become adept at employing purposeful mechanisms of social control and also at benefiting from unplanned or inadvertent mechanisms of social control, or else they cease at some point to be power holders. Indeed, social order within any complex social unit, and certainly within any sector, industry, or organization of a modern civil society, can rarely be attributed exclusively to power holders' purposeful designs. It is generally based in some significant part on informal, institutional, and systemic processes, and then, too, on actors' self-restriction. Consider only the following two reasons why this is the case.

On the one hand, physical or material sanctions need not be applied directly by the power holders who are benefiting most from their enforcement. Such sanctions may be applied by professional enforcers whom power holders no longer control, either directly or indirectly (Weber 1914–20: 214). Or, alternatively, sanctions may be "applied" by an "impersonal" marketplace, as systemic mechanisms of social control even further removed from power holders' direct or indirect control (Marx 1857–58). On the other hand, as noted above, heterogeneous actors' subjective interests and competing groups' immediate material interests may be manipulated, "distorted," or restricted from the outset. Thus, any given social order is likely a product of systemic forces of social change (such as rationalization, commodification, capitalization), structural and institutional obstacles, informal local interactions, and actors' self-restriction – rather than the product of purposefully enforced sanctions alone.

2.2. Social control in the literature

2.2.1. Social control sans social integration

The enormous American literature of social control, from Edward A. Ross's two articles in the first volume set of *American Journal of Sociology* in 1896 to impressive theoretical efforts by Jack Gibbs (1981) and Donald Black (1984), may be read as a sustained, collective effort by theorists and research-ers alike to fathom the relationship between purposeful and inadvertent mechanisms of social control. Yet, in recent years there has been a decided turn, for purposes of operationalization and empirical study, to concentrate on purposeful mechanisms. Gibbs focuses on these, for instance, and in no uncertain terms. What is increasingly being lost from sight, first conceptually and then empirically, is that many other mechanisms of social control often work to the benefit of power holders. This remains the case even when power holders fail to understand (a) that these mechanisms of social control work to their benefit, (b) how they operate, and (c) how their operation might be maintained or improved.

Even worse, all of the contributors to this literature collapse instances of heterogeneous actors' and competing groups' possible social integration into their analyses of (largely) purposeful mechanisms of social control. Indeed, this ongoing reduction, a manifestation of the lacuna of integrative possibilities, is what opened the way for researchers today to concentrate more and more one-sidedly on purposeful mechanisms of social control. Moreover, their longstanding failure to distinguish the *possibility* of hetero-geneous actors' and competing groups' social integration from the admit-tedly greater likelihood of their social control carries at least three other implications in this context:

> First, the possibility of eventually *specifying* when actors' self-restric-tion is unnecessary is eliminated by conceptual default. Scheff (1984a), for instance, asserts that there is unnecessary self-restriction, but then fails to specify how he knows when this is the case and when it is not (and his later concept of interpersonal "attunement" [1990] does not help researchers who are studying exercises of collective power at the macro-sociological level).

> Second, heterogeneous actors' and competing groups' *possible* social integration within any complex social unit is collapsed into the "suc-cessful" operation of institutional and systemic mechanisms of social control, rather than kept distinct conceptually. The very term "integra-tion" is thereby rendered intrinsically apologetic. It refers to situations in which *inadvertent* rather than purposeful mechanisms of social con-

trol largely account for actors' and groups' behavioral conformity (Parsons 1951, 1968c; Parsons and Platt 1973; Alexander 1978, 1980, 1982a, 1983b, 1987).

Third, sociologists' treatments of social control are rendered decidedly normative and relativist. They lack any claim to conceptual grounding, and thereby to critique. Their treatments may well be consistent with "conflict theory," to be sure, but the latter merely means that sociologists are refusing to consider the possibility that some existing social orders might be integrative rather than controlling (Collins 1979; Parkin 1979; Murphy 1988). More typically, sociologists' treatments of social control are apologetic. They are incapable conceptually of specifying when actors' behavioral conformity is excessive or unnecessary, other than to point to blatantly "coercive" controls (Etzioni 1961/1975; Gibbs 1981, 1982; Mayer 1983; Black 1984; Griffiths 1984; along with Parsons and Alexander).[9]

2.2.2. The distinct concept of social integration: a preliminary definition

Morris Janowitz's (1975, 1976) work is particularly influential within the American literature of social control. His approach is so internally at odds with itself conceptually, however, that, in a curious way, it exemplifies what needs to be done in order to distinguish social integration conceptually from social control. Janowitz fails to appreciate how readily his work falls victim to the first two implications just noted: He fails to detect when social control is excessive, other than in cases of manifest coercion. He also readily collapses the concept of social integration into an otherwise remarkably undifferentiated category of social control. Moreover, his study of the welfare state (1976) exemplifies yet the third implication – that of relativism. Ironically, it exemplifies *both* of this implication's manifestations: as an unsubstantiated "conflict theory" and as an unsubstantiated apologetics.

In his often-cited survey of the literature (1975), Janowitz traces the concept's evolution from the turn of the century to the 1970s. His thesis states that the discipline is best advised to return to the concept's earlier, more robust meaning. By his account, social control originally "referred to the capacity of a society to regulate itself according to desired principles and values." The antonym of this early concept was not entropy or randomness, therefore, but rather what Janowitz calls "coercive control." Given his social control/coercive control distinction, both an unsubstantiated apologetics and an unsubstantiated conflict theory pervade his subsequent study of the welfare state (1976). After all, any existing social order whose power holders do not typically resort to coercive mechanisms of social control automatically qualifies for inclusion into his otherwise undifferentiated master category. Then, with the concept of social control already shorn of the limiting case "coercive control," the former concept is rendered into a literal synonym for "social integration." Thus, the two terms are collapsed into a single concept that is relativistic or intrinsically uncritical. Janowitz's concept of social control permits him simultaneously to criticize most everything taking place within the welfare state, as he sees fit, even as he concedes that the welfare state does not rest on manifest coercion.[10]

As Janowitz would have it, the earlier, robust concept of social control was narrowed substantially in the 1950s (by Talcott Parsons, says he). Earlier references addressed how *collectivities'* institutionalization of their members' behavioral conformity contributes to the larger social order whereas later references concentrated on how *individuals'* internalization of norms contributes to the larger social order (see Scott 1971 for a captivating discussion of the latter). Thus, a concept once quintessentially sociological was narrowed, and rendered social-psychological. Janowitz instructs sociologists to return to the issue of how larger social units contribute to social order, or to sustaining national institutions. He is particularly interested in how these units regulate their own memberships *without* simply reacting strategically to the state's external threats of sanctions for misbehavior. Rather than instructing sociologists to balance their current treatments of purposeful mechanisms of social control with more methodical assessments of inadvertent mechanisms of social control, therefore, he instead calls on them to expand their studies of purposeful mechanisms to encompass larger social units.

In short, in both his review essay and subsequent study of the welfare state, Janowitz fails to address the phenomenon of manipulation at all, or instances when social control cannot be integrative even as it remains noncoercive. Put differently, by failing to distinguish the concept of social integration, the concept of social control becomes apologetic or uncritical at the moment that the discussion turns to systemic, institutional, or informal mechanisms of social control. In this respect, Janowitz's approach to social control is *consistent* with that of every other American sociologist who has used the concept, including those writing before the narrowing of the 1950s. Still, by distinguishing coercive control from social control, Janowitz at least intimates at times that the latter might be further distinguished from social integration. He at least intimates that: (a) he would like to make this distinction himself (but then never did), or else (b) he would adopt it if it became available. After all, the social control/social integration distinction would at least balance his otherwise one-sided concern about "coercive control."[11]

At this early point in the discussion, prior to the presentation of the

theory of societal constitutionalism, the distinct concept of social integration may be presented preliminarily by borrowing Janowitz's suggestions
regarding collectivities' self-regulation:[12]

> Heterogeneous actors and competing groups are *possibly* integrated
> rather than demonstrably controlled within any complex social unit
> when the shared social duties being sanctioned within it can at least be
> recognized and understood by them in common (even if *not* necessar-
> ily accepted by them in common).

Later in this volume it is demonstrated that this concept of social integration is intrinsically critical. It can credibly claim conceptual grounding
against normative relativism. After all, any set of shared social duties that
heterogeneous actors and competing groups can recognize and understand
in common is distinctive (chapter 6). If social scientists can specify when
such a set is being sanctioned within any complex social unit, then they
can credibly claim that it is *possibly* integrative. This means that social
scientists can specify when a set of shared social duties is capable of being
recognized and understood by such actors and groups in common, irrespective of: (a) the current (and possibly increasing) heterogeneity of
their internalized beliefs and subjective interests, and (b) their current
(and possibly increasing) competition for profits, power, and influence
within economic and political marketplaces.[13] Correlatively, any set of
shared social duties that lacks these qualities *is demonstrably controlling*.
If actors and groups cannot recognize and understand what their shared
social duties are, then, irrespective of anything else that may be said
about their behavioral conformity, it cannot be said to be possibly integrated rather than controlled.

2.2.3. Social control in social theory and political sociology

In the symbolic interactionist literature of "negotiated order" (associated in
particular with works by Anselm Strauss 1978), it is either argued or assumed
that social control rests on individual actors' ongoing, active self-regulation
within particular social situations, and not on norms actors have internalized
(see Maines and Charlton 1985 for a review; and J. Turner 1988 more generally). As one result of this eminently credible position, however, the terms
social control and social integration are employed interchangeably. Whenever interactionists see actors negotiating "definitions of the situation" in the
absence of either manifest rebellion or widespread deviance within any
sector of a civil society, they take this a priori as evidence of actors' social
integration (see Stelling and Bucher 1972: 432 for an influential example
applied to the medical profession). Interactionists correctly move beyond
Durkheim's, Freud's, and Parsons's emphases on actors' internalization of

norms, but they lack the conceptual apparatus required to recognize instances of actors' manipulation, latent coercion, and self-restriction, *in practice,* within any negotiated order (Sciulli 1988b).[14]

In both political sociology (Janowitz, Zald, Gibbs, Black) and general
social theory (Alexander 1978, 1982a, 1987; Giddens 1979, 1984), social
control also is equated either with actors' passive acquiescence or their
more active "self-regulation."[15] In one way or another, successful social
control ultimately is related to a social order's purported "legitimacy,"[16]
and, following Weber, the latter is treated as a widely shared subjective
belief (Giddens 1979: 101–3; Brennan and Buchanan 1985: 99–100): Subordinates believe subjectively that the acknowledged ranges of expectations
regarding acceptable behavior being sanctioned are themselves rational,
traditional, or habitual (or else purposive-rational, value-rational, or substantively rational). Given Weber's treatment of legitimation, issues of
latent coercion and manipulation, of whether actors' subjective beliefs are
themselves accurate or "distorted," are hastily subordinated to the more
superficial issue discussed at the opening of this chapter: Are authorities
(and the acknowledged ranges of expectations that they sanction) subjectively acceptable to most actors most of the time?

In the literature of political sociology devoted to the state, however,
power holders' purposeful mechanisms of social control as well as structural or systemic mechanisms of social control that work to their favor have
both remained central (see Evans, Rueschemeyer, and Skocpol 1985;
Block 1987; Gold, Lo, and Wright 1975; Skocpol 1980; Skocpol and
Amenta 1986 for reviews). By briefly surveying some of the major points
raised in this literature, the importance for comparative research of distinguishing analytically between heterogeneous actors' and competing groups'
possible social integration and their demonstrable social control begins to
come into view.

The capitalist state as instrument of purposeful social control. Ralph
Miliband (1969), G. William Domhoff (1967), and even James O'Connor
(1973), as well as many elite and Marxist theorists more generally, see the
state as capitalists' "instrument." With this, they emphasize the importance
of purposeful mechanisms of social control. They argue that capitalists
consciously maintain social control, first by maintaining their own intraclass solidarity, and then by either directly selecting or else directly
influencing policymakers. This same emphasis on purposeful mechanisms
of social control also explains why sociologists who are far less critical of
the state nonetheless study networks of elite solidarity, whether within
economic institutions such as interlocking directorships (Mizruchi 1982;
Burt 1983; Useem 1984; Mintz and Schwartz 1985) or within social organizations of intra-elite communication, including: private clubs (Domhoff

1974), trade associations (Sabato 1985; Laumann and Knoke 1987), and the mass media (Gans 1979). Elite solidarity is assumed to be central to social control and thus to social order.

"Instrumental theorists" have difficulties, however, accounting for actions taken by state agencies that turn out, in retrospect, to maintain capitalism but that were actively opposed by many capitalists when they were being proposed. Capitalists opposed these actions because they were convinced that they jeopardized their most basic material interests.[17] The problem, therefore, is that individual capitalists may well maintain intraclass solidarity, and may also secure routine access to policymakers through organized groups, if not as a class, and yet they may not have any idea, either as a class or an identifiable group or coalition within it, how best to maintain the capitalist system in the face of systemic crises.

The capitalist system as mechanism of inadvertent social control. This is the problem that Nicos Poulantzas (1973) and other structuralist Marxists (including Louis Althusser) long emphasized, as does Niklas Luhmann today (1982, 1986, 1990) and other non-Marxist systems theorists: Informal, institutional and, in particular, systemic mechanisms of social control maintain the (capitalist) system. Capitalists themselves need not be particularly skillful in coordinating their own activities more purposefully because their consciousness, or subjective solidarity, is ultimately not a crucial factor in successful social control. Capitalists also need not dominate the policymaking process, whether directly as a class or indirectly as a set of otherwise competing interest groups. The crucial factors maintaining any ongoing (capitalist) system are systemic. These factors broadly interrelate the interests of (otherwise diverse) capitalists and the policies of (otherwise independent) state agencies quite irrespective of whether capitalists establish a shared consciousness or exhibit particular solidarity. Once a (capitalist) system is in place, and once the legitimacy of its basic organizations and institutions has somehow been secured, whether by means fair or foul (Tilly 1985), systemic factors are then sufficient to sustain it. Capitalists themselves need not be particularly skillful in reaping the system's many advantages (Block 1977 and Therborn 1978; Block 1987 has since evolved away from this position).

In related approaches, Jürgen Habermas distinguishes between social situations in which actors' beliefs are purposefully "manipulated" and those in which they are more inadvertently or "systematically distorted."[18] Michael Useem's (1984) impressive study of the unplanned evolution of corporations within the United States and Great Britain across the twentieth century – from family capitalism to managerial capitalism and then to institutional capitalism – also demonstrates the increasing importance of systemic mechanisms of social control. Clearly, different sets of elites and power holders have benefited, both historically and today, from systemic social changes. Just as clearly, none of them controlled these changes or even necessarily understood their likely implications, even as they benefited from them.

Influentials' competition as mechanism of inadvertent social control. A third point of view is provided by researchers who retain a radical or critical intent but who are otherwise wary of orthodox Marxism and all related instrumentalist and structuralist positions. These researchers argue that the "causal agents" who initiated policies of the modern welfare state, for instance, were neither capitalists (and their agents within the state) nor strictly systemic or structural forces. Instead, the welfare state was initiated by coalitions of reform-minded capitalists, along with essentially noncapitalist and even anticapitalist political interests within and around legislatures and governmental agencies. Thus, contingent coalitions of reform-minded capitalists both responded to, and stimulated the mobilization of, working-class formations and other "progressive" interests within the wider civil society (Fulcher 1987 labels this "labor movement theory").

Given this dynamic process, the policies of the welfare state turned out over time to perpetuate and revitalize capitalism, even as this was by no means self-evident to any of the actors comprising the coalitions that proposed and defended these policies in the heat of political battle. It is only clear today, in retrospect, that many alternative policies would have likely precipitated sustained social and economic crises if they had been adopted instead. The central point of this third approach to the state, therefore, is not really that the state is "relatively autonomous" from capitalists' immediate interests. It is rather that shifts in domestic policymaking, both before and after World War II, were tied to the extent and intensity of working-class mobilization within the United States, on the Continent, and in Scandinavia.[19]

2.3. Conceptual limitations in political sociology?

What is clear from the discussion above is that the same fundamental distinction missing from the American literature of social control is missing as well from the international debate over the state:[20] the distinction between instances of demonstrable social control, whether purposeful or inadvertent, and instances of heterogeneous actors' and competing groups' possible social integration.[21] Marxists insist, of course, that actors who do not own or control the means of production cannot possibly be integrated, irrespective of what their subjective beliefs and interests happen to be. And, actually, this is a great virtue of Marxism as a tradition of theory and research. After all, actors' subjective beliefs and interests may be informally, institutionally, or systemically narrowed and "distorted" without actors being aware that this is the case. Moreover, the actors might operate on the basis of any number of self-restrictions and yet continue to believe that they are acting freely.

Still, as a tradition of theory and research, Marxism commits contemporary researchers *conceptually* (including Burawoy 1979; Therborn 1987; Wright 1985) to account for social order *exclusively* in terms of actors' manipulation, latent coercion, or worse – irrespective of any and all evidence to the contrary. Marxists are committed conceptually in this way, for instance, *quite irrespective of how actors happen to be organized within any sector, industry, or organization of a modern civil society, capitalist or otherwise.* Thus, to the extent that the proletariat is not actively engaged in rebellion against any capitalist society, Marxists have always had no alternative conceptually other than to conclude that workers' behavior is *reducible* to manipulation by an instrumental state, systemic mechanisms of social control, and workers' own self-restriction. There is not a single Marxist theory of heterogeneous actors' and competing groups' possible social integration within modern civil societies, nor can there be.

Even worse, given the conceptual and epistemological limitations of this remarkably methodical theoretical tradition, there is not a single Marxist theory of heterogeneous actors' and competing groups' possible social integration within *any* particular organization or institution. This holds true for labor unions within social democracies, communist parties either within the West or the former Eastern bloc, Solidarity within Poland, or popular movements of radical social change within the Third World. Marxists studying either "capitalist states" or "existing communist states" cannot link their theory to practice today precisely because they never developed a theory of what integrative institutions and organizations might look like even under the most favorable material conditions (Therborn 1977 and Sirianni 1981; Przeworski's 1985 account of social democracy revolves around the implications of this lacuna). Marx's original notion of the "withering away" of the state and of all other organizational and institutional forms (Ollman 1977) is as little a theory of possible social integration as his notion of absolute disalienation is a theory of possible praxis (Sciulli 1984).

At the same time, more mainstream political sociologists, whether critical of existing Western democracies or not (from Barrington Moore, Charles Tilly, and Theda Skocpol to Seymour Martin Lipset, Rheinhard Bendix, and even Daniel Bell, to cite only a few prominent examples), operate within and through conceptual frameworks that recapitulate many of the same limitations. Like Marxists, they also fail to isolate the organizational and institutional bases of heterogeneous actors' and competing groups' possible social integration. They instead focus on what they con-

sider to be the intrinsic interrelationships between (a) systemic and structural inequalities, (b) either class and status group behavior, and (c) liberal
political forms and economic practices. They lack the concepts to do anything other than to condemn in absolutist terms the extent of manipulation
and latent coercion in advanced societies (Bell 1976; Tilly 1985), or else to
elevate existing Western "freedoms" and "rights" to *the* standard of comparison (Lipset 1960; Moore 1966; Bendix 1978).[22]

This is why *critical* political sociologists working outside of the Marxian
tradition treat Western democratic institutions in terms that are altogether
consistent with this tradition's *conceptual* framework, even as they then
disagree with Marxists' findings. They treat these institutions conceptually
as sites to which purported "class conflicts" or broader "struggles" for
equality within civil society have been moved (e.g. aside from Tilly and
Skocpol, Katznelson 1978, Wolfe 1978, Quadagno 1988). They thereby
hold that social conflict and the potential for significant social change have
been moved to interest competition within and around governmental agencies, political parties, and peak associations (Janowitz 1976: 75–6; Skocpol
and Amenta 1986: 139–44). Indeed, when a "radical" political sociologist
today refers to "conflict" and "struggle," he usually is referring to robust
debate over policy-making within remarkably stable political institutions
(e.g. Kerbo's subtitle for his stratification textbook, 1983, is "class conflict
in the United States").[23]

Put differently, purported "conflicts" and "struggles" within existing
Western democracies are essentially policy debates. They are discussions
(and, of course, street demonstrations, too) that are altogether oriented by,
framed within, and mediated by governmental institutions, political party
organizations, and either interest group or peak association coalitions that
are themselves so stable, and so legitimate subjectively, that they escape
serious criticism. Indeed, these institutions, organizations, and coalitions
are typically elevated above any preliminary posing of possible alternatives. For instance, the leaders of working class organizations and other
"progressive" groups within the United States may very well question the
current composition of Congress. They may heartily ridicule the current
conduct of Congress. But, by contrast to the situation in Latin America in
particular, they never – never – question that Congress, as a political institution or agency of government, legitimately engages in law-making.

Across Latin America, this is precisely what is questioned (Anderson
1964 remains the most seminal statement, see chapter 9). What is subjected
to outright political competition and occasional social conflicts is precisely
which agencies and institutions of government, if any, legitimately engage
in law-making as such. This same questioning is underway within the
former Eastern bloc, albeit currently directed to the legitimacy of the
Communist Party apparatus rather than to emerging parliaments. As of

this writing, matters are being posed largely within the ideology of the presupposition of exhausted possibilities, and several Eastern countries seem primed to pay a dear price for this narrowness. Yet, there is no reason to believe that Easterners' questioning will or can remain confined in this way. Nor is there any reason to believe, for that matter, that questioning within the West will or can remain confined in this way for perpetuity (Habermas's 1989 tentative remarks). Regardless of how one reads the writings of *critical* political sociologists, however, one looks in vain for *concepts* that can possibly reveal whether or when questioning of any kind is moving beyond the presupposition of exhausted possibilities.[24]

The same political sociologists who concede, however implicitly, that the political institutions and practices framing "conflicts" and "struggles" within the West are themselves remarkably stable, go even further in their concessions to the presupposition of exhausted possibilities at the moment that they turn to the study of the Third World and the East. As noted in chapter 1, they presuppose that political institutions and economic practices of existing Western democracies utterly exhaust actors' possibilities for nonauthoritarian social order. They thereby presuppose that Eastern nation-states, for instance, can only become and remain nonauthoritarian by recapitulating the same political institutions and economic practices that these political sociologists otherwise criticize for being unrepresentative and unresponsive in the West (eg. Skocpol and Amenta 1986: 136; Laumann and Knoke 1987: 395–7; Schmitter in preparation).

Finally, even within the mainstream literature devoted to the study of social movements, the literature dedicated to studying precisely those social units that ultimately initiate any possible "emancipatory" social change, there is also not a single ideal type of heterogeneous actors' and competing groups' possible social integration *within* social movements. The resource mobilization approach, for instance, eliminates this possibility conceptually (McCarthy and Zald 1977; Oberschall 1973). The same may be said, however, of the core concepts informing more general theories of collective behavior (Turner and Killian 1957; Smelser 1962), as well as those informing case studies devoted to the civil rights movement (McAdam 1982; Morris 1984) and the farm workers' movement (Jenkins 1985).

Irrespective of the contributions that the resource mobilization approach in particular brings to empirical research, and they are considerable, this approach revolves around premises of rational choice theory, premises no less materialist than those underlying traditional Marxism (and, for example, Therborn 1987: 249, readily employs rational choice and public choice premises). The undiscussed assumption of even the most iconoclastic students working within this approach is that movement elites invariably manipulate their mass following. The only issue is whether they do so directly, through purposeful control of resources (see Olson 1965 and Hechter 1987 for the principles involved), or else indirectly, through ideologies that obfuscate how the movement's material base is secured and distributed.[25]

2.4. Implications of the concept of social integration

In short, even as radical and mainstream political sociologists broaden the American literature of social control by appreciating the importance of inadvertent mechanisms, they too fall victim to the lacuna of integrative possibilities. They too fail to appreciate that the issue of heterogeneous actors' and competing groups' possible social integration within sectors, industries, or organizations of a modern civil society is itself "relatively autonomous" from their strictly material situation. Both in principle and in practice, the issue is "relatively autonomous" from (a) the class composition of a civil society, (b) the material bases and extent of stratification more generally (other than the most extreme inequalities), and (c) how social movements secure their material resources and maintain a mass following (chapter 11).

At least three questions escape the debate over the state and social movements as well as the American literature of social control:

First, is it possible for social scientists to demonstrate empirically when power holders' purposeful exercises of collective power, as well as any and all inadvertent mechanisms of social control, are being restrained normatively rather than merely strategically within any sector of a modern civil society?

Second, is it possible for social scientists to isolate the particular social movements, institutions, organizations, or subdivisions of organizations that contribute to the social infrastructure of a nonauthoritarian direction of *social* change under modern conditions?

Third, is it possible, finally, for social scientists to demonstrate that there are certain qualities of shared social duties that determine without exception whether heterogeneous actors and competing groups can possibly be integrated within any complex social unit?[26]

Put into a more positive statement, these three questions may be converted into the conditional proposition that follows:

(a) If it is the case that very particular types of social movements, institutions, and organizations contribute to a social infrastructure of normative restraint on both purposeful and inadvertent mechanisms of social control;

And (b) if these restraints are indeed irreducibly necessary to the very possibility of sustaining a nonauthoritarian direction of social change under modern conditions, as well as to expanding heterogeneous ac-

tors' and competing groups' prospects for social integration within
complex social units;

Then (c) the presence of these normative restraints within any modern
nation-state – Western or Eastern, Northern or Southern – is an issue
independent of whether most Western political institutions and economic practices are otherwise present or not.

Once researchers find these normative restraints within any sector of a
modern civil society, they can no longer legitimately *reduce* actors' behavioral conformity to any combination of mechanisms of social control. To
distinguish sectors of possible social integration is to expand the breadth of
empirical social and political research considerably. It is to reveal where
conceptual gaps in postwar political sociology have resulted in researchers'
obfuscating significant empirical issues.

The theory of societal constitutionalism proposed in this volume does not
simply demonstrate that a modern nation-state may be relatively egalitarian and yet become more manipulative, controlling, and even coercive than
a nation-state that is more stratified. This was demonstrated in practice,
after all, in the 1920s and 1930s: Were Nazi Germany, Fascist Italy, or
Stalinist Soviet Union more or less egalitarian than Great Britain, France,
or the United States? The purpose of the theory of societal constitutionalism is rather to reveal when two other developments are also taking
place, in practice:

> First, modern nation-states may remain liberal-democratic or become
> social-democratic, and yet simultaneously become more manipulative,
> controlling, and even coercive within and across more and more sec-
> tors, industries, and organizations of their civil societies.

> Second, modern nation-states that are neither liberal- nor social-demo-
> cratic may nonetheless sustain a nonauthoritarian direction of social
> change, and expand heterogeneous actors' and competing groups' pros-
> pects for social integration within more and more sectors, industries,
> and organizations of their civil societies.

Put more concretely, neither Brazil nor the Soviet Union, as examples, is
likely ever to recapitulate all or most of the political institutions and economic practices of Western democracies, despite all of the reforms currently
underway within each nation-state. Does this mean, however, that irrespective of the social and institutional changes taking place within either nation-
state, comparativists cannot specify whether and when their direction of
social and institutional change is either becoming more or less authoritarian?
Does this mean that comparativists cannot specify whether and when any
social order is indeed based rather exclusively on mechanisms of social
control, and whether and when it is based on heterogeneous actors' and

competing groups' possible social integration? Does this also mean, conversely, that as long as Western democracies maintain their current political institutions and economic practices, comparativists cannot specify whether and when *their* direction of social and institutional change is becoming more manipulative, controlling, and susceptible to social authoritarianism? If these independent variations can be demonstrated conceptually, and then operationalized, they may be used to orient detailed comparative studies that jettison the presupposition of exhausted possibilities.

3. Liberalism and the Weberian Dilemma: from restraints on government to restraints on civil society

Social theorists, not political theorists or philosophers, most fully appreciated by the mid-nineteenth and then early twentieth century the effects that *systemic* pressures of social change were having on government and civil society. Among social theorists, it was first Karl Marx and then Max Weber who addressed most methodically modernity's negative effects. Marx examined these negative effects in terms of the relationship between capitalism, alienation, and systemic crises, and Weber did so in terms of the relationship between rationalization, bureaucratization, and authoritarianism.[1] In succeeding generations, each theorist responded to dislocations of industrialization that had been accelerating in Great Britain and Western Europe since the second and third decades of the nineteenth century, dislocations that affected the United States and Scandinavia later in the century (Alapuro 1988 on Finland, for instance).

In spite of social theorists' profound analyses of these dislocations, however, constitutional theorists and liberal theorists by no means altered their portrayals of the liberal state and a market economy. It is understandable, of course, that those writing before the mid-nineteenth century failed to address the negative social implications of industrialization. What is curious is that so many influential constitutional theorists and liberal theorists failed to address social theorists' concerns *conceptually* far into the twentieth century (from Hobhouse 1911 to Friedrich 1941; Lindsay 1943; Loewenstein 1957; Sartori 1958).[2] Today, legal scholars suffer greatly from this major conceptual limitation of their theoretical traditions. They have difficulty, for instance, assessing whether legal institutions are maintaining their integrity or are adrift, and increasingly they turn to social theory and social science for assistance (e.g. Ackerman 1980, Ely 1980, Dworkin 1986). This begins to explain why major law journals today are often more sociological, philosophical, and economic than juridical (e.g. *Yale Law Journal* 1988, *Pennsylvania Law Review* 1982, but also the Chicago, Harvard, Stanford, and Michigan journals generally).

The central problem facing those working within constitutional and Lockean liberal traditions is that their inherited concepts fail to address manifestations of *social authoritarianism*. Their concepts fail to address pur-

40

posefully and *inadvertently* arbitrary exercises of collective power *by power-ful private enterprises within civil society.* As was the case with their fore-bears, today's constitutional and Lockean liberal theorists have difficulty extending their inherited concepts from the legal individual's relationship to the state to the legal individual's relationship to powerful organizations within civil society (Selznick 1969; Evan 1976; Stewart 1987; Buchanan 1989). At best, they may at times extend their concepts to address selected sets of *purposefully* arbitrary exercises of collective power by private enter-prises within a civil society. Yet, a great many mechanisms of social control escape their attention, and they continue to be most comfortable discussing arbitrary government. The problem of *inadvertently* arbitrary exercises of collective power within a civil society falls entirely outside of the possible scope of application of their inherited concepts. This is the problem that the classical social theorists developed conceptually by exploring what Parsons later called the Hobbesian problem of order, and rejecting the alternative of Lockean and Smithean complacency. Weber's work is particularly instruc-tive in this regard.

3.1. Implications of rationalization: drift toward authoritarianism

As capitalism was expanding and maturing in the West, Weber's social theory proved a powerful tool not only for social theorists but also for researchers – at least until the late 1960s. His concepts greatly influenced Marxist theory before World War II (Jay 1973, Wellmer 1976), and both theory and research in American sociology after the war.[3] Within Marxism his work provoked both negative and positive reactions: from Lukacs (1920–22) and Michels (1911), to the first generation of the Frankfurt school, and then later to theorists as different as Habermas and Poulantzas. Within sociology, postwar concerns about "mass society" and even the "authoritarian personality" bear the imprint of Weber's social theory more than Marx's. Countless developments within the broad area of political sociology were in many respects direct responses of one kind or another to Weber's concepts, including works by Mannheim, Parsons, and Merton early on, to those by Lipset, Barrington Moore, and Bendix later. The same may be said of major developments within the area of organizations research, including works by Selznick, Gouldner, and Blau, and those by Etzioni and Crozier, and Perrow and Coleman.

Weber saw modernity "fragmenting" traditional societies' nonrational norms and practices as well as actors' habitual behavior more generally (see Rudolph and Rudolph 1979 for an influential counterargument).[4] The "fragmentation of meaning" that results is, by his account, much more likely to culminate in a drift toward authoritarianism than in stable liberal-democracy. Indeed, the disruptions or dislocations that fascinated him most were systemic rather than purposeful, and yet he fully appreciated that systemic social forces are manifested, in practice, by concrete groups and concrete actors competing for resources, power, and influence. What intrigued Weber was how this competition is structured within any modern nation-state, and which substantive goods attract groups' and actors' competition. In his view, where actors' and groups' normative behavior had once dampened both the extent and intensity of interest competition in earlier stages of modernity, ongoing disruptions at later stages accelerate both. Once actors and groups are dislodged from their traditional and habitual moorings, they adjust their behavior *independently* to systemic forces as they compete more immediately within economic and political marketplaces. As a result, they become incapable of resisting or controlling the larger drift of social change *collectively*. This process of fragmentation, accelerated competition, and accommodation of systemic pressures results, therefore, in a literal drift of social change (Weber 1914–20: 212–54, 926–38; Schluchter 1981: 20–23, 53).[5]

Looking at the impact on organizations and institutions in particular, Weber saw all complex social units within all modern nation-states responding in one way or another to at least the following four manifestations of "drift." These responses are to be found generally, in his view, or quite irrespective of the many particular qualities that institutions and organizations happen to retain within particular nation-states:

> *First, the problem of fragmented meaning.* Actors' once shared understandings of social events and social practices become differentiated by function, and then further specialized by task (as Parsons and Smelser 1956 later emphasized).[6] This is reflected in the subcultures and occupational factions that may be found within any modern civil society.
>
> *Second, the problem of instrumental calculation.* Given the fragmentation of actors' "lived" meaning, their most routine agreements increasingly revolve around their independent calculations of instrumental or strategic "success" (see note 11): Will alternative courses of action either increase or decrease an enterprise's efficiency or effectiveness, as measured *by quantifiable results?* The significance of actors' subjective interests, their social relationships, and their expectations and aspirations is increasingly tied to such calculations, and to the piecemeal reforms and compromises consistent with them (as Lindblom 1959 later emphasized).
>
> *Third, the problem of bureaucratic organization.* Again, given the fragmentation of actors' "lived" meaning, all informal mechanisms of social control become less effective in maintaining social order. Consequently, organizations and institutions rely increasingly on formal social controls. This process – which Maine captured in the phrase "from

custom to contract" – is progressive in that formal mechanisms advance where informal mechanisms recede. Put more concretely, bureaucratization advances within enterprises of economic production as well as agencies of political and legal administration (Hechter 1987 elaborates this).

Fourth, the problem of charismatic leadership. Not all social and political decisions can be reduced to actors' instrumental calculations of efficiency or effectiveness and the mundane reforms and compromises surrounding them. When power holders exercise leadership, when they are innovative, they essentially impose new social duties on actors (and possibly enliven their aspirations as well) in nonrational ways. Innovative exercises of collective power might go not only beyond actors' instrumental calculations of efficiency and effectiveness, but also beyond their earlier expectations and beliefs.

3.2. The Weberian Dilemma as negative liberalism

Taking these four manifestations of systemic drift together, they result in what may be called the Weberian Dilemma (Dryzek 1987: 424 for the phrase "Weberian anxiety"). Like Hobbes's view of market society earlier, Weber's view of social change is quite at odds with Lockean liberals' belief that a likely outcome of actors' and groups' pursuit of their own subjective interests within civil society is benign liberal-democracy (see Parsons 1937a on the "problem of social order" and "Utilitarian Dilemma").[7] By Weber's account, a more likely outcome is for informal social controls to give way: (a) to intense competition between power holders and social influentials, then (b) to formal social controls as one faction or another endeavors to maintain social order, and finally (c) to political (and social) authoritarianism. Weber also pointed out that *any* effort by social influentials or power holders to restrain these developments, *any* effort on their part to gain collective control over the drift of social change itself, can only *accelerate* the outcome just noted. Why? This may be answered by exploring each side of the Weberian Dilemma in turn: the problem of normatively unmediated drift, and the problem of placing resilient normative restraints on drift.

3.2.1. The problem of drift: Weberian pathos v. liberal complacency

By contrast to constitutional theorists and Lockean liberals, Weber clearly feared that informally mediated competition by essentially self-interested actors can only culminate in bureaucratization and an authoritarian reaction. For him, it can only culminate in impositions of formal social controls.[8]

Thus, one side of the Weberian Dilemma: If actors' competition for influence, resources, and power within economic and political marketplaces is not restrained by *institutionalized* norms that challenge – subordinate – the sovereignty of actors' subjective interests, then drift is the only outcome possible. After all, as actors' and groups' competition of subjective interests becomes further and further detached from any and all *shared* norms of mediation and restraint, it can only simultaneously intensify and extend to more and more areas of social life. Normative fragmentation and bureaucratization extend in tandem, and the inadvertent result is political (and social) authoritarianism.

Indeed, Weber never accounted *conceptually* for a more benign outcome of the sovereignty of actors' subjective interests. Unlike postwar pluralist theorists (chapter 4), for instance, Weber was not impressed by the idea that the competition between interest groups (and political parties) for power and influence is sufficient in itself (a) to ensure a benign "balance" between actors' subjective interests (Aleinikoff 1987), (b) to sustain meaning among actors, and thereby to allow them (c) to restrain social change from drifting inadvertently toward its fated outcome. Today, Brennan and Buchanan conclude their discussion of "constitutional economics" in a similar fit of pathos: "We must come to agree that democratic societies, as they now operate, will self-destruct, perhaps slowly but nonetheless surely, unless the rules of the political game are changed" (1985: 150; also Hayek 1973–9). What is ironic is that these two hard-headed economists, who insist throughout their argument that only the sovereignty of subjective interests provides a proper "model" of the individual behavior that political and social institutions must be expected to restrain or mediate, see only one way out of contemporary self-destruction: a new morality or "civic religion."[9] The other side of the Weberian Dilemma, however, speaks to why this leap into faith cannot succeed in practice.

3.2.2. The problem of nonrational restraints on drift

Even if a set (or sets) of nonrational norms were indeed institutionalized, and even if this restrained all groups and actors institutionally from competing more immediately in their own subjective interests, this too can have only one outcome by Weber's account: One particular set of actors or groups invariably imposes *its* interests and nonrational beliefs on all others. Since this is likely to involve a further rationalization of formal social controls, political (and social) authoritarianism can be expected to result sooner by this route than if actors and groups had simply acceded more immediately to drift.

Relatedly, Weber was decidedly inconsistent and ambiguous whenever he discussed the relationship between (a) purposive-rational action and both

(b) value-rational action and (c) substantively rational action (respectively, *Zweckrationalität, Wertrationalität,* and *materielle Rationalität*).[10] He never explored methodically the implications of the latter two types of social action somehow resiliently mediating actors' and groups' interest competition. This is why he failed to account conceptually, or in principle, for the possibility of a sustained nonauthoritarian response to modernization.

Weber saw no social stratum firmly anchored in Western industrial societies capable of replacing ethical salvation religions as an institutionalized carrier of ethical ratio- nality and value-rationalization processes. . . . If this trend is not reversed, the rule of authoritarian force will, according to Weber, inevitably spread and suppress all political freedoms (Kalberg 1980: 1176).

Brennan and Buchanan (1985) have come to the same conclusion today, and their call for a civil religion, like Robert Bellah's and Daniel Bell's earlier, fails to offer a way out of the Weberian Dilemma.

3.3. Unmediated drift as "rationalization"

In sum, "rationalization" meant for Weber that immediate – normatively unmediated – self-interest becomes the only standard of "reason" that *het- erogeneous* actors and *competing* groups can possibly recognize and under- stand *in common* under modern conditions (also Hechter 1987; and Brennan and Buchanan 1985). Such actors and groups can recognize and understand quantifiable increases and decreases in efficient production or effective administration *in common* even as they remain both fragmented in their normative beliefs and competitive in their subjective interests (chap- ter 6).[11] What *heterogeneous* actors and *competing* groups cannot recognize and understand in common, by Weber's account, is any standard of *rea- soned* social action beyond the quantifiable outcomes of such strictly instru- mental actions (Habermas 1973a; 1977; 1979; 1981a,b).[12]

Weber appreciated that one result of this approach to rationalization is a quite narrow standard of "reason." Despite its narrowness, he was never- theless convinced that this standard offers heterogeneous actors and com- peting groups the only normative orientation that they are typically capable of recognizing and understanding in common under modern conditions. Despite its narrowness, this standard happens to be generalizable within its scope of application. Actors' behavioral fidelity to, or encroachments against, this standard of reason may be specified within any modern nation- state or social setting. This is precisely why the idealized behavior of *Homo economicus* (Brennan and Buchanan 1985: 14) proves so useful in compara- tive analysis: Evidence of the presence or absence of this behavior escapes the fragmentation of meaning otherwise affecting social scientists them- selves. Still, it must be kept in mind that, by Weber's account, this narrow yet generalizable standard of reason orients actors and groups toward contributing inadvertently to an authoritarian rather than benign outcome.

Weber could understand Lockean liberals' optimism and complacency, therefore, even as he ridiculed their sophomorism. After all, the unmediated drift of social change likely takes longer to culminate in authoritarianism than any effort by any set of actors to institutionalize a resilient normative mediation. Weber rejected liberals' optimism and complacency because he refused, regardless, to posit that a nonauthoritarian social order is somehow sustained "automatically" on the basis of the sovereignty of actors' (unmediated) subjective interests itself. He refused to accept any reference to a "hidden hand," or to actors' "natural identity of interests," as somehow accounting mysteriously for a nonauthoritarian direction of social change under modern conditions.[13]

3.4. Can the Weberian Dilemma be resolved?

Still, Weberians have yet to account for considerable empirical evidence themselves, including the following two truisms of the late twentieth century: First, not all contemporary nation-states may be categorized as authoritarian a priori.[14] Second, systemic pressures of rationalization have nonetheless clearly intensified as well as extended to encompass more and more areas of social life. In short, the task facing Weberians today, now seventy years after Weber's death, is to provide *concepts* capable of answering either of the following questions:[15]

> (a) Why are all nation-states today not authoritarian, and in particular the most "advanced" nation-states? After all, the latter have experienced the most extensive and intensive systemic pressures of drift.

> (b) Alternatively, why are all nation-states today not more bureaucratic, and thereby more controlling and authoritarian, than they currently are?

With these two questions, the Weberian Dilemma is converted from the prospective issues that concerned Weber himself into retrospective issues that today's Weberians cannot avoid addressing. They cannot avoid addressing these issues because the conversion is accomplished using Weber's concepts alone.

3.4.1. Three points in retrospect: the importance of the "external"

Given the extension and intensification of systemic pressures of rationalization over the past seventy years, there is only one way in which bureaucratization and authoritarianism could have been mediated or restrained anywhere in the modern world. Heterogeneous actors and competing groups had to have institutionalized a set of norms (or alternating sets of norms, if one considers Pareto's social theory) and then subsequently maintained their integrity. These norms would have had to remain demonstrably *non-rational*, literally not-purposive-rational. That is, they would have had to exhibit over the years a most important quality, a quality revealed by their status as a residual category: They would have had to remain "outside" of, or "external" to, the drift of rationalization itself. Only by remaining "external" could heterogeneous actors and competing groups have possibly remained oriented by the same norms *in common,* even as they otherwise experienced intensified interest competition and a fragmentation of meaning. Only on the basis of a shared normative orientation, after all, could they have been capable of *resiliently* restraining *themselves* from otherwise competing more immediately, and thereby contributing to drift.

When actors compete immediately in their own subjective interests, their behavior may be thought of as "falling within," or being "internal to," the inadvertent drift toward bureaucratization and authoritarianism that Weber described. Given that this behavior is "internal" to the Weberian Dilemma and Lockean liberalism alike, any and all resilient normative *mediations* of, or *restraints* on, it are clearly "external." Since liberalism fails to address the Weberian Dilemma conceptually, and instead substitutes optimism and complacency for Weber's pathos, this sense of the "external" is as alien to liberal conceptual frameworks as it is to Weberian conceptual frameworks.

For instance, Brennan and Buchanan are liberal economists who nonetheless share Weber's pathos. Yet, they adamantly oppose all resilient normative restraints on drift because they clearly see that this challenges the sovereignty of actors' subjective interests.

The contractarian derives all value from individual participants in the community and rejects externally defined sources of value, including "natural rights." . . . [S]ocietal or communitarian influences enter through modifications in the values that are potentially expressed by the individual and not externally. . . . [Thus], a contractarian "explanation" of collective order [is that] individuals will be led, by their own evaluation of alternative prospects, to establish *by unanimous agreement* a collectivity, a polity, charged with the performance of specific functions, including, first, the provision of the services of the protective or minimal state and, second, the possible provision of genuinely collective consumption services. (Brennan and Buchanan 1985: 21–2, my emphasis)

Buchanan is opposed to elevating actors' "natural rights" to a resilient normative restraint on actors' subjective interests, and even Brennan takes exception to Buchanan's going this far. Thus, the Brennan-Buchanan collaboration nicely recapitulates the tensions riddling liberalism's Lockean and Hobbesian strands (see chapter 4). Regardless, the point stands that resilient normative restraints on actors' interest competition within economic and political marketplaces may be labeled *external normative restraints.*

Even as Weber never addressed them methodically, the very point of his social theory is that only the institutionalization of external normative restraints of one kind or another can account for a nonauthoritarian direction of social change despite modern conditions of drift.[16] Yet, ironically, this sense of the "external" is even more alien to Weber's social theory than it is to liberalism. It raises a distinct problem for today's Weberians precisely because *any and all* normative restraints on drift are invariably characterized by them as accelerating bureaucratization and the fated outcome. Still, two points stand up well *even within Weber's conceptual framework:*

> First, nonrational normative restraints of any kind are, by definition, external to the *inadvertent* drift of *rationalization.*

> Second, Weber's concern that rationalization culminates in authoritarianism rather than liberal-democracy distinguishes his social theory *in essence* from any and all variants of Lockean liberalism.[17]

Given these two points, a third point comes into view that is more revealing. Even as it is a mere corollary of the first two points, this third point begins to pose the Weberian Dilemma in such a way that the greatest limitations of Weber's conceptual framework and of Brennan and Buchanan's "constitutional economics" and both Hechter's and Coleman's rational choice theories begin to come into view:

> Third, if some set (or sets) of nonrational norms had not remained "external" in the sense just discussed, then, after seventy years of systemic pressures of rationalization, it would be highly unlikely that any nation-state today could have avoided drifting toward authoritarianism.

Again, the problem that today's Weberians face is that the third point follows directly from Weber's own conceptual framework itself, and yet it reveals unambiguously that Weberian social theory is incapable of accounting for considerable empirical evidence to the contrary: Some modern nation-states have clearly avoided authoritarianism, *in practice,* into the late twentieth century. There is also no good reason to believe a priori that authoritarianism is imminent in *every* modern nation-state's future.

3.4.2. Three questions in retrospect: an agenda for societal constitutionalism

The possibility of resolving the Weberian Dilemma conceptually, and thereby accounting for any possibility of a nonauthoritarian direction of social change in the late twentieth century, hinges on whether the following two questions can be answered:

First, how could any set of nonrational normative restraints have remained external in the sense noted above, after seventy years of actors' self-interested competition within economic and political marketplaces?

Second, is a single, identifiable set of such nonrational normative restraints to be found within each and every instance of nonauthoritarian social change in the late twentieth century? Or is the possibility of such a direction of social change contingent on circumstances altogether particular to each and every nation-state in which it is found?

If there is such a set, it would constitute the social infrastructure supporting a nonauthoritarian direction of social change. Put differently, it could credibly claim to ground the nonauthoritarian/authoritarian distinction in comparative perspective.

Looking at the first question, consider the difficulties actors would face in keeping any set of nonrational normative restraints external to their own self-interested competition. For instance, power holders in government and social influentials in civil society who are competing for material resources, political power, and social influence would surely also compete over how any set of purported external normative restraints is interpreted and then enforced. The debate among jurists in the United States over "strict constructionist" interpretations of the Constitution illustrates this only too well (Ely 1980). Clearly, power holders and social influentials would oppose any and all interpretations that challenged their material interests. As such challenges accumulated, this would lead eventually to radical questioning of the restraint's, and the interpreters', very legitimacy. Each action that power holders and social influentials took in their own material interests would involve their negotiating and renegotiating the restraints' very "meaning." Whatever "shared meaning" the restraints may have had when instituted would thereby steadily unravel under such everyday challenges.

This is what Weber so appreciated. Actors within modern nation-states never develop, let alone sustain, some "natural identity" of subjective interests. Nor, certainly, do they develop or sustain some shared understanding of substantive norms, whether those of founders' "substantive intent" or else those of some "civil religion" revolving around the cultural norms or "sacred" qualities of any lived social fabric. As soon as the "meaning" of any set of purported external normative restraints is *brought into* arenas of interest competition, moreover, it simultaneously loses its external status. It is *brought into* economic and political marketplaces, and thereby into the broader drift of social change.

Unfortunately, the Weberian Dilemma does not end here, with an already seemingly insoluble problem. Continuing with this retrospective portrayal, but turning now to the second question above, consider the difficulties that *social scientists* face in employing the concept of the external. They must specify some particular set of nonrational normative restraints whose sheer presence within any modern nation-state somehow accounts for its escaping authoritarianism in the late twentieth century. Moreover, if any purported set of external normative restraints turns out, *in substance,* to favor the strategic interests of only selected sets of actors and groups, as Weber clearly expected would be the case, then even if it somehow remained external, in principle, it would fail to account for a *non*authoritarian direction of social change *in practice.* After all, one set of substantive issues – the "meaning" of the normative restraints themselves – is being suspended from interest competition. This is likely to spawn opposition and outright conflict. Its external status could only be maintained, therefore, by the favored actors and groups extending formal mechanisms of social control in an effort to maintain social order regardless.

Weber failed to explore methodically one possible alternative, however, an alternative that at least remains consistent with his own conceptual framework: Those actors and groups expected to oppose the restriction on interest competition just noted may not rise in opposition because they have been successfully manipulated. By hypostatizing manipulation and actors' self-restriction, today's Weberians can offer an explanation for the presence of nonauthoritarian social orders in the late twentieth century.[18] But instead of this leading to sophisticated comparative analyses, it leads to a great irony. Weberians' *only* credible explanation for the presence of nonauthoritarian social orders in the late twentieth century may be reduced to the following proposition: It is precisely within today's *non*authoritarian social orders that heterogeneous actors and competing groups are *most* successfully manipulated.[19]

Yet, it may be, finally, that a way of responding to the Weberian Dilemma is beginning to come into view, however tentatively. The Weberian Dilemma may be resolved without resorting either to Lockean complacency or to an untheorized concept of manipulation if a positive answer can be provided to yet a third question:

> Third, are there external normative restraints, *in practice,* that (a) remain "external" to the drift of rationalization in some significant sense, *and* simultaneously (b) account for any and all instances of a nonauthoritarian direction of social change (and actors' possible social integration) under modern conditions?

This volume is dedicated to answering this question. With this, the Weberian Dilemma may be resolved; the questions posed earlier may be
answered; and the lacuna of integrative possibilities may be filled.

3.5. Illustration: "professional integrity" and limits of Weberian sociology

Social scientists rely on the concept of instrumental or rational action to
determine when social enterprises are becoming more efficient in production or more effective in administration. But as Weber demonstrated so
compellingly, this concept fails to reveal whether the larger direction of
social change is benign or threatening. It clearly fails to reveal whether
heterogeneous actors and competing groups are demonstrably controlled
or possibly integrated.

At this early point in the presentation of the theory of societal constitutionalism, it is best to illustrate the narrowness of the standard of rational
action, as well the problems attending any effort to restrain or mediate
rationalization, with a hypothetical example rather than grappling with the
details of an empirical example: Consider the possibility of leaders of a
professional association opposing the changes being proposed by administrators of universities, hospitals, or corporate research divisions. They do
so because of the effects these changes will have on how professionals are
organized at these sites.

On one side, the administrators' proposal is indeed a rational response to
commercial pressures. In fact, the proposed changes have already proven
to be successful (that is, efficient or effective) within, for example, department stores and insurance companies. On the other side, leaders of the
professional association cite their members' purported fidelity to (nonrational) "norms of professional integrity" as their rationale for opposing
these changes. They insist that their members' professional integrity takes
precedence over the narrow standard of rational action upon which the
administrators are operating. Professionals are not retailers or bean counters, they say in so many words; professionals are rather trained experts
who dedicate their expertise to their clients' (and the larger community's)
"best interests."

Are either the proposed changes or the opposition to them a manifestation of social integration, whether of members within the profession, the
profession within the larger organizations, or the professional association
within the larger civil society? Or, are they instead a manifestation of social
control, again whether of members within the profession, the profession
within the larger organizations, or the professional association within the
larger civil society? The fragmentation of meaning characteristic of modernity renders it impossible for social scientists (or actors) to address such

issues methodically using the conceptual frameworks of liberalism or Weberian social theory. Yet, these issues are far from abstract moral dilemmas. They are rather concrete policy problems that surface repeatedly, in a
variety of ways, within all modern nation-states. Only if the notion of
"professional integrity" can be rendered falsifiable and operationalizable,
however, can these issues be addressed by social scientists (to say nothing
of their being resolved by heterogeneous actors and competing groups, in
practice).

Weberians currently dismiss all such issues out of hand as hopelessly
"normative" or "ideological" (Waters 1989, chapter 8). But such labeling
restates the point made in chapter 2 and now in this chapter: These issues,
like so many others *in evidence* within modern nation-states today, fall
outside of the conceptual frameworks of social control that are currently
available. To employ *any* of these conceptual frameworks is to label such
issues "normative" a priori.

Consider how the hypothetical case above might be addressed by a Weberian today: On the one hand, the Weberian might reduce the issue of
"professional integrity" to two questions: First, what are actors' and
groups' immediate subjective or material interests? Second, what are their
substantive beliefs regarding the profession's social status and political
influence? In answering these questions, the Weberian *reduces* association
leaders' claims – that their members' purported fidelity to "professional
integrity" takes precedence over instrumental action – to discovering what
leaders' (or members') *particular* interests and beliefs are. Whatever these
turn out to be, they invariably comprise only one set of material interests
and substantive beliefs among many others to be found within any civil
society. Association leaders' opposition to administrators' proposals may
thereby be *reduced* to one of two *strategic* positions: It may be reduced to
association leaders' own immediate interests and beliefs. Or else it may be
reduced to the immediate interests and beliefs of prominent members
within (or influential constituencies outside of) the professional association
that the leaders are representing, either directly or indirectly. In either
case, it is impossible for the Weberian to demonstrate that association
leaders' opposition rests on any normative standard or "principle" that can
credibly claim precedence over instrumental action.

On the other hand, and an even more reductionist tack, the Weberian
might convert the issue of "professional integrity" to the following question: Is association leaders' opposition rational? Aside from their opposition being reducible to one strategic position or another, the Weberian
might now handily demonstrate that very notion of "professional integrity"
is not rational. Moreover, since the standard of rational action alone appears to Weberians to be *generalizable,* as a norm of reason that even
heterogeneous actors and competing groups might recognize and under-

stand in common under modern conditions, the Weberian can only conclude that the notion of "professional integrity" is devoid of reason altogether. Again, for a Weberian to label the notion of "professional integrity" first nonrational and then unreasoned is for a Weberian to be as generous to association leaders as he or she can be.

4. Conceptual foundations of societal constitutionalism: from internal restraints on government to external restraints on drift

It is only possible to escape the reductionist tacks noted at the end of the last chapter if a standard of "professional integrity" can be specified that is normative and yet also exhibits both of the following qualities. First, this normative standard must be capable of being recognized and understood *in common* by *heterogeneous* actors and *competing* groups even under modern conditions of drift. Second, this same normative standard must also qualify as at least possibly reasoned in some sense broader than the admittedly narrow standard of rational or instrumental action. If it turns out that there are no normative standards of professional integrity available that exhibit both of these qualities, then whenever professionals endeavor to maintain their purported "integrity" at the expense of other actors' subjective interests this is reducible to a power play on their part. As contributors to the "social closure" or "monopoly" approach to professions insist (from Larson 1977 and Collins 1979 to Murphy 1988 and even Abbott 1988), professionals are simply influencing power holders to impose on other actors the costs of whatever special advantages or "protected status" they are being accorded.

Four analytical distinctions fill the lacuna of integrative possibilities and open the way to responding directly to the Weberian Dilemma, including demonstrating that there is indeed a normative standard of "professional integrity" that exhibits both of the qualities just noted. The purpose of this chapter is to introduce these analytical distinctions, and in this way to propose a terminology with which to respond to the Weberian Dilemma directly.

4.1. Four analytical distinctions and four institutions of restraint

The first analytical distinction of societal constitutionalism has already been introduced in the discussion of the lacuna of integrative possibilities. This is:

> First, the distinction between (a) instances of demonstrable *social control* and (b) instances of *heterogeneous* actors' and *competing* groups' possible *social integration*.

54

Now three other analytical distinctions may be introduced. Together, they survey all of the normative and strategic restraints on group competition and on systemic pressures of drift that are to be found *empirically* within any modern social order as such, whether authoritarian or nonauthoritarian.

To anticipate the argument for a moment, one type of normative restraints comes to the fore within this survey that is present empirically only within *non*authoritarian social orders in particular. This is the type labeled external procedural restraints. Also coming to the fore is another type of normative restraints that is present empirically within any instance of heterogeneous actors' and competing groups' possible social integration within any sector, industry, or organization of a civil society. This is the type labeled internal procedural restraints. This volume is dedicated to (a) distinguishing these two restraints from all others, (b) specifying their analytical components as *procedural* norms, and (c) discussing the implications of their presence or absence within modern nation-states.

Returning to the overview of analytical distinctions, the second addresses the Weberian Dilemma directly by resting on the distinction between (a) the problem of arbitrary government that concerned liberal and constitutional theory and (b) the problem of drift that concerned Weber and other classical social theorists. This is:

Second, the distinction between (a) *internal restraints* on *purposeful* exercises of collective power by government (or by "private" enterprises in civil society) and (b) *external restraints* on *inadvertent* exercises of collective power that result from the drift of social change.

The key to whether such a distinction can be made, of course, is whether there are identifiable institutions and norms on which even heterogeneous actors and competing groups rely, in practice, whenever *a civil society* resists systemic pressures of drift toward control and authoritarianism. Only if such institutions and norms can indeed be found *empirically,* can the presence of nonauthoritarian social orders in the late twentieth century be described and explained in a way that responds directly to the Weberian Dilemma. It is institutions and norms of *external* restraint that enable heterogeneous actors and competing groups to respond collectively to drift, in practice, despite their own ongoing fragmentation of meaning and functional differentiation. Institutions and norms of *internal* restraint cannot assist them in this way since such restraints are by definition caught up in the drift of social change themselves.

The third analytical distinction of the theory of societal constitutionalism is drawn within each set of restraints. Some internal restraints on purposeful exercises of collective power are directly substantive whereas others are procedural mediations. Similarly, some external restraints on drift are directly substantive and others are procedural mediations. Thus, this results in:

> Third, the distinction between (a) normative restraints whose impact on power holders is immediate or directly *substantive,* and (b) normative restraints whose impact on power holders is first and foremost a *procedural mediation,* and only then substantive.[1]

Putting the second and third distinctions together, the theory of societal constitutionalism revolves around the relationship, in practice, between the following four basic sets of institutions of restraint:

> (1) Internal substantive restraints on purposeful exercises of collective power.
>
> (2) Internal procedural restraints on purposeful exercises of collective power.
>
> (3) External substantive restraints on inadvertent or systemic exercises of collective power.
>
> (4) External procedural restraints on inadvertent or systemic exercises of collective power.

The social integration/social control distinction revolves around whether the second of these basic sets of restraints is found empirically within any existing sector, industry, or organization of a modern civil society. The non-authoritarian/authoritarian distinction, in turn, revolves around whether the fourth of these basic sets of restraints is also found empirically within any existing social order.

Yet a fourth distinction comes into play as these four basic sets of restraints are discussed below, but it is less important than the first three. Institutions of internal restraint may be further distinguished. Each may be subdivided in terms of whether its impact on power holders rests on heterogeneous actors' and competing groups' (a) shared recognition and understanding of nonrational *norms,* or else on their (b) independent, and more or less rational, calculations of their own *strategic* advantages and opportunities (see note 4). By contrast, all external restraints are normative, irrespective of whether they are substantive or procedural; once they are reduced to strategic considerations, they simultaneously lose their status of being "external" to group competition and systemic drift.

4.2. The importance of institutions of external procedural restraint

It is the presence or absence of institutions and norms of external *procedural* restraint within a modern civil society that ultimately accounts for whether its direction of change is, respectively, (a) nonauthoritarian, and then possibly integrative, or else (b) one of increasing control and susceptibility to social authoritarianism. This emphasis on the importance of institutions and norms of external procedural restraint is what most essentially distinguishes *societal* constitutionalism from governmental constitutionalism and the liberal tradition more generally. On the one hand, it distinguishes societal constitutionalism from the latter's rather exclusive concern with arbitrary government. This is why constitutionalists once emphasized the inviolability of the division of powers, the separation of church and state, and the public/private distinction more generally, and why today they tend to emphasize the inviolability of individuals' "natural rights" within civil society.[2] On the other hand, it also distinguishes societal constitutionalism from liberals' preoccupation with extending economic and political competition into more and more areas of social life.

The theory of societal constitutionalism parts company with these traditions by methodically addressing the negative implications of systemic drift that concerned Weber and other social theorists. Western democratic institutions and practices fail to address these implications, either in principle or in practice (see the following discussions of pluralism and neocorporatism). This is widely recognized in the literature, from Arendt and Habermas to Hayek and Buchanan. The most succinct way of putting the problem is that the sheer presence of these political institutions and market practices alone fails to account for why control and authoritarianism are restrained within any modern *civil society*. After all, Western political institutions and market practices were never designed, either historically or today, to resiliently restrain *rational* exercises of collective power *by the leaders of "private" enterprises within civil society*.

But even more generally, and as demonstrated in chapter 2, there is no theoretical tradition institutionalized by existing Western democracies that distinguishes instances of heterogeneous actors' and competing groups' possible social integration from instances of their demonstrable social control. This distinction moves the theory of societal constitutionalism beyond liberal and constitutional traditions, and also beyond the conceptual frameworks inherited from the classical social theorists.

The four sets of restraints listed above are discussed in turn in the remainder of this chapter, and table 4.1 helps to visualize their relationship. Still, some of the examples filling this chart, and even the concept of external procedural restraints so central to the theory of societal constitutionalism, is not fully discussed in this chapter. This cannot be accomplished until Lon Fuller's legal theory (chapter 6) and then the concept of collegial formations (chapter 8) have both been presented. For that matter, even the basic analytical distinction between internal and external restraints is not really

Table 4.1. *Internal and external restraints: societal constitutionalism's threshold of institutionalization*

		Strategic	Normative
I Internal Restraints	(IA) Directly Substantive	Group Competition Patron-Client Networks	Religious Proscriptions Natural Rights Division of Powers
	(IB) Procedural Mediation	Elections Rational-Legal Enforcement	Interpretability of Law ↑ Societal Constitutionalism
II External Restraints	(IIB) Procedural Mediation	×	↓ Collegial Formations
	(IIA) Directly Substantive	Nationalism State Religion	Natural Law National Traditions

Notes: 1. The category of strategic restraints at IIB is left blank because it is oxymoronic: There are no external procedural restraints that are strictly strategic rather than normative. A strategic restraint is provided by individual or group actors' self-interested competition for resources or influence. It is precisely this competition that defines both the liberal market and Weberian drift, as opposed to any procedural restraint on them.

2. As noted in the text (page 56), all external restraints are normative. Because those that are directly substantive are blatantly exclusionary, all of the examples at IIA are imposed strategically under modern conditions. Nationalism, for instance, is what Arendt (1951) had in mind when coining the phrase "tribal nationalism": In a multicultural, modern society, groups' exclusion is imposed strategically, at extreme costs to all affected. Once natural law tenets or even more benign national traditions become contested and controversial, rather than remaining unquestioned and unchallenged, they too are upheld strategically. But because exclusion is more benign in these instances, or less costly to those affected, these tenets and traditions appear to be more normative than strategic.

3. Discussion of each of the sets of categories in table 4.1 may be found in the following pages:
IA at pages 60–64.
IB at pages 64–67.
IIA at pages 77–79.
IIB at pages 79–83.

sharpened sufficiently in this chapter to inform empirical research. This is accomplished only after voluntaristic action has been rendered into a distinct concept (chapter 7).

4.3. Four institutions of restraint: from liberalism to societal constitutionalism

4.3.1. Institutions of internal restraint: the legacy of Western democracy

Heterogeneous actors and competing groups rely on institutions of internal restraint whenever they recognize in common, and then restrain collectively, *purposeful* exercises of collective power. *These same actors and groups cannot rely on these institutions even to recognize in common, let alone to restrain collectively, systemic shifts in the direction of change whose impact is inadvertently controlling and authoritarian.* This impact is inadvertent precisely *because* heterogeneous actors and competing groups fail to recognize that their own subjective interests are leading them toward increasing both the extent and intensity of their own social control at the expense of their own prospects for social integration.

The discussion in this first section is dedicated to surveying internal restraints on purposeful exercises of collective power, many of which existing Western democracies place on arbitrary government. As a result, many of these restraints are quite familiar: the division of powers; elections and competing political parties; the competition for political influence between pluralist interest groups, patron-client networks, or neocorporatist peak associations; judicial review within common-law countries (chapter 6); and either religious, traditional, or constitutional proscriptions on the very scope of governmental power and authority itself.[3]

These institutions are indeed the major legacy of Western constitutional traditions, liberal democratic theory, and Western democratic practice. With the exception of the proscriptions, however, they were all designed explicitly to accommodate, not resiliently to restrain or mediate, *Homo economicus*'s self-interested competition within economic (and then political) marketplaces. They are all institutions of internal restraint that fail to address the Weberian Dilemma. Their significance is not being underestimated by pointing this out. Quite to the contrary, *these institutions have always appealed to liberals precisely because they remain forever "internal" in this sense.* Western democratic institutions were *designed* to be forever *incapable* of sustaining *any* resilient normative obstacles to *Homo economicus*'s self-interested competition within economic (and then political) marketplaces (Macpherson 1962; Lowi 1969).

Thus, rather than Buchanan's railings against "externally defined sources of value" being idiosyncratic, they are sentiments widely shared by liberal theorists (and economists) generally (Brennan and Buchanan 1985: 21). Similarly, it is because these institutions were designed to accommodate the sovereignty of actors' subjective interests that Weber never became much interested in them. He never discussed them methodically (see chapter 3, note 3). His central concern was how actors' normatively unmediated competition of subjective interests contributes to drift. It was eminently clear to him that liberal-democratic institutions are accomplices in drift, and by no means pose external restraints to it.

Keeping in mind the analytical distinctions of societal constitutionalism presented above, the institutions on which heterogeneous actors and competing groups rely as internal restraints on purposeful exercises of collective power fall into two broad types:

> First, institutions that are *directly substantive,* whether (a) strictly strategic,[4] such as interest group or political party competition, or else (b) normative, whether religious proscriptions on the scope of governmental power and authority or constitutional reifications of the division of powers or of actors' "natural rights" in civil society.

> Second, institutions that are *procedural mediations,* whether (a) strictly strategic, such as elections and the rational enforcement of positive laws, or else (b) normative – the threshold of interpretability of positive laws and of shared social duties.

Institutions of internal substantive restraint (IA): "natural rights" (normative) and group competition (strategic). Institutions of internal *substantive* restraint include *normative* restraints, such as religious, constitutional, or statutory proscriptions on the scope of governmental power and authority. These restraints often delimit government directly, but they also may do so indirectly. They may codify that which is inviolably "private," including property and individuals' "natural rights" (Fellman 1976; Dworkin 1977; McClosky and Brill 1983). Other normative restraints falling within this type include: the division of powers, the separation of church and state in particular,[5] and the distinction between the private and the public more generally (*Pennsylvania Law Review* 1982).

Still, the single most important institution of internal substantive restraint on purposeful exercises of collective power in comparative perspective is today, as always, an institution that is strictly *strategic* rather than normative. This is the institution of interest group competition, or, alternatively, of competition between peak associations, patron-client networks, or religious and ethnic sections. Whereas competitive elections (addressed in the next section) are not to be found within a great many modern nation-states,[6] *institutionalized* group competition for resources, power, and influence may be found everywhere. It may be found within and around all branches of government (e.g. pluralist theory, from Truman 1951 to Laumann and Knoke 1987),[7] as well as within and around all complex organizations of civil society (e.g. the power approach to organizations, from Thompson 1967 to Perrow 1979). Unlike all other institutions of internal *substantive* restraint, whether strategic or normative, the sheer *presence* of group competition is indeed generalizable, in practice. It may not be formally organized in every nation-state or organization without exception, but it is nonetheless present without exception. Everywhere power holders are in fact restrained by the extent and intensity of strategic opposition that *they anticipate* their actions are likely to stimulate among interested parties.[8]

Even as its sheer presence is generalizable, however, this institution's *impact* on power holders, and, of course, on the direction of social change, is particular. Its impact differs greatly from nation-state to nation-state, and from complex organization to complex organization. Indeed, the interests at issue, as well as the number, size, and relative influence of the groups competing, may change substantially within particular nation-states and particular organizations over even brief periods of time. Precisely because this institution's impact is so particular, so subject to change, and yet so significant, contributors to the literatures of comparative politics and political sociology have endeavored for more than forty years to describe, explain, and predict it. Their ongoing efforts account, for example, for the debate over pluralism and elitism in the 1950s and 1960s (from Truman 1951 to Lowi 1969), the debate in the late 1960s and early 1970s over the resilience of ethnic communalism in the Third World and its revival in Western democracies (Enloe 1973, Connor 1972, 1973), as well as the ongoing debate initiated in the mid-1970s over neocorporatism, labor mobilization, and social democracy (see Schmitter 1974; Fulcher 1987 for a succinct review; and Laumann and Knoke 1987 for an assessment in two U.S. policy domains).

Precisely because its impact is particular, *heterogeneous* actors and *competing* groups cannot rely on this institution to recognize *in common* whether either of two developments is unfolding in practice. First, the presence of even robust group competition cannot assist them in recognizing *in common* the significance of any *norms* of internal *substantive* restraint on government (or on private enterprises within civil society), irrespective of what these norms happen to be. After all, one interest group's support of, for example, a religious or constitutional proscription on the scope of governmental power and authority may be opposed stridently by many others. And either side in this dispute might eventually receive an electoral mandate for its strategic position. The same holds true ultimately for any group's support of, or opposition to, any and all constitutional and statutory proscriptions on government, including: the division of powers itself, the separation of church and state, actors' "natural rights" in civil society, and the private/public distinction more generally. The significance of *resiliently* upholding any of these normative restraints in the face of interest group opposition is not self-evident to actors (or researchers) under modern conditions.

Put in terms of the illustration in chapter 1, William may believe that Scott is violating either his "natural rights" or other "self-evident" proscriptions against purposeful exercises of power within the corporation, and many of his fellow chemists might well agree with him. But Scott and company managers may for their part simply dismiss all of this out of hand as either a most infantile normative belief on the chemists' part, or else as an outright power play by professionals – an interest group – within the corporation. It may also strike them, for that matter, that the chemists' belief evinces an utter lack of sophistication in grasping longstanding company practices, to say nothing of grasping which groups within the company currently wield the greatest power and influence (Goldner and Ritti 1967).

Second, and more importantly, competing groups and heterogeneous actors (including social scientists) cannot rely on the sheer presence of even robust group competition to recognize in common when exercises of collective power are *purposefully* arbitrary.[9] After all, any action taken by a state agency, or by a corporation, that the leaders of one interest group condemn as arbitrary may just as well be supported enthusiastically by the leaders of many other interest groups. And, once again, either side in this dispute may eventually secure an electoral mandate. Indeed, the most innovative policies and programs undertaken by any agency or corporation invariably test the outer limits of what was once proscribed, what was once labeled arbitrary.

Looking again at the illustration in chapter 1, William may believe personally that Scott is acting arbitrarily, and, again, other chemists within the corporation might well agree with him. But Scott is likely to respond that (a) William is not as fully aware of the company's "real situation" as are Scott and company executives, and that (b) the company pays the chemists' salaries and not any chemical association to which they might appeal for support. Is the company an innovator within its industry or a wielder of arbitrary collective power? Whatever the answer may be, what is certain is that the extent of mobilization of interested parties, whether within or outside of the corporation, cannot reveal what it is.

Within the United States as well as across Scandinavia and Western Europe, the outer limits of domestic policy-making processes are ceaselessly being tested, adjusted, and readjusted (Luhmann 1986, 1990 revolve around this). Often particular domestic programs fall somewhere between what is innovative and what is arbitrary, and perceptions of their impact are typically mixed (Habermas 1989 revolves around this problem). Consider, as examples, efforts to either retrench or redefine affirmative action (in the United States) or social welfare policies (in Scandinavia and Western Europe); attempts to institute prayer in public schools; controversies over the holdings of school and public libraries and over school curricula and school control; periodic "waves" of police corruption and public outrage (Goldstein 1977); the endless dispute over abortion as well as over health care generally; and emerging concerns over state governments' water rights, rights over other natural resources, and ecological policies. Which programs and proposals, if any, increase government's arbitrariness or the arbitrariness of "private" enterprises within civil society? Again, this is something that even robust group competition alone cannot reveal unambiguously one way or the other.

What robust group competition does reveal is something quite different: Political or corporate issues once assumed to be settled, and thereby "removed" from groups' ongoing competition within political marketplaces, may be repoliticized at any moment (again, Luhmann 1990 emphasizes this). This institution's supposed outer limits are never fixed once and for all but instead are endlessly being expanded or contracted over time (see Lowi 1969 and Dahl 1982 on the former; Habermas 1989 on the latter). As interest groups compete strategically, they quite often test what this institution's supposed normative (or strategic) limits really are. Indeed, those groups initiating tests may be rewarded in time for being "innovative." After all, which domestic issues today are unreservedly removed from politicization within any modern nation-state? Put differently, from which specific areas of social life is the state *unreservedly prohibited* from entering, under pressures from interest-group mobilization, either within the United States or any other modern nation-state? Is there any issue that a modern state is unreservedly prohibited from defining or redefining as "political," as falling within the reach of its own innovative actions or else those taken by "private" enterprises within its civil society?

To be sure, institutions of internal substantive restraint also include longstanding programs of political parties within parliamentary democracies, along with some remarkably stable coalitions of interests within their civil societies. For instance, once the organizations and institutions of a welfare state are in place, even President Reagan and Prime Minister Thatcher experienced formidable *strategic* obstacles in attempting to sidestep or reverse these domestic policies. This is the case even as each leader wielded significant electoral strength and interest-group support of his or her own.[10] This is a clear example of the capacity of the institution of robust interest-group competition to restrain purposeful exercises of collective power by government, and yet of its inability to reveal whether the proposed exercises are arbitrary – or, for that matter, whether normative restraints are arbitrary.

Institutions of internal procedural restraint (IB): elections, legal enforcement (strategic) and legal interpretation (normative). The impact that institutions of internal *procedural* restraint have on power holders is often more subtle and indirect than that of institutions of internal substantive restraint. Yet, the former institutions include *strategic* restraints which can be rather direct in their impact, as instrumental or rational procedures. The latter include, as examples, those procedures designed to render elections most effective and fair (Przeworski 1986; Przeworski and Sprague 1986), and also those designed to render law enforcement most effective and predictable (from Holmes 1897 and other American instrumentalists, e.g., Summers 1982 for a review; to Kelsen 1945; Hart 1961; and Luhmann 1972, 1982: 90–121; also see chapters 5–6). Being strictly rational or instrumental, these procedures offer social scientists generalizable standards for the detailed study of rationalization in comparative perspective: Are elections in Zaire effective and fair? Is law enforcement in Argentina effective and predictable?

However, as Weber clearly appreciated, precisely because these procedures are rational rather than normative, they are ultimately caught up in the drift of rationalization. They cannot resiliently restrain how actors and groups respond independently to systemic pressures. The theory of societal constitutionalism adds that these same procedures are also incapable of assisting heterogeneous actors and competing groups in recognizing, let alone in restraining, even *purposefully* arbitrary exercises of collective power – whether by government or by private enterprises. After all, wielders of arbitrary power may very well be fairly elected, or protected by the public/private distinction. Their decrees may also be enforced effectively, and ever so predictably.

The institution of internal procedural restraint most central to the theory of societal constitutionalism is a strictly *normative* restraint: a procedural threshold of interpretability of positive laws in particular and of shared social duties more generally. This threshold marks whether the positive laws of any modern nation-state, or the shared social duties sanctioned within any private enterprise, *can possibly be recognized and understood in common by heterogeneous actors and competing groups.* The procedures comprising this threshold are norms, and thereby decidedly *non*rational. And yet, this procedural threshold marks a standard for comparative research that can credibly claim generalizability: Whether actors and groups encroach against this threshold, in practice, is an issue that is as amenable to falsifiable empirical research as the issue of whether they encroach against the strictly rational procedures of effective elections or effective law enforcement. Are the positive laws of Zaire or Argentina interpretable or not? Are the shared social duties sanctioned within William's corporation, or within any private corporation in Japan, any stated-owned corporation in the Soviet Union, or any work unit in China, interpretable or not?

How can a procedural threshold be simultaneously normative or non-rational and yet generalizable? First, this procedural threshold is indeed nonrational analytically; it is not reducible to the instrumental means and quantifiable ends characterizing rational action. This issue is explored at length in chapter 7, but for now it can only be asserted that if laws or duties are kept consistent with this procedural threshold, and thereby kept interpretable, this might very well *reduce* the effectiveness of their enforcement. Put differently, the institutionalization of this procedural threshold by no means guarantees that the effectiveness or predictability of *enforcement* will be improved. Moreover, even should this prove to be the case in any particular instance, this would have little to do with why the actors involved are bothering to keep their laws and duties consistent with the procedural threshold.

Second, because this procedural threshold is *irreducible* to interpretability, both in principle *and in practice,* it is generalizable even though it is comprised of nonrational norms. Whenever enforced positive laws or sanctioned social duties encroach against this procedural threshold, they become incapable of being recognized and understood (let alone accepted) by *heterogeneous* actors and *competing* groups *in common.* They become demonstrably particular and controlling rather than remaining possibly generalizable and integrative.

One of the central points of the theory of societal constitutionalism is that (a) the *procedural norms* comprising the threshold of interpretability of laws and duties are indeed both irreducible and generalizable, and yet (b) these *analytically defined* procedural norms are nonetheless a distinct *historical* contribution of the common law tradition (chapter 10). Defining procedural norms analytically that emerged historically at selected places and times is never an easy matter. Indeed, common-law theorists and jurists, some of the finest minds (and most privileged persons) in the Anglo-American world, failed for more than four centuries to isolate the analytical principles underlying their ongoing practice. It was not until 1964 that the procedural norms comprising the threshold of interpretability of positive laws (and shared social duties) were first isolated analytically, by an American legal theorist born in Hereford, Texas, and raised in southern California (chapter 6). Lon Fuller demonstrated that a select set of procedural norms is indeed irreducible to legality as such, even as the historical record and contemporary practices of common-law countries certainly are not.

The analytical concept of *internal procedural restraints on purposeful exercises of collective power* is being coined here in order to capture these norms' irreducibility and generalizability as a procedural threshold. This concept is designed literally to isolate these procedural norms from the particularity of *any* nation-state's historical or contemporary practices of due process. The theory of societal constitutionalism proposes that this procedural threshold is as capable of informing critical studies of common-law countries as it is of countries of the civil-law world or, for that matter, of the Islamic-law world. It proposes that this threshold allows social scientists (as well as heterogeneous actors and competing groups) to specify when *any* set of shared social duties being sanctioned within any modern social unit can possibly be recognized and understood in common *by the heterogeneous actors and competing groups who are expected to bear them.* Whether any existing set of laws or duties is consistent with the procedural threshold indicates, therefore, whether *it* is recognizable and understandable. But this does not indicate whether heterogeneous actors and competing groups find it *acceptable* in terms of their subjective interests. As a result, its consistency with the procedural threshold is an issue independent of whether law enforcement agencies happen to enforce the set of laws or duties effectively at any given moment in time.

If heterogeneous actors and competing groups cannot possibly recognize and understand in common what their shared social duties are, then this reveals something of great significance about their enforcement, and about actors' possible subjective acceptance of them and behavioral fidelity to them. It reveals that effective enforcement, subjective acceptance, and behavioral fidelity are *reducible* to actors' *demonstrable* social control. Whenever laws and duties encroach against the procedural threshold of interpretability, social scientists cannot legitimately attribute *any* part of the resulting social order to heterogeneous actors' and competing groups' *possible* social integration. They can attribute it only (a) to the strategic advantages that certain actors and groups secure over others within economic and political marketplaces and, in turn, (b) to the support that these actors receive from both informal and formal mechanisms of social control, including actors' self-restrictions (chapter 2).

Thinking again of William's situation in the illustration in chapter 1, if he could appeal to *institutionalized* norms that are capable of securing heterogeneous actors' and competing groups' shared recognition and understanding of what purposeful arbitrariness *is,* then he could demonstrate, against Scott's and company executives' resistance, that Scott's demand is indeed particular and controlling. He could not possibly demonstrate this otherwise. As noted earlier, he could not do so by demonstrating that a significant number of chemists or other interested parties within or outside of the corporation share his sense of "natural rights" or of "professional integrity" more directly. Critics may reduce any such shared understanding to professionals' strictly strategic interests, given the fragmentation of meaning and functional differentiation taking place within any complex social enterprise (Bucher and Strauss 1961).

This particular institution of internal procedural restraint, the threshold of interpretability, is critical to the theory of societal constitutionalism. It can credibly claim grounding against the sovereignty of actors' subjective interests, including *Homo economicus*'s behavior within economic and political marketplaces.[11] It can credibly claim grounding against actors' (and social scientists') normative relativism and ongoing fragmentation of meaning. To the extent that the social integration/social control distinction is indeed grounded on procedural norms that are irreducible and generalizable, social scientists may employ it to draw sharp distinctions within ongoing social and political practice.

For instance, social scientists may employ the social integration/social control distinction to specify when the *outcomes* of interest-group competition are themselves extending or intensifying social control – even as these outcomes secure popular support and possibly an electoral mandate. The central issue is not whether the outcomes are popular or consistent with actors' subjective interests but whether they increase power holders' *behavioral* encroachments against the integrity of the procedural threshold. This issue is independent of whether interest-group competition within a particular nation-state is more or less robust than in others.

Yet, even resilient *internal* normative restraints on power holders' *purposeful* exercises of collective power remain incapable of assisting heterogeneous actors and competing groups in recognizing (or restraining) *inadvertently* arbitrary exercises of collective power. The latter include those exercises of collective power that are indeed instrumentally and strategically rational responses to competitive pressures, and that nonetheless contribute *inadvertently* to the drift of social change, as Weber warned.

Excursus: the contemporary crisis of internal restraints

Pluralism's critique of normative restraints. American pluralist theorists insisted as early as the turn of this century (Bentley 1908) that, more than any other institution of restraint, the robustness of interest group competition ensures democratic government under modern conditions. Pluralist theory essentially revolves around three assumptions (Lowi 1969), the first being *the sovereignty of actors' subjective interests:*

> First, it is assumed that actors' subjective interests can never be opposed to, or incompatible with, the public interest unless they entail a violation of existing positive law. Yet, any law may be changed in the political marketplace, including, ultimately, interpreta-

tions of the Constitution (on the latter, see Horowitz 1977; Ely 1980; Aleinikoff 1987).

Second, being sovereign, it is assumed that all subjective interests within civil society have about equal status (Brennan and Buchanan 1985: 37), even as they are certainly not assumed to be equal in financing and power, or in organizational and leadership skills. What is assumed is that no *moral* ordering may be drawn among subjective interests a priori; all ordering is strictly strategic, or tied exclusively to the outcomes of groups' competition for influence within political marketplaces.

Third, it is assumed that government secures actors' subjective consent, or legitimacy, for existing positive laws by ceaselessly accommodating the outcomes of group competition rather than by endeavoring to uphold any principle independent of these outcomes. Existing positive laws, along with courts' interpretations of them, ultimately mirror the ongoing balance of power between competing subjective interests. Beyond this, "the state's" role is *reducible* to that of a referee that dutifully enforces existing, ever-negotiable, "rules of the game."[12]

More than a century earlier, liberal theorists had emphasized the interrelationship between a relatively unfettered economic marketplace and a liberal state. They had similarly deemphasized the importance of institutionalized norms and *nonrational* restraints framing actors' conduct within the marketplace (Adam Smith's thoughts on "laws and institutions" notwithstanding, e.g. Buchanan 1989: 57–67).

Indeed, pluralist theory and liberal theory rest together on three assumptions (Lowi 1969) that Marx, Weber, and other major social theorists considered remarkably naive:

> First, both theories assume that every individual or interest group, in isolation, is the best judge of his or their own subjective interests, and that these interests are ultimately given or random. Because actors' subjective interests are sovereign, and a strictly "private" matter, they are beyond any "external" warrant or justification. As a result, they can only be treated as given or random. It is impossible to tell if they are reasoned (Buchanan 1989: 37–40, 61–2; Brennan and Buchanan 1985: 21–8, 37–9, 46–66; Hechter 1987: 31–3, 184–5).
>
> Second, both theories assume that the outcomes of actors' normatively unmediated, or merely informally mediated, competition within political and economic marketplaces are typically if not intrinsically benign.[13]
>
> Third, both theories assume that should arbitrary government ever result somehow from these outcomes, individuals comprising a "con-

stituent force" within civil society are certain to recognize this subjectively, each in isolation. As long as economic and political marketplaces are kept "free," or unencumbered by de jure obstacles to actors articulating their subjective interests, such a "constituent force" can be relied on to mobilize whenever necessary in order to uphold valued "rules of the game." In this way, governmental authoritarianism is either prevented or corrected (Truman 1951; Brennan and Buchanan 1985: 22, 26–32, 51, also 5–7).[14]

More than merely benign, therefore, actors' normatively unmediated or informally mediated competition over subjective interests within economic and political marketplaces is for liberals and pluralists alike positively virtuous: It fosters individual diversity and innovativeness, economic and political adaptability, and ethnic and cultural tolerance (see Hall 1987 for a statement; McClosky and Brill 1983 for an unsuccessful effort to document this in survey research). These theorists acknowledge, of course, that particular sets of actors and groups benefit most from robust interest competition. They also acknowledge that neither systemic nor informal mechanisms of social control are ever displaced entirely by the impersonal sanctions of political and economic marketplaces (chapter 2; Buchanan 1989: 32–5 on "norms" and customs; Hechter 1987: 62–73 on direct reinforcement, differential association, and reciprocity).

What is surprising is that this relatively unbridled, and unwarranted, optimism stands largely unchallenged *conceptually* in the social sciences today. This is the case precisely because of the lacuna of integrative possibilities and then the resulting ideology of exhausted possibilities. Within this context of conceptual default, liberals and pluralists readily dismiss out of hand the significance for social change of any and all imbalances of resources, power, and influence emerging from political and economic marketplaces – including the extent and intensity of social control accorded to "private" corporations within civil society. All such outcomes are for them unrelated to the issue of whether *government* remains "democratic" and whether the *market* remains "free." Because their complacency and optimism obfuscates the Weberian Dilemma, they fail to see any identifiable *social infrastructure* irreducible to the possibility of a nonauthoritarian direction of *social* change under modern conditions. They then fail to see, of course, whether and when this social infrastructure is jeopardized by certain outcomes of liberal-democratic economic and political marketplaces.

Pluralists' argument regarding the central importance of robust interest competition heavily influenced the works of many social scientists in many disciplines throughout the 1960s and beyond. Their argument is altogether consistent, for instance, with the tradition of symbolic interactionism in sociology (Blumer 1969). And yet, its great influence cannot be traced to its direct appeal. Its influence may be traced instead to how convincingly pluralists (and interactionists) revealed that all substantive and procedural *normative* restraints that once contributed to political democracy (in the United States and elsewhere) are today clearly in irreversible decline. By revealing that *all* normative restraints on government have become negotiable, in principle, and increasingly compromised, in practice, they left the social sciences with a compelling problem. This problem, in turn, enhanced the influence of pluralism (and interactionism): How can social scientists explain the remarkable stability of American democracy, for instance, *other than* to attribute this to the institution of robust interest competition itself?[15]

First, even by the mid-1950s, pluralists were pointing out that earlier norms of internal *substantive* restraint on government and the economy – norms of religion, natural law, and custom – were everywhere in flux in the West, rather than firm and resilient. Yet, these are the norms that once kept the private sharply distinguished from the public, and that thereby kept the state from encroaching into civil society *even in response to group competition*. As examples of these norms' flux and irreversible decline today, Supreme Court decisions in the United States regarding the substantive meaning of the equal protection clause of the Constitution are anything but consistent or unambiguous (Grossman and Wells 1980: 408–29, 564–608; Unger 1986). Sunday "blue laws" prohibiting commerce on the Sabbath are a thing of the past, as are countless other religious and natural-law proscriptions on economic and political marketplaces. Moving in the other direction, prayer in public schools is not something that is any longer beyond the possible reach of governmental action in response to group competition, despite the once presumed inviolability of the separation of church and state. Nor is the "privacy" of corporate investment or personnel decisions beyond the reach of government, despite the once presumed inviolability of private property (Note 1982; Stone 1982; Laumann and Knoke 1987: 381–2).

Second, pluralists were also insisting that even the integrity of earlier norms of internal *procedural* restraint on government is similarly in flux across the West, and in marked decline in the United States and other common law countries in particular. The integrity of nonrational norms of any kind, substantive or procedural, is difficult for heterogeneous actors and competing groups to sustain. This is the case because (a) pluralist group competition is embedded within a larger social order, and (b) the latter cannot be characterized as revolving around any identifiable lived social fabric. The larger social order is rather characterized by functional differentiation, actors' fragmentation of meaning, groups' competition, and (benign) systemic drift (Luhmann 1990 emphasizes this as compellingly as anyone in the literature today). Because pluralists insisted that American politics be studied coldly, "realistically," as it actually plays itself out in practice – rather than as "institutionalists" and "formalists" were once wont to idealize it – they insisted that even procedural norms of due process distinctive to common-law countries have become mere formalities (see Laumann and Knoke 1987: 383–5, 395–7 for the same conclusion).[16] These procedural norms, too, have become empty shells, like the substantive norms of natural law and natural right. By pluralists' accounts, these formalities are also readily adjusted and readjusted by the content of group competition, by power holders' ceaseless struggles for influence and strategic advantages. Indeed, on this point pluralists are in unreserved agreement with Marxists, Weberians, feminists, and contemporary sociologists of law.[17]

For all of these theorists and researchers, norms of due process are, at best, an accoutrement of robust interest competition itself. These norms can no longer be traced, if they ever could, to "principles" grounded against groups' competition and the sovereignty of actors' subjective interests. Instead, due process is itself reducible to how competing subjective interests countervail or balance each other within political marketplaces: the legislature, the administrative agency, and even the court. If there ever was a shared sense of the integrity of basic norms and nonrational procedures of internal restraint – including due process – it has clearly fragmented (Brennan and Buchanan 1985: ix, 146–50). This explains why it is so difficult today for legal scholars, for instance, to distinguish due process *conceptually* from the courts' accommodating of whatever outcomes individual and corporate persons negotiate within economic and political marketplaces. Legal scholars are increasingly aware that due process currently is being *defined*, in practice, as robust interest competition within and around the courts themselves. And they are increasingly aware, too, that this reduces the courts' role to "balancing," to acceding to drift; the courts are no longer mediating drift (if they ever did) on the basis of some relatively clear sense of direction (Aleinikoff 1987; *Yale Law Journal* 1988).

Given this growing awareness among legal scholars, it is an easy matter, then, for social scientists to insist in ever more direct terms that there are no internal procedural restraints on arbitrary government today that are either resilient, in practice, or grounded conceptually, in principle (Brennan and Buchanan 1985: 21, 37). Like pluralists and interactionists, Weberians take this to mean that internal procedural restraints cannot be independent of group competition. Marxists take this to mean that they cannot be independent of the bourgeoisie's interests and beliefs in particular. Feminists take this to mean that they cannot be independent of what MacKinnon calls the "male state." And mainstream sociologists of law (along with specialists on deviance) endlessly document how the integrity of procedural norms is subordinated to influentials' ongoing negotiations and compromises within criminal and civil justice systems.

Pluralism as critique of Western institutions and traditions. By substituting a "realist" appraisal of American democracy for institutionalists' and formalists' idealized portrayals (Garson 1978), pluralists successfully debunked the normative basis of American democracy. They accomplished this, ironically, as they simultaneously transferred Lockean liberals' optimism and complacency from the economic marketplace to the political marketplace (Lowi 1969). They successfully established that the *only* institution of internal restraint *both* necessary and sufficient to maintain American democracy, and, presumably, a nonauthoritarian direction of social change more generally, is robust interest competition. As long as the subjective interests emerging within a civil society are not blocked by de jure obstacles of any kind as they are being formulated, articulated, and mobilized, arbitrary government is restrained by definition. By implication, a nonauthoritarian direction of social change also is assured.

Putting this point differently, *purposeful* exercises of collective power by the state (or by any sector, industry, or organization of a civil society) can never be demonstrated by social scientists (or interest-group leaders) to be arbitrary in principle. They can only be demonstrated to stimulate unusually intensive, extensive, or sustained competition among interest groups. When the latter proves not to be the case, in practice, social scientists can only describe such exercises as acceptable responses to ongoing group competition, and, by implication, to systemic pressures of social change. If anything, these exercises now become a literal *virtue* of robust interest competition itself. By no means can they be condemned as particular, controlling, or otherwise threatening. Within the *conceptual framework* of pluralist theory, there are no grand "principles" that social scientists may cite that legitimate any other restraints on the state's actions.[18]

Once again, there is indeed a point to this "realist" appraisal of the admittedly dismal state of internal normative restraints *on arbitrary government.* But this point begins to move beyond pluralist theory itself, and beyond the other theories noted above: With the sole exception of Fuller's procedural threshold of interpretability, *it is indeed no longer possible today for competing groups and heterogeneous actors (or social scientists) to rely on existing Western political institutions and economic practices to recognize whether the state or any private enterprise is becoming more controlling and authoritarian.* The only changes that can possibly be recognized today on this basis are whether new social movements are emerging within a civil society, as one possible sign of unusual interest competition (Habermas ends up doing this, e.g. 1962: 181–250; 1989). Otherwise, the direction of social change cannot be fathomed, other than to keep track of any de jure obstacles to actors' articulation and aggregation of their subjective interests (or, in Habermas's case, de facto obstacles to actors' ideal speech).

Indeed, in terms of pluralism's "realist" approach, as in Weber's social theory earlier, if a democratic government ever cites any principle as it *hesitates* to accommodate the outcomes of ongoing interest competition, this can only *exacerbate* social tensions and conflicts. It can only result in "imbalance" and "crisis." As one example, if the separation of church and state were reified into some nonnegotiable principle, this might rigidify a mutual isolation of religious subcultures. By no means would it invariably foster a single "national culture" or any other social fabric of "shared meaning." Similarly, if either the division of powers or individuals' "natural rights" were reified, this might magnify heterogeneous actors' and competing groups' *difficulties* in coming to a shared "definition of the situation" regarding whether the direction of social change is benign or increasingly threatening (thus, Buchanan's opposition to any "external values"). In short, with the single great exception of their blind faith that the outcomes of normatively unmediated arenas of political and economic competition will invariably be benign, pluralists and interactionists otherwise follow Weber in discounting the significance for contemporary democratic government and for a nonauthoritarian direction of social change of all institutions and norms of traditional governmental constitutionalism.

European neocorporatism: an alternative to American pluralism? Studies of neocorporatism within Western Europe and Scandinavia since the mid-1970s (see Schmitter's works) find that on the Continent more centralized "peak associations" are substituted for America's decentralized pressure groups. Yet, these studies essentially recapitulate pluralism's optimism and complacency. They too discount the significance of the institutional legacy of governmental constitutionalism. But what are peak associations?

Standing at the "peak" or literal boundary between state agencies and the most powerful organized interests in a civil society, a peak association dominates one particular functional sector of a civil society, whether banking, housing, manufacturing, international trade, transportation, education, or any other. On the Continent (unlike the case in Latin America), it is a "private" trade association rather than an agency of government; its leaders are neither popularly elected nor appointed by popularly elected officials. Yet, these leaders bear enormous responsibilities for administering the *public* policies affecting their functional sector as well as for helping to formulate these policies in the first place.

Looking in the other direction, from the peak down to the enterprises and organizations within its functional sector, the leaders of each peak association dominate all of the organized interests and social units within its sector. Their domination is institutionalized in many ways, but the two which follow are as illustrative of the peak association's power as any others: First, leaders of peak associations directly or indirectly control the licensing of all enterprises within their functional sector; thus, they control their current and potential "membership." Second, leaders of peak associations formally or informally monopolize the political representation of all organized interests within their functional sector; thus, they literally control what the state hears from their "membership."

In short, peak associations simultaneously "intermediate" both (a) the public policy-making process taking place within the state that is directed to their sectors and (b) the "private" articulation and aggregation of interests taking place within their sectors that is directed to the state. As such, the leaders of peak associations typically are seen in the literature as a great stabilizing force in *all* democracies on the Continent. Neocorporatist theorists insist, and in no uncertain terms, that intermediation is more significant to democratic government, and by implication to a non-authoritarian direction of social change, than any and all traditions of governmental constitutionalism or norms of internal restraint. Like pluralist theorists' characterizations of decentralized group competition within the United States, neocorporatist theorists characterize centralized "intermediation" as a strictly strategic variant within the general type of internal substantive restraints. Yet, the dominance of peak associations *replaces* more robust interest competition, *and* it further subordinates the practical significance of the division of powers, individuals' (as opposed to groups') "natural rights," and the public/private distinction (Laumann and Knoke 1987: 381–2, 397 see similar results in the United States, albeit more informally developed).

Given (a) their dominance within functional sectors of civil society and (b) their responsibility for both formulating and administering the public policies affecting them, the presence of neocorporatist peak associations has substantial effects, of course, on the practice of Western democratic institutions. It also affects the latter's relationship to its own constitutional traditions. The following three effects may be included among them:

> First, as just noted, neocorporatism utterly eliminates interest-group competition. It replaces this with higher level negotiations between unelected leaders of peak associations, and then between them and both elected and appointed leaders of state agencies.
>
> Second, and as a result of this, neocorporatism institutionalizes a literal collapse of the public/private distinction. Depending on how one wishes to view it, neocorporatist "intermediation" either (a) brings unelected leaders of peak associations directly into the state or else (b)

brings elected and appointed leaders of state agencies directly into functional sectors of civil society.

Third, neocorporatism institutionalizes a literal collapse of the division of powers. Given that peak association leaders deal directly with managers of state agencies, and thereby typically bypass parliament and the courts, the division of powers has for all intents and purposes been rendered increasingly insignificant.

This is significant in that the division of powers is arguably the single most important institution of internal substantive restraint ever developed within the *tradition* of Western governmental constitutionalism.[19] Indeed, it was the division of powers, along with the public/private distinction underlying a truly liberal economic marketplace, that once provided actors and groups with an institutionalized "threshold." The integrity of this division and this distinction once allowed them the possibility of recognizing and understanding in common when government was becoming arbitrary.[20]

By contrast to Western democratic institutions and constitutional traditions alike, the neocorporatist intermediation of public policies and social interests is more like the "pacts" elites establish during periods of governmental crises. These are the periods when parliamentary democracy gives way to military rule, and vice versa (O'Donnell, Schmitter, and Whitehead 1986, vol. 5: 37–47). The one significant difference between neocorporatist intermediation and elite pacts is that elites forge pacts fully expecting their arrangements to be temporary. By contrast, peak associations' intermediation literally institutionalizes the collapse of the public/private distinction. This is why it is so unclear to social theorists today which exercises of governmental power on the Continent are extraordinary and which are ordinary, or which are innovative and which are arbitrary (Luhmann 1990, Habermas 1989). Peak associations' intermediation subordinates the significance of all restraints on arbitrary government to the literal end-in-itself of ceaselessly accommodating peak associations' own immediate responses to systemic pressures of drift (Streeck and Schmitter 1985).

Problems for Western traditions and Western institutions. Pluralism and neocorporatism both reveal, in short, that *Western democratic institutions and constitutional traditions, and in particular any and all norms of internal restraint, no longer operate as a reliable "threshold" or trip wire even in their originally limited way.* The integrity of the division of powers and of the public/private distinction once signaled to all actors and groups in common at least whether *government* was becoming unlimited, and thereby controlling and authoritarian (Friedrich 1974). The division of powers might very well remain today a most significant institution of internal substantive restraint on arbitrary government. But what would have to be done in order to reestablish its integrity within Western Europe, Scandinavia, or even the United States is no longer self-evident, even to specialists (Vile 1967).[21] As far as back as 1942, the American political scientist V. O. Key, Jr., pointed out (1942: 709) that the American government's growing complexity had "reduced to a fiction the theory of separation of powers and the parallel doctrine of the separability of politics and administration." Today, practicing politicians, leaders of interest groups and peak associations, and influentials within civil society fail to see this as a problem in the first place (Laumann and Knoke 1987: 383–7). The demise of the division of powers accounts only in part, however, for Western democracies' "crisis of public authority."[22]

Beyond this, none of the original restraints on arbitrary government codified in Western constitutional tradition operate any longer, in practice, even in their original, limited way. They no longer do so, ironically, *precisely because they were never extended, in practice, to the task of restraining at least purposefully arbitrary exercises of collective power by private enterprises within civil society.* Again, with the exception of Fuller's procedural threshold, restraints of governmental constitutionalism were never designed to support a *social infrastructure* on which competing groups or heterogeneous actors (and social scientists) might possibly recognize shifts in the direction of *social change.* As internal restraints, they are incapable of assisting heterogeneous actors and competing groups in recognizing the *inadvertent* arbitrariness of drift.

The restricted impact of internal restraints is most evident today within the civil law countries of the Continent. Yet, even within common-law countries, these restraints were never extended to *purposeful* arbitrariness by private enterprises.[23] As a result, since the turn of the century social influentials' once (relatively) shared recognition of the integrity of Western democratic institutions and norms of internal restraint has itself fragmented and withered. This is exactly what Weber expected, and *this* accounts for Western democracies' "crisis of public authority": *Whatever the social infrastructure may be today that is supporting a nonauthoritarian direction of social change within Western democracies, or elsewhere, it is no longer revealed by principles of Western constitutional and liberal traditions.* This disjunction between theory and practice explains why power holders and social influentials fail to recognize, first, what the social infrastructure underlying a nonauthoritarian direction of social change today is and, second, how it might be maintained despite systemic pressures of drift to the contrary. Pluralists' and neocorporatists' "realism" turns out, ironically, to document this disjunction, albeit indirectly, as they endeavor to account for the presence of political democracy (and, by implication, nonauthoritarian social order) in the late twentieth century.

A constitutional crisis in the United States is so likely today that the truly difficult problem is to predict which particular substantive issues will pre-cipitate it (Ely 1980; *Pennsylvania Law Review* symposium 1982; Aleinikoff 1987; Siedman 1987; *Yale University Law Journal* symposium 1988; Nagel 1989). Prospects for inducing or compelling government agencies to con-form more strictly to traditional constitutional restraints have been elimi-nated. In many respects American jurists' "strict constructionist" appeals are one last, fated effort to respond to drift in the traditional ways (Dwor-kin 1985: 33–71). The same is true of social scientists' appeals to "civil religion," including those by Bellah, Daniel Bell, and Brennan and Bu-chanan. Both types of appeals, coupled with (a) the increasing frequency of changes in Supreme Court opinions, and (b) the rise of both the Law and Economics movement and the Critical Legal Studies movement within major law schools, are cumulative reflections of the deeper crisis of internal restraints.[24]

4.3.2. Institutions of external restraint: tradition v. societal constitutionalism

External *procedural* restraints are the institutions and norms on which het-erogeneous actors and competing groups rely, in practice, whenever they recognize that exercises of collective power which are indeed rational are nonetheless contributing *inadvertently* to the drift of social change toward bureaucratization, control, and social authoritarianism.[25] Whether they rely on these restraints explicitly or implicitly, knowingly or unknowingly, is of secondary importance. What is of primary importance is whether distinc-tively external procedural restraints can be isolated, in principle, and then located unambiguously within existing civil societies, in practice. It is argued throughout the remainder of this volume that *social (and governmental) units organized in the collegial form institutionalize external procedural re-straints by their sheer presence.* The direction of social change can be said to be shifting inadvertently toward control and social authoritarianism, in prac-tice, whenever encroachments against collegial formations are increasing. The remainder of this volume is dedicated to demonstrating why this is the case. It is dedicated to demonstrating why the *sheer presence* of collegial formations within any modern civil society institutionalizes the distinctive *social infrastructure* underlying both a nonauthoritarian direction of social change and heterogeneous actors' and competing groups' possibilities for social integration.

Institutions of external substantive restraint (IIA): the anachronism of tradi-tion. Looking at external restraints generally, what exactly keeps any nor-mative restraint on the drift of social change "external?" What prevents any normative restraint from being generally perceived as favoring the subjective interests of selected actors only, and thereby from being politicized and drawn into interest competition itself? Institutions and norms lose their "external" status the moment that they can no longer credibly claim grounding. This means that they have lost any possibility of being recognized, understood, and accepted in common by heterogeneous actors and competing groups. Once they have lost this possibility, they are readily subordinated (a) to accommodating the outcomes of interest competition and (b) to accommodating social and governmental units' immediate responses to systemic pressures of social change in their own immediate interests.

This process of subordination is precisely what happened historically to external *substantive* restraints or all traditional norms and institutions with the onset of modernity and the fragmentation of meaning: One by one, substantive traditions and valued social fabrics lost their "external" status or capacity to sustain a credible claim to grounding against the emerging sovereignty of actors' subjective interests. Their claims to grounding were instead successfully challenged by emerging interests and systemic pressures within civil society (Habermas 1962, 1963a,b; Moore 1966; Friedrich 1972; Bendix 1978; MacIntyre 1981; Schluchter 1981; Luhmann 1990).

Institutions of external substantive restraint include, as one example, absolute religious proscriptions against various types of commercial practices, including usury (Nelson 1949; Meszaros 1972: 28–33). They also include, as other examples, absolute constitutional or statutory proscriptions (a) against interstate or international commerce, based on "natural law" tenets, or (b) against naturalized citizenship, based on ascriptive criteria. In short, all institutions of external substantive restraint without exception run directly counter to the very thrust of modernity itself. They run directly counter to the increasing heterogeneity of national populations and to the increasing functional differentiation of organizations and institutions within modern civil societies. Put more positively, these institutions can contribute truly external restraints only when actors somehow sustain a broad, unchallenged consensus regarding what is right and wrong, true and false, *in substance,* in their everyday social lives. This is rare in the modern world (but see MacIntyre 1981 and Braithwaite 1989 for intriguing calls for renascence, and Bloom 1987 for a polemic based implicitly on this).

Under modern conditions of drift, those who would endeavor seriously to maintain the integrity of substantive norms of religion or natural law must rely, ultimately, on precisely those mechanisms of social control that carry the greatest potential for degenerating into authoritarian excess. Moreover, as they do so, the institutions of external substantive restraint whose integrity they are endeavoring to maintain simultaneously lose their normative qualities.[26] They become strategic restraints, increasingly enforced by formal mechanisms of social control. This is the case, for instance, with those few nation-states that continue to uphold a state religion (e.g. Iran, Israel, and various Arab states) – irrespective of what the substantive merits of their institutions and practices happen to be. It is also the case with that far greater number of nation-states that continues to cast citizenship in terms of ethnic, religious, or other ascriptive criteria rather than in terms of more universal criteria.[27]

At this point a thesis of the theory of societal constitutionalism may be stated bluntly: If an institution of external restraint is to contribute to a nonauthoritarian direction of social change under modern conditions, and also to heterogeneous actors' and competing groups' possible social integration, *it must remain a procedural mediation.* Whatever its substantive impact might be on organizations and institutions within a modern civil society, its impact must remain mediated. It must remain consistent with actors' and groups' ongoing behavioral fidelity to certain procedural norms.

Institutions of external procedural restraint (IIB): the core of societal constitutionalism

Three qualities of external procedural restraint. Again, the only norms and institutions of external restraint that remain consistent with a nonauthoritarian direction of change as well as with heterogeneous actors' and competing groups' possible social integration are strictly *procedural mediations.* Being "external," these procedures allow such actors and groups first to recognize, and then possibly to restrain, the inadvertent arbitrariness accompanying the drift of social change at the heart of the Weberian Dilemma. This means that these procedures exhibit at least three distinctive qualities:

First, normativeness: These procedures are normative or nonrational rather than strategic or instrumental.[28]

When even heterogeneous actors and competing groups are capable of recognizing and understanding the integrity of *nonrational* procedures in common, these procedures also exhibit two other qualities:

Second, grounding: These procedures can credibly *claim* conceptual grounding against normative relativism, the sovereignty of actors' subjective interests, and the outcomes of interest competition.

Third, invariance: The impact of restraint which these procedures have on inadvertent arbitrariness, or drift, does not vary from nation-state to nation-state; it is instead a product of their sheer presence within any sector, industry, or organization of a civil society.

The distinctiveness of the collegial form. These three qualities are discussed at length in the remainder of this volume. For the moment, it is worth repeating that external *procedural* restraints are institutionalized exclusively by the sheer presence of collegial formations. And collegial formations may be defined in the following way for present purposes:

> Collegial formations are deliberative and professional bodies wherein heterogeneous actors and competing groups maintain the threshold of interpretability of shared social duties as they endeavor to describe and explain (or create and maintain) *qualities* in social life or in natural events.

This definition is repeated in chapter 8, and explored at length within the context of a discussion of organizational forms and a more developed presentation of the theory of societal constitutionalism. For now, the most that can be said is that these formations cannot be distinguished from other organizational forms by any of the substantive projects to which their members happen to dedicate them in any particular instance. They are rather distinguished by the procedural norms that distinguish this particular organizational form from bureaucratic, democratic, or partron-client forms of organization. At the moment that members of any collegial formation encroach *behaviorally* against the integrity of this form's distinctive procedural norms, they undermine this form's continued presence. Encroachments against these procedural norms do not affect any other organizational form in this way. Nor, certainly, do they affect economic and political marketplaces in this way.

Given that its members' *behavior* is distinctive, whether the collegial form of organization is in evidence within any sector, industry, or organization of a modern civil society is an eminently empirical question. Studies of its presence or absence within any sector, industry, organization, or organizational division are amenable to falsification and, ultimately, to operationalization. Moreover, because this formation's impact of restraint is invariant, this too renders the presence or absence of collegial formations amenable to empirical study.

Where is the collegial form typically to be found? To the extent that it is present at all within a modern civil society, it is *the* organizational form distinctive to the professions in particular and to rule-making and deliberative bodies more generally. To the extent that it is present at all, it is typically found not only within public and private research institutes, artistic and intellectual networks, and universities, but also within legislatures, courts and commissions, professional associations, and for that matter, the research divisions of private and public corporations, the rule-making bodies of nonprofit organizations, and even the directorates of public and private corporations.[29]

Still, how can it be said that the sheer presence of collegial formations institutionalizes external procedural restraints? How can it be said that these restraints can credibly claim conceptual grounding against normative relativism and the sovereignty of actors' subjective interests? How can it be said that the impact of these restraints on drift is invariant, in practice? Why do members of collegial formations exhibit behavioral fidelity to distinctive procedural norms, and how exactly do the members of these formations institutionalize external procedural restraints across entire sectors of a civil society?

These are all legitimate questions, and all of them, and many more, must be answered. But for now, in the context of this overview of internal and external restraints, it is possible only to state in the most general terms how institutions of external procedural restraint differ from institutions of internal restraint.

External and internal procedural restraints. Collegial formations institutionalize the social infrastructure underlying all nonauthoritarian social orders today, whether Western or non-Western. Only by maintaining the integrity of these formations can heterogeneous actors and competing groups simultaneously restrain social and governmental units' independent, immediate responses to the systemic pressures of social change that concerned Weber. If these responses are otherwise left unrestrained, they invariably contribute, however inadvertently so, to increasing bureaucratization, control, and susceptibility to social authoritarianism. Only the *presence* of institutions of external procedural restraint within a civil society can account for the possibility of nonauthoritarian social order under modern conditions, and thereby resolve the Weberian Dilemma directly. Correlatively, the absence of these institutions, or their loss of integrity and subsequent disappearance, both accounts for and reflects an authoritarian direction of social change under modern conditions. This holds true in comparative perspective *irrespective of whether most Western political institutions and economic practices are otherwise present within a particular nation-state or not.*

Thinking again of William's situation, consider the possibility that instead of Scott's demand being anomalous, it is consistent with the company's longstanding practices in approaching its research divisions.[30] Managers never have been instructed that research divisions are to be treated any differently than sales divisions, marketing divisions, or distribution divisions. Quite to the contrary, they have been instructed that if they need "results," then "results" had better be delivered – from any division. The problem is that "equal treatment" of all divisions results inadvertently in quite unequal effects and outcomes, precisely because research divisions differ from all others in the *form* in which they are organized.

Once social scientists see that this form also happens to institutionalize external procedural restraints by its sheer presence anywhere within a civil society, they may make the following distinction within William's lived situation: William's company may or may not be engaging in corporate crime. But it is indeed extending social control and contributing to social authoritarianism. This remains the case irrespective of whether corporate managers are doing so purposefully *or inadvertently*. By encroaching against the integrity of its research divisions' distinctive form of organization, *and thereby against the external procedural restraints that only this form institutionalizes, managers' behavior* is extending social control and reducing heterogeneous actors' and competing groups' possibilities for social integration. In this way, their contribution to drift at a microsociological level also contributes, however incrementally so, to a more macrosociological drift by their industry and sector of civil society. The concept of external procedural restraints permits observing social scientists to demonstrate this empirically, and in comparative perspective, irrespective of whether the civil society in question is Western or non-Western.

In short, the theory of societal constitutionalism revolves around the interrelationship, in principle and in practice, between:

(a) one particular set of internal procedural restraints: Fuller's procedural threshold of interpretability; and

(b) one particular institution of external procedural restraints: the collegial form of organization.

The distinctive characteristics of Fuller's procedural threshold are discussed in chapter 6 and collegial formations are discussed at length beginning in chapter 8. For present purposes, the following may be asserted outside of the conceptual context provided later in this volume: As long as members of collegial formations maintain the integrity of their organizational form, *this contributes to external procedural restraints on any and all manifestations of social authoritarianism, whether purposeful or inadvertent.* To say that collegial formations institutionalize "external" procedural norms by their sheer presence is to say that they do so: (a) irrespective of the subjective interests of the heterogeneous actors and competing groups comprising their memberships, and (b) irrespective of the substantive projects to which these members dedicate their formations (as long as the projects remain mediated).

Social scientists may locate collegial formations with precision within particular sectors, industries, and organizations, and even particular divisions of organizations. It cannot be assumed a priori, however, that all of the sectors of the civil societies in which these formations will be found, either today or historically, will invariably be those of Western democra-

cies. By contrast to the presupposition of exhausted possibilities, a central
thesis of the theory of societal constitutionalism comes to the fore: *The
extent of the presence of collegial formations within any particular civil
society – not the presence of political institutions and economic practices of
existing Western democracies in themselves – accounts for whether it, or any
particular sector within it, can become (or remain) nonauthoritarian and
possibly integrative, despite systemic pressures to the contrary.*[31] This thesis
is amenable to empirical falsification in case studies, and amenable as well
to eventual operationalization.

4.4. Social integration: again, a preliminary definition

Given the discussion of internal and external procedural restraints, the
concept of social integration may be defined a little more specifically than
in chapter 2. It may be defined in three related ways, and yet these definitions, too, remain preliminary.[32]

First, heterogeneous actors' and competing groups' possible integration within any complex social unit ultimately rests on whether *both*
sets of institutions of *procedural* normative restraint are in evidence:
(a) institutions of internal procedural restraint on purposefully arbitrary exercises of collective power, and (b) institutions of external
procedural restraint on inadvertently arbitrary exercises of collective
power.

Second, and put more positively, heterogeneous actors' possible social
integration rests, in practice, on whether they *share* a normative *orientation* of restraint on all arbitrary exercises of collective power. They
may share this normative orientation, moreover, *despite* their own
increasing differences in substantive beliefs, internalized normative
motivations, and subjective interests (see chapter 5, note 1; and chapter 8, note 4). A *shared* normative orientation of this type can only be
the product of the institutionalization of distinctively *normative procedures.* It cannot be the product of the institutionalization of substantive norms of any kind, nor of rational procedures.

Third, social integration remains a possibility, in practice, whenever
heterogeneous actors and competing groups exhibit *behavioral* fidelity
to the threshold restraints of the *collegial* form of organization. This
requires, however, that they resist systemic pressures of drift toward
bureaucratization or toward adopting any other organizational forms
that are more strategic or instrumental.

The continued presence, and then further extension, of the collegial
form of organization within a modern civil society remains as contingent a

possibility within Western democracies as it does within nation-states of the East and Third World. Nowhere in the modern world is this form's presence an "evolutionary universal." Nowhere in the modern world is its presence "overdetermined" by "cultural imperatives," "national traditions," or systemic pressures of "functional differentiation." Put differently, there is not a single social order in the world today that comparativists may legitimately treat as irreversibly nonauthoritarian, as intrinsically integrative. Quite to the contrary, each social order's direction of change remains an open, empirical issue, in research as well as in practice. The relationship between drift and direction remains forever subject to change. The theory of societal constitutionalism is designed to allow social scientists to specify empirically when these changes are occurring, in practice.

Origins of the analytical distinctions and conceptual foundations: retracing steps taken by Habermas, Fuller, and Parsons

5. Societal constitutionalism's grounding against relativism: from Weber's legal positivism to Habermas's communication theory

5.1. Taking stock and looking ahead

Unlike the principles underlying any other legal theory, Lon Fuller's principles of "procedural legality" are interrelated with the form of organization to which Talcott Parsons referred at various times as the "associational," the "*non*bureaucratic," and the "collegial." These Harvard colleagues team-taught a course at the law school during the 1966–67 academic year, and yet in two important respects Parsons's works remained unaffected by this "collaboration." First, he never drew any connection between Fuller's legal theory and his own explicit references to collegial formations, which began only in the late 1960s, (1969a) or after this "collaboration." Second, there is no evidence in Parsons's writings that he appreciated how incompatible *conceptually* Fuller's legal theory is with Weber's sociology of law.[1]

Parsons had been citing and referring to Weber's sociology of law for four decades, and he continued to do so into the 1970s. Yet, in order to work the conceptual implications of Fuller's view of law into his mature theory, the AGIL schema, he would have had to stop this practice, and he would have had to alter many of his own most basic concepts. This move would have eliminated many of the most noticeable dead ends of his mature social theory. But by the late 1960s and early 1970s Parsons was turning seventy, and was far too committed in too many ways to initiate a project of literal conceptual renascence.

Because such changes are not suggested in Parsons's writings, whether directly in texts or indirectly in footnotes, hermeneutics is not going to reveal what the results might have been. And this is not the place, anyway, to say another word about the AGIL schema. Instead, four steps may be taken to demonstrate the interrelationship between Fuller's legal theory and the collegial form of organization, and then to demonstrate the latter's centrality to the theory of societal constitutionalism. These steps also provide an overview of chapters to follow. However, a major obstacle stands in the way of taking even the first step: Fuller's work in particular and legal theory generally is unfamiliar to social scientists, and a more familiar backdrop is needed against which to proceed. The purpose of the present chapter is to provide this backdrop and simultaneously to demonstrate why it is untenable for any theorist to cite Fuller's approach to law and yet to retain basic concepts consistent with Weber's sociology of law.

5.1.1. A backdrop: critique of legal positivism

This chapter opens with references to Weber's sociology of law not because it is conceptually rigorous or intrinsically instructive but because it is familiar. Unlike Fuller's or any other legal theorist's approach to law, Weber's sociology of law remains for many researchers and theorists today, as for Parsons across his career, an unquestioned (and, regrettably, too often unargued) point of departure. The backdrop for the four steps taken in later chapters is not Weber's sociology of law in itself, however; it is rather a *critique* of it and of legal positivism generally. Jürgen Habermas's critique is so rigorous that it may serve as backdrop *even if not a single reader accepts that Habermas's communication theory is, as it stands, a viable theoretical vehicle for the social sciences.* His critique has the great merit of shattering the complacency of any reader who would continue to believe that Weber's sociology of law has more to offer the social sciences today than in fact it does. Equally importantly, by exposing the most important conceptual gaps in any positivist approach to law, his critique also opens the way to establishing in the next chapter the great merits of Fuller's procedural approach.

Unlike Parsons, however, Habermas is unfamiliar with Fuller's work even today. It goes without saying, therefore, that he has never made a case for the merits of Fuller's legal theory, directly or indirectly.[2] He believes instead that his own "theory of comunicative action" fills the gaps exposed by his critique. It is demonstrated in chapter 6, however, that (a) Fuller's concepts are superior to Habermas's in this regard, and that (b) these concepts are nonetheless intrinsically interrelated with Habermas's more abstract principles of "procedural reason." These theorists' very terminologies – procedural legality and procedural reason – suggest an interrelationship. In addition, Habermas's critique of Weber offers a convenient opportunity to explore (a) why he found it necessary to "twist" the traditions of neo-Marxism and critical theory, and European social theory more generally, with a "procedural turn," and then (b) why Fuller had come to the same conclusion regarding both European and Anglo-American traditions of jurisprudence.

For the moment, however, consider only in general terms what each theorist's procedural turn contributes to the other's concepts as well as to the distinction between internal and external restraints informing the theory of societal constitutionalism. On one side, Fuller defines "procedural legality" in terms of eight specific normative restraints. Unlike Habermas's idealized criteria of "procedural reason," these restraints may orient empirical studies. On the other side, the critique of positivism underlying Habermas's procedural turn offers Fuller the possibility of credibly supporting two claims for his normative restraints: First, his normative restraints challenge the sovereignty of actors' subjective interests within economic and political marketplaces. Second, these same normative restraints can credibly claim grounding against normative relativism rather than merely being asserted ad hoc, or for heuristic purposes.[3] Once it is demonstrated that Fuller's normative restraints are interrelated with Habermas's idealized standard of reason, the resulting synthesis opens the possibility of bringing a grounded concept of *reasoned social action* to detailed empirical research. This keeps open the *possibility* that specific legal systems may be demonstrated empirically to be consistent with actors' *reasoned* social action. The alternative is to assume that the legitimacy of any and all legal systems is ultimately *reducible* to a "balancing" of actors' subjective interests (Aleinikoff 1987).

Whether the possibility of conceptual grounding against normative relativism and the sovereignty of subjective interests is kept open or not (chapter 10) is critical to whether Fuller's standard of procedural legality can resist counterarguments from legal realists or legal positivists. The same holds true for whether the distinction between internal and external restraints can resist counterarguments from Weberians, pluralists, neocorporatists, feminists, and political sociologists generally. Putting this point more generally, the *possibility* of sustaining a *credible* claim to conceptual grounding is what distinguishes a social theory as critical or radical.[4] As a critical social theory, societal constitutionalism stands or falls on whether its claim to conceptual grounding can be kept open despite critics' most methodical efforts to close it (and Luhmann's systems theory is as formidable an effort as any).

5.1.2. The book as a whole: an overview

Given the backdrop provided in this chapter – Habermas's critique of positivism and his "turn" to a distinctively procedural standard of reason – the first of four steps may be taken to reveal the interrelationship between (a) Fuller's legal theory, (b) the collegial form of organization, and (c) the open possibility of conceptual grounding.

The first step, taken in chapter 6, is to bring into view a central implication of Fuller's approach to law: Precisely because it is procedural rather than substantive, it is consistent with Habermas's critique of positivism. It can thereby credibly claim conceptual grounding.

The whole matter of how *norms* of any kind, including procedural ones, can remain "external" to systemic drift and thereby challenge the sovereignty of subjective interests is very closely related to whether such norms can credibly claim grounding on any standard of reason. After all, if normative procedures cannot sustain such a claim, how can they be expected to assist *heterogeneous* actors and *competing* groups in recognizing and then restraining the inadvertent drift toward control and authoritarianism that concerned Weber? Yet, even if this claim is kept open, a question remains: How exactly can normative procedures assist such actors and groups in recognizing and restraining drift? These questions can only be answered by first sharpening the concept of "external":

> The second step, taken in chapter 7, is to reformulate Parsons's early concept of voluntaristic action. It is distinguished analytically from the broader concepts of normative action and nonrational action. Internal and external procedural restraints are then revealed to be distinctively voluntaristic (and possibly reasoned), and not normative or nonrational (and unreasoned).

The reformulated concept of voluntaristic action specifies how normative procedures can remain "external" to drift and yet contribute to heterogeneous actors' and competing groups' possible social integration rather than to their demonstrable social control. The voluntaristic status of external procedural restraints also keeps open their claim to grounding on a procedural standard of reason. In order for a nonauthoritarian social order to be a possibility in the late twentieth century, heterogeneous actors and competing groups must *institutionalize* external procedural restraints.

> The third step, taken in chapter 8, is to demonstrate that collegial formations institutionalize external procedural restraints by their sheer presence within a civil society. Unlike any other form of organization, the collegial form is *both* voluntaristic and procedural. This unique combination of analytical aspects simultaneously renders it "external" and also possibly integrative and reasoned.

> The fourth and final step, taken in chapters 9–11, is to elaborate the implications for theory, research, and practice of the presence (and absence) of collegial formations within modern civil societies.

5.2. Habermas's critique of Weber and later legal positivism

Weber's definitions of law are well known:

[L]aw [is an order] externally guaranteed by the probability that physical or psychological coercion will be applied by a *staff* of people in order to bring about compliance or avenge violation (Weber 1914–20: 34).

A "legal order" shall . . . be said to exist wherever coercive means, of a physical or psychological kind, are available . . . in other words, wherever we find a con-sociation specifically dedicated to the purpose of "legal coercion." (Weber 1914–20: 317; see Kronman 1983: 72–95; and Turkel 1980–1: 45–51 on Weber's concept of rational law in particular)

Weber defined the *legitimacy* of domination in related terms, as the "proba-bility" that actors will in fact develop the "appropriate" *subjective beliefs* for each ideal type of domination, whether rational-legal, traditional, or charis-matic (1914–20: 213). His reference to actors' subjective beliefs was his acknowledgement that *any* system of domination in time secures actors' subjective acquiescence, if not subjective support (Habermas 1973a: 95–6).

Habermas (1981a: 265–6) points out, however, that Weber's specific references to rational-legal domination rest on a line of argument that is at once circular and spurious. On the one hand, Weber treated domination as rational-legal (a) if enforcement agencies are organized rationally, that is if they are specialized and effectively organized within bureaucracies;[5] and (b) if citizens believe subjectively that enforcers' actions and commands are "right," or indeed lawful. On the other, Weber defined law as *any* set of rules that happens to be enforced effectively, or bureaucratically. As a result, at the moment that citizens, whose *behavior* is already controlled effectively, come to *believe subjectively* that stabilized social arrangements are also "rational" (rather than either traditional or charismatic), their domination is rational-legal. How enforcement agencies otherwise conduct themselves, either within or outside of their bureaucracies, is irrelevant to the concept of rational-legal domination. The only exceptions, of course, are when enforcers' conduct somehow brings the controlled citizenry to alter its strictly subjective beliefs that stabilized social arrangements are "rational."

Habermas considers Weber's treatment of law and legitimacy to be not only relativistic and uncritical but unnecessarily apologetic and, ultimately, simplistic. His alternative is to demonstrate conceptually that there is a generalizable standard of reasoned social action that is also "more compre-hensive" than Weber's narrow standard of purposive-rational action. Such a standard would allow researchers to determine (a) when actors' *subjective beliefs* are themselves "true" or "reasoned" and (b) when their subjective beliefs have been either purposefully manipulated or else systemically nar-rowed or "distorted":

In contemporary sociology, the usefulness of the concept of legitimation, which permits a demarcation of types of legitimate authority (in Weber's sense) according to the forms and contents of legitimation, is undisputed. What is controversial is the relation of legitimation to truth. This relation to truth must be presumed to exist if one regards as possible a motivation crisis resulting from a systemic scarcity of the resource of "meaning." Noncontingent [or non-relativistic] grounds for a disappearance of legitimacy can, that is, be derived only from an "independent" [*eigensinni-gen*] – that is, truth dependent – evolution of interpretation systems that systemati-cally restricts the adaptive capacity of society. (Habermas 1973a: 97; 1979: 205–12)

Still, Habermas's work is quite distinct from that of other theorists trained in either the Marxian or Frankfurt school tradition. He does not dismiss law out of hand as a veil or a "reification" that invariably distorts actors' subjective understandings of what their "real" situation is (1963b: 109–20; 1967a: 159, 165–7; other notable exceptions are Franz Neumann 1936 and Otto Kirchheimer in Burin and Shell 1969). Yet, like other neo-Marxists and critical theorists, Habermas nonetheless concludes that "capi-talistically modernized" legal institutions ultimately lack legitimacy. He also insists that these legal institutions invariably contribute to, rather than possibly slow or reverse, an inexorable, systemic drift toward what he calls "legitimation crisis." He sees this crisis as imminent within all Western democracies without exception (1973a; 1974; 1981a: 254–71, 412, note 49; 1982: 261–3, 281–3; 1984).[6]

Habermas's ambivalence toward law reflects the sophistication of his concepts. They permit him simultaneously to insist that: (a) on the one hand, Weber indeed was "basically a legal positivist" (1981a: 262; Kron-man 1983: 4), and yet (b) on the other, certain normative (that is, nonpositivist) qualities of law may be reasoned in a more generalizable sense. Thus, he sees that Marxists err in *reducing* actors' subjective accep-tance of any and all positive laws to their social control, manipulation, and distorted understanding. But he also sees (1981a: 258–9) that Weber re-duced the rationality of law to three characteristics. With these, Weber rendered his concept of rational-legal legitimation consistent with his "one-sided" view of purposive-rational social change more generally (see note 5):

(a) Weber's first characteristic of rational law, in Habermas's view, is "positivity." A rational-legal social order is regulated by a sovereign law-making body of one kind or another. This body, in turn, relies on what Habermas calls "juridical means of organizing" social control instead of coercing actors more directly.

(b) Weber's second characteristic of rational law is "legalism." Actors who are legally controlled or protected are not defined as moral agents. They are instead defined as possessors and consumers, as stra-tegic pursuers of their own subjective interests (Holmes 1897; Grey 1989 for nuances).[7]

(c) Weber's final characteristic of rational law is "formality." Entire domains of social life (economic and political marketplaces, in particu-lar) are defined legally as amoral, as relatively unmediated by norms.

Within such arenas, actors are permitted to compete strictly strategically, on the basis of immediate – unmediated – self-interest.[8]

Habermas accepts that these three characteristics may well represent the core of "bourgeois private law." But his point against Weber is that these same three characteristics cannot be said, by Weber or anyone else, to exhaust the normative (and possibly reasoned) components of law as such.[9]

Because Weber defined rational-legal legitimation so narrowly, so instrumentally, the only additional references to law that Habermas sees entering into his work, and in particular into his account of why actors ever believe that positive laws are "rational," are more ad hoc than methodical. These include Weber's occasional references, in Habermas's words, to "procedures through which it [law] comes to pass." Habermas (1981a: 255–8) ridicules Weber's references to procedures because the only procedures he has in mind are those that instruct specialized enforcers how to maximize the effectiveness of enforcement.[10] These sorts of procedures need not be directed to citizens at all since they are not designed to instruct citizens regarding what the positive laws are. Nor are they designed to instruct citizens regarding how they might adjust their behavior to avoid enforcers' sanctions. They are designed to instruct *enforcers* regarding how they might "rationalize" their exercises of collective power and other purposeful mechanisms of social control (also Kronman 1983: 30). [11]

Lon Fuller also saw that legal positivists *invariably* treat legal procedures as instructions that may, in principle, be directed *exclusively* to specialized enforcers. Indeed, this is the central point at issue in any critique of legal positivism: If the law is reducible to enforcers' instructions regarding how to maximize enforcement, then enforcers' camaraderie and fidelity to chains of command – not the interpretability of the law – becomes the only standard of legality as such. But if law is conceded to include instructions to citizens regarding what their shared social duties are, then interpretability – the duties' capacity to be recognized and understood in common even by heterogeneous actors and competing groups – becomes an *irreducible* criterion of legality as such. Far more than Habermas, Fuller specified the irreducible qualities of the law's (and duties') interpretability, and thereby drove home more methodically than anyone else before or since the central point at issue with legal positivism.

Fuller pointed out that it was Hans Kelsen, not Weber, who most explicitly and methodically elaborated the positivist approach to legal procedures (see note 13). For Kelsen, legal procedures need never inform citizens regarding the sorts of behavior prohibited (or facilitated) by positive laws. Nor, for that matter, need they inform citizens regarding how specialized enforcers are likely to act in typical (or possible) situations.[12] Quite to the contrary, the procedures Kelsen (and Weber) had in mind may be restricted, both in principle and in practice, to cues that enforcers exchange strictly among themselves as they endeavor (a) to maintain consistency across their own independent activities of enforcement, and thereby (b) to maintain their own camaraderie or esprit de corps as enforcers. In these ways legal procedures contribute exclusively to improving their effectiveness of enforcement, their rationalizing of purposeful mechanisms of social control.[13]

Habermas's (and Fuller's) point against Weber's (and Kelsen's) narrow approach to legal procedures is well taken. It reveals precisely why in the passage below Weber used *Autorität* when referring to the relationship of camaraderie between a chief and his staff, and why he then used *Herrschaft* when referring to the relationship of command between a staff of enforcers and the general population:

[A] system of domination may – *as often occurs in practice* – be so completely protected, on the one hand by the obvious community of interests between the chief and his administrative staff (bodyguards, Pr[a]etorians, "red" or "white" guards) as opposed to the subjects, on the other hand by the helplessness of the latter, that it can afford to drop even the pretense of a claim to legitimacy. But even then the mode of legitimation of the relation between chief and his staff may vary widely according to the type of basis [*Autoritätsgrundlage*] of the relation of the authority between them, and, as will be shown, this variation is highly significant for the structure of domination [*Struktur der Herrschaft*]. (Weber 1914–20: 214, my emphasis)[14]

Weber treated the *rationalization* of positive law, in short, in terms of two central factors: First, the increasing specialization of legal officials (from prophets, to honoratoriores, to secular power holders, to experts trained in the positive law). Second, the increasing bureaucratization and effectiveness of the agencies of enforcement. The result of this reductionism is precisely the three characteristics that Habermas isolates within Weber's account of rational law, and that Kronman (1983: 89–90) labels somewhat differently as "calculability," "comprehensiveness," and "organizational clarity." Weber expected to find these characteristics in *any* "true legal system," whether within an authoritarian or a nonauthoritarian social order. To concede his point is, of course, to acknowledge that these characteristics of law cannot support the nonauthoritarian/authoritarian distinction.

Habermas notes that later legal positivists, from Kelsen to Niklas Luhmann (1972; 1982: 90–137), and one could add H.L.A. Hart (1961) and Donald Black (1976), have remained remarkably consistent with Weber's lead. They continue to belittle the significance of legal procedures by reducing them, in principle, to cues exchanged among enforcers themselves. Habermas points out that Luhmann in particular treats all other legal procedures, all normative procedures, as a mere "secondary traditionalism" (Habermas's phrase, not Luhmann's): They habituate an already manipulated and controlled citizenry into believing, without warrant, that officials and enforcers would be capable of justifying their actions if questioned (Habermas 1981a: 255–6, 266, 269–70; also 1963b: 113–14; 1973a: 36–7). This subjective belief is unwarranted because, following Weber's definition of legitimacy, there is no generalizable, grounded standard of reasoned justification available beyond the narrow norm of rational action. Since authorities can appeal only to this narrow standard whenever they are questioned, other normative procedures cannot possibly be warranted:

Positive law is not valid because higher norms permit it, but because its selectivity [i.e. each particular positive law passed by a legislature] fulfills the function of congruency [with ongoing enforcement]. (Luhmann 1972: 156)

If an ordering of values is going to cross the lowest threshold of minimal complexity, it must become opportunistic [or strategic]. It must foresee the possibility of varying the order of values according to what actions are possible or urgent and according to how much the various values have been realized. This function corresponds to the normative regulation of norms in the legal domain. It is structurally analogous and necessary for similar reasons. (Luhmann 1982: 97–8)

The same presupposition, that citizens' questioning cannot possibly reveal a warrant for the positive laws beyond the latter's "congruence" with the norm of purposive-rational action and drift of rationalization, also explains why Weber based his ideal type of rational-legal domination exclusively on one particular interrelationship. He based it on the interrelationship between (a) specialized enforcers effectively maintaining social control, and (b) controlled subjects believing subjectively that their own control (and the social order that results) is "right" or "legal" rather than simply habitual or traditional (or charismatic). Thus, Weber's ideal type of rational-legal domination rests ultimately on whether enforcers reduce – or, better still, eliminate – citizens' questioning and their calls for warrants or justifications. When enforcers succeed in this, they simultaneously ensure that citizens' ultimately unfounded subjective beliefs in lawfulness and rightness will not be revealed to be unfounded (Habermas 1973a: 111–17). Thus, the phrase Habermas attributes to Luhmann's treatment of normative or nonrational legal procedures is quite apt for any legal positivist: Such procedures are merely a "secondary traditionalism," and not linked to any greater warrant or justification.

Habermas (also Parsons, surprisingly, 1958a; 1969a: 498–9) thereby reveals the most damaging flaw in Weber's (and then Luhmann's) circular reasoning: Rational-legal domination is not a distinct type of legitimation at all. Instead, it is "merely an indication of [some other] underlying legitimacy" (1981a: 266, 438 note 34). It is an indication of traditional legitimacy, or, even more simply, of actors' strictly habitual deference to power holders' and enforcers' instructions. After all is said and done, for Weber as for legal positivists ever since, *rational-legal domination is at its core as unreasoned as traditional domination; for that matter, it is as unreasoned as charismatic impositions of social control.* The increasing numbers of legal experts dedicated to enforcing legal domination, and the increasing complexity of the formalities and procedures by which they operate, merely "lengthen the path to [the citizens' questioning] legitimation" (Habermas 1981a: 269; 1982: 314–15). None render law any more reasoned or warranted.

5.3. Habermas's alternative: communicative action or procedural reason

5.3.1. Purposive rationality and procedural reason

Habermas insists that in order for any standard of reason to be generalizable today, in order for there to *be* a standard of reason grounded conceptually against normative relativism, *it must remain a procedural mediation.* He accepts from the outset Weber's pathos (chapter 3) regarding drift precisely because he concedes that modernity is indeed characterized by an ongoing fragmentation of meaning. Habermas *emphasizes* that the fragmentation of the "*substantial* unity of reason" is immutable. This is why he insists – against other neo-Marxists, and his own teachers – that *any* standard of reason today that can credibly claim grounding against normative relativism cannot itself be "objective" or directly *substantive* (1981a: chapter 4). Heterogeneous actors and competing groups cannot secure procedurally unmediated access to any "objective" or substantive standard of reason anyway. They cannot secure procedurally unmediated access to objective "facts" in the world, for instance, nor, for that matter, to an intersubjective recognition and understanding of complex social events.[15]

Indeed, one of the most important theses in Habermas's entire body of work is one that is both conditional and indirect: *If* there are irreducible qualities of reasoned social action that are indeed distinctively procedural, then *any* social action that *violates* the integrity of these qualities cannot contribute to reasoned social action.[16] It cannot do so irrespective of what the substance or content of these social actions happens to be, or what actors' normative motivations or subjective interests might have been in carrying them out. It also cannot contribute to reasoned social action irrespective of whether actors believe subjectively that their social action is otherwise legitimate, or whether they violated these procedural qualities unawares rather than purposefully.

What is a substantive standard of water pollution, for instance, that might reveal to social scientists when pollution enforcement is "reasoned"

Hawkins 1984)? What is a substantive rate of inflation or a substantive
evel of unemployment that might reveal when economic policy is "rea-
oned"? What is a substantive relationship between actors' concerns, say,
o maintain the integrity of their families, neighborhoods, communities,
or regions – however this is defined – and other actors' concerns to dis-
mantle all unnecessary obstacles to interstate (and international) commerce that might reveal when national planning is "reasoned"? What is a
ubstantive relationship between popular demands for greater egalitarian-
sm, on the one hand, and concentrations of wealth and power that leaders of either state agencies or private corporations insist are necessary for
effectiveness or efficiency, on the other, that reveals when social planning
s "reasoned"?

These questions may be multiplied endlessly. All of them revolve
around the same fundamental problem: How can social scientists (or
actors) recognize in common what *the* public interest is in substance?
What in substance is a reasoned or principled course of action, as opposed
o a passing agreement that interested parties accept at the moment,
subjectively as "legitimate"?[17]

The conditional thesis at the center of Habermas's social theory recapitulates Lon Fuller's central argument against legal positivism in the
950s and 1960s, albeit in a more conceptually sophisticated way. For all
of their many other differences, and in particular the great differences in
he theoretical traditions into which they were originally trained, these
two theorists nonetheless arrived independently at a most important point
of agreement: Possible manifestations of reasoned social action, in prac-
ice, can only be recognized by observing social scientists (or by the actors
and groups affected) through a procedural mediation. The latter, in turn,
an credibly claim to be grounded conceptually against normative relativ-
sm, the sovereignty of subjective interests, and the outcomes of interest-
group competition. Still, given the conditional thesis that Habermas and
Fuller essentially share, this procedural mediation can at best only reveal
when a social action is *possibly* reasoned. It can only reveal when a social
action does *not* violate the procedural requirements of reasoned social
action.

One other point must be emphasized. Any and all possible manifesta-
ions of reasoned social action will invariably be embedded within larger
ocial enterprises, larger social orders. The latter, in turn, are not likely to
be reasoned as a totality, as an undifferentiated, lived social fabric. More is
aid about this momentarily (and also in chapter 10).

Given his appreciation that the fragmentation of reason's "substantial
unity" is irreversible, Habermas sees more clearly than most other contemporary social theorists that he, and they, have a basic decision to make: On
he one hand, the concept of reasoned social action could be abandoned

altogether. This is precisely what mainstream theorists and researchers in the social sciences have done, including Talcott Parsons but not Lon Fuller. Systems theory, talk of postmodernism, and a recent renewal of interest in pragmatism, all add legitimacy to this basic decision rather than challenging it by proposing any alternative conceptual grounding that can support critique (see Antonio 1989 on pragmatism; Luhmann 1990 for systems theory; and Habermas 1989 on implications). On the other hand, the endeavor to specify *substantive* qualities that might somehow qualify social actions as reasoned could be abandoned in favor of focusing exclusively on the latter's irreducible *procedural* qualities. Only the latter, after all, can be recognized *in common* by social scientists (and heterogeneous actors and competing groups) in the face of functional differentiation and the ongoing fragmentation of meaning.

The importance of this second decision, to take a procedural turn rather than to abandon reason altogether, cannot be overemphasized. Because mainstream social scientists are typically not interested in critique, the moment that they come up against the fragmentation of the substantial unity of reason they readily accede to normative relativism and the sovereignty of actors' subjective interests (Brennan and Buchanan 1985; Hechter 1987). Indeed, the conventional wisdom in the social sciences holds that acceding to relativism and subjectivism are literal prerequisites of value-free research. Yet, this prevents social scientists from resisting the collective prejudices of the day, including the presupposition of exhausted possibilities. Because the conventional wisdom labels *any* talk of "reason" in social life as hopelessly "normative," and ultimately "ideological," this means that social scientists are convinced that the concept of reasoned social action cannot be rendered consistent with falsifiable research in the social sciences – before a single argument has been presented. Like any "aphorism" removed from discussion, this is more an article of faith than a scientifically sound point of departure. After all, it cannot be falsified empirically.

Nearly all neo-Marxist theorists other than Habermas also refuse steadfastly to take a procedural turn. Even worse, they then refuse to follow the conventional wisdom in abandoning the concept of reasoned social action altogether. Instead, they hold out the hope, and this is all it amounts to, that they will in the future specify what reasoned social action is in substance – despite the fragmentation of meaning, functional differentiation, and other manifestations of drift (Luhmann shatters this position 1982, 1986, 1990; and Wellmer 1976 brings Habermas's critique to it). Any and all references by Marxists (or by Giddens, Collins, and other British and American "conflict theorists" as well) to actors' alienation, exploitation, reification, fetishism, and "false consciousness" are nothing other than assertions that purportedly *substantive* qualities of reasoned social action are being unnecessarily restricted. These restrictions are then attributed, in turn, to the bourgeoisie's (or some "elite's") control over workers' access to the means of production, to a "dominant ideology," or to systemic social controls said to be intrinsic to capitalism but not to modernity more generally (this is Collins's assumption in calling for an end to credentials, 1979).

The problem with all of this is that if Habermas is correct, if only a procedural mediation can support critique today, then it is not possible for neo-Marxists or conflict theorists to escape infinite regress when they endeavor to demonstrate that particular social actions contribute to actors' alienation or exploitation (1981a: 171–2, 267–70, 218–22; Wellmer 1976). After all, if distinctively procedural qualities are indeed irreducible to the very possibility of anyone *recognizing* what reasoned social action is, how do neo-Marxists or conflict theorists know when reasoned social action is being unnecessarily restricted, in practice? Why aren't their descriptions of social events, like actors' subjective understandings of them, reflections of the false consciousness and inadvertent distortions of their subjective interests? How does the quite small circle of critical theorists, structural or systems theorists, or American and British conflict theorists manage to escape the dominant ideology and restrictions of reason that so effectively fetter everyone else?[18]

5.3.2. A procedural turn to truth and reason

Habermas's turn to the procedural mediation irreducible to the very possibility of social scientists (or anyone else) recognizing reasoned social action stems, therefore, from his early disillusionment with neo-Marxism. He became convinced that neo-Marxism as a tradition of theory and research suffers from serious conceptual limitations, and that these both contributed to, and were reflected in, communism's failures. His procedural turn also stems, however, from two other products of his training and early theorizing: First, he has been unwilling to abandon critique or to follow the conventional wisdom of the "bourgeois social sciences" in acceding to relativism and subjectivism. Second, he has rejected all *substantive* standards of truth and reason as a possible conceptual grounding for critique, *including those standards proposed in the philosophy of science by neopositivists who operate explicitly or implicitly with a copy theory of truth* (Habermas 1965, 1968a, 1973b, 1981a: 107–119; 1982: 274–8; Apel 1972, 1980).

The lessons that Habermas has drawn from these early positions are mutually supporting. To begin with, "truth" in the natural sciences cannot be traced, or reduced, to "objective" characteristics of natural events.

Individual scientists do not somehow discover or observe the "truth" of natural events as solipsistic researchers ("monads"). Nor do they, still in isolation, describe these "objective" characteristics in such a way that a particular set of descriptions somehow eventually strikes each monad to be "true." Similarly, "reason" in the social sciences (and in social life) cannot be traced, or reduced, to the substance or content of any lived social fabric. Social scientists do not somehow observe what is "reasoned" in substance in social life, as isolated observers.

At the same time, however, the scientific study of social life cannot be reduced to researchers' particular "perspectives," or "value commitments," in describing social behavior and in attributing subjective interests to actors. This would reduce the social sciences to a most mundane sociology of knowledge (Mannheim 1929 may legitimately be read in this way).[19]

Researchers' (or actors') *shared* recognition of what is "true" in natural events or "reasoned" in social life is indeed always and everywhere *normatively* mediated rather than objectively self-evident. This means, of course, that it is always and everywhere infused by researchers' value-commitments and attributions of subjective interests to actors. Yet, these commitments and attributions are themselves mediated by overarching normative orientations institutionalized within what Habermas calls researchers' (and actors') *communities of communication*. The question is not whether researchers ever accurately copy the "reality" of social events, but rather the extent to which communities of communication distort or manipulate researchers' (and actors') ongoing efforts to fathom the truth or reason of social events. By moving considerably beyond Habermas's own wording, however, this question may be sharpened: Is there a form of organization distinctive to any and all communities of communication that are reducing manipulation, and that are thereby approaching what Habermas calls "nondistorted communication"?[20]

Researchers (and actors) invariably operate within and through particular, identifiable communities of communication. This is the case irrespective of whether these communities are formal organizations or more informal networks. Habermas emphasizes this not because he turns to forms of organization – he does not – but because one key to recognizing whether any set of descriptions ever approaches the truth of natural events or the reason of social life is whether the communities in which these descriptions are presented *maintain the integrity of their communications*. For him, the integrity of communication includes irreducible procedural components. Instead of turning to forms of organization, he identifies these components, calling them both "universal pragmatics" and "formal pragmatics" (1976a). Only within communities that honor the integrity of these procedural components can actors (or researchers) literally recognize which of the competing descriptions, evaluations and explanations of natural phenomena and social events asymptotically approach "truth" or "reason." Whatever may be the objectively true qualities of natural events, or the substantively reasoned qualities of actors' lived social fabrics, these qualities cannot be described and explained by actors (or researchers) outside of such communities of communication.

5.3.3. A consensus theory of truth (and reason)

Habermas came to his communication theory by first methodically criticizing the rationales neopositivists offered for a "copy theory of truth."[21] He refused to accept the idea that natural scientists collectively correct errors, including faulty descriptions and interpretations of natural events, by somehow rendering their theories, hypotheses, and experiments into "copies" of what is "objectively true" within natural events. There is no scientific (or hermeneutic) standard available to them by which they might possibly gauge their own (or others') asymptotic advances toward such "copies." Thus, a "copy theory of truth" cannot be at the base of the natural sciences.

By contrast, a consensus theory of truth shifts the issue. It shifts the issue from whether certain *qualities* in natural events are or are not "copied" by scientists' descriptions and explanations, to whether certain *descriptions and explanations* of natural events are or are not distorted, and thereby capable of approaching the truth whatever it happens to be in substance. In the first case "truth" is something that may be grasped by monads. But in the second "truth" is something that can only be approached asymptotically be members of communication communities. And, again, Habermas's consensus theory of truth rests on a proposal that is quite conditional and indirect: *If* the procedural qualities marking *any* instance of "nondistorted" consensus among *any* set of speakers can be specified, then this establishes a limiting case standard, an "ideal speech situation." Against this standard, any existing communication community's institutions and practices might be described and evaluated. Moreover, because this standard is itself a strictly procedural mediation, and by no means an objective or substantive standard "in the world," it may be recognized and understood in common by heterogeneous actors and competing groups within and across existing communication communities.

In two respects, then, Habermas's consensus theory of truth and standard of procedural reason establishes something of an Archimedean point within the flux of actors' normative beliefs and subjective interests. First, this standard can credibly claim conceptual grounding, and can account for (a) how natural scientists ever recognize "objective" truth in their descriptions of natural events, (b) how social scientists ever recognize "reasoned" social actions, or (c) how actors ever approach "substantive reason" within their own lived social fabrics. Only within and through communication communities of one kind or another do researchers or actors ever discover that certain "protocol statements" – particular descriptions of natural or social events – are superior to others (see Popper 1934 on protocol statements). Second, the *quality* of communication within any particular community – whether it is distorted or not – may itself be described and evaluated on the basis of the limiting case of nondistorted communication.

Habermas insists that whatever limitations a "consensus theory" of truth and reason might have, it is nonetheless more fundamental epistemologically than any copy theory or any variation of realism or positivism.[22] Indeed, at the most basic level, the level of interpersonal communication, Habermas refers to these procedural qualities of truth or reason as "universal pragmatics." This term suggests conceptual grounding and generalizability: *Universal syntactics* (as presented by Noam Chomsky) proposes that a conceptually grounded grammatical code delimits those *sentences* that can possibly be constructed within any *written language*. Habermas's *universal pragmatics,* in turn, delimits those *"speech acts"* that can possibly be understood within any *spoken language*. It is only possible for speakers to arrive at mutual – nonmanipulated, nondistorted – understandings of each other's "speech acts" (Austin's term) if the latter exhibit fidelity to universal pragmatics under the conditions of the ideal speech situation. Speakers' mutual understandings of speech acts under these conditions, in turn, are the irreducible foundation upon which any intersubjective recognition of objective truth as well as of reasoned social action rests.[23]

5.3.4. The ideal speech situation: claiming an idealized grounding

Rather than exploring universal pragmatics in detail, it is sufficient for present purposes to address the "ideal speech situation."[24] Only within the latter, after all, can speakers' "discourse" and mutual understandings of speech acts be fully realized. Within the ideal speech situation: "[P]articipants do not exchange information [about states of affairs in the world], do not direct or carry out actions [in the world], do not have or communicate [particular] experiences. [I]nstead [they] . . . search for arguments or offer justifications" for their descriptions and evaluations of events or actions in social life that are of interest to them (Habermas 1971: 18–19).

A speech situation is ideal to the extent that it takes place under three conditions, and Habermas himself acknowledges that these conditions render this situation "counterfactual" and "unreal." It is a limiting case standard rather than a practicable situation. First, participants within the ideal speech situation "suspend" all of their presuppositions regarding "objective" constraints on social actions. All such purported "conditions" are treated, at least initially, as contingent or negotiable rather than as immutable.[25] Each participant temporarily treats any and all proposals for social action as potentially practicable. This community thought experiment permits participants (a) to "neutralize" not only whatever personal "motives" they may have for unduly limiting alternatives but also (b) to "neutralize" the influence of their institutional affiliations and material resources outside the situation.[26] In this way, participants develop a "cooperative readiness to arrive at an understanding" based strictly on each proposal's merits as an argument. Second, and as a result, the validity of any proposal is assessed independently of any consideration of the proposer's social standing outside of the speech situation. Third, participants "suspend" their earlier "assumptions" even regarding which types of statements or arguments are typically valid (1973c: 255–61; 1981a: 17–19, 22–42; 1982: 241).

Habermas insists that these three conditions ensure that all present *and potential* participants may "validate" statements, or influence others' assessments of statements, through the quality of their arguments alone. This is his "universalization thesis." It is, essentially, a thesis of absolute – unmediated, unconstrained – democratization within and around the ideal speech situation. Indeed, what Habermas means by the very term "ideal speech situation" is a situation in which *every* actor's unrestrained access to, as well as subsequently unrestrained participation within, artificially protected arenas of discourse is guaranteed without exception.[27] He refers to the same guarantee as the "symmetry-requirement" of discourse (1973c: 255–61; 1981a: 17–19, 22–6; 1982: 235–6, 241, 255–8, 262–3).[28] The social action that results from nondistorted communication is "communicative action." Unlike rational action, communicative action is tied to a "more comprehensive" concept of reason.

Habermas insists that the *substantive* impact of communicative action, in practice, is likely to vary greatly from group to group and from social unit to social unit. Yet, he also insists that all of the major institutions of the Western democracies are, without exception, too far removed from meeting the procedural requirements of communicative action to qualify as reasoned. One unfortunate result of this absolutism, however, is that Habermas cannot draw examples of communicative action from contemporary institutional or organizational practices.[29] He can draw examples only from interpersonal relationships.[30] He refers to psychoanalysis in particular as an exemplar of how willing participants push ordinary speech toward "depth hermeneutics" and communicative action: The analyst employs "depth hermeneutics" to remove phobias or deep-seated "distortions" in the analysand's understanding of his or her life-world. The analysand, of course, willingly visits the analyst precisely in order to have these removed. The analyst's task is to make it possible for the analysand to engage in reasoned discourse, and then in reasoned or communicative action (1968a: chapters 10–12; 1971: 28–32, 37–40; 1981a: 20–1, 41–2).

5.3.5. *Habermas's dead end, and a way out*

Precisely because Habermas accepts Weber's point that the "substantial unity of reason" has been fragmented, he dismisses out of hand many of the most basic presuppositions underlying Marxist theory. If substantive reason is fragmented, how can the proletariat be capable of nonmanipulated and nondistorted "consciousness" and "solidarity" on the basis of its "objective" material interests? If substantive reason is fragmented, how can Marxist theory itself be used – whether by the proletariat, a vanguard, or Marxist researchers – to reveal how relations of production might be dis-alienated consistently with a nonauthoritarian direction of social change? It is a rare Marxist theorist, historically or today, who has not ultimately based his or her work on the theory's *intrinsic* capacity to instruct actors on both counts. Yet, in many respects the crisis of Marxism since the 1920s has been a product of Marxists' increasing realization that the proletariat lacks any *intrinsic* capacity to establish consciousness and maintain solidarity on the basis of "objective" material interests alone (e.g. Olson 1965: 102–111).

Of course, Habermas also dismisses Weberians' presupposition that their conceptual framework somehow allows them to specify what a substantively *rational* action is, either in principle or in practice.[31] For Habermas, only actors' fidelity to admittedly idealized procedures of "discourse" allows anyone to recognize whether any social action is possibly reasoned rather than self-interested and "strategic." Weberians lack a theory of manipulation precisely because they lack a concept of reasoned social action against which to isolate manipulated action within the larger, strictly residual category of nonrational action (see chapter 7 for other distinctions within the nonrational).

Still, with his procedural turn, Habermas has painted himself into a corner. First, he can never posit that a particular group's way of life or a particular nation-state's institutions are reasoned or communicative in all of their parts or analytical aspects. Should he ever do so, he would have to explain how he arrived at this judgment, and he cannot possibly accomplish this. On the one hand, the limiting case of ideal speech clearly cannot be realized, in practice, by any existing group or nation-state. On the other, Habermas's own judgment would itself have to be filtered through the ideal speech situation since the latter alone certifies any judgment as reasoned rather than as distorted. Short of this, any such assertion by Habermas or anyone else marks either a return to a copy theory of truth, or, worse, a regression to dogmatism (Bernstein 1978, 1983; Dallmayr 1974, 1976). By contrast, if the ideal speech situation cannot be sidestepped by Habermas or anyone else, then the particular characteristics of any group's practices or any nation-state's institutions must be explored in very rich detail. Rather than launching an absolutist critique, one must endeavor to discover *those parts or analytical aspects that are consistent with irreducible procedural qualities of reasoned social action.* It is clear from Habermas's (1973a) absolutist critique of Western institutions, however, that the ideal speech situation is too blunt an instrument to inform such detailed study.

Second, Habermas has also painted himself into a corner because he is left with an idealized standard of democratic access to discourse as his only basis for describing and evaluating shifts in the direction of institutional and social change. Given the complexity of the latter, neither Habermas nor any of his proponents has to date provided the slightest hint regarding how the idealized standard might be used to specify whether any particular social movement, organization, or institution within any particular nation-state is becoming more reasoned or less "strategic" (e.g. Habermas's replies to critics in 1982, but consider the weakness of his position by 1989). Rather, the theory leaves Habermas no alternative other than to cling to an absolutist critique of all complex social units as ultimately manipulative and distorting. It is not surprising to be told that all Western democratic institutions and practices fail to exhibit fidelity to what Habermas himself acknowledges is an unreal standard. It is surprising to be told, however, that one unavoidable result of these failures is an imminent "legitimation crisis" (Habermas 1973a, 1974).

The interrelationship between Fuller's procedural approach to law (chapter 6) and the collegial form of organization (chapter 8) emancipates Habermas from the corner into which he has painted himself. This is accomplished, moreover, without jeopardizing the advances he has clearly made beyond copy theories of truth and both Weberian and Marxist social theories. If Habermas's idealized standard of procedural reason is to inform detailed research, it must be explicitly interrelated with a procedural threshold. It would have to be demonstrated, in turn, that this procedural threshold is (a) irreducible to any possibility of realizing the ideal speech situation, and yet (b) eminently practicable rather than counterfactual. What is clear, however, is that if Habermas's consensus theory of truth is to ground detailed research against normative relativism, the sovereignty of actors' subjective interests, and the outcomes of group competition and drift, then any practicable threshold must remain a procedural mediation.

Fuller offers the social sciences a specific set of procedural norms that are irreducible to any effort to restrain purposefully arbitrary exercises of collective power. Being irreducible in this respect, these procedural norms indeed mark an eminently practicable *threshold:* Heterogeneous actors and competing groups must successfully cross this threshold in their behavior *before* they can aspire to reasoned social action in Habermas's sense. Put differently, procedural reason will always remain a social aspiration at best (to borrow a term from Fuller). By contrast, Fuller's procedural restraints mark an irreducible and unambiguous social duty: Heterogeneous actors and competing groups must institutionalize their own *behavioral* fidelity to these restraints before they can take *another step* toward reasoned social action. At the same time, their behavioral fidelity to these procedural restraints by no means compromises or jeopardizes the credibility of Habermas's claim that procedural reason is grounded against relativism.

In short, even as Habermas's criticisms of Weber's views of rational-legal legitimation, and of rational-legal procedures, are sound in every respect, these criticisms cannot be transferred, in whole or in part, to Fuller's work. Quite to the contrary, Fuller's procedural restraints allow social scientists to demonstrate that particular sectors, industries, organizations, and even particular divisions of organizations are indeed legitimate in a sense that Habermas himself must acknowledge is reasoned. Yet, these same social units will certainly fail to realize the limiting case standard of ideal speech.

6. Societal constitutionalism's threshold in practice: from Fuller's legal theory to societal constitutionalism

The Harvard legal theorist, Lon Fuller (1902–78), and the Oxford legal theorist, H.L.A. Hart (1907–), were undeniably the English-speaking world's most respected and influential legal theorists from the 1950s through the 1970s, and their influence persists today. Robert Summers (1984: 2) calls Fuller the "greatest proceduralist in the history of legal theory," and ranks him as one of the four most important American legal theorists of the past 100 years, the other three being Oliver Wendell Holmes, Roscoe Pound, and Karl Llewellyn (1984: 1). Indeed, in 1948 Fuller succeeded Pound in the Carter Professorship of General Jurisprudence, after nearly a decade on the faculty at Harvard Law School. Aside from *The Morality of Law* (1964/1969), Fuller is best remembered for his debates over legal positivism in the 1950s, first with Ernest Nagel (see chapter 5, note 2), and then Hart.[1] The latter exchange "was perhaps the most interesting and illuminating exchange of views on basic issues of legal theory to appear in English in this century" (Summers 1984: 10).[2]

It is important to point out, however, that in the great debate over legal formalism and legal realism that raged in the United States in the 1930s, this future "greatest proceduralist" took the side of legal formalism's critics. Unlike the legal realists of his day who were advising legal scholars to describe judges' behavior as such, however, the young Fuller emphasized the importance of studying the reasons judges offer for their decisions and behavior. His point against Holmes (1897) and then the legal realists of his own generation was that the *meaning* of judges' behavior can seldom be gleaned from direct observation alone.[3] Judges' behavior can only be understood, and thereby accurately described and explained, he insisted, once observers have fathomed what the judges within any legal system are endeavoring to accomplish in the first place.

Put in more general terms, Fuller was intrigued by the social interactions underlying any legal system, and how increasingly complex social interactions are both reflected in, and shaped by, the law.

One can imagine a small group – transplanted, say, to some tropical island – living successfully together with only the guidance of certain shared standards of conduct,

107

these standards having been shaped in various indirect and informal ways by experience and education. What may be called the legal experience might first come to such a society when it selected a committee to draw up an authoritative statement of the accepted standards of conduct (Fuller 1964/1969: 130; also 205–6).

Though it can be said that law and [substantive] morality share certain concerns – for example, that rules should be clear – it is as these concerns become increasingly the objects of an explicit responsibility that a legal system is created (Fuller 1964/1969: 131).

Thus, Fuller saw the law framing complex social interactions, not behavior that is somehow accessible to discrete observations. Such an approach to law is, of course, as sociological as can be. In many respects, Fuller's legal theory may legitimately be labeled today a critical variant of symbolic interactionism. Whereas symbolic interactionists (and legal realists) accede to the sovereignty of actors' subjective interests and normative relativism as they describe social behavior, Fuller was confident that he had located something of a contemporary Archimedean point. He was confident that his claim to conceptually ground researchers' (or actors') critical descriptions of existing legal systems was credible. Yet, he explicitly acknowledged that his own work failed to establish this, and that it needed to be linked to a communication theory in order to do so (1964/1969: 184–6).

Why has Fuller's legal theory had so little direct impact on the social sciences, including the sociology of law? As is the case with any theory in the social sciences that claims conceptual grounding, sociologists hastily label Fuller's legal theory "normative." This happens whenever a conceptual framework is merely kept open to the possibility that there is a concept of reasoned social action beyond the narrow norm of rational action. With this conceptual openness, the theorist is refusing to accede a priori to relativism, and to the ideology of the presupposition of exhausted possibilities. Given the conventional wisdom in the social sciences regarding the acceptability of this presupposition and the unacceptability of the concept of reason, sociologists fail to appreciate the many respects in which their abandoning of the concept of reasoned social action narrows the scope of *empirical research* (see chapter 10 for elaboration).[4]

Still, as noted in chapter 5, Fuller team-taught a course at Harvard Law School with Talcott Parsons, the Harvard sociologist, and each theorist became noticeably influenced by the other's work and terminology. There are both personal and theoretical reasons why Parsons became increasingly attracted to Fuller's legal theory late in his career. On the one hand, each theorist already had reached the apex of his respective field when they met, and they were also age cohorts – born the same year (1902) and later passing away within one year (Fuller in 1978 and Parsons in 1979). Equally importantly, Parsons's analytical concepts *also were designed to challenge the sovereignty of actors' subjective interests and escape normative relativism* (see chapter 5, note 4). This renders his social theory intrinsically critical, irrespective of how Parsons himself happened to label it, and irrespective of how it has been labeled in the discipline (Sciulli in preparation, a). Indeed, it is fair to say that Parsons and Fuller independently developed the conceptual foundations of a decidedly non-Marxist approach to critical theory. Given that Habermas's communication theory departs so substantially from core concepts of the Marxist tradition, a synthesis of these three theorists' central concepts follows far more readily than might be expected at first glance.

6.1. Procedural legality as irreducible threshold: Fuller's contribution to the social sciences

Like Weber, Lon Fuller also rejected Lockean liberals' optimism regarding the drift of social change. Instead he operated implicitly on the basis of three very Weberian positions. First, he assumed that all social and governmental units within all modern nation-states respond in one way or another to systemic pressures of change. Second, he acknowledged that actors experience this as a fragmentation of "meaning," a literal sense of drift. Third, and most importantly, he insisted that any social order resulting from social and governmental units' normatively unmediated pursuit of their own interests under these conditions is more likely to be controlling and authoritarian than benign.

Unlike Weber, however, Fuller's central concern was to address directly how a nonauthoritarian social order is possible in the mid- and late twentieth century. By posing the following dual problem, he developed a distinction that anticipated Habermas's later critique of Weber and broader reasoned/unreasoned distinction: First, as bureaucratically organized enforcers enforce positive laws under modern conditions of drift, they are just as capable of effectively enforcing arbitrary decrees as they are capable of effectively enforcing responsible laws. Second, the actors subjected to effective enforcement are just as capable of becoming convinced subjectively that decrees are rational-legal, and thereby legitimate, as they are that responsible laws are rational-legal. In Fuller's terms, the question is: How can social scientists distinguish in comparative perspective when a nation-state's effectively enforced positive laws are becoming either more arbitrary or more responsible?[5]

The importance of Fuller's resulting lawless/lawful distinction is that it would allow social scientists to recognize *purposefully* arbitrary exercises of collective power irrespective of whether a nation-state's existing positive laws qualify as rational-legal in Weber's sense, and irrespective of whether actors accept their legitimacy as such. Just as importantly, Fuller's distinction is consistent conceptually with Habermas's communication theory, even as it remains a distinct contribution that cannot be derived directly or logically from Habermas's concepts. Finally, even as Fuller's dual problem and resulting distinction are consistent with longstanding concerns of constitutional and liberal traditions, they result in concepts capable of supporting a radical critique of any modern nation-state, including Western democracies. Because his concepts call into question the sovereignty of actors' subjective interests, they simultaneously open the way to addressing the Weberian Dilemma rather than sidestepping it with a facile optimism and complacency. Indeed, unlike any other legal theory drawn from Western constitutional and liberal traditions, Fuller's principles of "procedural legality" *begin* to address the problem of how social scientists might recognize the *inadvertently* arbitrary exercises of collective power that accompany the drift of social change.

6.1.1. Generalizing Fuller's threshold: from law to shared social duties

Fuller's contribution may be put into the terminology of societal constitutionalism rather than left restricted to references to law alone: He offers the social sciences an irreducible *threshold* of internal procedural restraints. Heterogeneous actors and competing groups rely on this procedural threshold, in practice, whenever they simply recognize and understand *in common* the *shared social duties* being sanctioned within any complex social unit. Social scientists may employ the same procedural threshold to *specify:*

(a) When the positive laws being enforced within any modern nation-state are arbitrary (and thereby controlling).

(b) When the shared social duties being sanctioned with any social unit are demonstrably controlling (and, of course, manipulative and distorting in Habermas's sense).

(c) When acknowledged ranges of expectations of what is acceptable behavior within any social unit contribute to actors' unnecessary self-restriction (chapter 2).

For two reasons, Fuller never extended his threshold in this way, from law in particular to shared social duties in general. First, he never explicitly interrelated his procedural threshold to a communication theory and grounded standard of procedural reason. Second, he never interrelated his procedural threshold to a particular form of organization. Given the presentation of the theory of societal constitutionalism to this point, this extension is incorporated into the discussion of Fuller's legal theory below even though these two interrelationships have yet to be explored methodically.

Critique of Weber: from effectiveness to interpretability. Weber's emphasis on the importance of effective law enforcement by specialized enforcers was not so much mistaken, in Fuller's view, as partial: It is certainly correct that social scientists can only recognize whether rules (or duties) are being *effectively enforced* by whether instances of lawbreaking are decreasing over time. Indeed, the effectiveness of law enforcement may be converted into quantifiable indices of lawbreaking of one kind or another, and, in this way, rendered increasingly consistent with strictly rational or instrumental calculations of success (chapter 7).[6]

But Fuller's point moves beyond such circular reasoning. Whether rules (or duties) are *successfully recognized and understood* by heterogeneous actors and competing groups cannot be reduced – by social scientists or actors – to indices of lawbreaking and the effectiveness of enforcement. Such indices fail to reveal whether such actors and groups are recognizing and understanding what their shared social duties *are*. After all, actors may purposefully disobey rules that are clearly understandable (as is the case, for example, with civil disobedience). Conversely, when rules or duties are not understandable – as is the case, for instance, with "laws" that prohibit "threats to the State" – actors' disobedience may be altogether inadvertent. For that matter, enforcement may be uneven, and again inadvertently so.

It is only possible for heterogeneous actors and competing groups, as well as the specialized enforcers themselves, to recognize and understand what the laws (or duties) are, in Fuller's view, when the laws (or duties) are kept consistent with a specific set of procedural qualities. This holds true, he insists, irrespective of: (a) what the laws' (or duties') positive content happens to be, (b) whether a legitimate lawmaking body drafted the laws (or duties) in an acceptable way, and (c) whether both their content and their legitimacy are consistent with the public's expectations. Put into the terminology of chapter 4, these procedural qualities mark a *threshold of internal procedural restraints*. This threshold cannot be reduced to surveys of enforcers' camaraderie, or of the public's strictly subjective beliefs regarding the legitimacy of the law, the lawmakers, or the enforcers (whether as rational-legal legitimacy, or any other).[7]

Procedural threshold: specifying the integration/control distinction. Fuller (1964/1969: 46–84) concentrated, therefore, on *specifying* those procedural qualities that distinguish law proper from any and all other mechanisms of social control, including well-enforced decrees (see Black 1984 for an impressive review of such mechanisms).[8] As noted above, he did not argue that these procedural qualities distinguish instances of heterogeneous actors' and competing groups' possible social integration from instances of their demonstrable social control (see Fuller 1966, 1969b, plus 1981). Yet, his references to law may be generalized in this way, and the first step is to substitute the phrase "shared social duties" for his references to law.[9]

With this substitution, it may be said that heterogenous actors and competing groups are capable of recognizing and understanding what their shared social duties are only when the latter are kept consistent with all eight of the following procedural restraints:

1. *Generality.* In order possibly to be integrative, a system of shared social duties must be applicable, in principle, to all actors and groups – irrespective of whether they are acceptable to them in substance or not. The case-by-case approach taken by regulatory agencies, Fuller notes, may in time become divorced from generality, and lead to inadvertent exercises of arbitrary power by entire agencies of enforcement (see Hawkins 1984: 33–5 for a clear example in Great Britain). Whether agencies' rulings are enforced effectively, or whether they continue to be accepted subjectively by most actors as "right" or "lawful," does not somehow keep them possibly integrative once they encroach against the principle of generality.

2. *Promulgation.* Although it is not necessary for every actor to be able to understand the meaning of every shared social duty, it must be possible for those who are most interested in, or affected by, particular duties to keep themselves informed regarding authorities' intent.[10] After all, actors less informed (the majority) tend to be influenced by the acceptance or criticism of sanctioned social duties by those more informed (the minority).

3. *Prospectivity.* Within a system of prospective rules, situations may well arise in which retroactive rulings are acceptable and necessary. This is the case when, as examples: courts confer validity on marriages that had not been conducted properly, appellate courts overturn lower court decisions or alter legal doctrine, and legislatures amend the tax code. But retroactive enactments of shared social duties must remain exceptional efforts, mere fine-tuning of prospective duties. It must remain clear to everyone that they are indeed exceptional. Thus, as appellate courts overturn or substantially alter their own decisions within ever shorter periods of time, or as the tax code is endlessly revised, the prospectivity/retroactivity distinction is being blurred.

4. *Clarity.* Beyond the obligation not to violate explicit constitutional provisions, any lawmaking body, whether in government or the "private" sector, has a responsibility to keep the shared social duties that it is sanctioning sufficiently clear. Both actors and enforcers alike must be able to recognize compliance and noncompliance unambiguously (Brennan and Buchanan 1985: 109).

5. *Noncontradiction.* Shared social duties are seldom in violation of "contrariety" (that is, A, not-A, or punishing an actor for doing what he or

she was ordered to do). But they must also avoid "contradiction." They must avoid becoming incompatible or repugnant, and thereby failing to correspond to any sensible legislative purpose. For instance, a right to freedom of assembly is meaningless if groups find it difficult to secure demonstration permits.

6. *Possibility.* All eight principles, according to Fuller, may be logically reduced to this requirement. Shared social duties must avoid requiring conduct of actors that is beyond their abilities to perform. For example, shared social duties cannot require actors to alter their ascriptive character-istics in order to enter the civil service or to escape prosecution. Impossible duties – duties that are secret, retroactive, unclear, or contradictory – allow power holders selectively to eliminate real or imagined political oppo-nents. Since all actors are in principle placed in jeopardy by such duties, particular power holders are free to select where and when to apply sanc-tions, quite irrespective of actors' behavior.

7. *Constancy.* This is self-explanatory, but it also provides the basis for the harshest criticism of contemporary rule-making in the United States and advanced societies generally. Across the West, legislatures, courts, professional associations, and many other organizations ceaselessly accom-modate interest lobbying (and political party logrolling) at the expense of institutional consistency or even institutional memory (Vile 1967; Lowi 1969; Hayek 1973–9; Luhmann 1990 sees this as a virtue of system "autopoiesis").

8. *Congruence.* Declared social duties must be in congruence with offi-cials' actions. Fuller says this principle is the most complex, and most interrelated with rule makers' substantive concerns. He notes that break-downs in congruence may be traced to many factors, including: mistaken interpretation, inaccessibility of the law, lack of insight into what is re-quired to maintain the integrity of the legal system, bribery, prejudice, indifference, stupidity, and a drive for personal power. The means used to maintain congruence also may vary from nation-state to nation-state, in-cluding: procedural due process, habeas corpus and right to appeal, and consistency in statutes and constitutional principles.

As noted above, these qualities do not merely ground the lawful/lawless distinction, as Fuller held. They mark a *threshold of interpretability* of (a) shared social duties (b) acknowledged ranges of expectations, and (c) the mechanisms of social control employed in their support. Whether the shared social duties sanctioned within any complex social unit remain con-sistent with these threshold restraints, and power holders do not in time resort to mechanisms of social control that encroach against them, is a strictly empirical issue. This is an issue amenable to detailed, falsifiable studies, and ultimately to operationalization. Unlike Habermas's limiting case of procedural reason, the threshold restraints are by no means counterfactual. They are rather the most irreducible *first* step that any set of heterogeneous actors or competing groups takes whenever they recognize in common, and then restrain collectively, *purposefully* arbitrary exercises of collective power or mechanisms of social control. This holds true within any sector, industry, or organization of a modern civil society, and, for that matter, within any division of a particular organization. Because this threshold marks an irreducible first step in recognizing the undue narrowness of even subtle forms of social control, it also opens the way to addressing the inadvertent arbitrariness of drift at the center of the Weberian Dilemma. This opening is carried through in chapter 8 by demonstrating that collegial formations *institutionalize* shared social duties that remain consistent with this threshold.

Preliminary criticisms of natural law, liberalism, and Marxism. Being procedural, Fuller's threshold restraints are much less robust and substantial than moral theories proper, including traditional theories of natural law and natural right. Their successful institutionalization by no means brings the "good life" any nearer to realization. Quite to the contrary, their successful institutionalization ensures only two things. First, it ensures that the "good life," whatever it might entail in substance, remains a possibility to which actors and groups may (or may not) continue to aspire. And, second, it ensures, in the meantime, that the most coercive, manipulative, or distorting *purposeful* mechanisms of social control can be recognized by heterogeneous actors and competing groups in common, and then possibly restrained by them collectively.[11]

Regardless, these threshold restraints are the most fundamental contribution of constitutional and liberal traditions. They are more basic to nonauthoritarian *social* order in the late twentieth century than the division of powers, individuals' "natural rights," a market economy, or competing interest groups, political parties, and timely elections. Rather than being intrinsically integrative, *all of these institutions are readily converted into mechanisms of social control once power holders encroach against the threshold of interpretability of shared social duties.* A democratic electorate that votes freely for candidates who issue unclear or contradictory decrees in the "national interest," for instance, converts elections, competing political parties, and even voters' own first amendment freedoms into mechanisms of actors' demonstrable social control. It increases a nation-state's susceptibility to social authoritarianism. Putting this point more generally, a sharp distinction can be drawn between (a) whether a candidate's claim to hold an office is warranted, either by an election or appointment, and (b) whether the candidate's (or the electorate's) subsequent actions are consistent with the threshold of interpretability. The former claim hinges entirely on actors' subjective acceptance of election outcomes, but the latter actions are quite independent of this. Thus, power holders' behavioral fidelity to the threshold does not guarantee that a social order will be subjectively legitimate (or popular) in Weber's sense. But a social order's popularity (or rational-legal legitimation) fails to reveal whether purposefully arbitrary exercises of collective power are increasing or decreasing (see the section below).

In addition to marking a threshold independent of rises and falls in subjective acceptance, and thereby of electoral outcomes, Fuller (1964/ 1969: 17–18) also used his procedural restraints to stake out a position independent of a view held, ironically, by liberal and Marxist theorists alike. This is the liberal view that the procedural integrity of law is only successfully institutionalized within modern nation-states that maintain robust market economies. Marxists convert this into the proposition that the procedural integrity of law only needs to be institutionalized where robust market economies are found.[12] Fuller ridiculed liberals who imagine that the interpretability of law is somehow *intrinsically* supported by a robust market economy. He also ridiculed "revolutionaries" who imagine that they may ignore the threshold of procedural restraints because their self-declared commitment to substantive justice or substantive rationality elevates their actions above all such "bourgeois" formalities.[13]

6.1.2. Between morality and positivism, aspiration and duty

Rather than merely exposing limitations in other approaches to law, Fuller preferred to demonstrate the generalizability of his procedural approach more positively. With this in mind, he saw that he had to steer clear of two shoals. First, he had to avoid succumbing to the conceptual imprecision of natural law theories in particular and moral theories in general. Contributors to these theoretical traditions typically treat categories of "natural law" as directly substantive.[14] Such categories are incapable of credibly claiming grounding against normative relativism under modern conditions. Second, he also had to avoid succumbing to the normative relativism of legal positivists, Weberians, and liberals. Contributors to these theoretical traditions treat the category of "positive law" as distinct from all that is nonpositive. But they fail to examine the latter residual category. They merely label it "morality."[15]

Relativism results from Weber's ideal types, to recall, because the norm of rational action, and the related type of legitimation, cannot in themselves account for the presence of nonauthoritarian social orders in the late twentieth century. Given this aporia in Weber's conceptual framework, this issue seems to hinge on strictly substantive, patently unreasoned factors, or factors distinctive to each instance of nonauthoritarian social order in and of itself. Consider, for instance, that in employing Weber's categories alone, one has no alternative other than to categorize contemporary Great Britain and the United States, as well as the Soviet Union and South Africa, as "rational-legal." All four nation-states, after all: (a) enforce positive laws through bureaucratically organized agencies, (b) adjudicate enforcement consistently with their respective country's positive laws, and (c) train both enforcers and jurists as specialists in these positive laws (Meador's 1986 intriguing discussion of legal training in East Germany is generally illustrative of civil law systems in the former Eastern bloc).[16]

Fuller did not develop his alternative to Weber and legal positivism, however, by turning immediately to natural law theories or other moral theories for guidance. Instead, and again like Habermas later, he developed his alternative by methodically addressing the conceptual limitations of legal positivism. Unlike Habermas, however, he turned his attention to legal positivists' unexamined category of "morality."[17] As a first step, he distinguished a "morality of duty" from a "morality of aspiration."[18] His challenge to legal positivists was that they could not describe (let alone explain) the positive laws of *any* modern nation-state, authoritarian or nonauthoritarian, without ultimately acknowledging that there is an irreducible interrelationship, *in practice,* between any set of positive laws and *both* moralities.

Two propositions. What did Fuller have in mind in drawing his distinction? Exemplars of the morality of aspiration are Aristotelian notions of "praxis" and the "good life," Nietzschean notions of "nobility," and Marxian notions of praxis as laboring under conditions of disalienation and unmediated access to resources. In all of these instances, actors aspire to a substantive ideal of self-development or cultivation that, at best, they ceaselessly approach asymptotically. By contrast, the exemplar of the morality of duty is basic criminal law. The limiting case of basic criminal law would place the most minimal, altogether nonnegotiable, social duties on all actors. It would impose that particular range of expectations regarding acceptable behavior most essential to maintain social order as such.[19]

What is ironic is that these seemingly polar types are simultaneously (a) analytically distinct in principle, and yet (b) intrinsically interrelated in practice. What Fuller had in mind in distinguishing them may be worded in the form of two propositions implicit in his writings:

> *First Proposition.* Actors are already exhibiting behavioral fidelity to *some* shared morality of duty whenever they are aspiring openly or publicly to *any* vision of the "good life," whether individually or collectively.[20]

Irrespective of how different actors' public aspirations may be, or how competitively and possibly conflictually they may pursue them, their ongoing behavioral fidelity to some morality of duty may be said to be in evidence whenever social order simply persists. Thus, Fuller's second proposition is more important:

> *Second Proposition.* Because the morality of duty is interrelated with social order as such, it may be thought initially that actors' mutual recognition and understanding of what their shared social duties are is more or less self-evident to them. *But actors no more readily recognize and understand in common what their shared social duties are than they recognize and understand in common what their aspirations are, or what any other public "morality" is that falls within positivists' residual category* (Fuller 1964/1969: 11).[21]

Fuller's point in drawing his distinction may be worded in the terminology of the theory of societal constitutionalism: The very notion of *shared* social duties is utterly meaningless in itself, even when the most basic social duties are being considered. This notion becomes meaningful only when the "purpose" intrinsic to *any* set of shared social duties is appreciated. Its intrinsic "purpose" is not to maintain social order as such. Its intrinsic "purpose" is to maintain *a social infrastructure that allows actors to pursue their aspirations* openly or publicly, whether independently or collectively. Legal positivists may well deny that this is the "purpose" of the positive law. But Fuller's challenge to them is simple: Account for judges' and enforcers' *behavior* without having this purpose in mind, either implicitly or explicitly.

Interrelated in practice; distinct in principle. To attribute any intrinsic purpose, including a substantively open-ended one, to any social enterprise is to attribute a telos to it; and any teleology is a "morality." This is precisely why Fuller calls heterogeneous actors' and competing groups' *mutual* recognition and understanding of even the most basic social duties a "morality." Put differently, consider what happens at the moment that it is conceded that shared social duties are intended to establish a social infrastructure that can support publicly pursued aspirations. At this moment (a) duty and aspiration, (b) enforcement and interpretation, (c) "fact" (description) and value (evaluation) have all been interrelated, *in practice.* Yet, neither side of these polarities has been reduced to the other *analytically,* in principle. Clearly, many publicly pursued aspirations are never enforced as shared social duties, or mandatory performances. Many shared social duties, in turn, are never treated as if they were aspirations, or optional performances.

Consider what happens when basic social duties are overextended, or treated as if they were optional performances rather than sanctioned as mandatory performances. Once truly basic criminal laws are treated in this way, those ranges of expectations regarding acceptable behavior that are indeed essential to the social infrastructure noted above become negotiable. Their enforcement becomes more uncertain than certain. Heterogeneous actors and competing groups no longer routinely acknowledge these ranges in common. Nor, of course, do they routinely exhibit behavioral fidelity to them. As a result, it becomes inordinately difficult for these actors and groups to devote as much time as they once had to publicly pursuing their own most lofty aspirations; the social infrastructure once supporting this is giving way to uncertainty.

To take an extreme example, breakdowns of basic law and order in inner-city residential areas have this unfortunate effect. Residents become so inordinately concerned about their personal safety that, too often, their publicly pursued aspirations tumble readily from lofty heights. Is it unfair to think in particular of selected neighborhoods within Harlem, the South Bronx, and Bedford Stuyvesant, to consider only three boroughs in New York City, as fluctuating back and forth in this respect from, say, the 1920s through the late 1980s? When personal safety turns out, in practice, to be more a personal and collective aspiration than part of an irreducible social infrastructure, all other publicly pursued aspirations are placed in jeopardy. More and more of them tumble from their lofty "ceiling" as the basic "floor" supporting them becomes shaky.

Consider what happens, in turn, when any *particular* public aspiration – any exemplary way of life or valued social fabric – is overextended by being sanctioned as a set of mandatory performances or basic social duties. Once enforcers treat any public aspiration in this way, they simultaneously (a) narrow the *range* of *aspirations* to which actors can possibly dedicate most of their time, *and,* for that matter, (b) reduce the amount of time actors can possibly dedicate even to those *optional* public aspirations that remain consistent with this narrow range. Enforcers are endeavoring, after all, to sanction some particular lived social fabric as a "duty," a set of mandatory performances. With this, the "floor" of any social order – its irreducible social infrastructure – is elevated. It is raised closer to the "ceiling" of public aspirations, as once optional or even exemplary performances are sanctioned as mandatory performances. Aside from narrowing the range of acceptable public aspirations, this renders truly *basic* social duties much more difficult for heterogeneous actors and competing groups to recognize in common, and for enforcers to enforce consistently.

Any state religion has this effect under modern conditions, irrespective of how benign its enforcement might be. Prohibition in the United States is another often-cited example of such an overextension. Contemporary examples in the United States include: current drug enforcement policies, the possible criminalization of abortion, and Catharine MacKinnon's (1983) proposed reform of rape laws.

Implications of Fuller's critique and threshold. Within any complex social unit, one comprised of heterogeneous actors and competing groups, many actors will readily discover that they cannot, and need not, comply with overextended aspirations (a lowered ceiling) or overextended duties (a raised floor). They will bring their remarkable abilities, their enviably diverse visions of the good life, to devising ever more clever ways of evading the announced "shared social duties." The problem, however, is not that evasion is predictable. The problem, unfortunately, is rather more general and more threatening: As either type of overextension occurs, it becomes more and more difficult for all actors to differentiate truly basic social duties from the overextensions. *A literal culture of evasion is being institutionalized.*[22]

Within such a culture, particular acts of evasion of shared social duties are just as likely to be inadvertent as purposeful. And particular acts of behavioral fidelity to shared social duties might just as well be products of actors' strictly strategic or habitual behavior as products of their reasoned or responsible action. Actors' behavioral fidelity to *any* set of shared social duties and to *any* acknowledged ranges of expectations regarding acceptable behavior is indeed converted into matters of their immediate subjective interests or local interactions. Or else, and even more contingently, it is converted into matters of their internalized normative motivations.[23] Actors' behavioral fidelity has been unhinged from the shared social duties that are unambiguous parts of the irreducible social infrastructure supporting all actors' publicly pursued aspirations.

Put differently, neither the undue lowering of the ceiling of aspirations to mandatory performances, nor the undue raising of the floor of shared duties to optional performances, is a problem in itself. After all, enforcement agencies cannot escape situations of selective enforcement (Klockars 1985: chapter 5; *Law and Contemporary Problems* 1984). Moreover, selective enforcement always takes place against *some* normative backdrop, against *some* set of acknowledged ranges of expectations regarding what is acceptable, *including what the "real duties" are.* And, any such normative backdrop is invariably comprised not only of truly basic duties but also of overextended aspirations and overextended duties. Thus, particular enforcers and particular agencies of enforcement invariably find themselves deciding, on an ad hoc basis, or else in terms consistent with an "organizational culture" unique to each enforcement agency, which "duties" they will enforce at particular times, and in particular places.[24] As lawyers are wont to say, reasonable men and women may disagree over the significance of any particular step taken in either direction of overextension.

But, again, the problem is quite different. It may be posed in two steps: The first step is to distinguish when exercises of *collective* power or mechanisms of *social* control are: (a) generalizable, and thereby *capable* of being recognized and understood in common even by heterogeneous actors and competing groups, and when they are (b) particular, and in principle incapable of being recognized and understood by such actors and groups in common. The second step, then, is to specify when enforcement agencies have indeed moved so far in either direction of overextension, whether purposefully or inadvertently, that heterogeneous actors' and competing groups' recognition and understanding of their shared social duties becomes contingent or uncertain. At these moments, a culture of evasion has been institutionalized.

Thus, selective enforcement under practical restrictions of scarce time and scarce resources is one thing (e.g. Goldstein 1977; Sherman 1978). *But selective enforcement that could not possibly be kept consistent with the threshold of procedural restraints, even if all practical restrictions were lifted, is quite another.* What must be emphasized is that the second step noted above may well be taken, in practice, as (a) the *effectiveness* of enforcement is improving impressively, as reflected in dramatic reductions in quantifiable indices of criminality and deviance. It may also be taken as (b) the popularity or subjective legitimacy of enforcement agencies either remains unquestioned or improves. Even acknowledging, therefore, that the "real world" of selective enforcement is immutably grey, aspirations and duties nonetheless remain irreducible *analytically.* And yet, what is equally certain is that heterogeneous actors' and competing groups' sense of when the encroachments marking the second step are occurring is not likely to be immediate. It is not likely to be based strictly on the *substantive* issues involved.

This is precisely why Fuller insisted that only a threshold of distinctively *procedural* restraints can possibly allow these groups and actors (and social scientists) to recognize in common when the very *direction* of change of rule-making and rule-enforcing enterprises is shifting (Fuller 1964/1969: 27–30). This is also why it was said earlier that the threshold of interpretability establishes something of an Archimedean point within the greyness of the "real world." There is indeed a most basic social duty shared by the members of any rule-making or rule-enforcing body that contributes in any way to heterogeneous actors' and competing groups' possible social integration rather than to their demonstrable social control. Their most basic social duty qua members of this body, rather than qua well-socialized individuals, is, simply, to maintain its integrity despite enormous systemic pressures of drift to the contrary. This holds true, moreover, irrespective of whether such a body is found within a Western democracy or not.

Indeed, members' ongoing refusal to allow this body's integrity to be subordinated to the end of maximizing the effectiveness of enforcement, or to becoming a strictly rational instrument of manipulation, control, and coercion, simultaneously becomes their loftiest, ongoing aspiration qua members.[25] By contrast, at the moment that they permit encroachments against the integrity of the threshold of interpretability, *they* are simultaneously permitting this body's integrity to be subordinated in this way. Whether permitted purposefully or inadvertently, such encroachments signal that the members of any law-making or law-enforcing body are failing to ensure that the shared social duties they are formulating, announcing, and enforcing are being kept recognizable and understandable. Encroachments signal that they are failing to maintain the only normative *orientation* that allows *them,* or anyone else, to recognize when their own activities of rule-making or rule-enforcing are anything other than manipulative, controlling, and coercive. Encroachments signal that the social infrastructure that can possibly support grander public aspirations of any kind, including actors' possible social integration, is being jeopardized.

5.2. Three foundations of societal constitutionalism: procedural grounding, procedural threshold, and procedural formation

Thinking again of the discussion of Habermas's communication theory in chapter 5 and the earlier discussion of internal and external restraints in chapter 4, the interrelationship between Habermas's procedural grounding and Fuller's procedural threshold may be characterized in three ways. All three also suggest the importance of the collegial form of organization, which is discussed beginning in chapter 8.

First, the threshold of interpretability specifies what is in effect an irreducible set of procedural *normative* restraints on *purposefully* arbitrary exercises of collective power. In chapter 4 these were called internal procedural restraints. Comparativists may employ this threshold to describe purposeful exercises of collective power by governmental agencies as well as those by private enterprises within a civil society. They may distinguish which purposeful exercises are demonstrably controlling and which are possibly integrative. Comparativists may also employ this threshold to *begin* to specify when systemic or inadvertent exercises of collective power are contributing to drift, and when they are being mediated to contribute to nonauthoritarian direction of social change. After all, if this threshold is being encroached against, then the social infrastructure supporting a nonauthoritarian direction of social change is being jeopardized.

Second, this is an irreducible threshold in another respect. Heterogeneous actors and competing groups must institutionalize these particular internal procedural restraints, in practice, if they are *possibly:* (a) to establish the collegial form of organization and then maintain its integrity, or (b) to aspire publicly to "communicative action" or reasoned social action in Habermas's sense. Neither of these grander projects can possibly be pursued, as ongoing public aspirations, if these actors and groups are failing to restrain even purposefully arbitrary exercises of collective power.

Third, in order to sustain a nonauthoritarian direction of social change in the late twentieth century despite systemic pressures to the contrary, heterogeneous actors and competing groups must also institutionalize *external* procedural restraints. This means, in practice, that they must institutionalize a network of collegial formations across a civil society, encompassing more and more sectors, industries, and organizations (chapter 8). The remainder of this volume is dedicated to presenting the rationale for what, at this point, is an assertion. Yet, even in the absence of a direct discussion of collegial formations, this chapter may be concluded by reviewing the three most basic institutional foundations of the theory of societal constitutionalism.

6.2.1. Procedural legality: normative means of societal constitutionalism

As noted above, Fuller's procedural norms stake out something of a contemporary "Archimedean point" in the greyness of the "real world." He saw that power holders on one side and actors on the other each face an unavoidable situation once law-making or law-enforcing bodies are permitted to encroach against the threshold of interpretability. On their side, actors find that there is no longer any *reasoned* basis for them to *feel a* moral responsibility to obey "laws" or bear shared social duties.[26] They may continue to obey power holders out of fear, indifference, or ignorance, of course. But officials' acts of encroachment nonetheless demonstrate – behaviorally, empirically – that power holders are implicitly (or worse, explicitly) oriented by the following presupposition: Actors are incapable of reasoning about, or taking responsibility for bearing, their shared social duties. What other presupposition might account for power holders' failures to ensure that the shared social duties being sanctioned are at least kept understandable?

On their side, power holders must realize that they have indeed crossed a most significant normative threshold. Having encroached against these procedural norms, they can no longer be *reasoned* in *feeling* any moral (or fiduciary) responsibility for honoring any restraints on exercises of collective power by rule-making or rule-enforcing bodies (see DeMott 1988 more generally on the notion of fiduciary obligation in the law). Their only consideration, at this point, is the strictly strategic restraints posed by competing power holders and social influentials. Ironically, these same encroachments and strategic considerations may increasingly jeopardize power holders' own rational action, including their ongoing efforts to improve the effectiveness of enforcement.[27] After all, they have exposed these efforts to a now normatively unmediated competition among interested parties for influence or particular strategic advantages within law making and law-enforcing bodies themselves. This is why Fuller noted that

[In]fringements of legal morality tend to become cumulative. A neglect of clarity, consistency, or publicity may beget the necessity for retroactive laws. Too frequent changes in the law may nullify the benefits of formal, but slow-moving procedures for making the law known. Carelessness about keeping the laws possible for obedience may engender the need for a discretionary enforcement which in turn impairs the congruence between official action and enacted rule. (Fuller 1964/1969: 92)

A radical critic might respond by insisting that internal procedural restraints on purposeful exercises of collective power are mere formalities (see chapter 4 for pluralists' similar response). As such, these restraints may be violated in the interests of attaining "substantive justice," or in the interests, say, of a revolutionary vanguard's strategy of initiating "emancipatory" social change. But the fundamental significance of the threshold of interpretability remains unaddressed and undiminished by this line of criticism: How might competing groups and heterogeneous actors (and social scientists) possibly recognize and understand in common whether substantive justice or an emancipatory strategy is really being attained? Given actors' fragmentation of meaning and organizations' functional differentiation, how might they recognize in common whether such public aspirations are being pursued at all, rather than being feigned for purposes of strategic advantage or mass manipulation?[28]

Because the threshold of interpretability is irreducible to the very possibility of heterogeneous actors and competing groups recognizing and understanding in common what their most basic social duties are, *the same normative procedures also are irreducible to any possibility of heterogeneous actors' and competing groups' social integration.* After all, it cannot be said that such actors and groups are ever integrated, within any complex social unit, if they cannot simply recognize and understand what the shared social duties are that are being sanctioned. Moreover, it is oxymoronic to refer to any possibility of these actors and groups aspiring to discourse, communicative action, or reasoned social action within complex social units that encroach against this threshold.

6.2.2. Procedural reason: conceptual grounding of societal constitutionalism

Habermas's oversight of internal procedural restraints. Habermas sees liberalism's tradition of "rational natural law" – its tradition of "natural rights" of private property, free exchange, and contract – as the "first to meet the [modern] demand for a procedural grounding of law, that is, for a justification by principles whose validity could in turn be criticized" (see 1981a: 264; also 1962; 1963; 1963b: 85–6 for his historical accounts). This attempt is instructive enough for Habermas that his reading of "bourgeois legality" is rendered ambivalent rather than left one-sidedly critical. He sees all legal and moral theories that fall within the broad category of "cognitivist ethics" endeavoring to secure "abstract universality" rather than "basing" normative positions on actors' mere habitual behavior or subjective interests. This category encompasses (a) liberal contract theories, (b) Kantian principles of morality, and (c) *Habermas's own theory of communicative action or "procedural reason."*

Another, related reason for Habermas's ambivalent reading of "bourgeois legality" is contained in the following passage:

Legal proceedings and the working out of compromises can serve as examples of argumentation organized as disputation; scientific and moral discussions, as well as art criticism can serve as examples of argumentation set up as a process of reaching agreement. (Habermas 1981a: 35)

Rather than treating courtroom proceedings as reducible to strategic or manipulative action, divorced entirely from reason or communicative action, Habermas sees them "as a special case of practical discourse" (1981a: 412, note 49).

Thus, *all* arguments . . . require the *same* basic form of organization, which subordinates the eristic means to the end of developing intersubjective conviction by the force of the better argument. (1981a: 36, my emphasis)

Like speech within any deliberative or professional body, that is, even Western courtrooms retain *elements* of communicative action.[29]

Yet, even with this ambivalence, Habermas nonetheless follows Weber (and Marx, and then Lukacs and neo-Marxism generally) in failing to appreciate the distinctiveness of the common-law tradition *within* liberalism, and its *critical* potential (this is particularly evident in his first work, *Strukturwandel* 1962). Whether shared social duties can be recognized and understood in common by heterogeneous actors and competing groups is an issue distinct from the sovereignty of subjective interests underlying all liberal contract theories, and Kantian ethics as well. The former issue cannot be reduced to whether actors are acting on their subjective interests "freely" or independently within economic and political marketplaces. To read the jurist Sir Edward Coke or Solicitor General of England William Murray (later Lord Mansfield) as unwitting apologists for the same market society that Thomas Hobbes depicted so methodically is as great a distortion as to read Hobbes as a "bourgeois" theorist preoccupied with internal procedural restraints on arbitrary power.[30] The threshold of interpretability of shared social duties indeed marks a *normative* standard of comparison rather than a rational – strictly instrumental or strategic – standard. Yet, it can credibly claim generalizability as possibly reasoned in Habermas's sense, and it underlies the social integration/social control distinction in forming the theory of societal constitutionalism.

Put differently, Habermas has never addressed the possibility that the claim to "abstract universality" by internal procedural restraints on government *is just as credible* as the claim he makes for his own principles of procedural reason. What is more, the threshold of interpretability at the center of these internal procedural restraints is irreducible to any possible non-authoritarian social order, and thereby generalizable. Yet, it is eminently practicable rather than idealized. The point at issue may be put to Habermas directly: Even if all actors who aspire to communicative action are as "rationally motivated" as he could ever hope, *they would nonetheless genuinely and sincerely disagree, and at every point along the way, as to whether their own actions were indeed progressing toward or regressing from this ideal.* Should they aspire to communicative action without first institutionalizing internal procedural restraints, that is, *they would invariably contribute to social control and increase a nation-state's susceptibility to social authoritarianism –* even if they did so inadvertently rather than purposefully.

Thus, even if universal pragmatics is generalizable at the level of actors' most basic interpersonal communications, as Habermas insists, he cannot expect *heterogeneous* actors and *competing* groups somehow to share "intuitively" a recognition and understanding of when exercises of collective power or mechanisms of social control are either controlling or integrative, arbitrary or responsible. To couple Habermas's lofty aspiration of procedural reason with the typical ambiguities, misunderstandings, and miscommunications that heterogeneous actors and competing groups invariably experience within any complex social situation is to reveal two flaws in Habermas's work, the first of which he himself acknowledges. First, it reveals that his communication theory is distanced from empirical application, in research (Habermas 1971). Second, it reveals that his communication theory offers unnecessarily wide latitude to demagogues, in practice. Demagogues may readily feign fidelity to "communicative action," as one aspiration within some purportedly long-term "plan" of social democracy (or of libertarian license). Even worse, they may cite the authority of what Habermas calls "therapeutic critique" to silence critics, those who question the sincerity of their self-declared fidelity to Habermas's principles (Habermas, 1968a: chapters 10–12; 1971: 28–32, 37–40; 1981a: 20–1, 41–2).

All of this changes, however, once the mediation provided by a practicable, procedural threshold is brought into the picture. The same critics, with the same demagogues among them, may now readily and unambiguously recognize in common, and at every step along the way, at least whether power holders' behavior exhibits fidelity to internal procedural restraints. The latter restraints differ in two important respects from Habermas's procedural aspiration: First, as noted above, these threshold restraints are practicable rather than idealized or "unreal." They may be, and indeed have been, institutionalized (however temporarily at times) within many modern nation-states. Beyond courts, legislatures, boards, and commissions, they have been institutionalized within universities; public and private research centers; research divisions of private corporations; professional associations; intellectual, literary, and artistic networks; and even selected corporate directorates.[31] By contrast, procedural reason has never been institutionalized, nor can it be. It is a social aspiration.

Second, and equally importantly, the threshold of internal procedural restraints differs from Habermas's procedural aspiration in that power holders may employ material sanctions and even physical force to uphold the threshold's integrity without placing all actors in jeopardy. Indeed, *sanctions supporting the threshold of internal procedural restraints remain consistent with actors' possible social integration even if these sanctions include manifest coercion.* In other words, social scientists cannot legitimately *reduce* any and all instances of coercion (or collective force) to social control *analytically.*[32] By contrast, coercive sanctions employed in support of actors' *unmediated* pursuit of the ideal speech situation cannot avoid extending and intensifying social control – irrespective of what actors' subjective interests or normative motivations happen to be.

Habermas's concern that Western democracies face an imminent legitimation crisis will remain insignificant empirically (Weil 1987, 1989), until some modern nation-state (a) begins to compete materially with Western democracies, and simultaneously (b) institutionalizes internal procedural restraints, at the very least. Neither of these projects is beyond the existing capabilities of several nation-states outside the West. There are no empirical, historical, or cultural factors that permit comparativists to presuppose, for instance, that existing economic advantages enjoyed by the Western democracies and Japan are anything other than a state of affairs quite idiosyncratic to the mid- and late twentieth century.[33] The matter of extending internal procedural restraints into civil societies outside of the West is addressed at length in chapters 9–10.

Interrelating the procedural threshold and procedural grounding. The relationship between the procedural threshold of interpretability and Habermas's procedural grounding may be elaborated in three steps:

> First, the threshold restraints provide social scientists with a generalizable standard that allows them to reevaluate critically Habermas's absolutist critique of Western democracies and his thesis of legitimation crisis.
>
> Second, the threshold restraints simultaneously close off any possibility of social scientists reverting to (a) the complacency and optimism of liberalism and pluralism, (b) the presupposition of exhausted possibilities, or, certainly, (c) the dogmatism of neo-Marxism's absolutist critiques of ideology and alienation.

Third, the threshold restraints open the way for social scientists to specify when any sector, industry, or organization of a civil society contributes exclusively to heterogeneous actors' and competing groups' social control and when it contributes in some part to their possible social integration.

The synthesis of procedural duties (the threshold restraints) and a procedural aspiration (the ideal of procedural reason) is one of two syntheses underlying the theory of societal constitutionalism. The other synthesis reveals that collegial formations are the *exclusive* organizational expression of *both* the procedural duties and the procedural aspiration.

Why is the first synthesis necessary at all? Why couldn't the theory of societal constitutionalism rest solely on the demonstration that internal procedural restraints can only be institutionalized by the presence of collegial formations? Why couldn't *this* synthesis alone be brought to comparative research, such that the theory of societal constitutionalism could avoid the entire controversy over whether Habermas's standard of procedural reason can credibly claim grounding? There are three reasons why the theory of societal constitutionalism rests on syntheses of the procedural threshold, the collegial form, and the procedural grounding rather than resting on a synthesis of the first two concepts alone.

First, even though it is indeed counterfactual, Habermas's proposed grounding of procedural reason is nonetheless clearly "more comprehensive" than the narrow norm of rational action underlying Weber's social theory and contemporary comparative research. It is also more generalizable conceptually, or more irreducible analytically, than either the sovereignty of actors' subjective interests underlying liberal contract theory *or the nonrational (normative) principles underlying the common-law tradition and lived social fabrics within Anglo-American countries* (chapter 10). By establishing that internal procedural restraints, as well as their organizational expression in collegial formations, remain consistent analytically with a "more comprehensive" concept of (*procedural*) reason, the theory of societal constitutionalism offers social scientists a standard of institutionalization that can credibly claim grounding against relativism. It exposes to view the *social infrastructure* that sustains a nonauthoritarian direction of social change under modern conditions, and that simultaneously expands heterogeneous actors' and competing groups' prospects for social integration within particular sectors, industries, and organizations of civil society. This standard allows them to describe and explain even subtle shifts in the direction of social change without reverting to the Europocentrism of the presupposition of exhausted possibilities.

Second, and equally importantly, this threshold's claim to conceptual grounding against normative relativism is not jeopardized even if it turns out that *Habermas's* communication theory is not the best one available. This threshold's claim to conceptual grounding is much more secure than this: It rests ultimately on the critique of neopositivism and copy theories of truth that is shared not only by Habermas and Apel but also by Popper, Lakatos, and many others. Thus, even if Habermas's communication theory is eventually jettisoned as inadequate, what is far less likely to be jettisoned is the thesis that (a) any concept of substantive reason is an oxymoron under modern conditions, and, correlatively, (b) only a concept of procedural reason can credibly claim grounding.

In short, comparativists may legitimately employ the social infrastructure noted above not only because it is practicable and already in evidence, but because it can credibly claim conceptual grounding, unlike the presupposition of exhausted possibilities. Any critic wishing to level the charge of particularism against the theory of societal constitutionalism must demonstrate that all possible concepts of procedural reason are particular and intrinsically relative (chapter 10). This is a much more formidable challenge than demonstrating that all possible substantive moralities and concepts of substantive reason are particular, including the presupposition of exhausted possibilities.

Finally, it should be kept in mind that Fuller's legal theory was by no means ever falsified, or rebutted directly, within the law journals. Instead, it was sidestepped. Critics typically acknowledged its compelling thrust but then insisted that it is unscientific, normative, and, actually, distractingly Anglophile. Critics complained that Fuller's legal theory merely selected tenets from a particular tradition of law, conveniently that distinctive to Anglo-American countries, and elevated these tenets to a purportedly generalizable standard of legality.[34] But only since the very late 1960s, at the earliest, has Habermas's (and Apel's) critique of neopositivism been available. And only since the mid-1970s has his communication theory really been presented in sufficient detail to be assessed. Taken together, this critique and this theory provide Fuller's procedural threshold with the theoretical framework that allows it to credibly claim grounding. This same theoretical framework closes off any possibility of sidestepping Fuller's legal theory today by merely pointing to its historical origin in the common-law tradition (chapter 10).

6.2.3. Collegial formations: qualitative ends of societal constitutionalism

With a credible claim to conceptual grounding, the foundations of an ideal type of nonliberal "democracy" are beginning to come into view, or, more accurately put, the foundations of an ideal type of *nonliberal or nonmarket social integration.*[35] The procedural concepts developed independently by

Fuller and Habermas are, respectively, the procedural duty or "floor" and the procedural aspiration or "ceiling" of the theory of societal constitutionalism. To bring this synthesis of concepts to detailed research, however, it is necessary to add something to the "middle," between "floor" and "ceiling." The "middle" of the theory of societal constitutionalism is occupied by the *only* organizational form that *either* the floor or ceiling can assume, in practice: the collegial *form* of organization (chapter 8).

As noted in chapter 4, to the extent that this form of organization is in evidence at all, in practice, it is to be found within deliberative bodies, rule-making bodies more generally, and sites at which professionals are employed collectively. The latter sites may be found within universities; public and private research divisions; professional associations; intellectual, literary, and artistic networks; courts; legislatures; public and private corporate directorates; and various commissions. Bringing this organizational form to comparative research opens the way for social scientists to describe and evaluate, and eventually to explain and predict, specific shifts in the *direction* of social change within any nation-state of the Third World or East, or within any Western democracy.

Collegial formations have already been formally defined in chapter 4 (page 80), and this definition is examined in detail beginning in chapter 8. The most that can be said about these formations at this point in the presentation of the theory of societal constitutionalism is to mention their interrelationship with the threshold of interpretability. Collegial formations *institutionalize* heterogeneous actors' and competing groups' behavioral fidelity to this threshold. They thereby institutionalize a distinctive normative orientation of procedural restraint *by their sheer presence within a civil society.* This is manifested, in practice, in two ways:

> First, *if* the integrity of collegial formations is being maintained, then, by definition, the members of these formations already exhibit behavioral fidelity to internal procedural restraints on purposeful exercises of collective power.

Why the sheer presence of these formations *also* restrains even the inadvertently arbitrary exercises of collective power that accompany drift is addressed methodically beginning in chapter 8. For the moment, the second manifestation of the sheer presence of collegial formations may merely be stated without elaboration:

> Second, *if* the integrity of collegial formations is being maintained, then the members of these formations also are "available" to extend internal procedural restraints on arbitrary exercises of collective power from government to sectors, industries, and organizations of a civil society.

Putting this second manifestation differently, professionals and other members of existing collegial formations remain a latent social force of procedural restraint within any civil society in which these formations are present. They remain a latent social force because they are members of collegial formations, not because they are properly socialized individuals. For the same reason, they share a normative orientation – irrespective of all of their remaining, and possibly increasing, differences in subjective interests and normative beliefs.

7. Societal constitutionalism's organizational manifestation, I: voluntaristic action as a distinct concept

.1. The importance of voluntaristic action

n chapter 4 institutions of external procedural restraint were distinguished analytically from three other types of institutions. What was left unclear vas how any *normative* restraint, procedural or substantive, can remain 'external" to group competition and systemic drift, and simultaneously contribute *intrinsically* to a nonauthoritarian direction of social change.)nce Parsons's early concept of voluntaristic action is reformulated into a listinct concept, it becomes clear how this is possible.

As a preliminary approach, voluntaristic action may be defined in the ollowing way:

> Voluntaristic action is an analytical distinction drawn within the broader categories of normative action and nonrational action. It is distinctive in that it alone is comprised of (a) qualitative worldly ends, and (b) the symbolic or normative means that allow actors to recognize such ends in common.

)nce voluntaristic action is distinguished analytically from purposive-ational action, on one side, and from nonrational and normative action,)n the other, the theory of societal constitutionalism may be seen clearly to evolve around normative restraints that are distinctively *procedural and 'oluntaristic*. The theory cannot be based on substantive restraints of any ⋅ind, whether normative or strategic. It also cannot be based on proce-lures that are rational rather than distinctively voluntaristic.

Still, what exactly is the relationship between voluntaristic action as a listinct concept and the internal and external restraints introduced in chap-er 4? What is the relationship between voluntaristic action as a distinct ⋅oncept and the procedural turns taken by Habermas and Fuller discussed n chapters 5 and 6? Finally, why was it said in chapter 4 and then again at he end of chapter 6 that Fuller's procedural threshold is intrinsically inter-elated with the *collegial* form of organization in particular? This chapter ays the conceptual groundwork for answering these questions.

131

7.2. Parsons's point of departure: the normative or nonrational

Across his career, Talcott Parsons dedicated himself to cataloguing and exploring *all* analytical aspects of social action and social order that are "nonrational," literally not-purposive-rational. He quite consciously drew his first major concept, voluntaristic action, from this residual category. Later in his career, most of his other important concepts were also drawn from the same residual category. Why did Parsons turn first to a strictly residual category, the nonrational? Why must his references to voluntaristic action be reformulated in order to reveal this concept's distinctiveness within this residual category?

7.2.1. Opening a social theory conceptually to nonrational action

Parsons's first published work in general social theory, "The Place of Ultimate Values in Sociological Theory," appeared in a philosophy journal in 1935, two years before the publication of *The Structure of Social Action.* Rather than summarizing his forthcoming book, he used this essay to present his rationale for saying that the social theory he was about to have published marked an "advance" beyond the contributions of Alfred Marshall, Vilfredo Pareto, Emile Durkheim, and Max Weber.[2] For all of his enormous respect for, and at times stultifying deference to, the ideas of the last three "classics" in particular, Parsons was nonetheless claiming as a young man of thirty-three that he was not merely standing on their shoulders but leaping over their heads.[3]

In 1935, Parsons discussed the importance of norms – actors' nonrational motivations, beliefs, and interests – in accounting for *social* action proper. He insisted that normative "factors" or "analytical aspects" account for social solidarity or those collective actions that cannot be reduced to an aggregation of individuals' self-interested behavior within (idealized) economic and political marketplaces. By concentrating on these aspects, Parsons moved far outside the possible scope of application of utilitarianism and methodological individualism. He also rejected John Locke's claim that social order rests on individuals' natural identity of subjective interests in establishing and maintaining a limited government.

Indeed, Parsons's very criterion for selecting his four theorists for methodical study was that each had turned to norms and other nonrational aspects of social action in order to account for solidarity and social order. When he discovered that the concepts each had developed independently "converged" in taking this "normative turn," he coined a new terminology. He did so in order to synthesize their contributions explicitly and to consolidate his own position: In his view, social theory already rested, albeit implicitly, on a new conceptual foundation. He was utterly convinced that

social theory could never again regress to utilitarianism and tenets of methodological individualism (Alexander 1982a,b; 1983a,b; 1987 updates this
argument). Of course, first Homans, then Coleman, and now Cook,
Willer, Hechter and others have since demonstrated that Parsons was somewhat hasty on this matter. Regardless, in the paperback edition of *Structure*
(1968d) he would refer to this new terminology as his "first conceptual
schema," and in 1935 and 1937 he used the phrases "voluntaristic means-
end schema" and "voluntaristic theory of action" to label it.

In short, the pervasiveness and salience of a distinctively nonrational
"reality" within everyday social life was Parsons's very point of departure
as a social theorist.[4] In his view, *any* methodical examination of the relationship between the means that actors employ and the ends that they pursue
within any solidary unit or collectivity must be kept open conceptually to
addressing directly the nonrational aspects infusing *both* the means and the
ends.[5] Utilitarianism, Marxism, rational-choice theory, and all other social
theories that rest on what Parsons then called a "materialist epistemology"
struck him as suffering first and foremost from conceptual closure. Their
conceptual frameworks were closed prematurely to the normative or
nonrational aspects of *social* action.[6] He did not reject Marxism, therefore,
because it is purportedly radical, nor, of course, did he reject utilitarianism
because it is purportedly conservative. He rather rejected all such theories
because they were closed conceptually in this respect, and because they
were unable to account for *social* action as such – let alone to account
either for conservative or radical social actions in particular.

7.2.2. Voluntaristic action in the literature today

Still, Parsons ultimately failed to distinguish his concept of voluntaristic
action from the more general concepts of normative action, nonrational
action, and even social action as such. As will be shown in this section, his
many exegetes and proponents have done the same ever since. When is
social action distinctively voluntaristic? Put more precisely, can voluntaristic *aspects* of social action be distinguished from aspects that are more
strictly nonrational or normative? One result of Parsons's own vagueness
and inconsistency in characterizing his first major concept is that at least
five definitions of this concept may be found in the literature today, including Parsons's own later references to it:

(1) Voluntaristic action as actors' free will.[7] This position is not claimed
explicitly today (except in treatments of Parsons's early works found in
theory textbooks), but it remains associated with John Finley Scott despite his objections (Scott 1963: 720, 724–5, 734; for the charge, see
Turner and Beeghley 1974a: 49; and Gerstein 1975: 11–12; for Scott's
denial, 1974: 59). It remains a position that is nonetheless implied by a

great many commentators (most recently Camic 1989: 92–3), including many of those cited below. For instance, Alvin Gouldner suggested this position throughout his critical treatment of Parsons's works (1970: 141–3, 156, 190–3).

(2) Voluntaristic action as actors' "formal" capacity, or capacity in principle, for "voluntary" or self-initiated action, regardless of whether this capacity is exercised by actors in practice at any particular moment or not (Proctor 1978: 44–7; Alexander 1978: 178–81; 1982a: 87, 96–8; 1982b: 65–6, 79ff, 197ff, 330ff; 1983a: 98–9, 107–8, 112–14; 1983b: 25–6, 120–7, 214; again, Camic 1989: 92–3).[8]

(3) Voluntaristic action as actors' autonomous action which, in turn, is always realized within and thereby "balanced" by some context of constraints, whether ideal or material conditions (Turner and Beeghley 1974a: 49; 1974b: 62; Gerstein 1975: 12; Mayhew 1982; Münch 1981a: 722–3, 727–8; 1981b: 312, 348; 1982: 773, 776–7; again, Alexander 1978, 1982–3; and also Parsons himself by the 1970s, e.g. 1974a: 56; 1975a: 108).

(4) Voluntaristic action as actors' autonomous action which is an inherently contingent and possibly disruptive factor within any social order (again Gouldner, but especially Luhmann 1976: 507–8, and Loubser 1976: 4–5, 19).

(5) Voluntaristic action as normative action, or as all of those factors or analytical aspects within any social action which may be categorized residually as not behavioral, conditional, or material (Scott 1963; Cohen, Hazelrigg, and Pope 1975; Bourricaud 1977: 33; Menzies 1977; Adriaansens 1980; Johnson 1981; as well as Münch, Alexander, and Camic).

None of the five meanings accounts for the concept's distinctiveness. If the concept is a synonym for "voluntary" action in particular, then it is commonplace rather than innovative. If the concept is a synonym for normative action in general, then it is redundant rather than distinctive (Warner 1978: 1319–20; and Parsons's weak reply 1978a: 1351–3).[9] Because Parsons failed to distinguish the concept, and commentators have fared no better, the case for its distinctiveness has yet to be made.[10]

7.3. The distinct concept of voluntaristic action

In the 1930s Parsons coined not only the phrase "voluntaristic means-end schema" but also the phrases "intrinsic means-end schema" and "symbolic means-end schema" (Parsons 1935: 300–5; 1936: 87; 1937a: 56ff, 133, 141, 109–18, 257–64, 285–8, 383–90, 404, 565–6, 645, 653–8, 673–7, 683–4). In his view, actors' solidarity or social action is comprised of some combination of these three "pure types," these three sets of analytical aspects (1935: 298–9; 1937: 79, 81–2, 209–15, 221, 251–61, 486 note 2, 645 note 1, 660–

1). By using his early references to each, but then reformulating them to clearly account for each type's or each set's distinctiveness, the concept of voluntaristic action may be specified:

(1) Formally rational aspects (or purposive-rational aspects) of social action comprise what Parsons in 1937 called the intrinsic means-end schema. The latter is distinguished by the intrinsic interrelationship between (a) physical means that are instrumentally effective and (b) empirical or worldly ends that are reducible to *interchangeable and quantifiable* physical units (such as utilities in economics).

(2) Nonrational aspects of social action comprise what Parsons called the symbolic means-end schema. The latter is distinguished by the interrelationship between (a) symbolic means that are normative (e.g. rituals) and (b) meta-empirical ends that are *transcendental* or ultimate.

Given these polar types, in order for voluntaristic action to be distinct it must be comprised of a distinct set of means and ends. For Parsons to coin a new term, presumably, this third combination of analytical means and ends of social action must indeed not be reducible to either of the first two combinations. Thus:

(3) Voluntaristic aspects of social action, and what Parsons called the voluntaristic means-end schema, are distinguished by the interrelationship between (a) symbolic means that are normative or noninstrumental, and (b) ends that are worldly *qualities* – neither reducible to interchangeable physical units nor attributable to transcendental matters of faith.

7.3.1. Rational action and quantifiable ends

In the 1930s (but not in his later works, e.g. 1977a) Parsons at times suggested that he was departing dramatically from Weber by defining rational action narrowly, that is analytically. At these times, it could be argued that he was establishing a foundation for comparative study – for "general social theory" – in the face of the sovereignty of actors' subjective interests and normative relativism as well as researchers' conceptual relativism (1935: 330–5; 1937: 432–3, 547–9, 564–6, 574, 673). On this foundation, shared by liberals and Weberians, positivists and utilitarians as well, he could move beyond the conceptual limitations of other theoretical traditions. He could do so by varying means and ends, and thereby distinguishing all of those combinations "external" to rational action's "intrinsic means-end schema." Even though Parsons was not consistent in referring to rational action in this way, this line of reasoning may be carried through consistently. One result is that the research potential of the reformulated concept of voluntaristic action begins to come into view.

Why the ends of rational action must be quantifiable. The ends of strictly rational action are reducible to discrete, interchangeable, physical units. Pushed to its limiting case, each unit lacks any and all worldly qualities that could distinguish it from any other. Because each unit is indistinguishable, each may be aggregated with all others and thereby converted into a quantifiable result. And this is of enormous significance to social scientists (as well as to actors) operating within a social context characterized by systemic pressures of drift and the fragmentation of meaning. Within this context, competing social groups and heterogeneous actors (and social scientists) are unlikely to recognize and understand *in common* when *qualities* in social life are either retaining or losing their integrity qua qualities. They are far more likely to recognize and understand in common when particular social enterprises or governmental agencies are becoming more or less efficient or effective – precisely *because* this issue can be reduced to quantifiable indices. Not only can actors (and observers) measure such ends, they can also attain them causally (or repeatedly) by employing strictly instrumental means.

For instance, qualities of taste, smell, or appearance that distinguish particular cuisines from others may be reduced to quantifiable indices, *if* one is interested only in recognizing, describing, and explaining the efficient production of foodstuffs. Such indices include, as examples, calories per serving, or, for that matter, bushels per acre. They establish an unambiguous foundation on which even heterogeneous actors and competing groups (and of course, social scientists) may recognize in common whether production is becoming more or less efficient. Companies that produce frozen dinners, dog food, or any number of snack foods no doubt calculate their efficiency in precisely this way.

By contrast, actors' subjective opinions regarding qualities in social life, including qualities of cuisine, cannot as readily provide an unambiguous foundation for *heterogeneous* actors' *shared* recognition and understanding. This remains the case even if these same opinions are observed "objectively" by social scientists, and then "quantified" into "indices" of survey analysis. These indices (a) are never unambiguous and (b) can never be causally or repeatedly reproduced in all social contexts using strictly instrumental means.

Purposive-rational action and survey research. A distinction must be drawn, both in practice and in principle, therefore, between the possible quantification of physical units in the world, which distinguishes purposive-rational action, and the possible quantification of heterogeneous actors' subjective opinions about qualities in social life. Researchers seeking "testable theories" are quite aware of this distinction, and the following statement by Jack Gibbs (1972: 387) is typical:

The most conspicuous limitation of [Gibbs's own proposed] scheme is that it does not permit a theorist to make empirical assertions about relations among qualitative properties. No attempt is made to belittle that limitation by arguing that all sociological terms actually designate quantitative properties. The recognition of unit terms is in itself an admission of the importance of qualitative properties, and the stipulation of referential formulas entails reference to qualitative units. The only mitigation is that virtually all sociological theories actually make assertions about relations between quantitative properties of social units, even though the distinction may not have been recognized by the theorist.

Two examples illustrate the distinction. The first also illustrates the interrelationship Weber had drawn between normatively unmediated drift of social change and bureaucratization. Bureaucracies are inordinately easy to recognize, by participants and observers alike, irrespective of whether they are found in government or in civil society. Following Weber's account (1914–20: 956–8), their characteristics are unambiguous because the performance of any bureaucratic agency may be described and evaluated in terms of quite discrete, quantifiable units, including the caseload that bureaus "process" per hour (or per day, week, month, or year). These units may be readily recognized and measured quite apart from subjective opinions regarding the quality of an agency's performance, whether those of officials or their clients. These units may be recognized and measured, that is, irrespective of whether survey research finds that officials or clients believe particular cases are genuinely well-handled or not, or whether they believe the agency performs a genuine "service" to the community or not. Moreover, either reformers or social scientists may explore how an agency's efficiency and effectiveness may be increased in these terms. They may, if they wish, disregard officials' and clients' subjective beliefs regarding the agency's "service" to the community.

By contrast, and as the second example, heterogeneous actors (and social scientists) face a great problem simply in recognizing, and then in defining, what a neighborhood is, and then, certainly, in describing neighborhoods over time and space (Warren 1977). The qualities of neighborliness, whatever they might be, and references to a residential unit as a neighborhood, whatever this might entail, are not reducible to any combination of quantitative indices of performance. Such indices might include: rates of property taxes, trees per lawn, schools per capita, residents' income per capita, or even local crime rates. It is very possible, however, for the most "neighborly" residential areas in a city to have a quite mediocre statistical record on every one of these scales without exception. It is just as possible for the most "anomic" residential areas to have exemplary statistical records on each without exception. Indeed, in order to discover how neighborhoods may be "improved" or "maintained," residents' subjective opinions *must* be surveyed; and opinions, of course, may be genuine or else manipulated and distorted. What is clear is that this question cannot be reduced to mere instrumental improvements of physical units within a residential area. It must include efforts to symbolize neighborliness, and to assess actors' subjective understandings of their own situation.

In short, survey research may "measure" heterogeneous actors' subjective opinions regarding qualities of cuisine, qualities of neighborhood, or regarding any number of other qualities in social life. But irrespective of how these opinions might be distinguished, gradated, and then aggregated, they remain subjective opinions about worldly qualities. They do not somehow become reduced to the discrete units of rational action. Indeed, resorting to survey research is in itself an acknowledgement (by participants or social scientists) that the ends involved in the social actions under study cannot be brought into the "intrinsic" interrelationship of means-end rationality. If neighborhoods could be instrumentally created, maintained, or improved, why survey actors' opinions?

Conceptual limitations of purposive-rational action. A final implication of the analytical approach to rational action implicit in Parsons's early writings also may be pushed beyond his suggestions. Parsons saw, of course, that the intrinsic means-end schema alone cannot account for *social* action, as opposed to *Homo economicus's* serially related actions within idealized marketplaces. Clearly, it cannot account for heterogeneous actors' possible social integration, nor for their contributions to a nonauthoritarian direction of social change. Quite the opposite is the case. Should actors ever reach the limiting case of sharing only a recognition of quantities of interchangeable units, and of the effectiveness or efficiency of instrumental means in attaining them, their "social" action would be reducible to strategic competition and, at best, strictly serial relationships. Only physical coercion, material sanctions, and other mechanisms of social control could account for actors' solidarity or longer-term social relationships, including social order itself (and Hechter 1987 and Coleman 1986 endeavor to demonstrate this).

Like Hobbes and then Pareto and Weber, Parsons carried this implication of rational action to its "limiting case:" for Hobbes, a war of all against all; for Pareto, cycles of normative breakdown and renascence; for Weber, bureaucratization and authoritarianism; for the young Parsons (1937a: 752), the possibility of "entropy." But because Parsons alone endeavored to account comprehensively for the nonrational restraints that typically prevent this limiting case from being realized, in practice, his analytical concepts accomplished something over the years that the others' social theories did not: they left open the possibility of specifying the social control/social integration distinction and the authoritarian/nonauthoritarian distinction. Parsons himself never characterized his work in this way, of course (Sciulli in preparation, a). For him, the dilemmas exposed by Hobbes, Pareto, and Weber illuminated the importance of nonrational aspects of social order, and this is what led him to coin the term voluntaristic action. The reformulated concept of voluntaristic action offered here begins to reveal why this particular set of analytical aspects of social order simultaneously restrains drift *and* contributes to a nonauthoritarian direction of social change.

7.3.2. Nonrational action and transcendental ends

Noninstrumental means of solidarity or social action are symbols and norms; in the limiting case, such means are ritual prayers and devout ceremonies. Regardless, all of these symbols and norms are by definition "external" to the intrinsic interrelationship of instrumental means and quantifiable ends that characterizes rational action (1937: 56ff, 133, 645, 653–8). When actors employ symbols and norms as means to secure quantities of physical units, for instance, their social action cannot be efficient or effective. Quite to the contrary, for them to employ symbols or norms in this way is for them to engage in magic: They are employing symbols and norms in an effort to "control" natural events or physical movements *instrumentally*. Magic, unlike religion, is in direct competition with science.

For its part, religion revolves around actors' dedication of symbols and norms to ends that are ultimate, or not worldly at all. This is the case when religious believers honor rituals as a means to their own putative spiritual salvation. The means to such ends are invariably symbolic and normative; they cannot possibly be instrumental or rational.

In so far as the common system of ultimate ends involves transcendental ends, it is then to be expected that it will be expressed in common ritual actions. From the empirical point of view the question whether such actions in fact attain their ends is irrelevant, for there is no possible means of verification. (Parsons 1935: 303; also 1936: 87; 1937a: 565–6)

Actually, once actors dedicate themselves to transcendental ends, it is no longer possible for them or social scientists to recognize whether *any* means secure these ends. It is senseless even to ask, therefore, whether certain means to such ends are instrumentally effective. As an example, if sociologists ask, what is an efficient way to get into heaven?, what could the members of any collectivity anywhere in the world *demonstrate* is an "efficient prayer" or an "efficient ritual"?

Parsons was clear that in the limiting case of strictly symbolic social action, actors' behavioral fidelity to symbolic and normative means must be scrupulously enforced precisely because the means' relationship to the transcendental ends can never be known. The means of the symbolic means-end schema must become ends-in-themselves, in practice. "Moral authorities" have no alternative other than to monitor actors' strict behavioral fidelity to these means because such behavior is their only evidence of ongoing symbolic social action as such (Parsons 1937a: 429–41).[11] It is clear from this, despite Parsons's failure to pursue the implications of this point explicitly, that the actors engaged in symbolic social action are far more likely to be homogeneous than heterogeneous. After all, ritual behavior ultimately rests on whether actors share cultural beliefs, internalized motivations, and subjective interests.

7.3.3. Voluntaristic action and qualitative ends

Given the rational/nonrational polarity, Parsons turned to a third pure type of social action,[12] and yet the great problem with his early works (and later references) is that he failed to specify the distinct set of analytical aspects comprising it. One result of this is that it has never been clear (a) what he meant by the term "voluntaristic action," whether in the 1930s or 1970s, or (b) why he thought it necessary to coin a new term in the first place. Indeed, with the exception of those rare moments later in his career when Parsons was specifically called on to clarify this term's meaning, the concept otherwise drops out of sight in his works after 1937.

Regardless, a two-step process of reasoning is implicit in Parsons's works of the 1930s, and it is depicted in table 7.1. By rendering these steps explicit, the reformulated concept of voluntaristic action comes into view. What also comes into view is how this concept can inform comparative research and directly address the Weberian Dilemma by accounting for the presence of nonauthoritarian social orders in the late twentieth century. It establishes why certain procedural restraints are accurately characterized as both "external" to drift and central to (a) maintaining a nonauthoritarian direction of social change and (b) enhancing heterogeneous actors' and competing groups' prospects for social integration.

Looking at the top of table 7.1, *all* analytical aspects of social action that cannot be *reduced* to the means and ends intrinsic to rational action fall into an enormous residual category. This is the category that Parsons appropriately labeled the "nonrational *realm.*" Irrespective of the characteristics that any of these analytical aspects happen to exhibit in practice, what is certain is that they are all: not quantifiable, not instrumental, not effective, and not efficient – in short, they are all nonrational.

Looking now at the middle of table 7.1, two pure types of social action or

Table 7.1. *The Rational, the nonrational, and the voluntaristic*

Rational Realm
Rational action: efficient means/quantifiable (empirical) ends
Residual Nonrational Realm
Voluntaristic action: symbolic means/qualitative (empirical) ends
1. If the means are substantive norms, they are tied to *homogeneous* actors' shared normative *motivations* – which they either internalize or else negotiate within local interactions.
2. If the means are procedural norms, they are tied to *heterogeneous* actors' shared normative *orientations* – which a form of organization may institutionalize, irrespective of actors' competing beliefs and interests.
Nonrational action: symbolic means/transcendental (nonempirical) ends; all of the means are substantive norms

two sets of analytical aspects of social action may be distinguished *within* this residual category: nonrational *action* proper (or strictly symbolic and ritualistic social behavior) and voluntaristic action proper. With this distinction, the residual realm of the nonrational is no longer left residual. Instead, it is exposed to further sociological inquiry.

But what, then, is voluntaristic action? Reformulated as a pure type, voluntaristic action is first and foremost a distinct concept *within the nonrational realm*. Irrespective of where this concept may ever be manifested in practice, that is, its status as a constituent of the residual nonrational realm can never be altered, by definition. However, since rational action revolves around ends that are worldly but quantifiable, and nonrational action proper revolves around ends that are transcendental rather than worldly at all, only voluntaristic action alone revolves around ends that are *both worldly and qualitative*. Magic is an oddity precisely because it brings the symbolic or normative means of nonrational action to the matter of attaining quantifiable ends. This is what places magic into direct competition with science.

By contrast to the polar types of rational and nonrational, voluntaristic action revolves around normative practices that actors dedicate to attaining or maintaining the integrity of qualities in social life. Since the ends involved are not quantifiable, and since the means involved remain symbolic or normative rather than becoming instrumental, voluntaristic action clearly remains nonrational. But, just as clearly, it is *neither* ritualistic nor magical. Voluntaristic action hinges on whether the actors involved can recognize *in common:* (a) what the worldly qualities are that they are seeking or maintaining, and (b) whether they are indeed maintaining, or else encroaching against, the integrity of these worldly qualities. The only means that actors have at their disposal in establishing or maintaining any such shared recognition among themselves, short of one faction imposing its will somehow on all others with material sanctions of one kind or another, are *shared* norms and symbols.

Thinking of voluntaristic action in Fuller's terms, when actors maintain the integrity of any qualities in social life, their ongoing solidarity and collective action to this end can rest either on obligatory performances or exemplary performances. In *either* case, their ongoing solidarity and collective action rests on their capacity to recognize in common *which* worldly qualities are worthy of attaining or maintaining. *This* is an irreducibly normative collective judgment rather than one that ever becomes amenable to scientific or rational calculation. Put differently, irrespective of whether the continued integrity of any qualities of social life rests on actors' shared social duties or on their independent aspirations, the actors engaged in voluntaristic action must themselves be able to recognize these qualities in common. If they lose this shared recognition under systemic pressures of drift, then these actors cannot prevent their voluntaristic action from "fragmenting." Their voluntaristic action will either be "reduced" to the instrumental means and quantifiable ends of rational action or else it will be "elevated" to the symbolic means and ultimate ends of nonrational action. In the latter case, worldly qualities will be treated as "sacred," and the symbolic means to upholding their integrity will be enforced as rituals.

As *qualities* in social life, analytical aspects of voluntaristic action proper may be found in families, schools, neighborhoods, communities, religious congregations, or ethnic sections within many modern nation-states. Continuing with the example of neighborhood, residents' views of *which* qualities merit their obligatory performances, and which may be left to their exemplary performances, might very well be far removed from a rational actor's calculations of the market values for housing. Residents may refuse to allow anyone to reduce the qualities that they prize in their neighborhood to such instrumental means and quantifiable indices. Even as housing is bought and sold in the marketplace, residents' working assumption may remain that any new owner is not permitted to conduct himself or herself strictly instrumentally or strategically. New owners may be informed, whether formally or informally, that reductionist treatments of their own property or, for that matter, of their own behavior, will be sanctioned, again either formally (by a neighborhood association) or informally (by concerned neighbors).

Being *worldly* qualities, however, these analytical aspects of voluntaristic action are not readily elevated by these actors, or any others, to transcendental qualities or ultimate matters of faith. Rarely are these qualities valued so widely or dearly that they are protected artificially from the outcomes of economic and political marketplaces, as "sacred." Actors' shared recognition that certain neighborly actions are obligatory and others are exemplary is not readily attributed to any sacred mandate (whether, as examples, to "God's will" or "natural law").[13] Their shared recognition is ultimately tied to quite local interactions.[14]

To be sure, there are institutions and landmarks within modern nation-states that may be honored quite literally as sacred, at least in certain of their analytically distinguishable aspects (e.g. Arlington National Cemetery or the Lincoln Memorial). But the point of Parsons's analytical approach to social action and social order is that, by definition, *these aspects of social action fall within the symbolic means-end schema or category of nonrational action proper.* These aspects do not fall within the reformulated concept of voluntaristic action. When residents share a recognition of their neighborhood's qualities, and none of them, of course, imagines for a moment that these qualities are tied to any sacred or transcendental mandate, their efforts to maintain the integrity of these qualities then remain strictly voluntaristic. For social scientists to attribute "sacred" qualities to these efforts is misleading and distorting in the extreme. The same may be said of attributing "sacred" qualities to related efforts by members of ethnic groups, schools, and families. Such an attribution discounts the enormous difficulties that modern actors everywhere experience in simply recognizing, and then in maintaining, the integrity of *any* qualities in social life. It obfuscates much more than it illuminates about the actual workings of local interactions, subcultural practices, and national institutions.

This point about voluntaristic "pattern-maintenance" may be put differently. It may be placed into the terminology employed in the preliminary definitions of social integration presented in chapters 2–3.

> Heterogeneous actors' and competing groups' *possible* social integration rests ultimately on whether they can recognize and understand (and then exhibit behavioral fidelity to) *some* qualities in social life, *and thereby institutionalize social action that is distinctively voluntaristic.*

Still, if voluntaristic action is to account for the solidarity and collective action of *heterogeneous* actors and *competing* groups under modern conditions, it must revolve around distinctively *procedural* norms and worldly qualities rather than around substantive norms and worldly qualities of any kind. First, it must revolve around the "means" of the threshold of interpretability. This frames their recognition and understanding of the *shared* social duties involved in their efforts to maintain the integrity of worldly qualities. Second, it also must remain consistent with the "end" that institutionalizes these voluntaristic procedures and other worldly qualities in social life: the collegial form of organization.

7.4. Three meanings of voluntaristic action

How is voluntaristic action related to the normative restraints discussed in chapter 4? As a distinct type of social action drawn from the residual realm of the nonrational, voluntaristic action is by definition "external" to the drift of rationalization. Still, how can it be said that certain types of voluntaristic action contribute to a nonauthoritarian direction of social change and to expanding heterogeneous actors' and competing groups' possibilities for social integration? Three interrelated meanings of voluntaristic action begin to answer this question. They also prepare the way for the discussion of collegial formations that begins in the next chapter. Taken together, these three meanings clearly distinguish voluntaristic action from normative action; they also distinguish it from even more general concepts, such as "action," "creativity," "effort," and the like.

Against the secondary literature, and against Parsons's own later references to the term, none of the three meanings below refers to actors' free will. Nor do any of them refer to actors' purportedly intrinsic capacity for solidarity or willingness to "volunteer" to act in common. Nor, finally, do any of the meanings refer directly to actors' personal "autonomy" or "independence" from given material conditions, from their own internalized beliefs, or from institutionalized norms and values. Rather than referring to qualities *that might distinguish the actors* who engage in voluntaristic action, these three meanings instead distinguish the *qualities of voluntaristic action* as such.

7.4.1. Voluntaristic action as restraint on drift

As noted above, precisely because voluntaristic action is not purposive-rational, precisely because it is a distinct type drawn from the nonrational realm, *any* manifestation of it, in practice, is "external" to the drift of purposive-rational social change. To be sure, this "external" status is shared by all actions drawn from the nonrational realm. The sheer presence of such actions within any social or governmental unit intrinsically restrains the unit from responding *most* immediately to systemic pressures of social change in its own immediate material interests.

The voluntaristic conception of action implies that there is resistance to the realization of the rational norm. . . . This problem of control [of collective recognition of qualities of social life] tends to be met by the subjection of action in pursuit of immediate non-ultimate ends [that is, worldly qualities] to normative rules which regulate that action in conformity with the common ultimate value system of the community [that is, a subgrouping of a society]. These normative rules both define what immediate ends should and should not be sought, and limit the choice of means to them in terms other than those of efficiency. Finally, they also define standards of socially acceptable effort. This system of rules, fundamental to any society . . . is what I call its institutions. They are moral norms, not norms of efficiency. (1935: 298–9; also, 1936: 79–80; 1937a: 74–9, 81–2, 209–15, 221, 251–7, 261, 486 note 2, 645 note 1, 660–1)

Given the Weberian Dilemma discussed in chapter 3, including how normatively unmediated responses to systemic pressures contribute to actors' fragmentation of "meaning" and then to bureaucratization and the extension of other mechanisms of social control, an important but implicit theme in Parsons's early writings comes to the fore: The presence of voluntaristic restraints of some kind is essential to the possibility of restraining drift under modern conditions. These same restraints are essential to the possibility of restraining bureaucratization as well as actors' fragmentation of meaning, if not all mechanisms of social control. The question, of course, is: Can any particular set of voluntaristic restraints be demonstrated to contribute intrinsically to a *nonauthoritarian* direction of social change, by its sheer presence alone? Or, alternatively, is Weber correct that any and all nonrational restraints invariably accelerate control and authoritarianism, however inadvertently so?

7.4.2. *Voluntaristic action as contingent institutions*

The institutionalization of voluntaristic action can be said to offer heterogeneous actors and competing groups their only *possibility* of escaping the Weberian Dilemma, provided that any of these institutions performs two tasks simultaneously. First, they must resiliently restrain bureaucratization and drift by normatively mediating how all social and governmental units are permitted to respond to competition and systemic pressures in their own interests. Second, they must avoid the excessiveness of restraint. They must avoid imposing greater homogeneity, collectivism, and ritualism on heterogeneous actors and competing groups than is necessary to restrain bureaucratization and drift. In the 1930s, Parsons clearly appreciated *both* of these implications of the Weberian Dilemma, and he endeavored to address them conceptually:

[Weber's] rationality occupies a logical position in respect to action systems analogous to that of entropy in physical systems . . . [I]t is the most fundamental generalization that emerges from Weber's work, his conception of the process of rationalization. . . . (Parsons 1937a: 752–3; also, 263, 392, 624–35; 675–6; 1935: 295–6; cf. Alexander 1983b: 167–8).

In many respects it is fair to say that Parsons anticipated Max Horkheimer's reading of Weber in the 1940s (1940, 1947; Horkheimer and Adorno 1944) when Horkheimer raised the spector of the authoritarian state, and Leo Strauss's reading of Weber in the 1950s (1953: 35–80) when Strauss argued that Weber's concepts result not merely in relativism but nihilism (Bloom 1987 resumes this argument; also see chapter 10).

Precisely because Parsons appreciated both of these implications, he explicitly *related* Pareto's and Durkheim's cyclical theories of normative and institutional change *to* Weber's more linear view of rationalization. Pareto and Durkheim saw periods of normative stability giving way to periods of normative breakdown: For Pareto, a "general law of rhythm" that includes "sentiments"; for Durkheim, "anomie" leading to atomization and even suicide. Nonetheless, all three theorists "converged," by Parsons's reading, on the following thesis: Systemic social forces cast all modern societies adrift, and power holders (or insurgents) invariably rationalize formal social controls during periods of normative breakdown. During periods of normative stability, informal social controls may replace some of the formal ones. But these periods are rare, and always appear only temporarily. Thus, normative breakdown:

[I]s essentially the process involved in Pareto's process of transition from dominance of the residues of persistence to those of combination, equally in Durkheim's transition from solidarity or integration to anomie. *It is a process the possibility of which is inherent in the voluntaristic conception of action as such.* Its complete absence from Weber's thought would have given grave reason to doubt the accuracy of [Parsons's convergence thesis and] analysis. But it is there. (Parsons 1937a: 685–6, my emphasis; also 710; 1962)[15]

Thus, Parsons's second implicit meaning for his concept: The institutionalization of voluntaristic action (and of any nonauthoritarian direction of social change based thereon) remains contingent rather than ever becoming firmly stabilized. In terms of the Weberian Dilemma, the polar types of strictly rational action and strictly nonrational action are each far more readily stabilized since each in its own way is *ultimately* consistent with extending bureaucratization. Rational action includes the rationalization of formal mechanisms of social control, of course, but nonrational action has the same result, albeit by a more indirect route. By institutionalizing ritualism, and thereby imposing homogeneous behavior on otherwise heterogeneous actors and competing groups, nonrational action ultimately relies heavily on specialized agencies of enforcement.

It is much more difficult, therefore, for heterogeneous actors and competing groups to institutionalize and maintain distinctively voluntaristic action. It is much more difficult for them to institutionalize their own recognition and understanding of shared social duties and other qualities in social life without moving to ritualism. The success of this project remains ever-contingent because it cannot be *reduced* to the effectiveness of formal mechanisms of social control, including the effectiveness of specialized agencies of enforcement. It also cannot be reduced to the purported "natural identity" of actors' and groups' subjective interests, to their purported internalization of shared substantive beliefs, or to their purported negotiation of shared definitions of the situation in local interactions. Indeed, were any of these reductions to occur, in practice, voluntaristic action itself would either be reduced to strictly rational action or else elevated to strictly nonrational or habitual action proper.

As noted above, voluntaristic action is in evidence within all social orders, both nonauthoritarian and authoritarian. But because the sheer presence of its means and ends restrains bureaucratization and drift, its institutionalization opens the contingent possibility that even heterogeneous actors and competing groups may contribute somehow to a nonauthoritarian direction of social change. This possibility is brought more clearly into view by noting that certain types of voluntaristic action may revolve around distinctively *procedural* norms (the threshold of interpretability of shared social duties) and distinctively *procedural* ends (the collegial form of organization). Thus, the external restraints placed on bureaucratization and drift may be procedural mediations rather than more directly substantive. The institutionalization of voluntaristic *procedures* provides the only foundation for a nonauthoritarian direction of social change under modern conditions. It also provides the only foundation for heterogeneous actors' and competing groups' possible social integration within any sector, industry, organization, or organizational division of a modern civil society.

Parsons never drew these distinctions within the concept of voluntaristic action, and yet his view of the contingency of institutionalizing voluntaristic action was far more radical than Niklas Luhmann (1976) and Jan Loubser (1976) appreciate. It remains more radical than Jeffrey Alexander's view (1984) of the contingency of interpersonal relations, and the related view long held by symbolic interactionists (also, compare Alexander's position in 1984 to that in 1987). Parsons agreed with Pareto's most pessimistic positions: Any particular set of substantive worldly qualities can only temporarily secure heterogeneous actors' and competing groups' shared recognition and understanding, to say nothing of their possible acceptance and behavioral fidelity. Systemic "drift," and the concomitant fragmentation of *substantive* meaning, *is immutable* (see Parsons 1962, 1970b for later statements of this position).

Substantive voluntaristic action, therefore, is as shaky a foundation on which to base a nonauthoritarian direction of social change under modern conditions as any that can be imagined. When power holders endeavor to enforce heterogeneous actors' and competing groups' fidelity to substantive norms and qualities of any kind outside of any mediation provided by voluntaristic procedures, they are repeatedly and persistently faced with situations wherein resorting to formal mechanisms of social control becomes their only hope of success (1936; 1937a: 284–8, 402). The great irony is that by resorting to these mechanisms, they are simultaneously subordinating the distinctive means-ends relationship of voluntaristic action either to that of purposive-rational action or that of strictly nonrational action. After all, they are treating substantive qualities either as ends that can be attained instrumentally or else as ends that merit actors' ritualistic behavior.

As a pure type, voluntaristic action isolates the *always* contested effort by actors and groups to maintain their own solidarity and collective action under conditions of drift, short of resorting to manipulation, coercion, or ritualism.[16] It sharpens the Weberian Dilemma by casting it into the following terms: First, periodic breakdowns in *substantive* voluntaristic action *are immutable,* rather than preventable or avoidable. Second, nonauthoritarian social order remains everywhere and always a contingent possibility, and by no means a state of "equilibrium" which systemic pressures themselves somehow intrinsically support rather than jeopardize.[17]

There are three logical possibilities of the general relation of a norm to the actual course of action. The first is the possibility that the mere existence of the norm, that is its recognition by the actor as binding, implies automatic conformity with it. The second is the opposite, that the norm is a mere manifestation, in the index sense, of the real [governmental or marketplace] forces governing action, but has no [independent] causal significance at all. Action [which is consistent with the norm] is then an automatic process. Finally, there is the possibility that while the norm constitutes one structural element in the concrete action it is *only* one. There are obstacles and resistances to its attainment. . . . The existence of this resistance and its (even partial) overcoming implies another element, "effort," which has no place in either of the other two views. (Parsons 1937a: 251; also 263, 285–6 and note 4, 288; 1935: 306–7; 1936: 80)[18]

The theory of societal constitutionalism proposes that only the institutionalization of voluntaristic *procedures* – the institutionalization of both internal procedural restraints on purposeful arbitrariness and external procedural restraints on inadvertent arbitrariness – can account for any sustained nonauthoritarian direction of social change under modern conditions.

7.4.3. Voluntaristic action as central to a conceptual schema

Parsons connected the first two meanings of voluntaristic action in his chapters devoted to Durkheim (1937a: chapters 8–11) rather than in either the introductory or concluding chapters of *The Structure of Social Action.* As he discussed Durkheim's work, he insisted that because voluntaristic restraints on drift are by definition nonultimate (that is, nonsacred), they are thereby always only contingently stabilized:

The further these immediate ends [of voluntaristic action] are removed in the means-end chain from the system of ultimate values sanctioning the system of rules, the more the rules will tend to appear to the individuals subject to them as morally neutral, as mere conditions of action. And since the ends *of the great majority* of practical activities are very far removed from ultimate values, there is a strong tendency to evasion. (1937a: 401, my emphasis)

Parsons failed to see, however, that this holds true only for substantive voluntaristic action in particular. It does not hold true, either in principle or in practice, for procedural voluntaristic action. This point is elaborated in the next chapter.

Given the concept's first two meanings, the third meaning of voluntaristic action implicit in Parsons's early writings is contained in his acknowledging that his first social theory is conceptually primitive. Even as he believed that it marked an "advance" beyond the contributions of the four theorists he examined, he knew he could not claim that it is "scientific." Instead, he claimed that it is voluntaristic: It offers sociologists a contingent possibility, but by no means any guarantee, that a suitable conceptual grounding had been laid on which knowledge in the social sciences might be accumulated. Parsons accepted that this grounding would likely have to be substantially reformulated, as well as supplemented with many other analytical distinctions, in order to inform empirical research.

The main framework of the present study may, then, be considered an analysis of the structural aspects of systems of action, in a certain sense their "anatomy." . . . Though all structures must be regarded as capable of analysis in terms of a plurality of analytical elements, and hence the two types of analysis [definition and specification] are closely related, it does not follow that only one choice of elements is possible in the analysis of a given concrete structure. . . . But this very possibility of different choices of elements explains why it is not advisable to attempt to jump directly from an outline of the structure of action systems to a system of elements. It is on the former, not the latter, level that the writers treated here [Marshall, Pareto, Durkheim, and Weber] converge almost explicitly upon a single system. (Parsons 1937a: 39; also 38–41; 1951: chapter 1)

8. Societal constitutionalism's organizational manifestation, II: from voluntaristic action to collegial formations

8.1. Again, the possibility of social integration

8.1.1. Four steps beyond Habermas, Fuller, and Parsons

The theory of societal constitutionalism draws comparativists' attention to those sectors, industries, and organizations of any modern civil society that contain norms and institutions that are distinctively voluntaristic *and* procedural. It does so because only the presence of these norms and institutions can account (a) for a nonauthoritarian direction of social change under modern conditions, and also (b) for heterogeneous actors' and competing groups' possible social integration within any sector, industry, or organization. The norms and institutions whose presence cannot resolve the Weberian Dilemma, either in isolation or in combination, are: (a) purposive-rational and strategic (for example, in economic and political markets), (b) nonrational and ritualistic (for example, in religious "protected spheres"), and (c) voluntaristic but also substantively immediate rather than procedural mediations (for example, in friendships, families, and neighborhoods, and also in ethnic solidarities and cultural "protected spheres").

Clearly, an emphasis on the importance of distinctively procedural norms and institutions informs the writings of Habermas and Fuller. Both of these theorists appreciated that only procedural norms and institutions can challenge the sovereignty of actors' subjective interests and yet credibly claim grounding against normative relativism. Neither appreciated, however, that the presence of these same norms and institutions within any sector, industry, or organization of a civil society places distinctively *voluntaristic* restraints on interest competition and systemic drift. Parsons's mature writings, in turn, do not as clearly emphasize the importance of procedural norms and institutions, and yet his steadily increasing references to the latter by the late 1960s and mid-1970s are in many respects as suggestive as Fuller's and Habermas's more developed approaches.[1]

These three theorists have been a focus of attention to this point precisely because each in his own way took a "procedural turn," albeit Parsons

150

less decisively so than either Fuller or Habermas. Still, the theory of societal constitutionalism takes four steps that each of these theorists failed to take.

First step: the importance of external (voluntaristic) procedural restraints. Habermas, Fuller, and Parsons each failed in his own way to appreciate, let alone elaborate, the unique impact of voluntaristic restraint that the presence of certain procedural norms and institutions have on organizations and their institutionalized environments (Meyer and Rowan 1977), and, in this way, on the direction of social change. This failure explains why each theorist also failed to appreciate how his own "procedural turn" might assist social scientists in addressing two related issues: First, how have organizations and institutions within nonauthoritarian nation-states actually responded, in practice, to the systemic pressures of drift that concerned Weber? Second, how have heterogeneous actors and competing groups ever managed to institutionalize restraints on drift *without* simultaneously extending or intensifying mechanisms of social control *inadvertently,* as Weber expected?

(a) Parsons failed to appreciate this because he never rendered voluntaristic action into a distinct concept in the first place. He also failed because he followed Weber in dismissing the possibility that a standard of reasoned social action more comprehensive than the narrow norm of rational action might be grounded conceptually against normative relativism (chapter 10).

(b) Fuller failed to appreciate this because he never developed methodically the more general implications of his legal theory: The latter establishes a procedural threshold of interpretability of shared social duties as such. In addition, Fuller never linked his legal theory either (1) to a grounded concept of reasoned social action, or (2) to its organizational expression within a particular form of organization. He acknowledged that he needed a communication theory (1964/1969: 138–45), but he never appreciated that he also needed an organization theory (1964/1969: 173ff for weak comments on "institutional design").

(c) Habermas fails, finally, because he has not linked his idealized standard of procedural reason to any practicable threshold of institutionalization. He also fails to appreciate the distinctiveness of voluntaristic action within the broader category of normative action. This explains why he correctly points out that communicative action is not legitimately treated as normative action, and yet why he wrongly insists that communicative action complements and contributes to rationalization. He fails to see that communicative action is voluntaristic, and thereby intrinsically restrains rationalization by substituting direction for drift.

Second step: differentiation of voluntaristic action in practice. Once these theorists' independently taken "procedural turns" are synthesized, the second step is to dedicate this synthesis to the methodical study of institutions and organizations that are distinctively procedural *and voluntaristic.* This step may be worded in the form of two propositions:

> *First Proposition.* Under systemic pressures of drift, voluntaristic action itself becomes functionally differentiated, *in practice,* within any *non*authoritarian social order. Those divisions of organizations and institutions in which heterogeneous actors and competing groups maintain the integrity of voluntaristic *procedural* mediations become more and more clearly differentiated, in practice, from those divisions in which their social action revolves more immediately around *substantive* qualities of life.

> *Second Proposition.* Correlatively, whenever this differentiation either fails to develop in practice, or else later collapses or *de*differentiates, the direction of change within a civil society ceases to be benign. It shifts to one of greater social control and susceptibility to social authoritarianism.

Thus, the theory of societal constitutionalism proposes that there will not be evidence of voluntaristic action's differentiation, in practice, within *authoritarian* social orders. It also proposes that within those *non*authoritarian social orders that are experiencing a shift toward greater social control, there will be clear evidence of increasing *de*differentiation of the divisions of substantive and procedural voluntaristic action.

Consider again the illustration in chapter 1. William could begin to protect himself against Scott, at least in principle, if he could demonstrate unambiguously that his "professional integrity" is compromised, as noted at the end of chapter 3. Now, by proposing an interrelationship between the threshold of interpretability and the integrity of the collegial form of any research enterprise – including William's research division – it is beginning to be seen how this might be done. The substantive projects to which William's research division is dedicated, or to which any other corporate research division in his industry and sector is dedicated, is an issue distinct from whether corporate managers are maintaining the voluntaristic procedures distinctive to any research division's collegial form.

Of course, even if he were aware of this threshold and its interrelationship with the collegial form, William would still face a very practical problem: When corporate managers lack any understanding of, or appreciation for, the worldly qualities that distinguish a research division's form of organization from all other organizational forms, neither William nor any other researcher can protect their "professional integrity" within such a corporate setting. Moreover, corporate managers typically endeavor to attain *most immediately* the corporation's *substantive* goals, whether quantifiable (purposive-rational) or qualitative (substantively voluntaristic). They seldom become dedicated to maintaining the purported integrity of any division's form or organization as an end in itself. Thus, if restraints are not firmly institutionalized on what can be called a corporate "culture of encroachment," then the threshold of interpretability of shared social duties cannot be extended to William and other researchers. This threshold cannot be extended from restraining arbitrary government to restraining arbitrariness within civil society. This means, however, that citizens' protections from arbitrary government are then, if anything, left exposed to increasing contingency. After all, these citizens are learning in their everyday lives that arbitrary exercises of collective power are acceptable, and commonplace, within civil society. They are learning that professionals' integrity is readily compromised in pursuit of corporations' prized substantive ends. How can these same citizens be expected to recognize when government is wielding its power arbitrarily as it, too, pursues worthy substantive ends?[2]

Third step: threshold of institutionalized external procedural restraints. The third step beyond Habermas, Fuller, and Parsons is to draw attention to the presence of the organizational form that *institutionalizes* a nonauthoritarian direction of *social* change under modern conditions: Heterogeneous actors and competing groups institutionalize restraints on drift that are distinctively procedural and external (that is, voluntaristic) only by establishing and maintaining collegial formations within a civil society. Actors' *behavior* within and around collegial formations is distinctive. Unlike their behavior within and around any other organizational form, it exhibits fidelity to the threshold of interpretability of shared social duties. This remains the case as long as the integrity of this particular form of organization is simply being maintained.

According to the theory of societal constitutionalism, it is the presence (or absence) of collegial formations, and of this *behavior* by otherwise heterogeneous actors and competing groups, that ultimately determines the direction of change within any sector, industry, or organization of a civil society. This, in turn, determines whether a nonauthoritarian direction of social change is being sustained within any modern nation-state or whether the latter is trapped by the Weberian Dilemma: either acceding to an inadvertent drift toward authoritarianism or institutionalizing substantive normative restraints that extend social control and increase its susceptibility to social authoritarianism.

Fourth step: specifying possibilities for social integration. Given that the presence (or absence) of collegial formations determines whether any complex social enterprise is contributing to direction (or to drift), the fourth step follows as a corollary: The presence of collegial formations allows social scientists literally to pinpoint heterogeneous actors' and competing groups' possibilities for social integration *within* any division of an organization or institution. Such possibilities may be found, as examples, within: particular divisions of a corporation, particular offices of a governmental agency, particular departments of a university, particular committees of a legislature, particular courts of a criminal or civil justice system, or particular networks of scholarship or the arts. By monitoring the presence of collegial formations, social scientists may pinpoint such possibilities even as ongoing mechanisms of social control continue to support the larger social order of the sector, industry, or organization within which these particular divisions are embedded.

Keeping in mind the reformulations of Parsons's trichotomy of concepts discussed in chapter 7, figure 8.1 places societal constitutionalism's framework of analytical concepts into the context of Weber's, Parsons's, and Habermas's contributions. As this figure portrays, the collegial form of organization is the last of the basic concepts of the theory of societal constitutionalism that needs to be discussed. A few more words of review set the stage for this.

8.1.2. Three characteristics of societal constitutionalism's threshold: a review

The theory of societal constitutionalism redefines Fuller's principles of procedural legality in two steps. The first step, noted in chapter 6, is to broaden the scope of application of what is now being called a threshold of interpretability. This threshold's scope of application is broadened from the interpretability of positive laws to the interpretability of shared social duties being sanctioned within any social unit. The second step is to define this threshold analytically as a set of *internal* procedural restraints on *purposefully* arbitrary exercises of collective power. By being defined analytically, the threshold is detached from the particularity of the historical experiences of common-law countries from which it emerged (chapter 10). And yet, since it remains a set of internal procedural restraints, this threshold cannot be said to address the Weberian Dilemma regardless.

What can be said about this threshold of internal procedural restraints as it stands? What can be said about it apart from the subsequent issue of whether, in any given instance, it is extended to a set of external procedural restraints on drift by being institutionalized by the presence of collegial

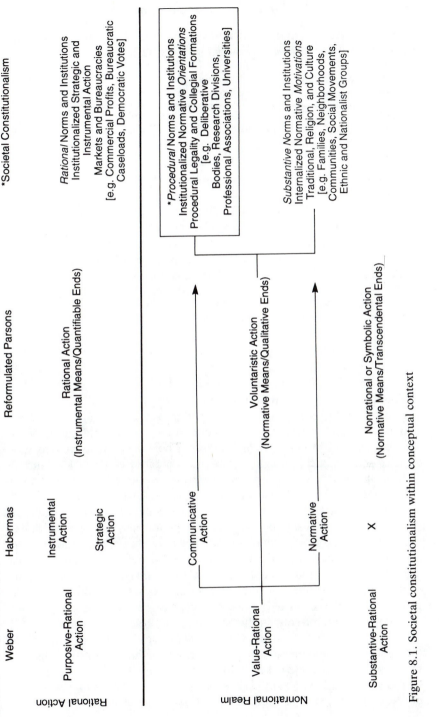

Figure 8.1. Societal constitutionalism within conceptual context

155

formations? As it stands, the threshold of internal procedural restraints brings three characteristics to comparative study:

First, the threshold is distinctively voluntaristic rather than either rational or more strictly nonrational.

Second, actors' behavioral fidelity to this threshold is irreducible, both in principle and in practice, to the possibility of their sustaining a nonauthoritarian direction of social change, and to the possibility of their being integrated rather than controlled anywhere within a civil society.[3]

Third, the threshold may credibly *claim* conceptual grounding against normative relativism (chapter 10). As such, it is not legitimate for any social scientist to *reduce* actors' behavioral fidelity to it to their subjective interests alone or to normative beliefs that are strictly relative to time and place. Such behavior instead rests, in principle, on a credible claim to contribute to *reasoned* social action as such.

By working the discussion of Fuller's legal theory (chapter 6) into the discussions of the reformulated concept of voluntaristic action (chapter 7) and Habermas's communication theory (chapter 5), each of these characteristics of the threshold of internal procedural restraints may be elaborated in turn.

Voluntaristic. One thesis cutting across chapters 5–7 is that most of the shared *social* duties being sanctioned within complex social units are neither rational and instrumental nor more strictly nonrational and habitual. They are rather distinctively voluntaristic. They are being sanctioned in the effort to maintain the integrity of worldly qualities in social life, and the success of this effort remains contingent rather than becoming overdetermined systemically. Such social duties can be recognized and understood by *heterogeneous* actors and *competing* groups in common only if the duties, as well as the sanctions supporting them, are kept consistent with the threshold of interpretability. If they are not kept consistent, then these actors' and groups' behavioral fidelity to social units' acknowledged ranges of expectations regarding acceptable behavior is indeed *reducible* to some combination of formal and informal mechanisms of social control. This proposition holds even if the actors involved are convinced subjectively that they are acting freely, in their own best interests.

Still, it is important to emphasize that if social scientists employ this threshold alone, independently of exploring whether it is institutionalized by the presence of collegial formations, their comparative research will be severely limited. It will be limited, even as it begins to challenge the presupposition of exhausted possibilities, because the reverse of the proposition

above does not hold: Actors' and groups' behavioral fidelity to this threshold at any given moment in time does not in itself, in the absence of
collegial formations, somehow guarantee that a nonauthoritarian direction
of social change is being sustained. Nor does it guarantee that these actors'
and groups' orderly behavior within any division of an organization or
institution is consistent with their possible social integration.

The threshold of interpretability of shared social duties is a voluntaristic
threshold of *internal* procedural restraints on *purposefully* arbitrary exercises of collective power alone. As such, it allows social scientists to go
beyond the presupposition of exhausted possibilities by specifying particular instances of control and arbitrariness within Western civil societies. But,
as a set of internal procedural restraints alone, this threshold fails to reveal
any *social infrastructure* that allows social scientists (or anyone else) to
distinguish shifts from direction to drift (or vice versa) within any given
civil society.

As one example, if particular corporate managers happen at any given
moment in time not to encroach against this threshold in their everyday
behavior, this does not mean that corporate research divisions in particular,
or corporate directorates, are organized in the collegial form. Nor does it
mean, therefore, that researchers within these divisions are maintaining
their professional integrity, and are thereby possibly integrated. Similarly,
even if particular researchers within these divisions happen to conform
individually to the threshold of internal procedural restraints, these divisions are themselves embedded within the larger institutionalized environments of the corporation, its industry, and its sector (Meyer and Rowan
1977). These environing institutions may be adrift themselves. Whether a
nonauthoritarian direction of social change is being sustained beyond actors' local interactions, therefore, hinges on whether *external* procedural
restraints on drift are also in evidence. This depends, in turn, on whether
collegial formations are present within research divisions' and directorates'
institutionalized environments, that is, within the corporation's industry,
sector, and the larger civil society (in chapter 11 these are called *sectoral*
collegial formations, as opposed to the *divisional* collegial formations
within any particular organization).

Thus, actors' and groups' behavioral fidelity to internal procedural restraints at particular moments in time guarantees only that (a) they happen
to be restraining purposefully arbitrary exercises of collective power at
these moments within their local interactions. And, as a result of this, it also
guarantees that (b) they remain capable, at least in principle, of recognizing
and understanding the shared social duties being *purposefully* sanctioned at
this level. Unfortunately, as symbolic interactionists richly document, local
interactions may alternate greatly, and within quite brief periods of time,
between fidelity to, and encroachments against, any set of normative re-

straints. Moreover, the theory of societal constitutionalism dismisses out of hand the likelihood that interactions within *any* complex social unit evolve or change in a unilinear direction. Indeed, one of the tasks of the social sciences is to monitor shifts of direction dispassionately, and not to assume, even provisionally, that interactions within Western democracies are tending in any certain direction whereas those in all other nation-states are tending in others.

Despite its limitations when brought to comparative research in isolation, the threshold of internal procedural restraints nonetheless offers comparativists at least three advantages over the presupposition of exhausted possibilities:

> First, encroachments against the threshold may be detected by any set of actors (including social scientists), and not merely by professionals trained in the law. Thus, when *professional enforcers* encroach against these restraints, this may be readily detected. Similarly, when *professional researchers* encroach against the same threshold within corporate research divisions, this too may be readily detected.

> Second, social scientists can demonstrate with precision when the shared social duties being sanctioned at local or interactional levels encroach against this threshold. They can demonstrate this with at least as much precision as they currently demonstrate whether local social units are becoming more or less efficient in production, effective in administration, or democratic in participation and responsiveness.[4]

> Third, the threshold of internal procedural restraints is *institutionalized* beyond local interactions by the presence of the collegial *form* of organization. This formation institutionalizes this threshold as a voluntaristic orientation that competing groups and heterogeneous actors (and social scientists) can recognize in common.[5] Moreover, because evidence of this voluntaristic *orientation* is strictly *behavioral*, its institutionalization has nothing to do with whether actors happen to internalize (or negotiate) *shared* normative *motivations* or subjective interests.[6]

Irreducible. As noted in passing above, the threshold of interpretability lays claim simultaneously to being practicable and yet *irreducible* to a nonauthoritarian direction of social change and actors' prospects for social integration. By marking the irreducible "floor" of actors' integrative possibilities, this procedural threshold permits social scientists to bring the social integration/social control distinction to even subtle changes within *any* complex social unit. By contrast, when social scientists undertake comparative research without employing this threshold, and without drawing this distinction, the most they can recognize is whether Western political institutions and economic practices are present or absent. In short, their research is then oriented, however implicitly, by the presupposition of exhausted possibilities.

The problem with this is that if actors freely vote and assemble, exchange and invest – even as power holders within a civil society typically encroach against the threshold of internal procedural restraints – then these actors are indeed being manipulated, controlled, and coerced in their everyday lives. When national institutions such as elections, civil liberties, and private property rest on such a social infrastructure, they may be demonstrated empirically to contribute to actors' demonstrable social control.[7] By no means can it be assumed that these national institutions somehow contribute intrinsically to actors' possible social integration within their lived social fabrics.

Grounded. One implication of the threshold's irreducibility in the sense above is that it can credibly *claim* grounding against the sovereignty of actors' subjective interests and normative relativism. Unlike the presupposition of exhausted possibilities, this threshold is consistent with Habermas's (and others') critique of copy theories of truth and subsequent "procedural turn" to a consensus theory of truth (and reason). Still, even as this threshold can credibly claim grounding, it cannot claim a universal scope of application in empirical research.

On the one hand, this threshold is legitimately applied only to *modern* nation-states and *modern* civil societies, and not to traditional societies. On the other hand, this threshold is not legitimately applied to the most microsociological interactions, or those that take place outside of any and all organizational forms. Such interactions include those taking place within families, and any and all other cathectic relations and relations of *personal* trust (rather than relations of institutional or fiduciary trust) (Barber 1983 on the former; Scheff 1990 more generally; and both DeMott 1988 and Frankel 1983 on fiduciary relations). Within its proper scope of application – to divisions of modern institutions and organizations – the threshold of interpretability is indeed generalizable rather than Europocentric or otherwise particular.

8.2. The organizational expression of internal procedural restraints

As actors establish and maintain collegial formations, they simultaneously *institutionalize* qualities in social life that are distinctively voluntaristic and procedural. The threshold of interpretability is included among these qualities. Once it is institutionalized by this organizational form, actors' behavioral fidelity to these qualities is no longer left to actors' ad hoc interactions. Indeed, as this organizational form is itself extended across entire industries and sectors of a civil society, actors' behavioral fidelity to the threshold of interpretability is extended into organizations' institutionalized environments.

What, then, are collegial formations? How may social scientists distinguish this particular form of organization from any and all others?

8.2.1. Defining collegial formations residually: nondemocratic

As a first approach, collegial formations may be defined in residual terms. This is precisely the tack that Parsons took late in his career. In occasional references, he emphasized what "associational" and "collegial" bodies are not: He found that they are not "competitive," bureaucratic, or democratic.[8] As was the case earlier with his treatment of voluntaristic action, here too he failed to specify any criteria that distinguish the collegial form positively. Within the theory of societal constitutionalism, however, the collegial form is distinguished positively in terms of two criteria. First, its members remain dedicated to describing and explaining (or creating and maintaining) qualities in social life. Second, its members' behavior remains consistent with the voluntaristic and procedural qualities of the threshold of interpretability of shared social duties. Before discussing why these criteria characterize actors' behavior only within the collegial form rather than within any other organizational form, it is worthwhile to consider first why the collegial form is nondemocratic.

Any democratic organization hinges ultimately on whether its members' subjective interests are treated equally, in accordance with the strictly rational procedure of majority rule (Offe 1983). This procedure is rational rather than voluntaristic because the counting of equal, and thereby interchangeable, subjective interests is consistent with the rational means-end schema.[9] Indeed, majority rule is the *normative orientation* institutionalized by any democratic formation, irrespective of how any particular one happens to structure its members' articulation and aggregation of their subjective interests (note 6). By definition, this normative orientation is shared by all members of this formation as long as the latter's integrity is being maintained. All of them are oriented to honor the outcomes of majority rule: (a) irrespective of what these outcomes happen to be in substance, (b) irrespective of the quality of information (if any) that they receive, (c) irrespective of the quality of discussion (if any) in which they engaged prior to voting, and (d) irrespective of all of their remaining differences in subjective interests and normative motivations.

Actors' *behavior* within collegial formations is inconsistent with this normative orientation. The collegial form does not orient its members normatively to exhibit behavioral fidelity to majority rule as such, but rather to exhibit behavioral fidelity to *voluntaristic or qualitative procedures* as such. This does not mean, of course, that members of collegial formations cavalierly ignore or contravene electoral results. Nor does it mean, for that matter, that they ignore or contravene other rational procedures, including basic techniques of administrative effectiveness or economic efficiency. It does, mean, however, that they are not normatively oriented first and foremost to rational procedures or to attain quantifiable outcomes of any kind, whether those of efficiency, effectiveness, *or majority rule*. As an organizational form that institutionalizes its members' behavioral fidelity to voluntaristic procedures, and to qualities in social life, the collegial form's normative orientation is *both* nondemocratic and nonrational.[10]

At the same time, collegial formations are clearly supported, in practice, by administrative staffs, and the latter, in turn, are organized in the bureaucratic form. These staffs are thereby oriented normatively to maximize efficiency or effectiveness rather than to maintain the integrity of deliberation or any other qualities in social life. Consider, as examples, the staff of the Supreme Court, the administration of a university, or the staff of a corporate research division. Just as clearly, members of collegial formations may ultimately finalize their deliberations by voting in a formally democratic way. Yet, what is distinctive about the *behavior* of the members of any collegial formation is that their behavior is oriented first and foremost (a) to keeping open the *possibility* of heterogeneous actors and competing groups recognizing and understanding what their shared social duties are, and then (b) to keeping open the *possibility* of their recognizing and understanding (or creating and maintaining) other worldly qualities in their social lives. For the members of any collegial formation to subordinate their behavioral fidelity to this institutionalized normative orientation is for them simultaneously to abandon this very organizational form. Actors cannot maximize their efficiency in production or their effectiveness in administration, as they are encroaching against this formation's threshold, and then expect that an essentially voluntaristic or nonrational form of organization can resist transformation under pressures of interest competition and systemic drift. Similarly, actors cannot vote in a majority, as they are encroaching against this formation's threshold, and then expect that this does not similarly jeopardize this organizational form.

Because this formation's procedural threshold is itself comprised of *worldly qualities* in social life, its sheer presence within any modern civil society means that its members' behavior already resists *reduction* to the instrumental means and quantifiable ends that characterize *any* rational social enterprise, *including democratic elections*. Put differently, this means that collegial formations cannot be *distinguished* by (a) the effectiveness of their administrative staffs, even as the latter might indeed be effective, nor by (b) the efficiency of their production units, even as the latter might indeed be efficient, nor by (c) the numbers of actors who participate in their elections or how the majority happens to vote, even as the latter might indeed be formally democratic. Collegial formations can be distinguished only by the *worldly qualities* orienting their members to resiliently *restrain* their administrators, producers, *and electoral majorities* from elevating effectiveness, efficiency, or even majority rule to their primary normative orientation.

Thus, the continued presence and integrity of collegial formations may well be compatible, in practice, with a great many of the economic practices and political institutions of Western democracy. But because the normative orientation institutionalized by these formations revolves around voluntaristic procedures rather than around rational procedures, *their sheer presence within a Western civil society just as intrinsically restrains one-sided democratization as it intrinsically restrains one-sided bureaucratization and all other immediate responses to the drift of rationalization.*[11] The sheer presence of collegial formations just as intrinsically restrains the social units' leaders from most effectively mobilizing voters as it restrains the social units' administrators from most effectively organizing personnel.[12] Within nonauthoritarian social orders, these and all other strictly rational actions are permitted and even encouraged – but only to the point where they begin to compromise the integrity of the voluntaristic procedural threshold institutionalized by collegial formations.

8.2.2. Three forms of organization

Whether efficient production, as measured by outputs, effective administration, as measured by caseloads, and even democratic participation, as measured by votes, are increasing or decreasing within any sector, industry, or organization of a civil society is, in each instance, an empirical question. But each of these empirical questions differs from the empirical questions raised by the theory of societal constitutionalism: Does the collective power wielded within and through these social units contribute exclusively to actors' social control, even if inadvertently so? Is the social order of these units, and then of the larger civil society, becoming more controlling and thereby susceptible to social authoritarianism?

The three types of ends characterizing the first three empirical issues noted above – outputs, caseloads, votes – are all quantifiable rather than intrinsically qualitative. As a result, none qualifies as a type of end consistent with voluntaristic action. Social enterprises dedicated primarily to attaining any of these three ends thereby fail to restrain the drift of rationalization intrinsically, by their sheer presence within a civil society. *For that matter, these enterprises do not instrinsically restrain even purposefully arbitrary exercises of collective power.* Thus, they fail to institutionalize *either* internal or external procedural restraints. Instead, because each revolves around rational procedures and quantifiable ends, each is marked by complicity in drift.

Unlike bureaucratic and democratic formations, as well as patron-client formations, collegial formations institutionalize external (voluntaristic) procedural restraints on both purposefully and inadvertently arbitrary exercises of collective power *by their sheer presence within a civil society.* Because they are oriented by voluntaristic procedures, members of collegial formations contribute to the social infrastructure of a nonauthoritarian direction of social change: (a) irrespective of the substantive goods or services that their formations provide, (b) irrespective of the sector or industry within which their formations are located, and (c) irrespective of their own subjective interests or internalized motivations. By contrast:

(a) Within *bureaucratic formations,* actors' orientation to voluntaristic procedures is clearly not emphasized. What is emphasized instead is their rational orientation to maximize the effectiveness of administration or efficiency of production. Thus, even as actors within a bureaucracy obey orders in a top-down chain of command, and thereby maintain the integrity of the bureaucratic form, they may nonetheless simultaneously encroach against the voluntaristic procedural threshold of interpretability of shared social duties.

(b) Within *formally democratic formations,* actors' orientation to voluntaristic procedures or other qualities in social life also is not emphasized. What is emphasized instead is their rational orientation to maximize the mobilization of formally equal votes, formally equal subjective interests. Thus, even as actors within a democracy mobilize voters, and thereby maintain the integrity of the democratic form, they may nonetheless simultaneously encroach against the voluntaristic procedural threshold.

(c) Within *patron-client formations,*[13] finally, actors' orientation to generalizable procedures of any kind, whether voluntaristic or rational, is not emphasized. What is emphasized instead is their substantive orientation to extend and intensify networks of personal loyalties that cover both material assistance and effective support (Gellner and Waterbury 1977; Schmidt et al. 1977; Eisenstadt and Roniger 1984). Thus, as actors within a patron-client network honor their personal loyalties, and thereby maintain the integrity of the clientelistic form, they may nonetheless simultaneously encroach against the voluntaristic procedural threshold.

A social order experiencing bureaucratization in response to the breakdown of meaning and other systemic pressures may maintain or even extend its popular appeal. Its political leaders may continue to be legitimated electorally in fair and free, and at least nominally competitive elections (as Mexico has long demonstrated, e.g. Hansen 1971; Purcell and Purcell 1980). It is even more likely that a bureaucratic-authoritarian regime (O'Donnell 1977) may steadily increase its effectiveness in administration and its efficiency in production, at least for a time (as Brazil once demonstrated, e.g. McDonough 1981). Mechanisms of social control may thereby remain rational and also secure ongoing popular support or, at least, the support of significant factions of social influentials. But to the extent that actors and groups maintain the integrity of collegial formations within any sector of a civil society, this sector simultaneously restrains *both* purposefully and inadvertently arbitrary exercises of collective power.

When voluntaristic action is institutionalized, whether substantive or procedural, this marks an external restraint on the drift of rationalization because such action is intrinsically nonrational (chapter 7). When the shared social duties being sanctioned within any institutionalized arena of voluntaristic action are kept consistent with the procedural threshold of interpretability, however, this marks the voluntaristic orientation distinctive to the collegial form alone. To institutionalize these shared social duties rather than leaving them to actors' ad hoc behavior is not merely to institutionalize internal procedural restraints on local arbitrariness. It is also to contribute to the social infrastructure that sustains a nonauthoritarian direction of social change and expands heterogeneous actors' and competing groups' prospects for social integration.

Thinking again of the young researcher within the pharmaceutical company sketched in chapter 1, how might company managers be restrained *institutionally* from pursuing the firm's material interests most immediately? They would be restrained the moment that they acknowledge that companies within their industry do not typically encroach against research divisions' collegial form even for "sound business reasons."[14] Indeed, within the industries or sectors where collegial formations are to be found, managements as well as interested parties both within and outside of particular corporations formulate and articulate *what* the company's (or their respective division's) material interests *are* within *an institutionalized environment that contains external procedural restraints.*[15]

8.3. The collegial form of organization

But, again, what are collegial formations? The following definition (see also page 80) brings some substance to the discussion of organizational forms:

> Collegial formations are deliberative and professional bodies wherein heterogeneous actors and competing groups maintain the threshold of

interpretability of shared social duties as they endeavor to describe and explain (or create and maintain) qualitative phenomena in social life or in natural events.

The collegial form literally ceases to exist when either one of two developments occurs, in practice: First, it ceases to exist when the members of this formation encroach against the integrity of its voluntaristic procedural threshold, whether purposefully or inadvertently. Second, it ceases to exist when the significance of the social or natural events that they are describing and explaining (or creating and maintaining) can be *reduced* to quantitative measurements of one kind or another. Each of these developments may be explored in turn, with the following proposition stating each more analytically:

Collegial formations institutionalize external (voluntaristic) procedural restraints on drift to the extent that: (a) Their members do not encroach against the formation's threshold. (b) The significance of the worldly qualities that these members are responsible for describing and explaining (or creating and maintaining) cannot be reduced to measurements or quantitative indices of any kind.

8.3.1. Encroachments against the collegial form

As deliberative and professional bodies, collegial formations may appear, in practice, as the networks of social interactions within and through which artists, intellectuals, or scholars exchange criticisms and evaluations. More importantly, they also may appear as the formally organized divisions of more complex institutions and organizations, including, as examples: the diagnostic units of hospitals, the research divisions and directorates of corporations, academic departments within universities, and refereed publications or prizes within disciplines or expert fields. Whether manifested as networks or as formally organized divisions, these bodies are distinguished by their *form* of organization, not by any of the substantive activities to which their members happen to dedicate them. In turn, their members are not distinguished by their subjective interests, nor by the particular value-commitments and motivations that they happen to have internalized as individuals either before or during their professional training.[16] Nor, finally, are they distinguished by any particular set of shared subjective interests they happen to bring to, or to negotiate within, their local interactions. As members of collegial formations, they are instead distinguished strictly and solely by their behavioral fidelity (a) to a shared voluntaristic procedural orientation, and, concomitantly, (b) to a shared voluntaristic procedural responsibility.

To the extent that individuals indeed remain members of collegial formations, they share a voluntaristic procedural orientation rather than any orientation that is either more rational or more immediately substantive. They share this orientation qua members of collegial formations irrespective of all of their remaining *and possibly increasing* differences in subjective interests and normative orientations qua heterogeneous actors and members of competing groups and factions.

First, they share the voluntaristic orientation institutionalized by the collegial form itself: They exhibit behavioral fidelity to the procedural threshold of interpretability of shared social duties.

Second, they also share a concomitant voluntaristic responsibility: They detect and sanction any and all encroachments against this formation's procedural threshold and, thus, against their shared orientation.

If members of collegial formations shirk this responsibility, in practice, then their own formations are placed in jeopardy. Still, in at least two respects, this responsibility is fiduciary rather than either self-interested or personal (see Frankel 1983 and DeMott 1988 on "fiduciary obligation" in law): First, the members of all other collegial formations are relying on the members of each particular collegial formation to bear this responsibility, however implicitly. Each set of members is being relied on to contribute to the *social infrastructure* that, in turn, supports the continued presence of all other nonrational or "protected" spheres within a civil society, including all other collegial formations. Second, and even more implicitly, the general public also is relying on the members of each collegial formation to bear this responsibility. The same *social infrastructure* is what ultimately supports *any* current or future effort to extend to the general public protection against greater social control and susceptibility to social authoritarianism. This social infrastructure is ultimately what underlies *any* effort, for instance, to extend even *internal* procedural restraints from arbitrary government to *purposefully* arbitrary exercises of collective power by private enterprises within a civil society (chapters 9–11 develop these two points).

If members of collegial formations either encroach against this form's institutionalized orientation themselves, or else shirk their concomitant responsibility to detect and sanction their own and others' encroachments, then there are no subjective interests or normative motivations that they can adopt, negotiate, or internalize that can insulate *them* from breakdowns of meaning, extensions of social control, and other manifestations of systemic drift. Only their behavioral fidelity to this orientation and to this responsibility can insulate *them,* even to some limited extent, from having *their own activities* subjected more immediately to the competition of subjective interests within economic and political marketplaces. This brings into view a second proposition (following the one on page 165):

Collegial formations are distinctive in that their members share an essentially voluntaristic procedural orientation and responsibility. Due to this, their members' *behavior* is distinct from the behavior of actors within any other organizational form.

8.3.2. Reducing qualities to quantitative measurements

Collegial formations and the contingency of qualities. Collegial formations are social units within and through which professionals in particular, and deliberators in general, describe and explain (and create and maintain) qualitative phenomena in social life or in natural events. Examples of such qualitative phenomena include (a) the "meaning" of a patient's physical or mental symptoms; (b) the "meaning" of social actions, texts, or works of art; and (c) the "meaning" of the "facts" in a court of law, a commission proceeding or, for that matter, a controlled experiment. Not being strictly reducible to quantification, actors establish "meaning" in each instance, from case to case and from social unit to social unit. Their shared "meaning" rests, in turn, on particular descriptions of qualitative phenomena somehow securing their shared recognition and understanding, and then possible acceptance.[17] *Collegial formations institutionalize professionals' and deliberators' ongoing efforts to establish and maintain a shared "meaning" of qualitative phenomena, qua heterogeneous actors and competing groups.*

When does the "meaning" of patients' symptoms or the "meaning" of the results of controlled experiments, as examples, remain irreducibly qualitative? Descriptions of such phenomena may be supplemented and greatly enhanced by any number of measurements, to be sure. But their "meaning" remains qualitative as long as their *significance for clients (or other interested parties)* resists reduction to such measurements. At the moment that reduction becomes a possibility, whether as a result of technological developments or advances in knowledge, collegial formations no longer remain central to professionals' and deliberators' everyday activities in the substantive areas affected. This is what occurs, for instance, at the moment that certain mental illnesses are discovered to be reducible to patients' chemical imbalances. Diagnosis is then reducible to laboratory technicians' measurements, and treatment is reducible to pharmacists' prescriptions – all outside of the collegial form (see Abbott 1988: chapter 2 on diagnosis).

Implications of collegial formations' loss of qualities. As the organizational form distinctive to working deliberative bodies (as opposed to honorific forums), collegial formations are *never* the most rational way to organize heterogeneous actors and competing groups for efficient production, effective administration, democratic participation or, for that matter, personal loyalty. Bureaucratic formations, democratic formations, and patron-client networks are *always* superior organizational forms for such ends. Precisely because this is the case, once the significance of qualitative phenomena is reduced to measurements, the continued presence of collegial formations becomes altogether unwarranted. These formations are by definition already voluntaristic or nonrational, and thereby incapable of being warranted on strictly instrumental or strategic grounds. With the reduction of qualities to measurements, they become patently nonreasoned as well: They can no longer be warranted even on communicative grounds. Within the broader social context of systemic pressures of drift, it becomes literally impossible for heterogeneous actors and competing groups to *resist* adopting some other, more strategic, form of organization, whether one more rational (in the cases of bureaucratic and democratic formations) or one more personal (in the case of patron-client relations).

The interrelationship between the collegial form and its members' independent and collective efforts to describe and explain qualitative phenomena carries two additional implications. On the one hand, at the moment that their descriptions can be reduced to quantification – whether technically or else strategically in competition with other occupations (Abbott 1988) – professionals' vulnerability to deprofessionalization increases dramatically. This is the case precisely *because* their continued membership within collegial formations is jeopardized. It is professionals' direct or indirect membership within collegial formations, and not any of the substantive activities to which they become dedicated, nor any of their own internalized beliefs or subjective interests as individuals, that ultimately distinguishes their expert occupations as professions (Sciulli and Jenkins 1990). The same membership is also what ultimately distinguishes any assembly as a working deliberative body rather than as an honorific forum.[18]

On the other hand, members of aspiring "professions" or aspiring "deliberative bodies" who fail either to establish or to maintain the integrity of the collegial form cannot succeed. Systemic pressures of rationalization, including ongoing competition with other expert occupations, ceaselessly pressure them to adopt organizational forms that offer their members more immediate protection and security within economic and political marketplaces. This is precisely what the bureaucratic and patron-client forms in particular offer to heterogeneous actors and competing groups under modern conditions. Through political lobbying or unionization, actors may for a time secure a monopoly over the services that they are offering within and through other organizational forms. This is what Abbott (1988) documents so impressively. But he does so by refusing to distinguish professions from "expert occupations." The problem is that successful monopolization or, in Abbott's terminology, successful control over a jurisdiction, by no means establishes that an expert occupation is either a profession or a deliberative body (Abbott follows Larson 1977, Collins 1979, and other "monopolist" theorists in thinking otherwise).

Qualities and the contingency of collegial formations. If professionals or deliberators *are* indeed endeavoring to establish and maintain an intersubjective understanding of qualitative phenomena, rather than subordinating this endeavor, for example, to maintaining personal loyalties within cliques or factions, *then* they have no alternative other than somehow to institutionalize their own ongoing exchanges of information. After all, if they are indeed presenting and discussing descriptions of *qualities* in social life and natural events, then they must expose their exchanges *institutionally* to public or at least peer appraisal rather than leaving them to personal or ad hoc exchanges. Whenever professionals or deliberators institutionalize such exchanges of information – whether in face-to-face proceedings, broader networks of exchanges, or publications and more formally organized forums – the *only* form of organization available to them in *this endeavor* is the collegial form. Still, this endeavor *remains* an intrinsically voluntaristic project, irrespective of how firmly they may institutionalize their exchanges within a particular network or organizational division at any given point in time. Given systemic pressures of drift to the contrary, as well as professionals' and deliberators' own increasing heterogeneity and competitiveness, *all of the networks and organizational divisions that they establish for the purpose of institutionalizing such exchanges are "artificial."* Their presence within any modern nation-state is never "natural," favored by the drift of modernity itself. *Precisely because all voluntaristic organizations and institutions are indeed nonrational,* their continued presence always strikes outsiders, those competing more immediately within economic and political marketplaces, as "artificial" and "monopolistic," unnecessary and unwarranted (Larson 1977 codifies this, and, ironically, Buchanan's approach to monopoly offers her theoretical underpinnings, 1989: 5–11).

The very presence of collegial formations means that "protected arenas" may be found within a modern civil society, arenas protected from what would otherwise be a more unmediated, and robust, interest competition within economic and political marketplaces. Only by great, sustained effort are such social arenas ever *kept* protected from competition's "natural" encroachments, and from two other sources of encroachment under modern conditions: On one side, these social arenas are exposed to outsiders' publicly presented, ideological proposals to *eliminate* all instances of "social closure" as intrinsically unnecessary and unwarranted (Collins 1979: 197–204). These typically include calls for (a) opening these social arenas internally to unmediated democratization and (b) opening them externally to unmediated strategic competition within economic and political marketplaces. On the other side, these social arenas are also exposed to their own members' personal cliques and factions.[19] These involve private or personal exchanges that compel or induce members to subordinate the voluntaristic orientation and responsibility institutionalized by the collegial form to the substantive goals of their own networks and to the patron-client form's normative orientation of personal loyalty. Professionals and deliberators operating within such networks scrupulously veil their activities from public and peer appraisal instead of announcing their activities publicly as a "school" of thought or a "tradition" of theory or practice (Crane 1972 collapses this distinction at times).

In short, heterogeneous actors and competing groups – including professionals and deliberators who have undergone the secondary socialization of expert training – never somehow maintain the integrity of voluntaristic networks and organizational divisions spontaneously or naturally. They never do so by default, as if more rational and strategic alternatives were not available to them every step of the way. Heterogeneous actors and competing groups never establish and institutionalize deliberation merely because (a) instrumental calculations cannot be applied at the moment to a particular task, (b) bureaucratic chains of command and record keeping cannot be applied to a particular task, or (c) personal networks of loyalty cannot be applied to a particular task. Even the greatest inappropriateness or inapplicability of all of these alternatives by no means improves the likelihood that collegial formations actually will appear, if actors are not already endeavoring to reach an intersubjective, public understanding of irreducibly qualitative phenomena.

Quite to the contrary, systemic pressures of rationalization, including actors' fragmentation of meaning, ceaselessly jeopardize the integrity of deliberation. They jeopardize the successful institutionalization of collegial formations as well as the continued presence of substantively voluntaristic "protected spheres" (from day-care centers to museums, and from monasteries to wildlife reserves). Indeed, collegial formations' vulnerability to encroachments *never diminishes with modernity.* There is not a single collegial formation anywhere in the world today whose continued presence and integrity is immune from encroachments as interested parties both within and around it mobilize resources in the effort to maximize economic efficiency, administrative effectiveness, "democratic" participation, or their own personal loyalties.[20]

8.4. Preliminary proposals for orienting empirical research

8.4.1. Proposals for organizations research

John Meyer's "rationalized myths." By emphasizing the significance of collegial formations' presence within sectors, industries, or organizations of a civil society, greater specificity may be brought to John Meyer's impressive studies of how organization leaders respond to competition within "institutionalized environments."[21] The question that Meyer poses may be put in the following way: Why do the leaders of corporations, labor unions, schools, and other complex organizations often *fail* to maximize their organizations' efficiency in production or effectiveness in administration, even as they endeavor to remain economically and politically competitive within their sector or industry? Meyer's answer to this question is that some of the norms institutionalized within their sector, as ranges of expectations regarding acceptable behavior, are "rationalized myths." They are "myths" regarding what qualifies as "rationalization" within their sector.

This is an unfortunate term *because the institutionalized norms to which Meyer is referring are neither rationalized nor myths, at least within nonauthoritarian social orders.* He resorts to his oxymoron because of two conceptual gaps in his work. First, he fails to differentiate voluntaristic action from rational action. As a result of this, all norms other than the narrow norm of rational action are labeled "myths," a term more consistent with nonrational action proper than with voluntaristic action. Second, he then fails to distinguish voluntaristic procedural restraints on drift from the more immediately substantive or strategic restraints posed by organizations' ongoing economic and political competition within any industry or sector. Given these conceptual gaps, Meyer coined his oxymoron because he *accurately* observed the following two phenomena: First, the norms or expectations institutionalized within many sectors and industries of modern civil societies are by no means consistent with the narrow norm of rational action. Second, these norms do not pose absolute obstacles to leaders steadily rationalizing their organizations' production and administration, but they do mediate how they accomplish this.

Meyer may refer to these norms as "rationalized myths," however, only because he is assuming, implicitly or explicitly, that leaders' fidelity to these institutionalized expectations compromises their organizations' efficiency and effectiveness *objectively.* Only on the basis of an implicit or explicit objective (or intersubjective) standard of efficiency and effectiveness, after all, can Meyer suggest that norms are "myths," that they *distort* organization leaders' strategic decisions and actions.

Bracketing this issue for a moment, consider two other issues that

Meyer's oxymoron raises. First, why would organization leaders who are attempting to gain advantages over their competitors ever conform to such norms rather than take steps independently to rationalize their organization's production and administration? They do so, presumably, because these norms are indeed *the* ranges of expectations regarding acceptable behavior that are widely acknowledged within their industry or sector. Second, even if this is the case, how are such "myths" institutionalized? According to Meyer, governmental funding, customer or supplier loyalty, camaraderie within and across the subdivisions of each organization itself, and each organization's prestige and reputation within its industry, all hinge, in practice, on whether organization leaders appear to conform to these expectations. Within the context of these ongoing interrelationships, organization leaders who endeavor to maximize the efficiency of production or the effectiveness of administration "objectively" may simultaneously challenge the expectations of suppliers, clients, and regulators. Thus, their efforts would be sanctioned formally or informally as disorderly. The result would be that the organization's costs of operation would escalate, and its efficiency or effectiveness would not be improved at all.

Meyer's work cannot be faulted as it stands either for the accuracy of his descriptions of organization leaders' behavior, or for the sophistication of his methodology. It can be faulted, however, for its two conceptual gaps, and thereby for its lack of analytical precision. This, in turn, distorts the implications that he draws from his methodologically sound descriptions of organizational behavior.[22] These implications also have a vague or indefinite quality to them at times because every organization is embedded within an "institutionalized environment" of one kind or another. And nonrational norms of one kind or another are invariably to be found within all of these environments. To point this out fails to assist researchers who are interested in empirically specifying how particular organizations respond to particular "environments," or, conversely, how particular "environments" affect either the internal structure or the external performance of particular organizations. The implications that Meyer draws are equally applicable to the most controlling sectors of a civil society as to the most integrative. Something is wrong with any framework of concepts, however, that fails to assist researchers in drawing detailed distinctions between sectors and between organizations within different industries.[23]

Five empirical issues for the organizations literature. Meyer leaves at least two central questions unanswered: First, what qualifies any institutionalized norm as a myth in the first place? Second, why does Meyer also contend that some of *the same* institutionalized norms are nonetheless "rationalized" in some sense? Bringing the discussion of collegial formations to Meyer's work, it can be seen that the distinctively voluntaristic procedural norms that these formations institutionalize are nonrational, by definition, *and* yet are also at least as generalizable as the narrow norm of rational action. Social scientists can as readily recognize actors' fidelity to, and encroachments against, the collegial form as actors' fidelity to, and encroachments against, the narrow norm of rational action. Moreover, because the presence of these formations means that actors' behavior remains consistent with the procedural threshold of interpretability as well as with Habermas's proposed procedural grounding of reason, it is a distortion for social scientists to attribute this behavior to the impact of myths of any kind. Quite to the contrary, instances of actors' behavioral fidelity to the collegial form of organization qualify as *possibly contributing to reasoned social action,* even as this behavior remains nonrational.

By contrast to Meyer's analytically undifferentiated concept of "rationalized myths," therefore, the theory of societal constitutionalism approaches the issue of organizational behavior within institutionalized environments with a question capable of orienting detailed empirical studies: Are collegial formations to be found within the sector or industry of the organizations under study? This question can be answered with precision. In turn, the answer opens up numerous specific issues for detailed, falsifiable, empirical studies, issues buried somewhere within Meyer's institutional approach. In particular, the theory of societal constitutionalism poses such historical and cross-national issues as:

First, in which sectors of a modern civil society do organization leaders (or others) typically institutionalize collegial formations first, at the point of initial industrialization?

Second, what do the "alternative" environments look like, those in which actors fail to institutionalize collegial formations even as industrialization matures?

Third, is the institutionalization of collegial formations ever state-initiated, or does this invariably "percolate" up from civil society to eventual state recognition (and possible cooptation)?[24]

Fourth, are there particular sectors of civil societies in the former Eastern bloc, the Third World or, say, China, North Korea, or Cuba in which actors have indeed institutionalized collegial formations, even as most Western political institutions and economic practices continue to be absent?

Fifth, and conversely, are there particular sectors of Western civil societies within which actors are increasingly permitting or encouraging encroachments against the integrity of collegial formations, whether purposefully or inadvertently?

Three presuppositions and an orienting hypothesis. Rather than resting on the reductionist claim that when collegial formations institutionalize procedural voluntaristic restraints this somehow squelches or ameliorates interest competition, or occasional group conflicts, the theory of societal constitutionalism rests on quite different presuppositions:

> First, the theory of societal constitutionalism presupposes that individual actors and particular groups within all networks and organizational divisions act primarily on the basis of their immediate material interests, not on the basis of procedural mediations of any kind.

With this, the theory of societal constitutionalism is consistent with rational-choice theory in sociology and public-choice theory in political science, along with neocorporatism, pluralism, and liberalism, Yet, this theory adds that wherever and whenever collegial formations are present within a civil society, actors' and groups' self-interested *behavior* is indeed being restrained normatively, *in practice.* With its second presupposition, the theory of societal constitutionalism is rendered consistent with Hobbesian and Weberian approaches to social order:

> Second, the theory of societal constitutionalism presupposes that heterogeneous actors' and competing groups' immediate material interests are always sufficiently diverse and competitive that they never lose their capacity to foster disorder and outright social conflict.

Instead of downplaying the significance of the material and substantive bases of group competition and social conflict, yet a third presupposition of the theory of societal constitutionalism emphasizes it:

> Third, the theory of societal constitutionalism presupposes that whenever *heterogeneous* actors and *competing* groups *share* subjective interests or immediate material interests outside of any *mediation* provided by distinctively voluntaristic procedures, this is *always* the product of their manipulation, control, and coercion.

Heterogeneous actors' and competing groups' sharing of subjective interests is never a "natural" product of their unmediated recognition and understanding of an "objective" situation that they purportedly share in common. It also cannot be treated as empirical evidence of their possible social integration. This third presupposition distinguishes the theory of societal constitutionalism from the theories and approaches noted above, as well as from others, including: symbolic interactionism, network analysis,[25] exchange theory, Giddens's structuration theory, and both Parsons's functionalism and Luhmann's systems theory. Given these three presuppositions, an orienting hypothesis follows:

Collegial formations must be present in an increasing number of sectors of a civil society in order for (a) group competition and mechanisms of social control to be restrained, (b) a nonauthoritarian direction of social change to be sustained, and (c) heterogeneous actors' and competing groups' prospects for social integration to be expanded.

With this orienting hypothesis, the theory of societal constitutionalism proposes that the presence of a particular organizational form is *more fundamental* to a nonauthoritarian direction of social change and to heterogeneous actors' and competing groups' prospects for social integration than the presence of Western political institutions and economic practices in and of themselves. It thereby fills the lacuna of integrative possibilities and opens the way to revealing the prejudice, the normative relativism, of the presupposition of exhausted possibilities.

3.4.2. Proposals for comparative research

In which ways can this orienting hypothesis inform research in comparative political sociology and comparative politics? How can it inform comparative research that is amenable both to falsification by critics and to operationalization by proponents?[26]

Comparative research beyond left and right. As one illustration, it is not self-evident that "left-wing" regimes (social democracies or increasingly egalitarian social orders) uniformly encroach against the threshold of interpretability in a particular way, or that "right-wing" regimes (liberal democracies or increasingly inegalitarian social orders) uniformly encroach against it in a particular way. Put more generally, the implications that comparativists routinely draw from the types of class structures and stratification systems that they find within a particular nation-state may have to be altered or amended once they consider the organizational forms that dominate particular sectors, industries, and organizations. By exploring which sets of the eight procedural norms comprising the threshold are violated within particular sectors and industries, a new typology can be expected to emerge that cross-cuts or otherwise challenges more traditional, strictly materialist approaches to comparative research.

For instance, students of social democracy currently offer "left" and "right" interpretations of recent trends in Scandinavia: respectively, labor-movement theory (exemplified by the works of Walter Korpi, Gosta Esping-Anderson, and John Stephens) and the theory of neocorporatism developed by Philippe Schmitter and subsequent proponents). The prob-

lem, however, is that this way of approaching contemporary social democracies is less instructive than counterbalancing studies of their stratificatior
systems by exploring whether arbitrary exercises of collective power are
increasing or decreasing across their civil societies. Adam Przeworsk
(1985) in essence demonstrates that the left-right dichotomy is misleading
from the outset, given Social Democratic parties' acceptance of more anc
more practices of liberal-democracy. Social Democratic parties have long
ago abandoned a truly radical policy agenda. Even to approach their pro
grams today in terms of any traditional left/right dichotomy is to inject a
language of class struggle into scholarly research that has long been anachronistic in practice.[27]

Because the standard of the presence or absence of the collegial form car
credibly claim grounding against relativism, and also can be brought witl
precision to particular sectors, industries, and organizations, any new
typology of social orders that results will reflect the complexity and diver
sity of modern civil societies. As one example, comparativists have no
reason to assume a priori that power holders and social influentials within
each nation-state of the former Eastern bloc (say Poland, Yugoslavia, Hun
gary, and Romania) violated the same norms of the procedural threshold
before 1989. Nor do they have any reason to assume a priori that they
violated the integrity of nascent collegial formations within and across the
same sectors of their civil societies.

Quite to the contrary, there *may* be particular professional enterprise
within particular sectors of the civil societies of each Eastern nation-state
that have long been organized in the collegial form.[28] Some professiona
enterprises, that is, may have long resisted the state's and the party's exer
cises of collective power. They may well have provided insurgent leader
with a social base from which to challenge power holders. Or, their pres
ence may have restrained power holders sufficiently that independent trade
unions or state agencies emerged that were not themselves organized in the
collegial form. What is clear is that these sites of resilient restraint were no
formally institutionalized anywhere in the East before 1979, just as they
have yet to be formally institutionalized anywhere in the West. This is why
they readily escape researchers' attention.

The theory of societal constitutionalism directs comparativists' attentior
to the issue of the presence of collegial formations irrespective of whethe
the latter are formally institutionalized or not. With this shift in focus
studies of the relationship between nascent collegial bodies and broade
opposition groups within particular sectors of any Eastern or Western civi
society may result today in predictions of further changes in its politica
institutions and economic practices. Given this same focus, studies of Japa
nese civil society, for instance, may escape the increasing speculation re

garding whether it is more authoritarian than liberal-democratic (or vice versa). Social scientists may get on with the business of empirically exploring changes within particular sectors and industries of Japanese civil society over time. Relatedly, as Germany unifies and once again becomes a world economic and political power, shifts in its direction of social change may be monitored with far greater precision in this way than by concentrating on its stratification system or on whether it continues to maintain relatively free markets.

By exploring how Western and Eastern nation-states differ from each other in these specific respects, each nation-state, and then each sector of its civil society and each agency of its government, may be placed along a spectrum of *types of social order*. This spectrum would range from the most controlling and least integrative to the most integrative and least controlling:

(a) Strict authoritarian social control. This is marked by routine encroachments not only against the integrity of professionals' formations and practices but also against internal restraints, whether procedural or strategic.

(b) Efforts to introduce and then routinize the resilience of internal substantive restraints on government. This includes the institutionalization of interest-group competition and the rise of spheres of social life protected from immediate economic pressures (chapter 11).

(c) Efforts to introduce and then routinize the resilience of internal procedural restraints on government. This includes the institutionalization of particular guarantees of due process at least, and then of the threshold of interpretability on enterprises of law making and law enforcing.

(d) Efforts to extend internal procedural restraints from government to more and more sectors of civil society, and to more and more exercises of collective power by state-owned or state-controlled organizations.

(e) The rise of distinctively collegial forms of organization at least within selected divisions or particular organizations and agencies.

(f) Fully institutionalized and stabilized collegial formations within some major organizations and institutions of civil society and some agencies of government.

(g) A public policy of maintaining the integrity of the collegial form within more and more sectors of civil society and agencies of government – that is, the institutionalization of a public realm proper (chapter 11).

Such a typology begins to reveal possibilities for nonliberal (or non-Western) "democracy" in practice. Better put, it reveals possibilities for

expanding heterogeneous actors' and competing groups' prospects for social integration, whether within Western or non-Western nation-states. It
exposes possibilities that comparativists have long obfuscated because of
(a) their presupposition that Western political institutions and economic
practices exhaust the possibilities for "democracy" under modern conditions (including Schmitter 1983), or (b) their preoccupation with whether
public policies within a nation-state maintain private property (including
Przeworski 1985) or else a substantive way of life (including Popenoe 1988
and Bloom 1987). Even though some Western democracies may have
moved furthest to date in spanning the above spectrum of types of social
order, the very real possibility remains open of a nation-state of the East
or Third World "leaping ahead" to the final point in the spectrum, by
maintaining the integrity of its collegial formations as a matter of public
policy.

   The same typology also allows social scientists to specify points at which
manipulation, control, and latent coercion are increasing across sectors of
a civil society, whether within a Western or non-Western nation-state. It
allows them to specify this without concentrating exclusively on whether
state agencies resort at times to manifest coercion. Like any other substantive standard of comparison (note 27), state agencies' physical control of
rebels, demonstrators, or emigrants is not in and of itself an infallible
reflection of the extent of social control or the prospects for social integration to be found across a civil society. To take extreme examples, the
shootings at Kent State likely reflected as little about the prospects for
social integration across the sectors of American civil society in 1970 as do
the obstacles that state agencies within nation-states of the West, the East
and the Third World currently place on professionals and other skilled
workers who wish to emigrate on demand.

   By monitoring *all* exercises of collective power that encroach against the
integrity of collegial formations and its procedural threshold, social scientists
may study each sector, industry, and organization of a modern nation-state
in detail and in comparative perspective. They may describe and evaluate
the substantive accomplishments of each social unit, as well as the ideologie
with which actors symbolize these accomplishments. By employing a standard that allows social scientists to *specify* excesses or encroachments, *social
scientists need neither accept nor reject out of hand any of the ideological
claims that organization leaders are offering to justify their actions.* These
claims become data that researchers may take into account as they monitor
behavioral encroachments. Such data is the equivalent, at the macrosociological level, of "mitigating circumstances" or "subcultural mores" that social scientists take into account in microsociological studies of criminality or
deviance. In both instances, social scientists acknowledge that actors' beliefs

re part of the lived social fabric within which particular types of organiza-
ional behavior are to be understood and possibly explained.

Comparative research beyond the presupposition of exhausted possibilities.
A second illustration of how comparative research may be informed by the
heory of societal constitutionalism is that there is no reason for social
cientists to assume that Latin American nation-states that hold elections
re less controlling or less authoritarian than those that do not. There is no
eason for them to assume, for example, that Mexico has been less control-
ing than either Cuba since 1960 or Brazil since 1964. The theory of societal
onstitutionalism permits social scientists to draw important distinctions
vithin existing models of "authoritarianism" (from Linz 1964) and "cor-
oratism" (from Schmitter 1974), models that emerged largely from case
tudies of Latin America and the Iberian peninsula.

The major conceptual contribution to date of the neocorporatism litera-
ure, for instance, has been two sets of ideal types developed by Philippe
chmitter (see his works in the bibliography). Schmitter first distinguished
eocorporatism from pluralism (and, more vaguely, from syndicalism):

> In pluralism (within the United States), interest groups compete inde-
> pendently for political influence.

> In neocorporatism (within Western Europe, Scandinavia, and Latin
> America), a single peak association dominates each sector of a civil
> society, and other interest groups are unable to compete for influence
> independently.

chmitter then distinguished between what he calls "societal" and "state"
eocorporatism:

> In societal neocorporatism (within Western Europe and Scandinavia),
> peak associations and major labor unions were founded independently
> of the state. As a result, they remain potential social bases of internal
> substantive restraints on state policy-making bodies.

> In state neocorporatism (within Latin America), peak associations and
> major labor unions were founded by the state, whether directly or
> indirectly. They remain mechanisms by which the state controls the
> demands that emerge from civil society.

Schmitter fails to consider two significant issues, however. First, why is it
ot possible in time for state-created peak associations to restrain arbitrary
xercises of collective power by state agencies (or by private corporations
ithin civil society)? Second, why is it not possible, conversely, for indepen-
ently created interest groups or peak associations in time to provoke or

even initiate arbitrary exercises of collective power by state agencies or by "private" corporations? These are empirical issues that Schmitter's distinction between state and societal neocorporatism obfuscates. Regardless of whether any interest association is independent of the state, either at its founding or later in its development, the theory of societal constitutionalism orients social scientists to address these issues in each particular case.

Implications of the analytical distinctions and conceptual foundations

9. Procedural institutionalization beyond the Western democracies: three bases of voluntaristic restraint

Is the integrity of corporate directorates' collegial form upheld by law in any nation-state (Note 1982, Useem 1984)? Is the integrity of the collegial form of corporate research divisions upheld by law in any nation-state (Braithwaite 1982), or that of research facilities within public or private universities (Parsons and Platt 1973)? Do professional associations uphold by law the integrity of collegial formations at their members' various work sites, whether within universities, corporations, hospitals, or other complex organizations (Abbott 1988)? Do artistic, intellectual, or scholarly networks uphold by law the integrity of the collegial form framing their members' exchanges of information, including their anonymous refereeing and independent reviewing of publications and prizes (Crane 1972)?

The integrity of collegial formations is not currently upheld by law in any modern nation-state. As a result, not a single modern nation-state protects and expands heterogeneous actors' and competing groups' prospects for social integration as a matter of public policy. Yet, collegial formations are to be found, both historically and today, within different sectors, industries, and organizations of different civil societies. By no means are all of these sectors located within civil societies of Western democracies exclusively. Yet, in every instance to date, actors who have adopted the collegial form of organization have done so on their own, independently of the support of legal or formal sanctions. One result of this ad hoc activity, of course, is that collegial formations are distributed quite unevenly across the civil societies in which they are found at all. Another result is that everywhere their presence remains as contingent today as it has ever been historically.

What is intriguing to consider in comparative perspective is how different this present state of affairs could be in most modern nation-states, *given their existing material conditions, forms of government, patterns of stratification, and cultural traditions.* It is well within the material means of a great many modern nation-states, East and West, North and South, for their leaders *immediately* to mandate an extension of collegial formations across their civil societies *as a matter of public policy.* This same policy proposal also happens to be consistent with many of their national traditions and historical experiences. Thus, even though this public mandate is not in evidence, it is nonetheless eminently practicable. Nothing about it is utopian, idealistic, or ideological – unlike many existing and proposed public policies, including: President Bush's proposals to curtail the drug trade and never to raise taxes; many of the details of President Gorbachev's policy of perestroika; President Reagan's commitment to balance the federal budget – to say nothing of his proposed Strategic Defense Initiative; President Carter's wish to reverse a perceived "malaise" in the American body politic; and, for that matter, many of President Johnson's and then President Nixon's Great Society programs, including the "war on poverty."[1]

It is well within the material means, political power, historical experiences, and cultural traditions of *many* modern nation-states to support their existing collegial formations immediately with legal sanctions and to mandate the creation of others. And yet this public policy is not likely to be adopted soon in any modern nation-state, Western democratic or other. It is not on the policy agenda today because the Weberian Dilemma itself goes largely unnoticed, as it does at any historical moment when drift seems more benign than immediately threatening.

What go unnoticed today are two important points about institutions' and organizations' ongoing responses to systemic pressures of rationalization: First, the reason why actors within a very select set of modern nation-states do not experience greater social control and arbitrariness today, and thereby experience drift as more immediately threatening, is that collegial formations are indeed present within some sectors of their civil societies. Their presence can continue for a time today, as it did historically, even in the absence of support from legal sanctions; but in this absence, the eventual collapse of existing collegial formations is as fated today as it was historically (see pages 199–200). Second, the only practicable and prudent way for the leaders (or insurgents) of any modern nation-state to respond to systemic pressures in such a way as to *sustain* a nonauthoritarian direction of social change is for them to uphold existing collegial formations by law, as a matter of public policy.

Why does it matter at all whether such a public policy is ever adopted within any modern nation-state? Are heterogeneous actors and competing groups within the United States or Great Britain, as examples, rendered more vulnerable to increasing manipulation, control, and possible social authoritarianism, if their policy makers fail to adopt such a public policy? Can such actors and groups within the Soviet Union and China, or Brazil and Mexico, as examples, become less controlled and manipulated, and also reduce the likelihood of their leaders reverting to authoritarian excesses, if such a public policy is adopted? The answer to both questions is positive.

If either answer seems startling or disturbing, then what needs to be asked is whether the Weberian Dilemma remains salient in the late twentieth century. Or, alternatively, have the Western democracies, as well as other modern nation-states, somehow developed *systemically* in such a way that they have safely escaped its implications once and for all?

9.1. Once again, the Weberian Dilemma

When government agencies act instrumentally or strategically in response to systemic pressures of social change, and social influentials believe subjectively that these actions are literally unavoidable, *this context of subjective belief* renders these actions seemingly self-justifying. Within this context, these actions appear to social influentials not merely to be rational. Because they seem unavoidable or "natural," they are elevated implicitly to a broader, but conveniently unarticulated, standard of "reason." Social influentials believe that the warrant for these actions exceeds that provided by the narrow norm of rational action (and Luhmann 1982, 1986, 1990 codifies this by treating their warrant as systemic). These actions appear to be determined (Luhmann) or principled (traditional liberalism), even as they remain strictly strategic and narrowly self-interested. That this appearance is a distortion is readily revealed in two ways.

First, since *quantitative* indices of efficient production, effective administration, and democratic participation may improve steadily as the *quality* of actors' everyday lives deteriorates, it cannot be assumed a priori that instrumental and strategic action exhausts reason as such. Consider, as examples, when urban zoning policies remain rational even as inner-city decay increases or when the actions taken by government agencies remain rational even as their responsiveness to clients narrows and declines (to use two of Habermas's examples, 1980).[2] Second, governmental actions that seem unavoidable, within the context of belief just noted, cast a quite different appearance once they are placed outside this context. They then appear to be *particular* responses to pork-barrel politics (in the United States), partisan politics (in parliamentary democracies), drives for personal gain or career advancement (in all Western democracies and elsewhere), or utter confusion in the face of the complexities of drift. The latter was the case, for instance, during the energy crisis of the mid-1970s, and then during the recession that followed (Laumann and Knoke 1987: 69–72, 160, 166, 183–5, 283–4, 298–9).[3] Jill Quadagno (1990) has found, in turn, that a remarkably narrow coalition of interests defeated President Nixon's proposed family assistance plan in the early 1970s.

Within the context of belief noted above, social influentials' preeminent concern is whether particular governmental actions happen to stimulate unusual levels of group opposition, either from other agencies of government (including legislatures or courts) or from interests in civil society (Laumann and Knoke 1987: chapter 14). Within the same context, social influentials assume that all interests in civil society, including all interests stimulated to opposition, are subjective and thereby *intrinsically* particular rather than possibly principled or reasoned (see Lowi 1969 on American pluralism). Indeed, beyond the wax and wane of levels of group opposition, social influentials operating within this context of belief are inclined to assume from the outset that any resilient *normative* restraints placed on government's instrumental or strategic actions invariably fuel prejudices of one kind or another.[4] They assume, in short, that the leaders of any "reasonable" group or movement would never endeavor to resiliently restrain government's instrumental or strategic responses to systemic pressures.

And there is a point to this skeptical view of normative restraints. What is *unambiguously* principled or reasoned about contemporary tax policies, or policies of affirmative action – or opposition to them? What is unambiguously principled or reasoned about (proposed) policies of prayer in public schools, or, for that matter, the protection of academic freedom within universities – or opposition to them? What is unambiguously principled or reasoned about extending first amendment freedoms of speech from the "natural person" to the "corporate person"[5] – or opposition to this? What is unambiguously principled or reasoned about Brazilian labor policy or monetary policy, or about many of the details of President Gorbachev's domestic policies – or opposition to them?[6] Putting these issues more generally: Does the Weberian Dilemma loom still in the background in the late twentieth century, or have the United States, Japan, and the Continent safely escaped it once and for all, unawares and unannounced?

The context of belief discussed above is itself not attached to any principle or standard. As such, it cannot inform social influentials (or anyone else) regarding *what* the contemporary direction of social change is. Rather than addressing the Weberian Dilemma either directly or indirectly, this context of belief instead simultaneously (a) disenchants officials' actions and (b) elevates these same actions above significant criticism. In this way it is a reflection of the Weberian Dilemma itself, not a manifestation of any successful escape from it.

On the one hand, this context of belief disenchants officials' actions by reducing them to indices of efficiency, effectiveness, or popular acceptance. It thereby detaches these actions from *any* possible source of principled justification, including, of course, any "sacred" or strictly nonrational mandate. Is there a single student of contemporary politics who believes that the president, Congress, or the courts and federal agencies are doing God's work, or toiling in *the* public interest? Yet, on the other hand, this same context of belief simultaneously elevates these same domestic policies above radical or sustained criticism. Social influentials acknowledge that government's actions are detached from *any* generalizable standard of reason against which these actions might possibly be criticized radically or fundamentally. They thereby reduce officials' actions to the self-justifying products of *whatever* coalitions of interests happen to prevail within any policy domain at any particular point in time (Laumann and Knoke 1987 revolve around this belief by influentials and power holders).[7]

Still, this whole matter of the relationship between reasoned restraint and instrumental rationality, between qualities in social life and quantifiable outcomes, may be sharpened. It may be converted into discrete, researchable issues rather than left to speculation.

9.2. Three bases of voluntaristic restraint

It has been noted at several points in this volume that the presence of collegial formations within any sector, industry, or organization contributes to a literal *social infrastructure* of nonauthoritarian social order and possible social integration. Actually, the presence of these formations provides up to three related *social bases* on which even competing groups and heterogeneous actors (or social scientists) may recognize when government's actions are first purposefully and then inadvertently arbitrary. They may recognize this even when these actions remain rational in every respect, and thereby seemingly "natural" and unavoidable.

> First, collegial formations provide a social basis on which heterogeneous actors may at least *recognize* the broad direction of social change, despite the particularity of their own subjective interests and normative beliefs.

> Second, collegial formations provide a social basis on which heterogeneous actors and competing groups may resuscitate the integrity of internal procedural restraints on government by extending these restraints at least to *purposefully* arbitrary exercises of collective power *by private enterprises within civil society.*

> Third, collegial formations institutionalize external procedural restraints on *inadvertently* arbitrary exercises of collective power, whether by government or private enterprises.

Each of these social bases is discussed in turn.

9.2.1. The problem of recognizing drift and direction

With John Willard Hurst, the University of Wisconsin legal historian, Talcott Parsons (1962) believed that behind the American government's instrumental and strategic actions there "lies a system of order which, while not centrally directed, is in fact directional in its main influence on society." Indeed, Hurst characterized this "system of order" in the United States in terms that Parsons at times adopted: the relationship between the "drift" of self-interested competition and the "direction" of normative mediation. Hurst also characterized it as the relationship between the substance and the form of American politics. The substantive drift of American politics is fueled by what he called the "bastard pragmatism" of interest-group pluralism. The form or normative mediation of American politics is provided by the "directionality" that Hurst saw law bringing to bastard pragmatism. In the terminology of the theory of societal constitutionalism, "directionality" can only refer to a procedural voluntaristic orientation that enables heterogeneous actors and competing groups, first, to recognize social control and arbitrariness in common, and, with this, to bring some direction to the drift of interest competition.

Parsons's (1962: 561) most significant criticism of Hurst was a telling one, however: Hurst failed to see that (a) what heterogeneous actors and competing groups *recognize* to be "drift," in practice, and (b) what they *recognize* to be a more directional pattern of social change, in practice, *must itself be mediated by norms*. And this normative mediation, in turn, must itself be insulated from the bastard pragmatism of interest-group politics. If it is not, then any recognition of drift or direction would be a product of bastard pragmatism itself, and thereby incapable of supporting the "system of order" to which Hurst referred.

> Hurst, in his understandable anxiety to be realistic, has himself fallen a victim to the tendency to bastard pragmatism. By assimilating the categories of legal and political so closely together as he has, he has tended unnecessarily to give away an important part of his case, which I take to be that the relative directionality of American history (including the containment of, if not immunity to bastard pragmatism) is primarily explained by the institutionalization of a distinctive normative framework which is the core of what he calls the legal element. It is indeed precisely the containment of shorter-run interests by this normative framework, and the stimulus to redefine them in longer-run terms which is the feature of development serving as the focus of his discussion. (Parsons 1962: 564, my parenthesis)

Clearly, a shared recognition of which governmental policies contribute to drift and which ones contribute to "directionality" is not something that heterogeneous actors and competing groups develop intuitively. It is also not something that they negotiate "naturally," outside of economic and political marketplaces. For this very reason, Parsons's reference to a "distinctive normative framework" that, he believed, already supports such a shared recognition within the United States is vague in the extreme. Here and in his later works Parsons failed to specify any *social basis* on which social scientists – let alone actors and groups – might possibly recognize directionality within the United States, to say nothing of doing so in comparative perspective.

In fact, because Parsons's references to "directionality" from 1962 to the end of his career are so vague, they perpetuated a longstanding, and unfortunately ultimately correct, impression of his work overall: His accounts of social order hypostatize the "success" of socialization and of actors' *internalization* of *shared* subjective interests and normative beliefs. In the 1930s, Parsons labeled these internalized interests and beliefs "voluntaristic" (in some vague sense). Throughout the remainder of his career, he labeled them "integrative" and "directing."[8] Yet, if the *same* shared interests and beliefs were externally sanctioned rather than successfully internalized, Parsons's concepts left him with no alternative other than to label them deterministic and controlling.

To hinge the social control/social integration distinction on whether shared interests and beliefs are internalized or not fails, of course, to move beyond Hurst's vague notion of "directionality." Both theorists' concepts turn out, therefore, to be relativist and uncritical, and incapable of informing detailed comparative studies. By contrast, the increasing presence of collegial formations within a civil society provides a social basis on which direction may be distinguished from drift. The absence of these formations is clear evidence that drift is unmediated by direction.

9.2.2. Internal procedural restraints and purposeful arbitrariness

Constitutional theorists of the seventeenth and eighteenth century had a point: The division of powers and other internal restraints on arbitrary government are central to limited government. It bears repeating (from chapter 4) that *these* restraints are the core of governmental constitutionalism, not popular elections, competing mass political parties, interest-group lobbying, nor, for that matter, *broad* first amendment freedoms of property, speech, assembly, and religious worship.[9] However, none of the nation-states today whose governments are limited in this sense have yet extended internal procedural restraints to *purposefully* arbitrary exercises of collective power *by private enterprises within their civil societies* (Braithwaite 1982; Stewart 1983, 1987).

This next step is by no means systemically "overdetermined," whether within Western democracies or elsewhere. Yet, both William Evan and Philip Selznick come very near to treating it as if it is. Evan (1976) does not hold that an extending of internal procedural restraints in this sense is overdetermined, but he does insist that an extending of actors' citizenship status or "natural rights" is overdetermined. He sees the latter being extended to actors' sites of employment within both public and private organizations, but he fails to provide any rationale for why he assumes this. After all, corporations are not typically treated as if they are legislatures dedicated to ensuring their employees' (or stockholders') increasingly equal representation within their decision-making bodies. Philip Selznick (1969) also does not contend that the extension Evan has in mind is overdetermined, but he does see it as an increasingly likely possibility. He also fails to provide a rationale for why he assumes this, or how it escapes confusing corporations with legislatures. In the decade and more that has passed since their publications, there has been no discernible movement in this direction within the United States. More importantly, even if there were an extending of actors' "natural rights" into civil society, this would by no means be equivalent to extending internal procedural restraints (see note 30).[10]

The second social basis provided by the presence of collegial formations differs, therefore, from Evan's and Selznick's vision of extending actors' citizenship status or "natural rights" to actors' sites of employment. Along with the division of powers, internal procedural restraints on purposeful arbitrariness are the single most significant contribution of governmental constitutionalism in general, and of Anglo-American legal theory and practice in particular (Haar and Fessler 1986). To restate this contribution as an analytical concept, however, not only begins to elevate it conceptually above the particularity of its historical origins (chapter 10) but also above the tendency today to equate it with actors' "natural rights" (see chapter 4, note 2). Indeed, by taking this step and two others, the quite particular historical contribution of the threshold of interpretability is elevated to a generalizable standard, one suitable for the comparative study of drift and direction:

> The first step, just noted, is to restate this contribution as internal procedural restraints on purposefully arbitrary exercises of collective power, irrespective of whether these exercises are undertaken by governmental agencies or private enterprises.

Any analytical concept properly defined is generalizable because it isolates aspects distinctive to types of social action, whether historical or contemporary. Moreover, these aspects may appear, in practice, in various combinations, *and many of these combinations are likely to cut across the types in which they originally appeared historically.* Thus, the appearance of these aspects is by no means somehow tied intrinsically to their sites of historical origin – even as their appearance may remain tied broadly to time (that is, to modern conditions as such). As one example, the most irreducible aspects of interest competition may be found within many nation-states, including those that fail to exhibit any of the characteristics of either American pluralism or European neocorporatism.

Similarly, the concept of internal procedural restraints is "freed" from its sites of historical origin in Anglo-American experiences and the common-law tradition once it is defined analytically (chapter 10). Irrespective of the admittedly particular historical origins of modern limited government, evidence of internal procedural restraints may well be found within a great many networks, organizations, and institutions of modern civil societies in comparative perspective. Put differently, these aspects of restraint may well *disappear,* in practice, within particular Western democracies, and they may well *appear,* in practice, within particular nation-states outside the West.

The second step is to use this analytical concept to sharpen the distinction between drift and directionality. By being defined analytically, a distinction may be drawn, for instance, between (a) internal procedural restraints on government and (b) internal procedural restraints on private enterprises.

This distinction advances beyond constitutional and liberal traditions,[11] including Evan's and Selznick's and others' emphases today on extending actors' "natural rights." Yet, it fails to address the Weberian Dilemma directly. The third step finally accomplishes the latter, and it is the proposed contribution of the theory of societal constitutionalism.

The third step is to monitor the institutionalization of collegial formations within and across a civil society, rather than following rational-choice theorists and pluralists in monitoring the robustness of economic and political marketplaces, and rather than following Evan, Selznick, and others in monitoring the extension of natural persons' (or corporate persons') "natural rights" into these marketplaces.[12]

The institutionalization of economic and political marketplaces is a significant achievement, both historically and today. The former is today often labeled "liberalization" and the latter "democratization." Whenever actors' individual and collective ends can be quantified, these marketplaces effectively institutionalize the mobilization of instrumental and strategic means to attain them (Williamson 1985). But, in themselves, liberalization and democratization fail even to maintain, let alone to extend, any voluntaristic *procedural* restraints on arbitrary exercises of collective power, whether by government or private enterprises. Indeed, political marketplaces extend *Homo economicus's* self-interested competition for capital and possessions to the bastard pragmatism of group competition for power and influence within legislative and administrative bodies. Thus, "democratization" at best institutionalizes internal *substantive* restraints on government, and this alone extends drift at the expense of (traditional) directionality.

First step: analytical restatement of Anglo-American tradition. What is the significance of the first step, restating the historical contribution of Western constitutional theory and Anglo-American practice analytically, as internal procedural restraints? This step "frees" this contribution from the particularity of its historical origins in two respects, and thereby renders it generalizable and amenable to comparative study: First, by defining this contribution analytically, specific *qualities* of restraint are isolated that are significant for the comparative study of purposefully arbitrary exercises of collective power. Second, by emphasizing that these qualities happen to be procedural mediations rather than directly substantive, this further "frees" this contribution from *reduction* to the particularity of *any* national experience or lived social fabric. The latter revolves first and foremost around substantive qualities of life, and not strictly procedural qualities. A British or American "way of life," for instance, is not reducible to procedural qualities of any kind, nor is a Soviet, Chinese, Iranian, or Brazilian "way of life."

The purpose of the next chapter is to elaborate why this is the case: Why are particular procedural restraints on arbitrary exercises of collective power more "available" for transfer across modern nation-states today than substantive restraints of any kind? The purpose of the present discussion, however, is to explore this from the side of non-Western nation-states to which such procedural restraints are transferred today. That is, even if these restraints *are* somehow "available" for transfer, why do power holders and social influentials *outside of the Western democracies* ever consider introducing them into their nation-states? Why do they consider this even when their nation-state's historical experiences, current economic and political marketplaces, and cultural and national traditions differ markedly from those of any existing or historical Western democracy?[13]

As power holders and social influentials in the East and Third World become more heterogeneous themselves, and as their civil societies become more functionally differentiated, they face the same problems that all other sets of heterogeneous actors and competing groups face: They too endeavor to establish and maintain a *shared* recognition of which purposeful exercises of collective power are arbitrary and which are innovative. They too must discern which exercises of collective power are threatening and which are initially controversial but by no means controlling. If they fail to establish such a shared recognition, then *their own* subjective interests – and, for that matter, their own persons – are increasingly exposed to jeopardy by the state's actions. In addition, they too are increasingly exposed to jeopardy by the actions taken by powerful social movements, organizations, and institutions within civil society.

As power holders and social influentials become more heterogeneous themselves, and as the social units that they own, control, or influence become more functionally differentiated, their earlier reliance on patron-client networks and informal understandings no longer suffices to protect their interests and persons (see Luhmann 1982: 140–1 on the transition from expectations "mediated by personal identities" to a "loss of security"). These networks of personal loyalties once were extended sufficiently to encompass literally all power holders and social influentials. But, as a result of the changes just noted, they no longer comprise *one* social fabric of substantive restraints. They no longer provide *all* power holders and social influentials with a reliable trip-wire. They no longer signal to all power holders and social influentials *in common* when purposeful exercises of collective power are controlling and arbitrary.[14] In short, *power holders and social influentials outside the West are steadily losing the social infrastructure that had once permitted them to recognize in common what direction is, and what drift is.* For the reasons discussed in chapter 4, the internal substantive restraints provided by robust group competition (or by robust competition between patron-client networks) are incapable of providing such a social infrastructure in and of themselves.

Illustration: regime changes in Latin America. Looking at Latin America first in general terms, Charles Anderson, a University of Wisconsin political scientist, concedes in a 1982 updating of his 1964 "general theory of Latin American politics" that personal networks no longer provide resilient substantive restraints on exercises of collective power. He fears that violence by state officials as well as by "power contenders" within civil society can be expected to escalate as Latin American elites' once shared meanings fragment, and their negotiated settlements periodically break down. For Anderson, the great variety of power contenders in Latin American countries in this century, and their ceaseless struggles for material resources, political power, and social influence, best explains why many of these countries have alternated between civilian and military rule.

Consider, on the one hand, that only certain power contenders within any civil society in Latin America are particularly adept at mobilizing mass electoral support. On the other hand, many other power contenders are adept at mobilizing investments, military power, general strikes, or, for that matter, street demonstrations, public disruptions, and threats of vandalism or property damage. None of these latter power contenders accepts that any single "power resource" is the most legitimate power resource of all, *including that of mobilizing mass electoral support.* Each power contender instead operates on the assumption that the power resource it monopolizes is at least as legitimate as the power resource of electoral mobilization.

Thus, a great many power holders and social influentials within Latin America have never believed at any time in this century that the results of elections are legitimate or decisive a priori. They have never believed that electoral results alone legitimately determine: (a) who is to hold public office; (b) how material resources and political power are to be distributed, whether by government or private enterprises in civil society; or, ultimately, (c) *what the form of government itself is to be.* They have never believed that the single set of power contenders that happens to control the single power resource of mobilizing voters somehow has an unchallenged right to determine what the form of government is to be. Why, they wonder, should the very form of government itself guarantee that elections are held in the first place, let alone that all other power contenders are to defer to their results as legitimate or decisive?

For many power contenders and social influentials in Latin America, therefore, and particularly those in Brazil and Argentina, as prominent examples, periodic turns to military rule counterbalance those turns taken earlier that favored the power resources wielded by other sets of power contenders – nothing more. This is why regime changes are more the norm than the exception for many Latin American countries. Rather than being an unambiguous sign of "political decay," regime changes are rather manifestations of the robustness of power contenders' competition for power, resources, and influence. Instead of following North Americans in competing over government policies alone, social influentials and power contenders within Brazil and Argentina compete over the very form of government itself. If anything, they wonder why North American elites in particular and Western elites in general are so naive as to ignore that any form of government benefits only a fraction of the entire set of social influentials and power contenders within a civil society. In addition, there is precious little empirical evidence to support a proposition that appeals intuitively to Westerners: That stable civilian rule, as opposed to military rule or, for that matter, periodic regime changes, invariably fosters higher rates of economic growth (see Friedland and Sanders 1985 on the West alone) *or* more egalitarian distributions of resources (Bollen and Jackman 1985).

Illustration: a closer look at Brazil. Looking more specifically at Brazil, Peter McDonough (1981) discusses Brazilian elites' alliances and coalitions, and he notes that their dedication to their own patron-client networks squeezes out consideration of broader norms, including Western "rules of the game" (Higley and Burton 1989; O'Donnell, Schmitter, and Whitehead 1986 more generally on elites during transitions to civilian rule). Luciano Martins (1986) demonstrates indirectly, in turn, how broader normative restraints of some kind are needed today in order for "liberalization" to secure a foothold in Brazil in the face of competing influentials' immediate calculations of strategic advantages. Put differently, Brazilian influentials are finding that they must respond in some way as systemic pressures of drift *affect them*. Yet, they are not likely to abandon their own patron-client networks at local, regional, and national levels. Nor are they likely to abandon the corporatist structures dating from Getúlio Vargas's rule in the 1930s, structures that include state-dominated peak associations that have for so long blurred the public/private distinction in Brazil. This means, in turn, that it is highly unlikely that Brazilian elites can firmly institutionalize (a) a truly professional civil service, (b) truly pluralist group competition, or, for that matter, (c) truly competitive political parties *independent of these personal networks and state-dominated structures.*

Given that Brazil's massive state apparatus dates to the 1930s, and given that power holders' and social influentials' patron-client networks antedate this, it is unlikely that Brazilian elites will institutionalize a resilient division of powers within the government itself. They are just as unlikely to institutionalize truly effective governmental regulation of powerful enterprises within civil society. The blurring of the public/private distinction has gone so far in Brazil that these policy options are impractical. Although commonplace in (early) Western democracies, these policy options are decidedly idealistic and utopian when considered in the context of Brazil's existing social infrastructure. And yet, Brazilian power holders and social influentials (or insurgents) can find some way to restrain *their own* fragmentation of meaning, and *their own* competition across patron-client networks. They can find a way of doing this, moreover, that takes into account their embeddedness within the permanent government of corporatist peak associations and the permanent social infrastructure of patron-client networks. They can establish *social bases* of some kind that permit *them* to recognize direction and drift – even as they themselves continue to compete in their own subjective interests across a permanently blurred public/private distinction.

To this end, institutions and norms of internal procedural restraint are available to them *for their own self-interested, strategic purposes.* Brazilian power holders and social influentials may introduce internal procedural restraints on purposely arbitrary exercises of collective power by government, or else by "private" enterprises within civil society (including peak associations), as *social duties that, at first, they share (and sanction) only among themselves.* They may institutionalize these restraints in order to protect *themselves,* as they continue to compete across their patron-client networks. They may fail to extend these restraints to protect others, either from governmental control and arbitrariness or from corporate control and arbitrariness across Brazil's civil society.[15]

Any move by Brazilian power holders and social influentials to institutionalize internal procedural restraints on purposeful arbitrariness, even if only to protect themselves, would be a voluntaristic undertaking consistent with the theory of societal constitutionalism. Although admittedly a small step in itself, the public/private distinction in Brazil is so blurred that social scientists seeking unambiguous evidence of a shift to a market economy (liberalization) or a liberal state (democratization) in any sense familiar to Westerners are unlikely to find it.[16] The theory of societal constitutionalism may assist social scientists studying Latin America's largest economic and political system precisely because it is not a theory of Western democratization or liberalization. It is also not a theory of egalitarianism, nor, certainly, a theory of elite magnanimity. It is rather a theory that addresses when interest competition is being restrained in any way that remains consistent with a nonauthoritarian *direction* of social change, and with heterogeneous actors' and competing groups' possible social integration. The first steps taken in this direction may well be small, but they are significant nonetheless.

Second step: internal procedural restraints as voluntaristic action. Internal procedural restraints on purposeful arbitrariness are generalizable *qualities* in social life. Yet, they are procedural mediations rather than more directly substantive. The discussion of Fuller's legal theory demonstrated that these analytically distinct qualities are irreducible to any nonauthoritarian direction of social change under modern conditions. Yet, their irreducibility and generalizability *in principle* does not explain why they are found *in practice* within modern nation-states. Nor does it rule out the possibility that actors may place these restraints *first on "private" enterprises within selected sectors or industries of a civil society rather than on government.*

The significance of the second step for comparative research is to emphasize that systemic pressures of social change do *not* improve the likelihood that power holders and social influentials (or insurgents) will in fact extend internal procedural restraints either (a) from government to civil society or (b) from civil society to government. Systemic pressures do not improve the likelihood of the first extension within Western democracies, nor would they improve the likelihood of the second extension within Brazil or any other nation-state that happened to institutionalize these restraints first in civil society. The significance of this second step may be elaborated in three ways:

> First, even the continued presence of internal procedural restraints on government is an intrinsically contingent or voluntaristic project. It, too, is never systemically overdetermined – even within Western democracies.
>
> Second, yet internal procedural restraints are indeed to be found within a great many modern nation-states, Western and non-Western alike. This is the case not *because* these restraints are generalizable qualities, in principle, but because they remain attractive to actors *by default,* in practice: Whenever power holders and social influentials (or insurgents) wish to institutionalize resilient *normative* restraints on purposeful arbitrariness, more practicable alternatives are not available to them as *their* own subjective interests become more heterogeneous and *their* sites of employment become more functionally differentiated.
>
> Third, collegial formations proper revolve around qualities that are generalizable in principle. But the presence of collegial formations

unlike the presence of internal procedural restraints alone, never attracts the attention of heterogeneous actors and competing groups by default of practicable alternatives. Quite to the contrary, these formations suffered a rather sudden decline *within Western civil societies* during the mid-nineteenth century, even as internal procedural restraints on arbitrary government remained in place (at least within Great Britain and the United States, not within France or Germany). Systemic pressures today have by no means reduced the possibility of another collapse of collegial formations within Western civil societies.

The contingency of internal procedural restraints on government. The likelihood that heterogeneous actors and competing groups will institutionalize internal procedural restraints *on arbitrary government* has not improved over the years. The systemic pressures that clearly improved the likelihood of actors institutionalizing first economic markets and then political markets, for instance, did not simultaneously improve the likelihood of this.[17] This may be said with the same certainty in reference to seventeenth-century England, as in reference to (a) the American colonies of the late eighteenth century, (b) France, Italy, Germany, and then Scandinavia in the early twentieth century, and (c) the Iberian Peninsula and Latin America in the late twentieth century. Heterogeneous actors' and competing groups' institutionalization of the threshold of interpretability on positive laws has always been, and remains today, a strictly voluntaristic project rather than becoming either more rational or more habitual.

Indeed, it must be kept in mind that Western governments today encroach against this threshold quite often. Their encroachments largely are ignored by social scientists because the latter emphasize the significance of pluralist politics or peak associations' "intermediation," and downplay the significance of all normative restraints (chapter 4).[18] Yet, current encroachments may well extend and intensify rapidly under conditions of economic crisis. Systemic pressures in the late twentieth century do not somehow reduce the likelihood of this happening. Quite to the contrary, the continued integrity of threshold restraints on government is, if anything, increasingly jeopardized by the drift of social change – unless collegial formations are firmly institutionalized within a civil society to counterbalance this drift with direction.

What is intriguing to consider is that social scientists may well find empirical evidence of increasing *failures* to institutionalize internal procedural restraints *on government* even as they find empirical evidence of two other developments instead. On the one hand, social influentials within an Eastern or Third World nation-state might fail immediately to institutionalize internal procedural restraints on government and yet institutionalize these same voluntaristic restraints on (or within) selected sectors, industries, and organizations *of their civil society.* As examples, they may institutionalize the integrity of the research divisions of private or state-run corporations within a particular industry. Or else they may institutionalize the integrity of university departments or, for that matter, artistic networks or deliberative bodies controlling prestigious exhibitions or publications.[19] Only at a much later date, if ever, may these or other social influentials successfully pressure policymakers to institutionalize the same voluntaristic restraints on agencies of government themselves. As examples, they may move internal procedural restraints to bureaus of the secret police, to particular offices of regulatory agencies, to caucuses of a ruling political party, or to the decision-making bodies of neocorporatist peak associations.[20]

On the other hand, encroachments by policymakers and specialized enforcers against internal procedural restraints on government may very well increase in frequency within a Western democracy. This may happen as either one of the following developments is taking place simultaneously: First, social influentials within the same nation-state may be endeavoring to extend these voluntaristic restraints to selected sectors, industries, or organizations of their civil society. Second, open elections, competing political parties, and broad first amendment freedoms might continue to be upheld rather than being suspended or restricted.

Where social influentials (or insurgents) first institutionalize internal procedural restraints within a modern nation-state – and, later, where power holders (or insurgents) first encroach against them – is very much an empirical issue. Comparativists have yet to explore methodically the rise and fall of internal procedural restraints, and yet this empirical issue begins to reveal whether direction or drift characterizes *social change.* At the very least, the methodical study of these shifts is as worthy a *sociological* undertaking in itself as the methodical study of organizations, social movements, patterns of stratification within economic and political marketplaces, welfare policies, "social closure," deviance, or, certainly, revolutions.

In short, the voluntaristic restraints on arbitrary government that are the hallmark of constitutional theory and practice may well be found outside the West. But they may be found in civil society, rather than where comparativists have been looking for them, oriented by the presupposition of exhausted possibilities. Similarly, many non-Western nation-states' pre- and postwar institutions and practices not only lack but fundamentally resist many of the substantive norms and social practices that comparativists associate with the social infrastructure of Western democratization and liberalization. As examples, social influentials within these nation-states may never assume a priori that: (a) individual actors ultimately possess "natural rights," whether first amendment freedoms in general or the right to own industrial capital in particular,[21] or that (b) policymakers (or social influentials themselves) ultimately are accountable to some distinct branch of government (or, certainly, to some "natural law" overarching a nation-state's positive laws).[22] Yet, these same influentials might well institutionalize internal procedural restraints within selected sectors of their civil societies regardless. Why they would do so has already been discussed in reference to Brazil, and this point may be restated in more general terms now.

The proliferation of internal procedural restraints by default. A more optimistic way of addressing the intrinsic voluntarism or contingency of extending internal procedural restraints from government to civil society comes into view with the Brazilian illustration. Common-law countries need neither promote nor impose their particular institutions and practices on the social influentials and policymakers of other nation-states. This is unnecessary precisely because there are no alternative, *substantive* norms of internal restraint, nor strategic restraints of any kind, available to social influentials and policymakers who wish to restrain purposeful arbitrariness *in their own subjective interests.*

Put differently, there are no internal substantive and strategic restraints on purposeful exercises of collective power that can be recognized in common by heterogeneous and competing social influentials as they are experiencing a breakdown in meaning and other manifestations of drift. There are no alternative internal restraints available to them which provide a social base on which they might recognize when purposeful exercises of collective power are becoming arbitrary. Even more clearly, substantive and strategic restraints fail to provide them with as secure a social base on which they might recognize when specific exercises of collective power are maintaining or extending their own possibilities for social integration.

Historical decline of collegial formations. As emphasized in chapter 8, actors exhibit fidelity to the threshold of interpretability of shared social duties whenever they maintain the integrity of the collegial form. But, again, the collegial form is never the most effective, efficient, democratic, or personal way of organizing heterogeneous actors and competing groups. Being voluntaristic, and thereby not rational, it fails to maximize efficient production, effective administration, or democratic participation. Being procedural, it is impersonal.[23]

Across the West in the mid-nineteenth century, including the United States and Great Britain, social influentials subordinated their fidelity to these threshold restraints and to this organizational form as they pursued both substantive and quantifiable ends more immediately. They abandoned existing collegial formations in civil society in favor of alternative organizational forms that were either more rational or more personal. Put more precisely, they abandoned the deliberative bodies of the "bourgeois public" that had emerged in the early eighteenth century *as liberalization and democratization were being extended.* Thus, this was a period marked by a significant historical shift from direction to drift under systemic pressures of change (but see note 24). Consider the following approaches to this period of decline:

(a) Weber codified this period in the very way that he approached what he called "collegiate bodies" in *Economy and Society,* a work written in the second decade of the twentieth century (1914–20: 271–82, 994–98, 1089–90). He treated these bodies as decidedly anachronistic holdovers from a premodern era. His working assumption throughout was that these bodies are nonrational and thereby incapable of surviving ongoing systemic pressures.

(b) Maurice Duverger (1951) chronicled this same period, albeit more indirectly, by tracing the contemporaneous rise of mass political parties. He explored how the latter affected not only voting patterns but also patterns of coalition formation within legislatures themselves. They thereby contributed to the waning political significance of government's deliberative bodies.

(c) Looking more directly and more methodically at the rise and decline of deliberative bodies within civil society, Habermas (1962) explored what he called the "bourgeois public." He studied the formally and informally organized deliberative bodies that landed and merchant middle classes established within coffee houses, salons, inns, and reading groups. These informal collegial formations were originally dedicated to criticism of the arts, but they soon moved to criticism of politics.

(d) Hannah Arendt (1951) turned Weber's argument on its head by emphasizing that what she called the "council system," a network of collegial formations across a civil society, is far from anachronistic in the twentieth century. She thought, in fact, that collegial formations might be resuscitated *outside* of the Western democracies, her exemplar being Hungary in the mid-1950s (see Sitton 1987 for discussion, and Sciulli 1990 on the councils' relationship to the theory of societal constitutionalism).

(e) A prominent American law review (*Yale Law Journal* 1988) devotes an issue to the fall of the "republican civic tradition" in the United States during this same historical period, and the subsequent rise of interest-group politics. The working assumption is that American pluralism today is casting the courts adrift, and that a return to republican principles of one kind or another is a possibility.

It is not by accident that the early nineteenth century marked the rise of mass political parties, beginning in the United States in the 1820s. Their rise set the stage for two subsequent, interrelated developments. The first was the emergence, by midcentury, of the party "machine." Dedicated to maximizing voter turnout, machines were organized in the patron-client form (and Latin American clientelism is often compared to American politics prior to the Progressive reforms). The second development, in turn, was the rise of reform politics by the late nineteenth and early twentieth century, as a reaction to the perceived corruption of party machines. These reforms essentially subordinated the machines' patron-client form to more rational and impersonal techniques of political mobilization and recruitment. On the one hand, democratization was extended by the direct election of senators and the steadily increasing use of primary elections rather than party caucuses for nominations. On the other hand, bureaucratization was extended by both a marked reduction in the offices subject to election (and party patronage) and a marked increase in those subject to civil service appointments.

The point, however, is that *the decline of collegial formations within civil society* antedated the rise of party machines as well as the subsequent reforms that continued into the 1960s. It does well to recall that when American political parties emerged in the 1820s, on a rising tide of Jacksonian democracy that so captivated Tocqueville, the framers were anxious and suspicious. They had been witnessing since 1789 the rise and rigidification of voting factions and interest coalitions *within* state legislatures and Congress. As these factions curried popular support, and the electorate steadily expanded, the most entrepreneurial leaders of these factions steadily developed the skills of "machine politics." Indeed, the period from the 1820s through the 1890s established the high-water mark of electoral participation in the United States (Chambers and Burnham 1969; Burnham 1970; Ladd 1970: chapter 4). Moreover, legislative rules at the time accommodated the rising power of political-party caucuses, both by allowing the latter to control legislative committee assignments and by institutionalizing a "strong Speaker" in the House of Representatives and state legislatures. After the 1890s, electoral participation steadily declined in the United States while industrialization and urbanization accelerated.[24]

On the Continent, the period from the 1820s through the 1890s was marked by national governments' increasing interest in steering their economies and their ongoing effort to develop the administrative capacity to do so. It was a period marked generally by a coupling of an ambivalent view of liberalization and democratization with a decidedly romantic view of science and technique (as exemplified by the writings of Comte and Marx). Both the ambivalence and the romanticism ended dramatically with World War I, the Soviet Revolution, and the Fascist and Nazi reactions; such an ending was presaged in the writings of Nietzsche, Michels, Weber, and Freud; Mosca and Pareto; and Sorel and Durkheim.

In short, the decline of the collegial form of "bourgeois" talking clubs in civil society antedated the rise not only of mass political parties in the United States and then in Europe, but also the rise of European and then American industrialization and urbanization. It was also coupled with a decline of the collegial form *within* European parliaments and American legislatures. All of these developments contributed, of course, to an ongoing fragmentation of meaning among social influentials and power holders. Their earlier sense of shared meaning had at one time rested rather securely on shared substantive beliefs within relatively stable social fabrics of preindustrial cities and communities (see chapter 10 on the allegory of the "constituent force").

As noted many times throughout this volume, manifestations of rationalization such as the fragmentation of meaning and functional differentiation could not then, and cannot today, be halted or reversed without authoritarianism *invariably* resulting. The only practicable, nonauthoritarian response to systemic pressures of rationalization, whether historically or today, is for social influentials (or insurgents) to counterbalance drift by institutionalizing a normative direction that is both voluntaristic and procedural. To attempt to institutionalize substantive values of preindustrial cities and communities is invariably to extend and intensify mechanisms of social control, and thereby to increase a nation-state's susceptibility to authoritarianism. The point of this section is to illustrate that the decline of deliberative bodies that occurred across Western civil societies in the mid-nineteenth century under systemic pressures of social change might well be repeated in the late twentieth century. It might occur, for instance, under the even greater systemic pressures of international economic, political, and cultural competition. The fall of the Berlin wall, and the welcomed opening of the former Eastern bloc, does not somehow ameliorate the impact of these systemic pressures. It instead extends their most immediate impact from West to East, without reducing their intensity within the West itself.

Third step: external procedural restraints as voluntaristic action. Whenever the meaning of shared social duties (or of research findings or professional practice) becomes unclear to the actors affected, whenever meaning is typically contested rather than typically assumed, two outcomes are possible. First, the actors involved may be increasingly subjected to formal rather than informal social controls, including stricter chains of command or harsher (or more alluring) material sanctions (Olson 1965; Hechter 1987). Or, second, actors' voluntaristic deliberations over meaning may be moved closer to the center of their *everday* concerns. Actors' deliberations may be institutionalized more firmly at selected sites that are protected "artificially" from actors' more immediately rational and nonrational behavior.

During initial moments of confusion over meaning, moments of contestation and ad hoc deliberation, actors experience great personal stress and anxiety. After all, their personal responsibilities for securing shared meaning, and for sustaining deliberation, increase dramatically. Their everyday lives are disrupted. Whether they know it or not, moreover, they are endeavoring to institutionalize a voluntaristic direction of social change that runs quite counter to enormous systemic pressures of drift. As obstacles to their success multiply, their stress and anxiety escalate.

During these moments, actors within particular divisions of social networks or complex social enterprises *may* adopt the collegial form of organization *precisely in order to reduce their personal stress and anxiety.* Once again, this is a choice that actors may make strictly in their own self-interest, and not out of any sense of altruism or magnanimity. For actors to remain devoted *personally* to securing shared meaning is for them to bear an inordinately burdensome responsibility. It is much easier for them to accede at some point to decrees, material incentives, or personal loyalties than to bear this burden. For any set of *heterogeneous* actors and *competing* groups to bear this burden outside of forms and procedures mediating their own interest competition within economic and political marketplaces is unthinkable.[25]

As a practicable alternative, the same actors and groups, facing the same obstacles, may endeavor to *institutionalize* deliberation over worldly qualities and to *institutionalize* their own shared social duties within deliberative bodies. They may approach the problem, that is, in terms of establishing and maintaining shared meaning more indirectly, *and more impersonally.* This is precisely why these actors and groups may adopt the collegial form of organization – at least within selected, "protected" arenas of a civil society. This is also why they may agree to sanction by law actors' ongoing fidelity to these formations' distinctive procedural threshold and concomitant voluntaristic orientation. Yet, this move has yet to be taken within any modern nation-state.

What happens if actors within any social network or complex enterprise remain convinced that the integrity of their own deliberations is less significant, and less rewarding personally, than their strategic competition within alternative organizational forms? What happens if they prefer personally to maximize the effectiveness of administration, the efficiency of production, the scope of democratic participation, or the loyalty of personal networks? At such moments, the voluntaristic project of institutionalizing the collegial form of organization remains for them an unnecessary *personal* burden. It is a burden that they will refuse to bear. This voluntaristic project will not seem sensible, let alone practicable.

These two choices convey the significance of the third step for comparative research: The sheer presence of collegial formations institutionalizes a voluntaristic orientation of external procedural restraint on *how* heterogeneous actors and competing groups within civil society are permitted institutionally to compete strategically (irrespective of whether the economy in question is market- or state-dominated). It also institutionalizes such restraints on *how* they are permitted institutionally to rationalize administration, mobilize voters, and cultivate loyalties within personal networks (again, irrespective of whether any of the enterprises involved are "private" or state-controlled). Because Western democracies have taken neither the second step of extending internal procedural restraints from government to civil society, nor this third step of institutionalizing external procedural restraints by extending collegial formations as a matter of public policy, the theory of societal constitutionalism reveals that comparativists currently lack a rationale, conceptual or empirical, for operating with the presupposition of exhausted possibilities. They lack a rationale for employing concepts that suggest directly or indirectly that Western social orders rest primarily, or to any great extent at all, on heterogeneous actors' and competing groups' possible social integration rather than on their demonstrable social control. Once this is exposed as a strictly empirical issue, it can no longer be presupposed in lieu of being studied – even if the former tack has long been supported (and encouraged) by the conventional wisdom of the social sciences.

It *may* turn out, for instance, that leaders within Western democracies are indeed merely more sophisticated than their counterparts in the Third World and the East in employing purposeful mechanisms of social control and in benefiting from systemic and informal mechanisms. Conflict theorists insist that this is the case, but they fail to demonstrate this empirically. Clearly, Western leaders currently have enormous material resources at their disposal. They can readily substitute both positive and negative economic sanctions for cruder, and ultimately more costly, formal social controls. This is precisely why the resource mobilization approach to social movements is so cogent, and why rational-choice theory in sociology or public-choice theory in political science will never wane. This may also be why social influentials and power holders in the East and Third World are so amenable today to adopting many Western democratic institutions and practices: They are increasingly appreciating that the latter rest on far less costly mechanisms of social control (see chapter 8, note 7).

Some of the specific respects in which the theory of societal constitutionalism directly challenges traditions of Western constitutionalism and liberalism (as well as social-democratic practice) are addressed in the next two chapters. Because this theory instructs social scientists to seek *evidence* of the presence of collegial formations, and thereby of resilient external procedural restraints, it remains critically distanced from existing institutions and practices of Western democracies.[26] The continued integrity of collegial formations is as little supported by these institutions and practices, in and of themselves, as it is by systemic pressures of social change. The *possibility* of heterogeneous actors and competing groups linking the threshold of interpretability of shared social duties with the only organizational form that institutionalizes external procedural restraints on drift hinges at some point on whether this becomes a matter of public (or corporate) policy.[27]

9.3. Institutionalizing collegial formations as public policy

9.3.1. A coming challenge to the West?

Beyond instructing social scientists to monitor actors' fidelity to the threshold of interpretability, the theory of societal constitutionalism also instructs them to monitor whether and when power holders uphold the integrity of collegial formations as a matter of public policy. *What alone casts this public policy as unusual today is that it exceeds the scope of application of the presupposition of exhausted possibilities.* It is not merely conceivable but rather eminently practicable for a nation-state in the East or "advanced" Third World (e.g. Brazil, Argentina, Cuba, South Korea, Taiwan, or India) to "leap ahead" of Western democratic institutions and practices by *introducing* collegial formations into more and more sectors, industries, and organizations of its civil society *as a matter of public policy.* To be sure, such a public policy might well be coupled, in practice, with policies of democratization or liberalization designed to institutionalize robust competition within political and economic marketplaces. But it need not be. Indeed, such *coupling* is not likely to be in evidence where national marketplaces already are constricted by peak associations and patron-client networks (e.g. Brazil and Mexico, to say nothing of Cuba's formal controls). Moreover, such coupling may not prove successful in Eastern Europe as the costs and disruptions involved in institutionalizing unmediated marketplaces begin to be experienced. Again, even to entertain the empirical issue of the coupling or decoupling of (a) a public policy of introducing or maintaining collegial formations and (b) a public policy of democratization and liberalization is already to move beyond the presupposition of exhausted possibilities.

Because the collegial form's voluntaristic orientation is both nonrational and nondemocratic, it may be introduced into a civil society as a matter of public policy in the absence of policies of liberalization or democratization.

The question of whether this voluntaristic orientation is in evidence within any particular civil society, then, is independent of the question of whether a nation-state's economy is market-based or state-controlled, or whether its political marketplace is pluralist or neocorporatist. It is illegitimate for social scientists' very concepts to obfuscate the significance of any modern nation-state adopting the former public policy. Indeed, greater decoupling might very well *prove attractive to citizens within Western democracies themselves,* as the disruptions of unmediated liberalization accumulate, and as unmediated democratization becomes more a matter of ascriptive and functional group representation than a matter of individual citizenship.

Western democracies today by no means provide the majority of their citizens with the best of all possible worlds, either material or normative. Notwithstanding the comforting ideology of the presupposition of exhausted possibilities and liberalism's traditional complacency and optimism, Western democracies are no more insulated from the positive challenges posed by viable alternatives than they are from the negative challenges posed by the Weberian Dilemma. Quite to the contrary, the emergence of a nonauthoritarian alternative either inside or outside of the West that decouples the institutionalization of collegial formations from (now unmediated) liberalization may well stimulate great disaffection among actors *within all other Western democracies.* Such an alternative can be said to emerge: First, once a modern nation-state offers the vast majority of its citizens not more consumer goods or creature comforts but instead greater protection from everyday contingencies, including, as examples, the anxieties attending possible economic hardships, general health care and environmental safety, and fear of violent crime.[28] Second, once a modern nation-state offers the vast majority of its citizens more certain protection from breakdowns of "meaning" by purposefully expanding their *possibilities* for social integration at their various sites of employment. In the face of such a practicable alternative, actors' disaffection within existing Western democracies may escalate so suddenly that survey researchers might indeed be startled.

9.3.2. Two policy options

Many social controls are enforced by law within nonauthoritarian and authoritarian nation-states alike. Certain actors, including police officers, are mandated by law to bear the responsibility for enforcement, and encroachments are formally sanctioned by courts and other bodies (see Berman 1972 on postwar Soviet alternatives). What is critical in all of this is that these responsibilities are not left to voluntary associations (such as bar associations) or professions (such the legal profession); encroachments are not left to informal sanctions. What the theory of societal constitutionalism reveals is that the responsibility for maintaining and extending heterogeneous actors' and competing groups' possibilities for social integration can no longer be left to voluntary associations and professions today. Similarly, encroachments against sites of possible social integration cannot be left to informal sanctions within civil society. Given pressures of drift, this responsibility and these sanctions must be mandated by law or else actors' prospects for social integration can be expected to decline. *If the institutionalization of collegial formations is not mandated by law in particular, then systemic pressures yield fewer possibilities for social integration. In this way, the social infrastructure underlying a nonauthoritarian direction of social change is steadily eroded.* Still, social influentials and power holders (or insurgents) might adopt such a public policy either indirectly or directly, and each of these possibilities may be considered in turn.

- *Extending substantive restraints: from religious to secular "protected spheres."* An indirect way of adopting such a public policy is for enterprises performing certain functions or tasks within a civil society to be explicitly protected by statute or constitutional provision from immediate interest competition within economic and political marketplaces – irrespective of the organizational forms that actors within these enterprises adopt. The historical separation of church and state is an instructive example of this, as one particular manifestation of the public/private distinction. Yet, it is otherwise not consistent with the theory of societal constitutionalism. Within multireligious nation-states, the church/state distinction is more consistent with mechanisms of social control, however benign, than with *heterogeneous* actors' and *competing* groups' possibilities for social integration.[29]

By placing religious enterprises of any and all kinds into a *legally* sanctioned "protected sphere" of civil society, the state in essence buffers these enterprises "artificially" from all other spheres' more "natural condition," that of immediate competition within economic and political marketplaces. *This is a voluntaristic public policy* even as it results in protecting enterprises and arenas of nonrational action. Indeed, the state often subsidizes these enterprises at taxpayers' expense, whether indirectly, by granting them tax-free status, or more directly, by paying clerics' salaries as civil servants (see Popenoe 1988 on Sweden). Still, a voluntaristic public policy cannot ensure that these nonrational enterprises will in fact wield moral authority. Whether increasing numbers of churchgoers become disaffected, and at some point no longer believe that the clerics and churches being legally protected wield moral authority – as opposed to political influence or economic patronage – is a matter that, ultimately, the state can neither prevent (in the West) nor promote (in the former Eastern bloc).

The principle of a legally sanctioned "protected sphere" may be extended, in practice, to cover enterprises performing any number of identifiable functions, including many of more direct concern to the theory of societal constitutionalism. Enterprises dedicated to quite secular pursuits might be defined by statute, or in constitutional provision, as comprising such a sphere. Indeed, this is already the case in many civil-law countries on the Continent where, as examples, the state buffers labor unions or trade associations from immediate economic and even political competition (e.g. the chapters in Streeck and Schmitter 1985 survey the Continent). In Japan, corporations have more or less formalized an "internal labor market" into which loyal employees are promoted, another sphere artificially protected from immediate pressures of competition in the economic marketplace. In the United States, dominant firms in expanding markets establish similar internal labor markets, albeit less consistently so (Hechter 1987: 141–3). More importantly for present purposes, this practice of "artificial protection" could be extended to include deliberative bodies within modern civil societies as well as professional associations and sites of professionals' practice within corporations, universities, hospitals, artistic networks, and elsewhere.

As is the case with legally protected religious bodies, and with corporations' internal labor markets, some nation-states also buffer certain social and cultural enterprises from immediate competition within economic and political marketplaces as a matter of public policy. These include enterprises dedicated to the arts, architectural preservation, environmental protection, rehabilitation of the handicapped, and, for that matter, certain types of schooling and day care. But whether actors are actually integrated rather than controlled within any of these legally protected enterprises is also a matter that, ultimately, the state cannot guarantee *in this way* (also see chapter 11, pages 257–8 on moral authorities). It cannot guarantee this simply by declaring that these enterprises comprise a legally "protected sphere." It can only guarantee this by moving to the next step: ensuring legally that enterprises of deliberation and professional practice adopt and then maintain a particular form of organization in order to qualify for inclusion within a "protected sphere." This moves the discussion, however, away from a public policy that *may* contribute indirectly to the theory of societal constitutionalism. It moves the discussion to a public policy that directly institutionalizes heterogeneous actors' and competing groups' possibilities for social integration at their various sites of employment.

Extending procedural restraints: from government to civil society. Public policies within Western democracies currently permit and, for that matter, encourage (a) legislators and public administrators to be lobbied by competing interests, (b) judges to be influenced by interested parties (through amici curiae briefs), and (c) leaders of enterprises within legally protected spheres to be influenced by their clients and patrons. None of this institutionalizes the "rule of law." Quite to the contrary, these policies extend the bastard pragmatism of interest competition from markets, legislatures, and administrative agencies to the courts and then to "protected spheres" within civil society.[30] When deliberators and professionals alter their decisions because interested parties have mobilized, or because they are wary of being sued for malpractice, rather than because they anticipate how peers would likely evaluate their decisions in anonymous review, bastard pragmatism has been extended, not the rule of law. The rule of law proper is extended when the integrity of the threshold of interpretability of shared social duties is legally sanctioned within appropriate protected spheres as a matter of public policy. It is extended when internal procedural restraints are established and maintained by law anywhere within a civil society.

But consider this distinction between institutionalizing bastard pragmatism and institutionalizing the rule of law from a different angle. If interest competition were extended by law to the self-governance of protected spheres in civil society, then *neither* purposefully nor inadvertently arbitrary exercises of collective power would be intrinsically restrained. Neither would be restrained *even as* "liberalization" and "democratization" were being extended successfully from the economy and government to once protected spheres of civil society. For good reason, Weber treated democratization in particular as more a "leveling" of the governed than as a significant restraint on drift. For the same good reason, Buchanan today remains an anxious Hobbesian rather than becoming a complacent Lockean.

What is important to keep in mind is that as long as actors' and groups' *behavior* exhibits fidelity to the threshold restraints, then, whatever else their behavior might entail in substance, observing social scientists cannot legitimately *reduce* it to interests that are strictly subjective and particular. Quite to the contrary, their behavior remains consistent with *intersubjectively* recognized and understood social duties, even as it otherwise remains competitive and at times conflictual. Moreover, actors' and groups' competition and occasional conflicts may be classified as a public good (Samuelson), social capital (James Coleman), communitarian (Selznick), or a noncommodity value (Stewart).[31]

Historically, a democratic franchise, regular elections, and competing political parties all emerged as alternatives to the nonrational rituals and external substantive restraints of premodern societies (chapter 10). These institutions *replaced* the latter with new rituals. The new rituals were both rational and procedural rather than nonrational and substantive. At best, the interests in civil society that the new rituals protect place strictly strategic restraints on purposeful exercises of collective power alone. They fail to distinguish arbitrary exercises from innovative ones. More importantly for present purposes, modernity's rational, procedural rituals historically undermined and replaced the informal collegial formations of the early "bourgeois public realm." And any set of collegial formations institutionalizes external (voluntaristic) procedural restraints on all manifestations of rationalization, *including* unmediated liberalization and democratization.

When the democratic franchise, regular elections, and competing political parties are compared exclusively to the external substantive restraints once posed by nonrational rituals and traditions, the former institutions appear *intrinsically* liberating or emancipatory. However, when the rational, procedural rituals that they institutionalize are compared to the voluntaristic procedures institutionalized by collegial formations, everything suddenly appears in a different light. The impact of the former institutions now appears more ambivalent than one-sidedly progressive. Indeed, the great strength of Habermas's study of the early bourgeois public sphere is that it explores this ambivalence: These early talking clubs excluded the working classes, and yet they were nonetheless critical deliberative bodies; mass political parties included the working classes, and yet they were from the start available for apologetics – and worse.

Still, Habermas fails to distinguish organizational forms methodically. He fails to specify a procedural threshold of restraint irreducible to a nonauthoritarian direction of social change and also distinct from the new procedures that simultaneously replaced both the bourgeois public realm and nonrational traditions. Because he sees that the new rituals are more manipulative and controlling than critical and emancipatory, he tries desperately, and fails, to discover some alternative. But he cannot say much more about the new rituals even today other than to note, unsurprisingly, that they are at odds with the ideal speech situation (Habermas 1989). What Habermas finds is that as the working class struggled to broaden the franchise, the public sphere's distinctively critical qualities steadily gave way to the strategic mobilization of electoral majorities within mass political organizations. The coffee houses, salons, reading societies, and other informal deliberative bodies of the bourgeois public sphere gave way to the political "machine." "Public opinion" became more passive and acclamatory than active and critical.

Putting this differently, wherever democratization is institutionalized in response to interest competition, social time and social space are subordinated to the drift of rationalization.[32] Because none of the Western democracies maintains the integrity of the collegial form within their civil societies as a matter of public policy, all existing "protected spheres" are based on function or task rather than being tied as well to organizational form. As a result, these spheres may restrain governmental agencies and social enterprises from acceding immediately to drift. But they do not contribute by their sheer presence to heterogeneous actors' and competing groups' possible social integration.

What does it mean, in practice, when electoral majorities acclaim manifestations of drift? Looked at in the most positive light, and thereby most narrowly, they legitimate particular leaders' claims to hold public offices (again, Charles Anderson discusses why this is often not the case in Latin America). They also pose a rational, procedural restraint – the possibility of losing reelection – on a rather small set of power holders: public officials. Yet, elections were substituted historically for the *external* substantive restraints that traditions (including natural law) had once placed not only on absolute monarchy but also on *all other* power holders and social influentials affiliated with the court, *and thereby on drift itself.* Unlike the rigidity of external substantive restraints, the great appeal of the new rituals for an emerging landed and commercial bourgeoisie was that the *substantive outcomes* of rational procedures are not merely quantifiable but also eminently flexible, negotiable, and reversible: Particular office-holders might be changed in the next election, and particular public policies as well.

Looked at more broadly, once again everything appears more ambivalent. Elected officials have every reason to hypostatize their "popular mandate" to rule, and to encroach against the threshold of interpretability as well as the collegial form, as they accommodate competing interests.[33] In this respect, the new rituals prove to be too flexible (cf. Luhmann 1990). Their flexibility means that they are potentially manipulative and controlling, not intrinsically integrative.[34] By contrast, the threshold of interpretability might be extended by introducing collegial formations into those sectors, industries, and organizations of a civil society in which this form of organization is possibly appropriate. These areas would not include, as examples, those containing mass political parties or other electoral majorities, those containing labor unions whose members are tied to primary and secondary sectors of the economy dedicated instrumentally to attaining quantitative ends, or, for that matter, those containing elite occupations on Wall Street and elsewhere that are dedicated to the same means and ends.

9.3.2. External procedural restraints and "wasted" time and space

The threshold of interpretability may be extended quite dramatically beyond government's deliberative bodies into civil society. This may be done by extending these restraints from covering positive laws to covering shared social duties being sanctioned within any social enterprise. The ranges of expectations of acceptable behavior typically acknowledged by actors within social enterprises are part of the shared social duties in question. These ranges, too, can be kept consistent with the collegial form of organization and its threshold restraints. In this way, social influentials (or enlightened insurgents) within any modern nation-state, and not simply Western democracies, may institutionalize the time and space that heterogeneous actors and competing groups need in order to respond to the Weberian Dilemma collectively.[35] They may institutionalize deliberative bodies, networks of interpretation, and a great diversity of self-regulating "protected spheres." Together, these social units mediate even inadvertently arbitrary responses to systemic pressures, and they do so by their sheer presence within a civil society.

Thus, *both* nonrational traditions historically and voluntaristic collegial formations today *elevate* time and space above the drift of unmediated liberalization and democratization. The point of enforcing the integrity of collegial formations as a matter of public policy is that such time and space are no longer elevated habitually or ritualistically. The rational procedures institutionalized as rituals of liberalization and democratization, in turn, were never designed to support or extend "protected spheres" within civil society, and thereby to elevate social time and social space above drift.

The external procedural restraints institutionalized by collegial formations both support, and are supported by, the presence of other "protected spheres" within a civil society. Protected from immediate interest competition within economic and political marketplaces, all of these social units are permitted institutionally to "waste" time and space. Ironically, to the extent that more traditional principles of governmental constitutionalism, such as the division of powers or actors' "natural rights," are hypostatized today as "sacred" restraints on electoral outcomes and interest competition, their strictly nonrational or symbolic quality comes to the fore. These principles have indeed become mere formalities. However revered they might remain in some quarters, they are today quite far removed, in practice, from affecting how collective power is exercised in everyday life within modern civil societies. This is particularly apparent within the neocorporatist policy making processes of Western Europe and Scandinavia today, but it holds true as well for the United States, Great Britain, and other common-law countries.[36]

A public policy of maintaining the integrity of collegial formations is *more practicable* today than any public policy designed somehow to preserve the integrity of the "sacred" division of powers, actors' "sacred" natural rights, and the "sacred" church/state and private/public distinctions (see chapter 11). But why would extending collegial formations across a civil society ever become a matter of public policy within a modern nation-state? Why would it ever become the organizational policy of any particular corporation, or, for that matter, of any particular professional association? Are there concrete interest groups within modern nation-states that already operate in terms of a *normative orientation* consistent with such a policy? Can researchers demonstrate that identifiable groups have an immediate *material interest* in supporting and promoting such a policy?

10. External restraints: prospects for reason and "tradition"

10.1. Why Parsons and Weber distorted restraints

10.1.1. Abandonment of reason

Like the social theorists whose works he helped elevate to the status of classics, Parsons assumed that when social scientists (or actors) describe a social action as "reasoned," rather than as rational and either instrumental or strategic, this is at best normative and at worst ideological (see also Stinchcombe 1986, even as he endeavors to distinguish reason from rationality). For Parsons and the classics alike, the concept of rational action is generalizable. It can credibly claim grounding against actors' subjective interests and normative relativism, as well as against the relativism of researchers' own value commitments. By contrast, the concept of reasoned social action cannot. As a result, there is no "Archimedean point" available to the social sciences other than the narrow norm of rational action.[1]

By labeling the concept of reasoned social action normative, however, social theorists leave social scientists with an enormous problem. Every researcher's description of social events ultimately contains, among other things, the researcher's attribution of subjective interests to actors and the researcher's own value commitments. As a result, the obstacles to recognizing shifts in the direction of social change other than those either toward or away from rationalization are seemingly insuperable. This is why Parsons thought that the "directionality" that social scientists might possibly recognize in common are shifts (a) toward or away from the narrow norm of rational action,[2] or (b) toward or away from realizing social scientists' own shared value-commitments. He could readily concede, moreover, that it would be rare indeed for social scientists to share any particular set of value-commitments. Yet, one example of this is the presupposition of exhausted possibilities. The latter may well be a collective prejudice, but it offers social scientists a standard of "directionality" that they (and many actors) seemingly share in common beyond the narrow norm of rational action. This is what makes this prejudice extremely valuable, and inordinately difficult to jettison, even in the face of mount-

214

ing evidence that it obfuscates more about contemporary social change than it illuminates.

There is something else about this prejudice that makes it difficult to jettison. In dismissing out of hand the possibility that any concept of reasoned social action can credibly claim grounding, social theorists simultaneously dismiss another possibility out of hand, and here rightly so. They dismiss the possibility that the social sciences can ever challenge actors' subjective interests and researchers' value-commitments on the basis of a substantive grounding or an "objective" standard of social change. It is clearly beyond the capabilities of the social sciences to locate any such grounding or standard.

At the same time, social theorists are going far beyond this when they dismiss the possibility that *any* concept of reasoned social action can credibly claim grounding. In acceding *conceptually* to the sovereignty of actors' subjective interests and to social scientists' own value relativism, they are failing to appreciate the many implications that their own conceptual frameworks have not only for theory construction but also for research and practice. In theory construction, one implication, of course, is that social theorists fail to leave their frameworks or theories *open conceptually*. They close them to the very possibility that any concept of reasoned social action might prove in time to credibly claim grounding and generalizability. Their seemingly plausible rationale in opting for conceptual closure rather than openness is that they endeavor to keep the social sciences: falsifiable (Popper 1934), value-neutral (Weber 1914–20; Merton 1949/1957), and conceptually consistent with actors' subjective interests and lived understandings (from Weber 1914–20 to Brennan and Buchanan 1985 and Hechter 1987). They wish to avoid any unnecessary risk of appending the prestige of the social sciences to *any* normative posture or ideology (Mannheim 1929).

The great irony is that social theorists' *decision* to close their theories and frameworks conceptually in this way *is itself decidedly normative*. It is not a decision tied to any scientific finding or tenet. After all, it is not scientific to decide a priori to close all conceptual frameworks to the possibility of particular concepts or analytical distinctions proving in time that they can credibly claim grounding. What *exactly* are the costs to scientific research of leaving this matter an open issue *in theory construction?* How are the prospects for value-neutral and falsifiable research in the social sciences jeopardized as a result of opting for conceptual openness and yet remaining critical of all concepts that purportedly isolate reasoned social action? Moreover, is it really intrinsically impossible to falsify a purportedly generalizable claim regarding whether certain social actions possibly contribute to reasoned social action or are demonstrably unreasoned? Conversely, if one insists that theories and frameworks are to be kept closed conceptually to all concepts of reasoned social action, how exactly does this a priori decision insulate the social sciences from ideology? Does it not instead place unnecessary obstacles in the path of possible empirical, falsifiable discoveries in the social sciences?

Still, the decision to close theories conceptually in this way neither explains nor justifies why social theorists also fail to appreciate the many implications that this decision carries *for research and social practice*. Its implications for research cannot be halted, for instance, at the point where social scientists (and actors) respect, and neutrally describe, differences in national traditions, subcultures, and lived social fabrics (see Winch 1958 as an exemplar, but also labeling theory and symbolic interactionism more generally). After all, once any existing tradition, subculture, or lived social fabric is disrupted or challenged, in practice, this in itself begins to push social scientists' conceptual relativism beyond equanimity. It can result in social scientists' outright nihilism or else in their respectful, neutral descriptions of social controls that are sophisticated and manipulative rather than blatantly coercive. What else can it mean when symbolic interactionists insist that *all* interests and norms are negotiable in *all* social orders, and thereby refuse to address the "normative" issue of distinguishing non-authoritarian from authoritarian social orders?

Relativism in the social sciences is readily pushed to nihilism, in practice, at the moment that any social movement becomes committed to "radical reform" of the larger social system of which it is a part. The Nazis' organizing slogan at local levels was not accidental in this regard: "To each his own" (Allen 1965). This slogan was designed precisely to test the limits of relativists' equanimity. It certainly beckons social scientists at least to consider that conceptual relativism may be incapable of resisting nihilism.[3] To be sure, during unusual historical periods, periods of sustained domestic tranquility, conceptual relativism appears resistant to this. The social sciences in particular then seem incapable of contributing to one-sidedness or harshness of any kind. But such periods are unusual. A few Western democracies have happened to experience such a period in the postwar era, but the vast majority of modern nation-states have been experiencing quite different domestic situations. Moreover, ethnic and religious competition, and moments of outright conflict, are increasing not only across the Third World (with the exception of Latin America) and the former Eastern bloc but also across the Western democracies as well. As regards Latin America, consider what the result would be of bringing symbolic interactionists' or rational-choice theorists' concepts to elites' competition over power resources and forms of government (chapter 9). If concepts are indeed value-neutral, should they not hold up equally well within any and all modern social contexts – including those charged by escalating tensions?

If the most basic conceptual decisions in the social sciences hold up best during unusual historical periods of sustained domestic tranquillity, it is likely that the social sciences will seem remarkably short-sighted during moments of domestic disruption, the very moments when they are called on for their richest insights (see pages 4–5). Even more ironically, the social theories and social research tied to these basic conceptual decisions are those that zealots may heartily embrace – as they longingly await *their* opportunities to negotiate some interests and norms of their own. The alternative to these decisions, however, is by no means to base social theory on any substantive standard or "objective interest." Nor, of course, is it to turn to any normative posture or ideology for instruction or "value orientation." It is simply to leave the social sciences open conceptually to the possibility that a concept of reasoned social action might prove in time to credibly claim grounding. It is to leave the social sciences open conceptually to the possibility that sharp *empirical* distinctions might be drawn in time between *types* of social orders, between concrete instances of integration and control, and between the ways in which interests and norms are negotiated within these types and in these instances.

One significant result of the alternative of conceptual openness is that it reveals that when relativists posit that all interests and norms are ultimately negotiable – in all "social orders," in all places and at all times – they abandon *any* possibility of distinguishing drift from direction. In defending an a priori decision of conceptual closure, they label any and all efforts to draw the latter distinction "normative" and "ideological." The problem today is that even the most basic conceptual distinction, the authoritarian/nonauthoritarian distinction, is dismissed out of hand as intrinsically normative and ideological. The presupposition of exhausted possibilities rests ultimately on domestic tranquility continuing in the Western democracies – for perpetuity – because, within a context of conceptual closure, it is as normative or ideological a stance as any other. Yet, does it make sense to assume a priori that within *non*authoritarian social orders, and within sites of heterogeneous actors' and competing groups' *possible* social integration, *all* interests and norms remain negotiable, either in principle or in practice? Equally importantly, does it make sense to assume a priori that the interests and norms distinctive to these orders and these sites are *reducible* to those characterizing the presupposition of exhausted possibilities? Ironically, *these two assumptions can themselves only be warranted or justified if they are based on a standard of reason that can credibly claim grounding or generalizability.*

10.1.2. Why Parsons's decision was particularly unfortunate

Parsons's decision to close his social theory conceptually in this way means, of course, that his social theory is, as it stands, ultimately closed to the central proposal of this volume: Institutions of external procedural restraint offer social scientists (and actors) a standard that can credibly claim grounding in distinguishing drift and direction. Parsons's decision is more disappointing than those by other classical or contemporary theorists, however, because among all major non-Marxist theorists of the twentieth century only Talcott Parsons built his social theory on *analytical distinctions*. Analytical distinctions are the contemporary social theorist's claim to conceptual grounding against the sovereignty of actors' subjective interests and researchers' value relativism (chapter 7). *All* analytical distinctions rest on a claim to irreducibility, and thereby to generalizability. *A social theorist has no reason to draw analytical distinctions other than to claim conceptual grounding.*

By contrast, ideal types or cruder generalizations rest solely on a claim to heuristic fruitfulness. Weber's ideal type of bureaucracy, for instance, portrays one particular set of analytical concepts as if they were permanently interrelated, in practice, as a single, irreducible social whole. In this way, it casts researchers' sights away from the analytical concepts comprising it and turns their sights toward what the whole illuminates. In portraying an undifferentiated whole, the question this and other ideal types raises is: Which existing social actions or social units most closely approach this idealized whole in practice? In this instance, which existing organizations in the world come closest to the ideal type of bureaucracy?

Analytical distinctions isolate the most irreducible building blocks of ideal types or cruder generalizations. As such, they cast researchers' sights away from the whole and toward its constituent parts. Given this focus, the question they raise is: Which analytical aspects may be found, in practice, within existing social actions or social units that have nothing to do with the ideal type, and which analytical aspects are indeed found exclusively within those actions and units that approach the ideal type? For instance, aspects of "disinterestedness" may be observed in actors' behavior not only within bureaucratic organizations but also within professional-client relationships. Fewer of these aspects are typically observed in parent-child relationships or in patron-client relationships. Instead, aspects of affect are more prominent.

Where ideal types orient research in terms of polarities – which existing organizations are becoming bureaucratic and which nonbureaucratic? – analytical distinctions orient research in terms of mixtures or gradations of aspects. Some mixtures are typically in evidence whereas others rarely appear: Are professional-client relationships always characterized by the prominence of aspects of "disinterestedness," either in comparative perspective or historically? When did parent-child relationships become marked by aspects of affect, either in the West, or, for example, in Brazil or Indonesia?

Are there limits, in practice, to the aspects of disinterestedness or those of affect that can be present or absent within any of these relationships?

Parsons quite consciously based his social theory on analytical concepts precisely because he wished to ground the findings of social science *research* against the relativism, and concomitant distortions, of findings informed by ideal types and cruder generalizations. He was convinced that only a framework of analytical concepts could accomplish this and thereby render knowledge in the social sciences cumulative. He was convinced that a comprehensive inventory of all analytical aspects to be found within any of the complex social events or social units under study can offer the social sciences their only opportunity to overcome the current incommensurability of their substantive findings. Incommensurability in the social sciences results from the different levels of analysis, ideal types, and generalizations that researchers employ. It also results from (a) differences in the subjective interests that social scientists attribute to the actors they are studying, and (b) differences in social scientists' own value-commitments. A framework of analytical concepts offers researchers an opportunity literally to "translate" all of their diverse findings into a single body of cumulative knowledge *despite all of these differences and many others* (Bershady 1973). It offers them a framework of concepts that claims to be irreducible, and thereby generalizable; a literal "common language" of translation.

What is so disappointing, therefore, about Parsons's decision to close his framework of concepts to the concept of reasoned social action is that this single decision in theory construction undermined everything else he was endeavoring to accomplish. On the one hand, it prevented him from ever considering the possibility that a framework of analytical concepts might address the Weberian Dilemma directly, and thereby allow him (and other social scientists) to jettison the ideology of the presupposition of exhausted possibilities. On the other, it also prevented him from seeing that *any* effort to escape relativism brings a "critical edge" into the social sciences. It pushes the social sciences closer to critical theory than to Lockean complacency (Sciulli and Gerstein 1985).[4]

Parsons never saw either of these points because, like the classics that he studied so methodically, and like his own students and exegetes both in his own day and today, his decision to opt for conceptual closure in theory construction simultaneously committed him to two decisions: First, he had to assume a priori that the concept of reasoned social action is substantive or "objective," and thereby intrinsically normative and ideological. Second, he had to close his social theory *conceptually* to any possibility of accommodating *any* concept of reasoned social action, *even if the latter turns out to be distinctively procedural and intersubjective.*

10.1.3 Bringing reasoned social action to comparative research

The theory of societal constitutionalism does not rest directly on a grounded standard of reasoned social action. It need not in order to differ considerably from Parsons's social theory as well as from other social theories that rest on theoretical frameworks already closed conceptually to this very possibility. The theory of societal constitutionalism differs from these social theories simply by remaining open *conceptually*. It differs simply by refusing to assume a priori that the concept of reasoned social action is substantive or "objective."

The conceptual openness of the theory of societal constitutionalism carries at least two implications.

> First, the theory of societal constitutionalism remains open conceptually to the possibility that some normative (that is, voluntaristic) *aspects* of existing or historical social actions and social units can credibly claim to contribute to reasoned social action even as they remain decidedly nonrational.

> Second, as a result, social scientists' *descriptions* of the social actions or social units that *contain these aspects* cannot legitimately be *reduced* to any combination of (a) researchers' attributions of actors' subjective interests, (b) researchers' own value commitments, and (c) researchers' evaluations of whether these actions and units are consistent with rationalization or the presupposition of exhausted possibilities. The impact that these actions and units have on the direction of social change may be demonstrated to transcend all of these factors.

The theory of societal constitutionalism posits that social scientists' descriptions of social actions and social units *containing voluntaristic procedural aspects* can, at the very least, be kept as generalizable as their current descriptions of those containing rational or instrumental aspects. The concepts that keep the theory of societal constitutionalism open to this possibility include: the distinct concept of voluntaristic action (chapter 7), the positively defined concept of collegial formations (chapter 8), and the analytical distinctions drawn between normative restraints (chapter 4) and heterogeneous actors' and competing groups' possible social integration and demonstrable social control (chapters 1–3).

The theory of societal constitutionalization is designed conceptually to accommodate a grounded standard of reasoned social action whenever this becomes available to the social sciences – as long as it is procedural rather than directly substantive. Unlike Parsons's social theory, as well as the diverse social theories of Niklas Luhmann, Jeffrey Alexander, Richard Münch, and others working broadly within the Parsonian tradition, this possibility is left open rather than closed a priori. Conceptual closure is what ultimately blocks these theorists from bringing a critical edge into neofunctionalist research. Lacking a critical edge, the latter ends up recapitulating one version or another of Lockean optimism and complacency, alongside those versions already provided by researchers employing the concepts of symbolic interactionism, rational-choice theory, and systems theory.

10.1.4. Distinguishing societal constitutionalism from other non-Marxist theories

It was pointed out in chapter 9 that the project of institutionalizing and then maintaining collegial formations is voluntaristic rather than either rational or more strictly nonrational and habitual. The success of this project is never overdetermined systemically. Yet, its relative success or failure within any modern nation-state, and within any sector of its civil society, provides social scientists with a generalizable standard that can support the direction/drift distinction.

Three points about societal constitutionalism's response to the sovereignty of actors' subjective interests and social scientists' value relativism demonstrate this standard's generalizability, and the credibility of its claim to conceptual grounding:

First, not all of the nation-states in which collegial formations are to be found, whether historically or today, are Western democracies.

Second, not all Western democracies have been, or are today, equally successful in meeting this standard of institutionalization. Some allow the integrity of collegial formations to be undermined inadvertently, and others undermine their integrity purposefully as well. Moreover, Western constitutional and liberal traditions fail to inform power holders and social influentials that collegial formations institutionalize external procedural restraints on drift.

Third, there is not a single nation-state today that either maintains or extends collegial formations within its civil society as a matter of public policy, and thereby institutionalizes external procedural restraints on drift.

These three points distinguish the theory of societal constitutionalism from: (a) the Europocentrism of the presupposition of exhausted possibilities; (b) the normative relativism and potential nihilism of Weberian ideal types; and (c) Parsons's unfortunate decision to close his social theory conceptually.

A public policy of maintaining and extending collegial formations is a voluntaristic project of institutionalizing a *public realm* or a *public sphere* proper *within a civil society.*[5] To draw attention to this in the last decade of the twentieth century is to draw attention to a *practicable alternative* to the earlier theory and practice of (a) the "bourgeois public sphere" of the Continent from the mid-eighteenth through the early nineteenth century (Habermas 1962), and (b) the "constituent force" of seventeenth-century England and eighteenth- and early nineteenth-century American colonies (Friedrich 1941, 1972, 1974). Against constitutional theorists and liberal theorists who even today operate on the basis of the empirical generalization that limited government is exclusively interrelated with the presence of a market economy (which drove Arendt 1951 to distraction by its illogic), the theory of societal constitutionalism operates on the basis of a quite different presupposition: It presupposes that heterogeneous actors' and competing groups' prospects for institutionalizing a public realm within civil society are neither invariably based on, nor at all restricted to, the historical experiences, socioeconomic conditions, governmental forms, and cultural traditions of existing Western democracies. Instead, these prospects are equally voluntaristic in any modern setting, and they are by no means impaired within modern nation-states that can be expected to retain an enormous administrative state and a relatively controlled economy (*Perestroika* notwithstanding, e.g. Battle 1988; Birman 1988; Rosefielde 1988). This point is elaborated momentarily.

10.1.5. From relativism to nihilism: theorists' complicity in drift

A problem that Parsons failed to address as a result of his decision to close his social theory to the concept of reasoned social action may be stated in the following way: When normative restraints on drift are approached conceptually as ultimately reducible to particular sets of subjective interests rather than as possibly reasoned, it is being assumed that they can only be maintained by mechanisms of social control, whether informal or formal. To follow Parsons and the classics in closing social theory conceptually in this way is to take two further steps by conceptual default: First, it is to assume that external *procedural* restraints on drift are ultimately inconsistent with heterogeneous actors' and competing groups' *possible* social integration. Second, it is to bracket the Weberian Dilemma from further discussion, including any effort to resolve it conceptually or, for that matter, any effort to demonstrate that it has been rendered irrelevant in practice.

If the implications of drift are pondered rather than bracketed, then a haunting, unyielding sense of pathos accompanies *the same decision* to close social theory to the concept of reasoned social action. This was the case with Weber, and it is the case today with Hayek and Buchanan.

Parsons was an optimist not because he was an American (although this probably helped), but because he failed to appreciate fully that this single decision in theory construction meant that he was acceding *conceptually* to the sovereignty of actors' subjective interests and researchers' value relativism. He failed to appreciate this, ironically, because his ongoing effort to escape normative relativism with analytical concepts was far more sustained than that by any other liberal theorist. The irony is that for all of the critical potential left latent within his analytical concepts, Parsons's decision in theory construction rendered his social theory *more* apologetic than Weber's and other liberals': *Like Weber, Parsons treated manipulation conceptually as both immutable and inescapable, but, unlike Weber, he labeled noncoercive social control "integration." This allowed him to convert Weber's pathos into an optimistic portrayal of the prospects for system "equilibrium" and "social order."* Today, Luhmann has carried this conversion to the point of assuming that systems operate on the basis of a natural identity of interests (1982, 1986, 1990).

As the literature review in chapter 2 makes clear, such apologetics are not unique to Talcott Parsons (or Niklas Luhmann). Many of Parsons's harshest critics are equally guilty of complicity in drift. His critics "reveal" that all normative restraints on actors' interests and negotiations are ultimately particular, and thereby unreasoned. Consider two respects in which this position results in complicity in drift. First, the specialized enforcers wielding formal mechanisms of social control cannot be expected to operate with any greater sophistication than the theorists and researchers studying their behavior.[6] Like the latter, the enforcers, too, find that it is very difficult to recognize which "protected spheres," if any, simultaneously restrain drift and contribute to heterogenous actors' and competing groups' possible social integration. It is an easy matter for them (and other actors) either to allow, or themselves to contribute to, inadvertent encroachments against such spheres. Put differently, enforcers cannot be expected by anyone, least of all by the social theorists who have already decided that the social sciences are to remain closed to the concept of reasoned social action, to take any special pains in maintaining the integrity of those particular spheres that are sites of actors' possible social integration. They may instead maintain other "protected spheres," those that contribute exclusively to actors' demonstrable social control (chapter 11).

Second, the heterogeneous actors and competing groups employed within the protected spheres that are sites of possible social integration find that they face an enormous obstacle under modern conditions of drift. As they restrain encroachments, and as they seek the support of social influentials and power holders to this end, *these efforts of normative restraint* appear – to actors and social scientists alike – to be particular, and thereby unreasoned. If they persist in these efforts, they run the risk of being seen as extending or intensifying social control rather than as endeavoring to protect the sites of (their own, or others') possible social integration.

The result of social theorists' and researchers' acceding conceptually to the sovereignty of actors' subjective interests and normative relativism, therefore, is by no means dispassionate or value-neutral observation of ongoing social events and existing social units. The result is rather the social sciences' complicity in drift. Shifts in the direction of social change are left undifferentiated conceptually, and thereby left literally unobserved and unresearched empirically. Enforcers (and actors) are never informed of the full implications of their actions by the social sciences (this paragraph specifies the point on pages 216–7).

This explains why social scientists find themselves at times facing the following situation: On the one hand, they become convinced personally that the quality of life of the actors they are studying is deteriorating, or clearly not improving, and yet quantitative indices of their material condition and of their subjective approval of their lived situation are either stable or improving. On the other hand, social scientists find that they lack the concepts with which to convert their personal conviction into falsifiable descriptions and explanations. Turning to social theory for assistance, they discover that non-Marxist theorists declare the entire issue of directionality to be off-limits conceptually, unredeemably "normative." By conceptual default, the whole matter is left to survey researchers, the reporters of record of actors' successful manipulation and control.

10.2. Are restraints on drift intrinsically unreasoned?

10.2.1. From Weber's pathos to Parsons's optimism: rendering "tradition" benign

The prospect of infusing external restraints on drift with political power or legal sanctions clearly troubled Parsons. The three reasons why it did unite him with Weber as the two most conceptually sophisticated non-Marxist social theorists of their respective generations:

First, neither Weber nor Parsons distinguished internal from external substantive restraints *conceptually*, even as both theorists clearly appreciated the great differences between resistance to arbitrary government and resistance to modernity itself.

Second, and more importantly, neither theorist distinguished external procedural restraints from external substantive restraints *conceptually*.

As a result, each failed to distinguish between voluntaristic directionality and traditionalism or substantive fundamentalism. Each also failed, of course, to explore methodically the relationship between internal and external *procedural* restraints.

Third, because neither theorist really distinguished the concept of voluntaristic action from nonrational or normative action, neither kept his social theory open to the possibility that certain normative social actions might credibly claim to contribute to reasoned social action.

Still, Parsons turned away from Weber's rather one-sided treatment of rationalization because he saw that it led to "entropy" (1937a: 752), and could not, in itself, account for the evidence of ongoing social order by mid-century. Far more methodically than Weber, Parsons explored the *substantive* normative restraints that continue to be found within modern societies. Rather than employing this terminology of restraints, however, he instead referred to norms, values, solidarity, morality, and the like. He was particularly interested in studying: kinship (1943; 1965; 1971b,c); race, ethnicity, and religion (1945, 1952b, 1958b, 1966c, 1969b, 1973b, 1974c, 1975c); community (1957); value commitments (1968b); and culture more generally (1972, 1976b, 1978b).

Because Parsons did not distinguish between procedural and substantive external restraints, nor between voluntaristic and nonrational action, he classified all of the topics just mentioned as, ultimately, manifestations of religion and tradition. He did so because he saw that all of them revolve around actors sustaining *shared substantive beliefs.* To be sure, Parsons treated all of these topics as complexes of analytical aspects amenable to comparative study rather than as manifestations of particular lived social fabrics tied to time and place. The problem that Parsons faced is that once substantive normative *aspects* are isolated analytically from the lived social fabrics in which they originated historically, *their patently unreasoned qualities come to the fore in stark relief.* Religious and traditional aspects are indeed substantive prejudices. The reasons why they happen to appear within any lived social fabric, in practice, are invariably particular rather than ever generalizable. Thus, these aspects may be placed into comparative perspective by being defined analytically as norms and values. But their appearance, in practice, cannot be generalized because they cannot be justified to *disbelieving* outsiders with reasons.

Weber's very concept of "substantive rationality" is his relativist substitute for the concept of reasoned social action. And this concept codifies the problem: *Substantive* restraints on drift are indistinguishable from prejudices, both in practice and conceptually.[7] Aside from collapsing the distinction between substantive and procedural restraints, and that between internal and external substantive restraints, Weber's concept does not permit any social theorist or researcher to specify what exactly is "rational" about any purported instance of *substantively* rational action (see Habermas 1981a for the best discussion of this problem). When residents in a neighborhood band together to resist commercialization, is this substantively rational or not? When executives in a corporation fail to organize either sales or research personnel most effectively, is this substantively rational or not?

Putting the problem more generally: Is there a single social theorist or researcher who has contributed to the vast Weber literature who directly or indirectly refutes the proposition that *any* purported instance of substantively rational action, in practice, is actually an instance of "substantively prejudiced action"? Why are there so few examples of substantive rationality in Weber's writings, and, surprisingly, even fewer in the Weber literature?[8] The fact of the matter is that no one has specified conceptually, nor illustrated with concrete examples, what is unambiguously rational about any purported instance of substantively rational action. This failure explains why Weber, and then Parsons, assumed that any effort to infuse external restraints of any kind with political power or legal sanctions is, respectively, "regressive" and "dedifferentiating." They shared this assumption because the only alternative to acceding to drift that they saw available to modern actors is some variant or another of substantive prejudice. Each tried desperately, and failed, to demonstrate that certain substantive prejudices are "more rational" than others.[9] With this, both the optimistic American and the pessimistic German ultimately fell victim to the ideology of the presupposition of exhausted possibilities.

10.2.2. Parsons's conceptual limitations and dilemma

Parsons failed to take three steps that would have pushed his framework of analytical concepts toward addressing the Weberian Dilemma directly and challenging the presupposition of exhausted possibilities:

> First, external *procedural* restraints may be infused with political power, without simultaneously imposing prejudices on "outsiders" or disbelievers. They may be infused with political power just as the rationalization of economic growth or the rationalization of law enforcement, as counterexamples, are infused with political power.
>
> Second, and relatedly, to infuse external procedural restraints with political power is not to shift social change from direction to drift, nor from possible social integration to demonstrable social control. As one example, this does not contribute intrinsically to shifting law enforce-

ment from routine discretion or selective enforcement to unmediated manipulation, control, and coercion.[10]

Third, even should law enforcement agencies (and other organizations) resort to discretion, and even should they extend formal mechanisms of social control to outright coercion, all of their actions remain consistent with heterogeneous actors' and competing groups' possible social integration *if* their actions remain consistent with external *procedural* restraints.

Rather than taking any of the steps, Parsons instead followed the classical social theorists in failing to distinguish external procedural restraints conceptually. Like them, he too collapsed these norms into more general categories of solidarity, morality, tradition, religion, and the "sacred." The problem with all of the latter categories is that they may be reduced by critics to strictly nonrational social action – just like Weber's oxymoron, substantive rationality. All of these categories address external substantive restraints at the very core of lived social fabrics, and they collapse into the latter the external procedural restraints found, in practice, only within certain traditions and lived social fabrics.

Parsons's failure to draw these analytical distinctions accounts for his lifelong interest in exploring how cultural values and nonrational social solidarities of all kinds maintain "equilibrium" and "social order." He lacked the concepts to address *explicitly* the problem of *non*authoritarian social order in particular (Sciulli 1988b). Late in his career, for instance, he expected middle-class professionals to bear a "fiduciary responsibility" for "pattern-maintenance." In other words, he expected professionals to become increasingly responsible for maintaining social order *within every modern nation-state without exception.* He expected this to occur, moreover, despite the ongoing fragmentation of meaning affecting professionals in the same ways that it affects all other actors.

Aside from the unlikelihood of either expectation's being realized, in practice, each also lacks conceptual support in Parsons's own social theory. Ultimately, his view of the professions illustrates the great weakness of retaining Weber's concept of substantive rationality instead of keeping a social theory open to the concept of reasoned social action. Just as the former concept can be rendered synonymous with substantive prejudices, so too Parsons's approach to professions cannot account for the possibility of *non*authoritarian social order in comparative perspective (see chapter 11, pages 251–4 for an alternative account of professionals' responsibility).

Still, Parsons's approach to professions raises a legitimate problem. Since he lacked the conceptual apparatus to resolve it directly, this problem is fittingly labeled the Parsonian Dilemma: How is it that professionals, whether acting independently or collectively, can recognize and understand the "meaning" of *substantive* norms of restraint *in common?* How is it that they can accomplish this despite: (a) their own increasing heterogeneity and increasing diversity in their patterns of primary socialization; (b) the increasing functional differentiation of their professional training and thereby of their secondary socialization; (c) the increasing functional differentiation of their sites of employment and thereby of their duties and aspirations; and, finally, (d) the increasing diversity of their styles of life, subjective interests, and substantive beliefs?[11]

10.3. Rethinking tradition: lived distinctiveness v. transferable qualities

10.3.1 Two conceptual possibilities exposed by Parsons's mature works

The discussion of the theory of societal constitutionalism to this point reveals two ways in which Parsons's treatments of norms and values might be significantly improved. First, quite distinctive social units – collegial formations – are for a variety of reasons becoming increasingly significant under modern conditions, at least in principle. Within *non*authoritarian nation-states, this is indeed the case in practice. Second, and equally importantly, Parsons's residual references to collegial formations, and then to procedural institutions and the law generally, provide an opening to an alternative way of thinking about his treatments of norms and values.

To Parsons's credit, he saw members of collegial formations (particularly within the United States) as bearing a fiduciary responsibility for somehow maintaining the integrity of national (and cultural) "traditions." The Parsonian Dilemma, however, results from his assumption that professionals would indeed bear this responsibility within all modern nation-states. This dilemma may now be traced specifically to Parsons's failure to relate this assumption to his treatment of traditions. On the one hand, he failed to account *conceptually* for why professionals can be expected to assume such an onerous fiduciary responsibility *in common*, despite systemic pressures to the contrary (chapter 8, note 16). Yet, on the other, he acknowledged that within common-law countries at least, *national traditions* cannot be reduced to *substantive* norms and institutions. These national traditions also include longstanding principles of governmental constitutionalism *as well as other analytical aspects of distinctively procedural norms and values.* This suggestion, presented by Parsons ever so tentatively, carries three important implications. Once developed, they move progressively beyond Parsons's writings:

> First, comparativists cannot legitimately treat all analytical aspects of all national (or subcultural) traditions as if they are exclusively substantive.
>
> Second, comparativists cannot treat all analytical aspects of "tradition" as if they are intrinsically *reducible* to the lived social fabrics within which they originated historically.[12]
>
> Third, professionals and other members of collegial formations may well institutionalize the external procedural restraints distinctive to *non*authoritarian social order, even as they simultaneously maintain this order's "traditions." They may accomplish this as long as the "traditions" involved contain voluntaristic procedures rather than being reducible to some combination of rational procedures and more immediately substantive qualities.

Parsons acknowledged the distinctiveness of procedural norms within certain national traditions, and in particular within those of Great Britain and the United States. But he failed to work this insight into his conceptual framework. It is precisely the procedural norms of any national tradition, both rational and voluntaristic, that can *possibly* claim generalizability, not the norms of its substantive core and lived social fabrics. It is the former analytical aspects of any national tradition, moreover, that are capable of being transfered overseas *without having to be imposed on "outsiders."* It is these analytical aspects, finally, that can credibly claim to contribute to reasoned social action rather than being reducible a priori to prejudices.

Indeed, these analytical aspects of tradition have been transfered historically to "alien" locales, short of imposition. They have been successfully detached, in practice, from *the substantive core and lived social fabrics of the national traditions within which they originated historically.* Still, it must be keep in mind that even as procedural norms include rational norms, such as those involved in advances of science and technology, only distinctively voluntaristic procedures are significant for the theory of societal constitutionalism.

10.3.2. Two conceptual developments beyond Parsons

Actors' *lived social fabrics* (or *Lebenswelt*) within any modern nation-state indeed revolve around particular sets of substantive norms (and material interests). The actors living *within* any particular fabric only pass these substantive norms to future generations through relatively successful primary socialization. Many of these substantive norms may be lost from actors' *Lebenswelt* even within a single generation. This happens, in practice, whenever institutions of family and primary education, as examples, are disrupted or substantially altered. Being difficult to pass along successfully even from generation to generation, these norms are clearly not readily transferred overseas short of being imposed by conquest, colonization, or cultural imperialism.[13] They are not available for transfer because they are particular rather than generalizable; they are ultimately supported by a particular social infrastructure of lived social fabrics. This is why even after 300 years of direct military occupation Brazil is not Portugal, and Mexico and Argentina are not Spain. With far fewer years of occupation, the New England states and Guyana are not England, Louisiana and Haiti are not France, and Zaire is not Belgium.

Nevertheless, *analytical aspects* of traditions, whether substantive or procedural, are indeed transferred to new sites, in practice. At times they are transferred during quite brief periods of imposition, as was the case, for example, with French occupations of Algeria and Vietnam or American occupations of Japan, Germany, and Vietnam. The important point for comparative research, however, is to consider methodically which *analytical aspects* of any tradition are "most available" for transfer *without having to be imposed on "outsiders" or disbelievers in any respect whatsoever*.[14] Put differently, comparative researchers cannot legitimately treat all *analytical aspects* of all national traditions as equally confined to their social infrastructure of lived social fabrics, and thereby equally unavailable for tranfer. Two possible lines of theoretical development left unexplored by Parsons are beginning to come into view, based on the two steps taken in the preceding section.

"Tradition" as transferable, generalizable, and invariant in impact. The first line of theoretical development is to consider that if at least certain analytical aspects of certain national traditions are indeed distinctively voluntaristic and procedural, then these aspects are possibly generalizable, in principle. As such, they are also available for transfer, in practice.[15] In addition, unlike all other analytical aspects comprising the *same* national traditions, these analytical aspects also have an *invariant impact* on the direction of social change of any modern nation-state to which they are transferred.[16] They restrain arbitrary exercises of collective power by their sheer presence. This means that they do so: (a) irrespective of the particular nation-state to which they are transferred; (b) irrespective of the substantive projects to which they become attached within this nation-state; and (c) irrespective of the primary socialization, substantive beliefs, and subjective interests of the actors participating in these substantive projects.

Once the availability for transfer of distinctively voluntaristic and procedural aspects of a national tradition is brought into view, along with an appreciation of the invariance of their impact upon transferal, the prominence that Parsons gave to primary socialization, and to Durkheim's and Freud's analyses of actors' internalization of shared *substantive* norms, is challenged conceptually. Comparativists cannot legitimately treat national traditions as undifferentiated wholes which, in principle as well as in practice, are altogether fixed social facts. They cannot legitimately employ conceptual frameworks that a priori treat all analytical aspects of all national traditions as if they were exclusively or ultimately tied to actors' internalization of shared substantive beliefs. Nor, for that matter, can they employ conceptual frameworks that treat all such aspects as reducible to actors' local interactions and cultural "tool kits" (Swidler 1986).[17] This first line of theoretical development beyond Parsons is pursued in the remainder of this chapter and the next.

Resuscitating the integrity of internal procedural restraints. The second possible line of theoretical development left unexplored by Parsons is that actors within *non*authoritarian social orders either develop or adopt both internal and external procedural restraints. They do so irrespective of the substance of national traditions and the particularity of the social infrastructure that is comprised of lived social fabrics. Moreover, they may innovate by infusing any newly transferred restraints with political power or legal sanctions. In other words, the nation-states to which voluntaristic procedural norms of restraint are transferred may, in principle, initiate the establishing of a public realm within their civil societies *well in advance of the nation-state within which these voluntaristic procedural norms originated historically.* There is no theoretical or empirical reason why this cannot occur, in practice. Such a move beyond the public policies of existing Western democracies exposes limitations in the presupposition of exhausted possibilities.

By contrast to Parsons and Weber alike, therefore, it cannot be assumed a priori that one invariant result of infusing norms of external restraint with political power or legal sanctions is institutional regression or functional dedifferentiation. Quite the opposite is the case: When exercises of political power and legal sanctions are dedicated to maintaining the integrity of internal and external norms of *procedural* restraint, they are always and everywhere *possibly* integrative. By distinguishing voluntaristic procedural analytical aspects within any national tradition, and by considering the implications of supporting their integrity with political power or legal sanctions, the discussion has moved significantly beyond the literature of Western constitutional theory and practice. It has moved beyond this literature by revealing that a public policy of introducing collegial formations into a civil society may be initiated *even within nation-states whose substantive cores of national traditions are quite different from, and possibly incompatible with, those of any and all Western democracies.* This too exposes limitations in the scope of application of the presupposition of exhausted possibilities. This second line of theoretical development beyond Parsons is explored somewhat further in the next chapter.

10.4. Prospects for "tradition"

10.4.1. Societal constitutionalism v. governmental constitutionalism

The first line of theoretical development beyond Parsons as noted previously is that researchers may *predict* that procedural and voluntaristic aspects of national traditions are "available" for transfer short of impositions and not any part of their core substantive norms and social infrastructure of lived social fabrics. This first possibility may be specified in three distinct steps:

> First, any corporation or complex social unit anywhere in the world that maintains the integrity of collegial formations simultaneously institutionalizes external procedural restraints on drift, at least within its sector or industry. Yet, the voluntaristic and procedural norms underlying collegial formations originated historically within common-law countries.
>
> Second, the sheer presence of collegial formations within any corporation or complex social unit also contributes to a *social infrastructure* that permits even heterogeneous actors and competing groups to revitalize the integrity of internal procedural restraints on government. They may revitalize these restraints by extending them from government to purposefully arbitrary exercises of collective power by private enterprises within civil society. This extension bears a striking resemblance to the (purported) contribution of the "constituent group" in seventeenth-century England and eighteenth- and early nineteenth-century American colonies, which is discussed momentarily. Once again, the theory (and purported practice) of the constituent group originated historically in legal and constitutional struggles against absolute monarchy within common-law countries.[18]
>
> Third, the external procedural restraints institutionalized by collegial formations not only render the constituent group's (purported) historical contribution "available" for use by social influentials (and insurgents) within non-Western nation-states. They also extend its contribution from establishing strictly internal procedural restraints

to establishing external procedural restraints on how sectors, industries, and organizations respond to systemic pressures of drift. Unlike the particularity of the constituent group's (purported) narrower contribution, moreover, the external procedural restraints institutionalized by collegial formations are eminently transferable. Just as importantly, their impact of restraint on any sector, industry, or organization of any modern civil society is invariant.

It is instructive to consider more closely the major differences between governmental constitutionalism's "agent of change" and that of societal constitutionalism. Governmental constitutionalism's agent is homogeneous actors and consensual groups, first within an amorphous "constituent force" and then within a temporarily organized "constituent group." Societal constitutionalism's agent is heterogeneous actors and competing groups within collegial formations. In exploring the differences between these agents, the reasons for collegial formations' greater "availability" for transfer or generalizability, and for their invariant impact, come into view.

10.4.2. From the constituent group to collegial formations

Constituent group: restricted impact, temporary presence. The "constituent group" of seventeenth-century England and eighteenth- and early nineteenth-century America is, according to Anglo-American legal and constitutional theory, the social agent that, respectively, institutionalized a limited government (in England) and framed a republican constitution (in America) (see Friedrich 1941, 1963, 1972, 1974; Milsom 1981; *Yale Law Journal* 1988 on republicanism). In both instances, this group placed *both* substantive and procedural restraints on arbitrary government or, more accurately, on absolute monarchy. The constituent *group* is explicitly distinguished, however, from a much more amorphous social force: the "constituent *force.*" According to this same theoretical tradition, this social force literally pervaded English and American civil societies at the time of their respective revolutions. The constituent force, it is said, was comprised of that entire set of social influentials who opposed arbitrary government, whether commercial landowners, emerging bourgeoisie, or others sympathetic to limited government. Anglo-American legal and constitutional theory holds that it was from these ranks that the much smaller set of political activists comprising the constituent group eventually emerged, by a process of self-selection. The constituent group's popular mandate continued to rest, however, on whether the constituent force accepted that the limits it placed on government were proper. Once acceptable limits were placed on government, the constituent group disbanded immediately, receding into the amorphous constituent force from which it had emerged and to which it had remained responsible.

Legal and constitutional theorists distinguish the constituent group from the constituent force for a most important reason. By their accounts, the constituent force is in itself incapable of either establishing or maintaining a republican or limited government. Indeed, these theorists insist quite adamantly that if this social force were ever mobilized en masse it would be unable to *avoid* authoritarian excesses. They said this because with the delegitimation of the natural right of kings – the "natural law" that a monarch's sovereignty is as removed from challenge as is God's rule over man or a parent's rule over a child – the *constituent force* became sovereign, and sovereignty is ultimately indivisible.

Thus, once the monarch's sovereignty could no longer escape challenge, the constituent force became the ultimate source of political power within the nation – as the totality of republican-minded social influentials. Like the monarch's sovereignty before it, however, the constituent force's sovereignty also is ultimately absolute, beyond challenge. Its power is never legitimately limited or restrained by any group or faction because any and all other interests are particular whereas the interest of the constituent force is general, the literal "public interest." The major difference between the monarch's sovereignty and the constituent force's sovereignty, however, is critical to this tradition of legal and constitutional theory: Unlike a monarch, the new sovereign is likely to remain forever a latent social force, or what Habermas (1962) calls a "bourgeois public sphere." The theorists within this tradition could not imagine the circumstances under which the constituent force would ever, or could ever, mobilize fully. But then again these same theorists failed to anticipate the rise of mass political parties in the mid- and late nineteenth century, to say nothing of the numerous mass-based authoritarian (and occasional totalitarian) regimes of the twentieth century.

Regardless, Anglo-American legal and constitutional theory revolves around the presupposition that whenever government exceeds its "natural" limits, a *faction* of the constituent force – the constituent *group* – can be expected to organize, albeit temporarily. It can be expected to organize only for as long as it takes to complete its single task: to return government to "natural" limits, limits popularly recognized by the latent constituent force. The constituent group accomplishes this at the moment that it frames (and has ratified) a republican constitution, and in particular at the moment that it successfully introduces (or resuscitates) the division of powers (see Vile 1967 for the best account). Once this is accomplished, the constituent group simultaneously loses *its* legitimacy to remain organized. It properly disbands, receding into the amorphous, ever-vigilant constituent force from which it came.

If the constituent group fails to disband, it cannot *avoid* authoritarian excesses because, as legal and constitutional theorists insist, as long as it remains organized it takes into itself the nation's sovereign power. As long as it remains organized, *its* exercises of collective power are not legitimately limited or restrained by *any* opposition from *any* quarter, strategic or normative.[19] As the literal sovereign, the constituent group can never be trusted *to govern*. It can be trusted only *to limit government*. In the terminology of societal constitutionalism, it can be trusted only to institutionalize internal substantive and procedural restraints.

Indeed, according to early Anglo-American legal and constitutional theory, the members of the constituent group not only must recede into the amorphous constituent force but also must forego communicating among themselves through formal channels. They cannot remain organized within any identifiable groups or "factions" purporting to represent the constituent force. It can be appreciated at this point why the American founders and framers so feared the rise of fledgling political parties in the 1820s. Only in the face of renewed arbitrariness by government are members of the larger constituent force ever to establish formal channels of communication or to seek organizational expression. Otherwise, none of this is necessary. According to this theoretical tradition, the individuals comprising the constituent force are ever-vigilant regardless. They are certain to recognize *in common* any increases in government's arbitrariness. Given this faith in dispersed individuals' capacity to sustain a shared recognition and understanding within civil society of government's actions, these theorists were convinced that a faction of the constituent force would invariably organize in sufficient time whenever government became threatening. This is why these theorists also were certain that this faction, once self-selected, would arrive rather readily at consensus regarding how best to proceed, and then when it is appropriate to disband.[20]

Like neopositivists' implicit portrayals of how individual scientists conduct themselves in order for a copy theory of truth to be a possibility, these early legal and constitutional theorists assumed that each social influential comprising the amorphous constituent force is capable, in isolation, of recognizing unambiguously what governmental arbitrariness is. Given this assumption, it was not problematic for these theorists also to assume that the same individuals, still operating in isolation or at best through the informal channels of communication that Habermas documents in his study of the bourgeois public sphere, can readily agree when it is time to institutionalize internal procedural and substantive restraints on government. The constituent group can readily get on with the task of framing a republican constitution *precisely because the constituent force's shared recognition of the problem antedates its formation.* Correlatively, the constituent group can organize itself on short notice, with scarce resources and informal leadership, *precisely because it does not face legitimate strategic or normative opposition from any quarter within the constituent force proper.* The only opposition it faces comes literally from traitors or monarchists, and the latter are already riddled by the problem of delegitimation. As the constituent group carries out its sole task, its opponents are encouraged to leave the country – and to leave their property behind.[21]

Still, even if all of these assumptions are conceded, the only normative and strategic restraints that concerned early legal and constitutional theorists were *internal* procedural and substantive restraints *on government.* Systemic pressures of rationalization, including actors' fragmentation of meaning and the reactions of bureaucratization and steady extensions of formal *social* controls, were not salient issues for theorists in the seventeenth, eighteenth, and early nineteenth centuries. This is why the issue of challenging the sovereignty of actors' subjective interests, of institutionalizing *external* procedural restraints on the drift of social change, falls far outside the scope of application of the *concepts* that these theorists developed.[22] Just as early legal and constitutional theorists assumed that the constituent force would remain forever latent and unorganized within civil society, so too they assumed that the sole legitimate product of the constituent group – a republican constitution – would have at most a strictly latent and indirect impact on *civil society.*

To this day, this tradition of legal and constitutional theory lacks the concepts that would allow social scientists to address even the possibility that *permanent* organizations and institutions *within a civil society* might comprise the *social infrastructure* of a nonauthoritarian direction of social change. First, this would be the social infrastructure on which a contemporary "constituent force" (and social scientists) might establish and maintain a shared recognition and understanding of what governmental arbitrariness is in the late twentieth century. Second, this would be the same social infrastructure on which social influentials (and social scientists) might recognize and understand in common when arbitrary exercises of collective power by private enterprises are increasing within a civil society.

Habermas fares no better than this constitutional and legal tradition when he explores the rise of popular opposition to absolute monarchy in Western Europe in the mid-eighteenth century. (He excludes the American colonies from his discussion.) As noted in passing above, he refers to this opposition not as an amorphous constituent force but rather as an informally organized "bourgeois public sphere:" "[A] forum in which the private people, come together to form a public, readied themselves to compel public authority to legitimate itself before public opinion" (pp. 25–6). Habermas traces this sphere's steady rise to prominence through the early nineteenth century, and then its subsequent rapid decline in influence beginning in the mid-nineteenth century as premodern absolutism dropped from the scene and both liberalization and democratization were extended.

Consistent with constitutional and legal theorists' accounts of the constituent group in England and the American colonies, a great irony informs Habermas's account of the bourgeois social sphere on the Continent: It was most critical, and seemingly most reasoned, when its participants were most homogeneous – in class, in ethnicity, in religion, and in style of life.[23] This informally organized "sphere" was most critical when admission to its talking clubs was most restricted, when the vast majority of the population, the working classes and rural populace, was both impoverished and illiterate. An individual's admission to the early public sphere was contingent on the security of his or her property base as well as on the suitability of his or her education or "cultivation." The richest part of Habermas's account is indeed his careful exploration of the talking clubs comprising this amorphous sphere: the coffee houses, salons, reading societies, and intellectual networks that sprang up across Western Europe as expanding market societies generated both investment opportunities and a consumer market outside the control of court and estates.

Within these talking clubs, first the arts and then politics and public affairs were *critically* discussed. Consider the following items selected from the tapestry of Habermas's excellent discussion:

(1) The earliest private "publications" are circulars exchanged by merchants engaged in long-distance trade (1962: 15).

(2) "Political journals" then appear by the early seventeenth century, first weeklies and then dailies; again, they are first written in response to the needs of merchants, and they continue to fall under the watchful eye of the state administration (1962: 21–2).

(3) By the end of the seventeenth century, periodicals begin to appear not merely with trade information but also with educational instructions as well as literary criticisms and reviews (1962: 24–5). There is a rise of coffee houses in Britain (3,000 in London) and of salons in France (1962: 32–3).

(4) During the eighteenth century, apolitical literary expressions of the private lives of the bourgeois family begin to appear (1962: 29). For the first time in history, mediocre novels become best-sellers (1962: 43).

(5) Also by the mid-eighteenth century, serious reading by an interested public emerges simultaneously with the rise of theaters and concerts independent of the court (1962: 38). The very term "public" refers to this new theater audience.

(6) Only by the late eighteenth and early nineteenth century, however, did large daily newspapers emerge (such as the *Times of London* in 1785) (1962: 64); newspapers were permitted to report the votes of Parliament in 1771 and by 1803 places were set aside in the gallery for journalists (1962: 62).

(7) Three decades later, the press began to distance itself from ideological position-taking and to become more commercial (1962: 184); by the 1870s, publishers wielded more power than editors (1962: 186).

Habermas's point in exploring such details is to demonstrate that *public opinion* was intrinsically critical of public authority for about a century, and then it became increasingly acclaiming. The bourgeois public sphere proper was a decentralized network of distinct talking clubs, each with its own public meeting places and publications. The public opinion emerging from these clubs initially provided, in Habermas's view, a relatively reliable standard against which the "truth" or "reason" of public officials' actions might be broadly gauged. Public opinion was not yet a measurable sentiment that advertisers and other experts might manipulate, if not control, with symbols detached from reasons. Indeed, the survey analyst, the public relations expert, and the media consultant would all have to wait a full century before the object of their handiwork, a seemingly speechless mass, and before their own clients – the political party and corporate leaders seeking to manipulate this object – would become available for their techniques.

Habermas's account of the early bourgeois public sphere, and its demise, is much richer sociologically than the accounts of the constituent force provided by classical liberal and constitutional theorists. Yet, incredibly, the account of the constituent force is ultimately what underlies Lockean liberals' complacency and optimism in the late twentieth century. By contrast to this allegory, Habermas provides more than 100 pages of rich detail of the specific social units that comprised the so-called constituent force. Just as importantly, he explores how the integrity of these social units was steadily undermined with the onset of industrial capitalism, mass political parties, and the administrative state. He concludes by trying, and failing, to find substitutes for these social units within postwar Western democracies. This leaves him with the dilemma that he inherited from Marx and Weber alike, the dilemma that he has yet to resolve now nearly three decades after his first book appeared: How is nonauthoritarian social order possible in the late twentieth century given that the social infrastructure once provided by the bourgeois public sphere is not in evidence?

Habermas's concepts, like Marx's and Weber's, fail to yield answers to this question. In turn, liberal and constitutional concepts are tied to this tradition's vague allegory, and to complacency and optimism, rather than offering an answer to this question. A major reason for Habermas's failure in particular is that since 1962 he has been looking too directly, too literally, at political parties, interest groups, and social movements for the social infrastructure once provided by the public realm. He then finds, of course, that they fail to measure up as arenas of critical discourse, and thereby fail to account for the possibility of nonauthoritarian social order. His later, absolutist critiques of Western democracy (1973a; 1981a,b) clearly signal that his conceptual apparatus, an achievement of the first order in other respects, is leading him further and further away from answering the question above and resolving the Weberian Dilemma. Yet, this question and this dilemma are being answered every day, in practice. There is indeed a social infrastructure underlying nonauthoritarian social orders today, and it is indeed under threat from systemic pressures of social change. But it is comprised of collegial formations largely located within formal organizations. It is not comprised of a more amorphous set of social influentials operating within informal talking clubs or broader social movements.

In sum, the constituent group has the following characteristics:

(a) The constituent group strategically restrains government's excesses, and then institutionalizes both substantive and procedural internal restraints, including the division of powers in particular.

(b) The constituent group's emergence not merely straddles but collapses the public/private distinction. But because the constituent group brings the sovereign power of the constituent force to bear on the single task of restraining arbitrary government, civil society is not directly affected by its actions.[24] It is not to be trusted when it defines its mission any more broadly, to include exercises of collective power by private enterprises within civil society itself.

(c) The constituent group places both substantive and procedural restraints on government, but it does not do so by its sheer presence within civil society. Nor, certainly, does the sheer presence of the more amorphous constituent *force* or bourgeois public sphere yield internal restraints. The constituent group places these restraints on government by organizing temporarily as a faction of the constituent force or bourgeois social sphere.

Collegial formations: invariant impact, permanent presence. The problem of arbitrariness in the late twentieth century is not as confined as it once appeared to be in the days of the (purported) constituent force and the bourgeois public sphere. Corporations within American civil society, for instance, are larger, more powerful, and more influential than the largest state governments, and often two or three of the latter taken together. The problem of arbitrary exercises of collective power can no longer be kept confined to maintaining or resuscitating the integrity of internal restraints on arbitrary government. The problem instead becomes: Is it possible to address the Weberian Dilemma by institutionalizing external restraints on drift, and yet simultaneously avoid extending social control and increasing a nation-state's susceptibility to social authoritarianism? It has been argued throughout this volume that collegial formations restrain drift, and that they do so in a way that remains possibly integrative rather than becoming demonstrably controlling. It is intriguing, therefore, to consider points of comparison and contrast between collegial formations and the constituent group.

Collegial formations are permanent organizations, and they also are distributed far more widely across the sectors and industries of a civil society than was the constituent group in its day. Again, Habermas's account of the exclusivity of the larger "bourgeois public sphere" from which the constituent group is drawn speaks to its restricted presence within civil society. By contrast, the collegial form of organization potentially could be extended to cover literally all of the professions (and their clients) as well as all of the deliberative bodies of an entire civil society. It could be extended further into the working classes than might be expected, even as it is likely to *exclude* elite positions that are dedicated to corporate finance and investment but cannot credibly claim to be professional or deliberative. Yet, like the constituent group, members of collegial formations will likely always remain a distinct faction within any civil society – unlike, say, the potential membership of mass political parties or of national social movements.

Put most succinctly, collegial formations have the following characteristics:

(a) Collegial formations are permanently organized, and by their sheer presence institutionalize external procedural restraints not only on government but also on how private enterprises are permitted institutionally to act in their own interests.

(b) Collegial formations pose invariant, generalizable restraints on any and all exercises of collective power, again by their sheer presence within a civil society.

(c) Collegial formations may be present within and across countless sectors of a civil society as well as within and across countless agencies of government. By their sheer presence, they establish a *social infrastructure* on which even heterogeneous actors and competing groups might resuscitate the integrity of internal procedural restraints on government by extending them into civil society.

Actors' voluntaristic project of establishing and then maintaining this social infrastructure may be thought of as one of institutionalizing and then maintaining *a public realm within civil society*. This project is much more complicated than the constituent group's project of framing a constitution and then receding into civil society, and yet this project is decidedly practicable rather than idealized or allegorical.

A public realm proper is literally the commons *within a civil society* (cf. Selznick 1987). No one is excluded, in principle, from participating within and contributing to the organizations and institutions comprising this realm. Yet, these same organizations and institutions are not themselves democratic in any strict sense. They are not organized in the democratic form, and their impact on civil society and government, while invariant, is by no means synonymous with that of the "public opinion" that survey research codifies. The organizations and institutions at the center of this public realm are a decentralized network of collegial formations. The same social and political conditions supporting this network simultaneously support *other* "protected spheres" that fail to adopt the collegial form. The latter are functionally defined spheres of religion, the arts, environment, leisure, and family or local life protected artificially from unmediated competition within economic and political marketplaces.

11. Collegial formations as external procedural restraints: prospects for a public realm

The discussion in chapter 9 addressed why power holders and social influentials can be expected to institutionalize internal procedural restraints in particular. This was followed, in chapter 10, by a discussion of why procedural voluntaristic restraints in general are "available" for transfer. Now it is possible to assess *conceptually* collegial formations' current status and future prospects within contemporary nation-states. Along the way, other issues come to the fore as well, including: First, the relationship between the theory of societal constitutionalism and other theoretical approaches to social order. Second, how the presence of collegial formations affects the stratification system. Third, how both authoritarian and nonauthoritarian directions of social change develop beyond the limiting case of authoritarian social order. And, fourth, how the presence of collegial formations within selected sectors of a civil society can affect how power holders act and propose actions across an entire civil society.

11.1. Speculations on collegial formations today: two restraints not institutionalized

Collegial formations today fail to restrain two sets of social activities that they could restrain to some greater extent if their integrity were upheld as a matter of public policy. Yet, they restrain a third set of social activities because, by definition, their members' behavior is oriented by voluntaristic procedures. This third contribution of restraint is what accounts for the collegial form's modest links to social power today. It also provides social scientists with a standard by which to gauge whether collegial formations are maintaining or losing their integrity.

11.1.1. Collegial form and possessive individualism

The first set of normative restraints that collegial formations fail to institutionalize by their sheer presence within a civil society has to do with orienting economic activity within market economies. The presence of collegial formations fails to restrain consumerism and possessive individualism

Macpherson 1962).[1] Prominent members of collegial formations may endeavor at times to influence others by ridiculing the mindlessness of consumerism and possessiveness, and by rejecting the latter in their own styles of life. The same may be said of selected leaders of other protected spheres, including religious leaders and others dedicated in word and deed to maintaining the integrity of the substantive core of a national or cultural tradition. But more typically these members and leaders accommodate, and themselves recapitulate, this behavior.

This presents a problem, of course, and one may label it "motivation crisis" if one wishes (Habermas 1973a). Or else, one may label it the problem of maintaining "social solidarity" (Hechter 1987), the "free-rider problem" (Olson 1965),[2] or the problem of "social order" (Parsons 1937a). But this is a manifestation of systemic drift that is not intrinsically related to the problem of whether social order is becoming more controlling and arbitrary.[3] The mindlessness of consumerism and possessiveness may be regrettable. But free riders and other narrowly motivated actors in abundance do not invariably threaten heterogeneous actors' and competing groups' possibilities for social integration, nor their possibilities for maintaining a nonauthoritarian direction of social change.[4] Quite to the contrary, the reformers who endeavor to eliminate free riders, and to "cultivate" the narrowly motivated, might well pose a greater threat. This is clearly the case the moment that even the best-intentioned efforts at "cultivation" entail either purposeful or inadvertent encroachments against collegial formations or against the threshold of interpretability of shared social duties.

1.1.2. Collegial form, social stratification, and social order

The second set of restraints that collegial formations fail to institutionalize today by their sheer presence within a civil society is a corollary of the first. Consider the relationship between the collegial form of organization and the substantive inequalities found within a civil society: the relationship between collegial formations, social stratification, and social order. In exploring this relationship, points of contrast between societal constitutionalism and competing approaches to the "problem of social order" come to the fore. Again, social order is any situation wherein actors conform to ranges of expectations regarding acceptable behavior that are widely acknowledged by the members of any social unit (chapter 2).[5]

Societal constitutionalism v. consensus theory
Social order within *collegial formations: acknowledged expectations.*
When actors maintain the integrity of the collegial form within any division of a more complex social enterprise, this means that their behavior *within*

this division already exhibits fidelity to a normative orientation that is distinctively voluntaristic and procedural. Correlatively, their behavior within this division is *in*consistent with the rational actions being taken within the larger social enterprise; principles of rational choice cannot account for this observed inconsistency.[6] Yet, as noted above, their behavior *within this division* need not present any obstacle whatsoever to most manifestations of consumerism and possessive individualism *in the larger economy*. After all, the latter typically take place outside of the collegial form, and they need not jeopardize the integrity of collegial formations either directly or indirectly.

Still, all members of all collegial formations *share an acknowledged range of expectations regarding the behavior that is acceptable within (and then around) their own divisions and social units*. They expect any interested party seeking to influence their behavior qua *members of collegial formations* to (a) present "acceptable" proposals and (b) present these proposals in "acceptable" ways. "Acceptable" behavior is any behavior that, at the very least, does not compromise these members' own ongoing behavioral fidelity to the threshold distinctive to this organizational form itself. Thus, to the extent that its members are indeed maintaining this formation's integrity they are dismissing all *proposals* submitted by interested parties that threaten the "social order" – the acknowledged ranges of expectations – institutionalized by this organizational form.

As one obvious example, bribery certainly fails to qualify as an acceptable *way* to present otherwise acceptable proposals to members of collegial formations. Bribery is an equally unacceptable way to approach members of bureaucratic and democratic formations, to be sure. But it is by no means as unacceptable to members of patron-client formations. More importantly, and less obviously, there are *types of proposals* that are unacceptable to members of collegial formations and yet acceptable to the members of all other organizational forms: These are proposals whose adoption by members of collegial formations would entail their encroaching against the threshold of interpretability of shared social duties.

Collegial social order as group competition and potential conflict? When actors maintain the integrity of the collegial form, they institutionalize a procedural voluntaristic orientation; they institutionalize ranges of expectations that set unambiguous limits to acceptable behavior within and around existing collegial formations. But these same ranges of expectations by no means set unambiguous limits to *types or levels of stratification within the larger civil society*. Does this mean that the impact of collegial formations on the stratification system is neutral? Does this mean that, ultimately, the theory of societal constitutionalism is a "consensus" theory, a social theory consistent with even extreme material and substantive inequalities?

Unlike collegial formations' impact on arbitrary exercises of collective power, which may be captured conceptually because it is invariant, their impact on the stratification system is more open empirically. The only thing that can be said about it a priori, and thereby stated conceptually, is that their impact on the stratification system (a) is not likely to be neutral, and (b) is no more likely to be apologetic than critical. The best way to conceptualize this impact is to think of collegial formations introducing a "wild card" into the stratification system of any modern civil society (cf. Collins 1979 focuses more narrowly on the relationship between credentials and stratification). As actors introduce these formations into sectors, industries, and organizations of a civil society, the presence of these formations does not immediately affect the substantive inequalities that actors are experiencing in their everyday lives. Yet their presence does begin to affect *how these substantive inequalities are symbolized and justified, in practice* (chapter 7). As a consequence of this, their presence does indeed begin to alter *how* substantive inequalities are maintained, and whether they are likely to be reduced or increased.

Still, the presence of these formations could, in any given instance, just as conceivably (a) lend support even to extreme inequalities as (b) direct sustained challenges to minor inequalities. The key to the type of impact they are likely to have, in practice, hinges on two factors: First, can existing substantive inequalities be justified with reasons that, at the very least, can be kept consistent with the ranges of expectations that these formations institutionalize? Second, are the actors benefiting most from the inequalities competent in formulating and presenting such reasons? If this can be accomplished, in principle, and if the actors are competent in demonstrating this, in practice, then the impact of introducing collegial formations into a civil society is likely to be more apologetic than critical. But if this cannot be accomplished, or if the actors are not particularly competent, then the impact of introducing collegial formations is likely to be critical, and it could be radicalizing.

Consider what happens as actors introduce collegial formations into a civil society. Power holders and social influentials within (and around) the organizations and divisions immediately affected begin to reformulate all of their policy *proposals* accordingly, including those designed to maintain or enhance existing substantive inequalities. All proposals – and, thus, any inequalities that they symbolize – are cast into terms consistent with the ranges of expectations regarding acceptable behavior that members of collegial formations acknowledge qua members. This seemingly benign and restricted activity of adjustment is not likely to be neutral in its impact on the stratification system. Substantive inequalities heretofore unquestioned, in part because of the ways in which they had been symbolized, are now being symbolized differently (e.g. Gouldner 1976 revolves more generally around such changes). This may either convert them into controversial issues or bolster them with new sources of legitimacy.[7] What is ironic about all of this is that *as* the power holders and social influentials who benefit most from existing substantive inequalities *conform most fully to the acknowledged ranges of expectations institutionalized by collegial formations,* their very *behavioral conformity* to the "social order" of collegial formations might *exacerbate* interest competition and foster outright social conflict.

Collegial formations and middle-class sensibilities. Few social and governmental units within any modern nation-state ensure that the "most reasoned" interests typically prevail within their decision-making processes. Habermas's point about the pervasiveness of purposeful manipulation and inadvertent distortion is well taken. Indeed, most complex social units fail to ensure that the "most reasoned" interests are typically afforded a hearing. Given contemporary systemic pressures, actors' fragmentation of meaning, and both organizational complexity and functional differentiation, it is likely impossible to ensure even this. As noted in chapter 5, Habermas's ideal speech situation has never been institutionalized, nor can it be.[8]

It is also likely impossible for the members of any complex social enterprise today to institutionalize the expectation that interested parties are eventually to arrive at some "consensus," whether reasoned or not.[9] Interested parties gaining access to any complex enterprise's decision-making processes are going to be differentiated by function, if nothing else. This alone renders them competitive rather than predisposed to consensus, even on the "rules of the game." Yet, as long as their *competing* proposals do not threaten the procedural theshold of *existing* collegial formations, as long as their proposals remain "acceptable" merely in this sense, interested parties may be said to be *competing* collegially. This may be said *even as their behavior becomes ever more disorderly within the wider civil society, departing ever more from other acknowledged ranges of expectations to the point of conflict.*[10]

In short, when actors exhibit behavioral fidelity to the integrity of the collegial form within particular divisions of larger organizations, this does not somehow guarantee simultaneously that the "social order" of these divisions is consensual, pleasant, or tranquil. Quite to the contrary, the integrity of these formations may be maintained even as the sensibilities of middle-class professionals and deliberators are increasingly being assaulted. The "social order" of these divisions may well be competitive, unpleasant, and stressful for all involved. After all, like any other set of substantive norms and lived social fabrics, the sensibilities of the middle class are particular. The voluntaristic orientation of the collegial form, however, is ultimately a procedural mediation, and not more immediately substantive or particular.

It is as detached from the middle class's sensibilities as it is detached from the sensibilities of the upper class, working class, or lower class. Clearly, it is also detached from the sensibilities of any and all ascriptive groups, whether those of majority or minority groups. In short, the collegial is an impersonal organizational form, in this respect much like the bureaucratic and democratic forms. The great difference between them is that the latter forms revolve around rational procedures and quantifiable outcomes whereas the collegial form revolves around voluntaristic procedures and outcomes that are qualitative, and far more amenable to politicization and controversy.

The empirical issue of whether members of collegial formations retain the integrity of the latter's distinctively procedural voluntaristic orientation is altogether independent of any and all substantive empirical issues. As one example, this issue is independent of whether college or high-school curricula are either too "European" or insufficiently "Third World" in substance (a longstanding debate in the United States fueled a few years back by Bloom 1987). It is possible for the "Europeanists" to prevail by acting arbitrarily; it is possible for the "Third Worldists" to prevail by acting arbitrarily; it is possible for their dispute to escalate from competition to occasional conflicts *without either side acting arbitrarily.* In the latter case, even occasional social conflicts can be said to remain collegial, to remain consistent with a nonauthoritarian direction of social change, and, ironically, to remain consistent with actors' possible social integration.

In short, domestic tranquillity or consensus is not a synonym for social integration. The former may well be a product of actors' demonstrable social control, whereas actors' social integration may well result in their experiencing increasing personal stress and anxiety. The sheer presence of collegial formations: (a) frames particular spheres *within which* heterogeneous actors and competing groups *may* be integrated, and simultaneously (b) institutionalizes external procedural restraints on drift. It does not, however, guarantee that actors will defer to the sensibilities of middle-class professionals and deliberators. It also does not guarantee that there will be any reduction in (a) the extent or intensity of interested parties' competition and occasional conflicts, (b) the levels of substantive inequalities and types of stratification to be found within a civil society, or (c) the levels of stress and anxiety that actors experience within any integrative social order.

In terms of the theory of societal constitutionalism, the central empirical issue is never whether participants or observing social scientists find actors' behavior within and around collegial formations to be tranquil, consensual, or personally pleasing. The central empirical issue is rather whether the latter's voluntaristic orientation is being maintained by actors' behavior. Middle-class professionals' and deliberators' personal sensibilities regarding which policy proposals and which ways of presenting them are acceptable have little bearing on whether heterogeneous actors and competing groups are possibly integrated rather than demonstrably controlled. After all, these same sensibilities may be respected, to the point of being elevated to the status of the "sacred," even as "cultivated" middle-class professionals and deliberators are repeatedly and cavalierly violating the integrity of the collegial form. Indeed, middle-class sensibilities may be respected scrupulously as power holders and social influentials are engaging not merely in manipulation and control but in outright social and political authoritarianism. Arendt's phrase "the banality of evil," first applied to Adolf Eichmann, often is applied today to middle-class professionals engaging in corporate crime. The same phrase may be applied to those who are either purposefully or inadvertently encroaching against the collegial form as they champion middle-class sensibilities.

Calling to mind the illustration in chapter 1, the managers of research divisions who compel their researchers to meet the division's production schedule at all costs might be widely respected and admired for their cultivation and panache within the corporation. The same may hold for their reputations in the industry and the corporation's local community. In terms of the theory of societal constitutionalism, however, there is no class, group, or faction which monopolizes a "culture of sensibility" that is intrinsically nonauthoritarian or integrative under modern conditions. As noted in chapter 10, there is no substantive core of any national tradition or lived social fabric that is intrinsically nonauthoritarian and possibly integrative under modern conditions.[11]

Heterogeneous actors' and competing groups' fidelity to the collegial form's voluntaristic orientation clearly mediates each class's, each group's, and each faction's most objectionable *behavior*. Within the collegial form, all actors and interested parties are prohibited institutionally from resorting immediately to mechanisms of social control that encroach against the form's threshold restraints. Thus, the Ku Klux Klan, for instance, would have a difficult time conveying its members' hesitancy to encroach against this threshold. Nazis' *Führerprinzip* and Leninists' notion of "democratic centralism" are outright antitheses of such fidelity. Still, Klansmen, Nazis, and even Leninists are rarities today, not only in the West but in the East and Third World as well. And yet, very great ranges of unpleasant and stressful social behavior remain quite common. These are by no means eliminated or even muted by the presence of collegial formations. The theory of societal constitutionalism cannot be read as making grand claims to the contrary. It is not a social theory of egalitarianism or consensus. Nor is it a sociological rendering of Robert's Rules of Order or of table manners at black-tie dinners. It is not a sociological rendering of the conduct found (ideally) within graduate seminars or within any other arena of (relatively) dispassionate colloquy. As the subtitle of this volume indicates, the theory of societal constitutionalism is not a consensus theory of any kind, left or right (see Habermas 1981a,b; and Brennan and Buchanan 1985 respectively).

Societal constitutionalism v. symbolic interactionism. The presence of collegial formations accounts for how nonauthoritarian social orders have addressed the Weberian Dilemma, in practice, in the late twentieth century. It also accounts for how heterogeneous actors and competing groups have established and maintained possibilities for social integration, at least within selected sectors of selected civil societies. But, bringing symbolic interactionists' most central point into the discussion, whether concrete interactions are pleasant, comfortable, and orderly or stressful, uncomfortable, and disorderly is something that actors and groups negotiate locally, and then renegotiate endlessly. Symbolic interactionists (Blumer 1969; Turner and Killian 1957; Strauss 1978) correctly point out that *any* form of organization, or any institutionalized normative orientation, can, at best, only broadly *frame* actors' and groups' local interactions (also see Leifer 1988 on "local action," and Swidler 1986 on cultural "tool kits"). Within the latter, actors and groups invariably negotiate and renegotiate their recognitions and understandings of shared subjective interests, shared meanings, shared social duties, and acknowledged ranges of expectations. None of this is somehow reduced or eliminated by whatever norms actors have internalized prior to interacting, nor by whatever normative orientations forms of organization have institutionalized.

The theory of societal constitutionalism radicalizes this position, however, by pointing out that local negotiations of meanings within (and around) collegial formations are nonetheless distinctive, in practice. The interactions taking place within and around these formations are insulated not only from manifest coercion but also from many subtler mechanisms of social control, whether formal or informal, purposeful or systemic. *This cannot be said of the interactions or local negotiations of meaning taking place within any other form of organization, or, clearly, within economic and political marketplaces.* By emphasizing the distinctiveness of the former negotiations and interactions, the theory of societal constitutionalism brings a critical edge to symbolic interactionism. It brings critical potential to an otherwise disappointingly relativistic approach to local social action, one that otherwise asserts that *all* interests and *all* norms are ultimately negotiable at local levels. This approach fails to address how organizational forms, and other meso- and macrosociological factors, affect the *type* of local social order being studied.

As it stands, symbolic interactionism is sociology's version of Lockean liberalism. It rests on concepts that prevent social scientists from appreciating that certain institutionalized normative orientations serve all actors and groups as reliable trip wires marking shifts in the direction of change, including those taking place within local social orders. But where liberal theorists at least addressed the issue of directionality in some way, albeit by positing that drift is intrinsically benign, symbolic interactionists simply bracket the whole issue from sight and mind. Their conceptual framework rests on the presupposition that ongoing shifts of social change, like the effects of all other institutional and structural factors, cannot affect actors in ways that escape their cognition and behavioral reaction within local social orders (the same may be said of Giddens' structuration theory, 1979, 1984; thus, Alexander's charge, 1987, that interactionists are "ptesentist" is right on the mark). Yet, only on the basis of procedural voluntaristic restraints that remain "external" to actors' ongoing negotiations and interactions at local levels may *heterogeneous* actors and *competing* groups possibly recognize in common whether *they themselves* are being controlled or integrated.

Countless mechanisms of social control affect local interactions, of course, including those framed by the collegial form: from structural or inadvertent restrictions on acknowledged ranges of expectations regarding acceptable behavior, to actors' informal feelings of pride and shame (e.g. see Mayer 1983 on the former and Scheff 1988, 1990 on the latter). The sheer presence of collegial formations does not somehow reduce or eliminate the appearance of these mechanisms of social control. But the critical edge that the theory of societal constitutionalism brings to the relativism of symbolic interactionism may be put in the following way: *To the extent that actors maintain the integrity of the collegial form, they do not permit even structural or informal mechanisms of social control to push them (or others) into either purposeful or inadvertent behavioral encroachments against the threshold of interpretability of shared social duties.* Whether the shared social duties being sanctioned within local interactions are at least being kept recognizable and understandable to those affected is a matter of some significance. Symbolic interactionists cannot merely bracket this issue from consideration a priori by refusing to account for institutional continuity, and rigidity, and by concentrating exclusively on describing actors' subjective understandings of, and reactions to, their immediate situation; again, Giddens's "structuration theory" suffers from the same problem (see Stryker 1980 for the best treatment of interactionism's limitations).

Consider the situation today in many American cities where health-care professionals strike and take other actions to protest what they believe is the inadequate health care being provided to those lacking health insurance or needing emergency treatment (note 7). The professionals may sincerely see themselves as serving the interests of those least influential in civil society. Others, including hospital administrators, may sincerely believe that the professionals are largely operating in their own interests, that they are mobilizing (news media) support outside the hospital in order to compete more strategically for influence and control within the hospital. The theory of societal constitutionalism reveals that both sets of actors may be in error, and it also reveals when and how such strikes contribute to shifts in social change regardless.

How can it be possible for both sides to be in error? To the extent that an inadequate level of health care places professionals into lived situations where they cannot avoid encroaching against the threshold of interpretability of shared social duties, where they cannot avoid meting out health care capriciously, strikes are related directly to the issue of *professionals'* integrity. Ironically, strikes are then related only indirectly to the level of health care as such. They are not *reducible* to: professionals' instrumental or strategic interests, hospital administrators' policies, patients' scope of insurance coverage, or even the supposed "objective" health-care needs of the general population.

How do such strikes contribute to shifts in the direction of social change? Clearly, the quality and accessibility of health care that any nation-state affords its citizens varies greatly in comparative perspective, even across the Western democracies. It is clearly impossible to select any particular standard as "objectively irreducible" or "nonnegotiable," one that is unambiguously indicative of whether national health care is improving or declining.[12] *But it is possible to specify levels of provision of health care at which professionals are placed into lived situations where they cannot avoid capriciousness and encroachments against the threshold of interpretability of shared social duties at their sites of employment.*

The theory of societal constitutionalism reveals, therefore, that *whatever* the "objective" level of national health might be, this is an empirical issue quite distinct from the following empirical issue: What level of health care must be provided in order for professionals to maintain the integrity of their collegial formations within and around health-care facilities? When any nation-state fails to provide a level of health care that can at least support professionals' collegial formations, then hospitals and other health-care facilities are rendered into sites where breakdowns in professionalism, and both inadvertent and purposeful contributions to social authoritarianism, are common. This may be demonstrated by social scientists empirically, and in comparative perspective. It may be demonstrated by them independently of officials' (too often politicized) "objective" indices of public health, and independently of professionals' (too often self-serving) "subjective" impressions of whether any particular level of health care is adequate or not (see Sciulli and Bould in preparation for an example and an initial approach to this issue).

Societal constitutionalism v. functionalism's accounts of professionals' motivations. Parsons conveyed the wrong impression entirely when he argued that "all professions, sociologically, are 'mechanisms of social control' " (1956: 64–6). The quotation marks notwithstanding, this statement reveals his failure to distinguish instances of possible social integration from instances of demonstrable social control. More fundamentally, it reveals his failure to distinguish analytically between individual professionals' internalized normative motivations and the collegial form's institutionalized voluntaristic orientation. Parsons held that individual professionals within complex social enterprises bear "fiduciary" responsibilities. In his view, they are responsible for maintaining the integrity of (a) their own particular *substantive* value-commitments,[13] (b) the substantive core of national traditions or lived social fabrics, and (c) a form of organization that he described only residually, as nondemocratic, nonbureaucratic, and noncompetitive. Having failed to distinguish either voluntaristic action or the collegial form in more positive terms, he had no alternative conceptually other than to posit that individual professionals somehow bear all of these responsibilities as a result of their *shared* internalized substantive beliefs and normative *motivations* (Colomy and Rhoades 1988 continue this approach to the professions).

The problems this raises are apparent in two respects. First, individual professionals may be structurally exposed at their various sites of employment to increasing opportunities to compromise their professional integrity. Second, individual professionals simultaneously experience the same systemic pressures that all other actors in civil society experience: functional differentiation, organizational complexity, *and an increasing fragmentation of meaning.* Thus, individual professionals' sense of what professional integrity *is* can only be sustained under these conditions if either one of two measures is taken. On the one hand, the issue of professional integrity may be linked directly to political power, if the continued integrity of collegial formations is made a matter of public policy. On the other, the issue of professional integrity may be linked directly to social power, if the continued integrity of collegial formations is made a matter of formal corporate policy in those sectors, industries, and organizations in which professionals are employed collectively.[14]

In the absence of either of these measures, individual professionals cannot be expected by Parsons or anyone else to be any more capable than any other sets of individuals in civil society in avoiding succumbing to drift. Indeed, there are many manifestations of their failure to do so today, including:

(a) Breakdowns in individual professionals' abilities to detect, and then collectively to prevent and regulate, increasing instances of malpractice, corporate crime, and other illegal and unethical practices.

(b) Distortions in individual professionals' advice to clients and other interested parties as a result of their own calculations as *Homo eco-*

nomicus, driven by possessive individualism, rational-choice ethics, and systemic pressures of rationalization.

(c) Ongoing declines in the aura with which the public perceives professionals, coupled with the public's increasing cynicism regarding professionals' concerns for their clients' interests as well as the longer-term interests of "the public."

(d) Individual professionals' own increasing, public expressions of cynicism, and their increasing agreement with social scientists who view professions first and foremost as instruments of "status closure" or group competition rather than as worthy vocations in themselves.

Parsons saw the issue of professional integrity quite differently, of course (as have Barber 1963; Merton 1976; and Alexander 1986, 1987 since; also see chapter 8, note 16). For him (and them),[15] the issue was how "pattern-maintenance," the maintaining of the integrity of substantive norms and values of national traditions or lived social fabrics, might simultaneously be supported by individual professionals and, in turn, support these influentials' senses of professional integrity. With this in mind, he failed to distinguish the "value-commitments" that professionals share qua members of collegial formations from the nonrational beliefs that other actors share qua individuals properly socialized within religious, ethnic, or other nonrational bodies.[16] For him, *all* value-commitments are ultimately grounded on *individuals'* internalization of *shared* substantive beliefs of one kind or another (1970c: 342–5; Parsons and Platt 1973: 6–7). Parsons had no other way of approaching the professions, even as evidence mounted that individuals professionals' value-commitments are persistently challenged and compromised by the much more focused "energy" of material incentives at local sites of employment. All evidence to the contrary notwithstanding, he had to persist in hypostatizing actors' successful internalization of norms.

Moreover, having closed his social theory to the concept of reasoned social action, Parsons (and Barber, Merton, and Alexander) also had to concede from the outset that individual professionals are like all other actors within complex and functionally differentiated enterprises: They too cannot possibly provide *generalizable justifications or reasons* for their value-commitments (chapter 10). They cannot justify their value-commitments with arguments capable of persuading nonprofessionals, or those actors who have not already undergone the secondary socialization of expert training. As a result, whatever it is that is sustaining the integrity of professionals' residually defined "associations," it cannot be the justifications professionals are providing for artificially protecting them from more immediate competition within economic and political marketplaces. What must be sustaining these associations' integrity as well as each individual professional's sense of integrity, by Parsons's account, is the drift of rationalization itself. That is, he correctly posited that functional differentiation is a systemic social force. Inordinately high levels of "energy" (or material incentives) would have to be mobilized in order for power holders to dedifferentiate complex social units in general. But he incorrectly drew the conclusion that this meant it is becoming increasingly difficult for power holders to encroach against professionals' associations and professionals' integrity in particular.[17]

Once again, the assumption on which Parsons (and Barber, Merton, and Alexander) had to be operating was that, in addition to (a) Weber's view of rationalization and (b) Parsons's own view of functional differentiation, as related systemic pressures, there must also be (c) *systemic* tendencies toward "integration" and a benign "social order" (Alexander 1987: 36–51, 63–4, 68–9, 83–8 cannot escape this account of social order). This assumption is simply posited. It lacks conceptual support in Parsons's own social theory and empirical support in practice.

11.2. Collegial formations today: institutionalized restraint beyond left and right

Collegial formations today institutionalize procedural voluntaristic restraints on a third set of social activities. This set revolves around the *possibility* that professionals and deliberators contribute to reasoned social action *in the larger social order* – qua members of collegial formations rather than qua properly socialized individuals who happen to have undergone expert training. Put differently, the contributions that *these* heterogeneous actors and competing groups make to the larger social order is by no means reducible to those made by *Homo economicus* (Coleman 1986, 1990; Hechter 1987) or by expert occupations competing for "jurisdictions" within economic and political marketplaces (Abbott 1988).

But in which specific respects can the actions taken by *individual* professionals and deliberators *outside* of the collegial formations at their sites of employment be said to contribute to reasoned social action in the larger social order? In answering this question, these individuals' *cognitive* contributions to the resilience of external procedural restraints, and thereby to a *non*authoritarian direction of social change, must be isolated from whatever *normative* contribution they may also make to social order *as such* (see chapter 2, note 6, on R. Stephen Warner).[18] Put differently, the cognitive contributions that individual professionals make to a nonauthoritarian direction of social change qua members of collegial formations is analytically distinct from whatever normative contribution they happen to make to social order as such, qua properly socialized individuals who happen to have undergone expert training.

11.2.1. Collegial formations' subtle restraint

One possible set of cognitive contributions that individual professionals and deliberators may make qua members or collegial formations is to present purportedly "reasoned" cases for those interests in civil society that are otherwise inarticulate or ineffectively mobilized. Such interests would include those of the physically, mentally, or socially disadvantaged. This is what health-care professionals believe they are doing when they strike to protest inadequate emergency care. The problem, however, is that this set of cognitive contributions, taken alone, does not contribute intrinsically to maintaining the integrity of the collegial form and external procedural restraints on drift. Thus, it does not contribute to a nonauthoritarian direction of social change, nor to expanding heterogeneous actors' and competing groups' prospects for social integration. More importantly in this context, this set of cognitive contributions *cannot be said to contribute to reasoned social action in the larger social order.* Quite to the contrary, these cognitive contributions are consistent with Parsons's use of the term "reason" rather than Habermas's: Individual professionals and deliberators are merely wielding their social influence in the interests of others.

Because Parsons closed his social theory to any possibility of accommodating a standard of reasoned social action more comprehensive than the narrow norm of rational action (chapter 10), he had no alternative conceptually other than to define "reason" in terms of the social status of the *presenter* of arguments. He lacked any standard by which to define reason in terms of *the quality of the presenter's arguments itself.* In this way, he *reduced* the concept of reasoned social action to actors' relative (and competitive) social influence within *any* existing social order.[19] This renders "reason" intrinsically relative to time and place, of course, as does liberalism's hypostatization of the sovereignty of actors' subjective interests and pluralism's hypostatization of interest competition (chapter 10). Because Habermas proposes a standard of reasoned social action that revolves around the procedural qualities of the arguments themselves, his social theory is capable of moving a significant step beyond this. It can support the issue of whether and when the actions and proposals of particular social influentials *possibly* contribute to reasoned social action, and when they are demonstrably unreasoned. This issue is independent of what these actors' relative influence actually turns out to be within any given social order.

Thus, the first set of possible cognitive contributions that individual professionals and deliberators may make to the larger social order is tied exclusively to whether, and how, they wish to wield their social influence. But by moving beyond Parsons's residual references to "associations," and beyond his reductionist treatment of "reason" as social influence, another set of cognitive contributions comes to light. This is the set of cognitive contributions that individual professionals and deliberators may make to the larger social order *qua members of collegial formations*. The continued presence of collegial formations within a civil society means that even those social influentials and power holders who present their interests most articulately, and who are mobilized most effectively, anticipate a distinct possibility, a palpable contingency, within their institutionalized environments. They anticipate that their actions and proposals may at some time be scrutinized and criticized methodically by individual professionals and deliberators. (This point is developed further below.)

Even if it turns out, in practice, that they are seldom questioned, the sheer presence of collegial formations within power holders' institutionalized environments nonetheless renders them permanently vulnerable to this contingency, in principle. It is, of course, strategically rational for them to endeavor to limit their vulnerability. This is why power holders at least *prepare* rationales for their actions and proposals. These rationales, in turn, *are themselves voluntaristic*, even if only indirectly so. Any rationale that contributes in the slightest way to a nonauthoritarian direction of social change goes beyond the action's or proposal's instrumental rationality or strictly strategic implications. It also affirms, in one way or another, that the action or proposal does not threaten the ongoing direction of social change itself. Such assurances, however implicitly stated, may be thought of as power holders' expressions of a procedural "public good," and their contributions to a procedural "social capital."[20]

Three points may be made about the subtle impact of restraint that this institutionalized environment contributes to the larger social order, and these points also relate it to the issue of reasoned social action:

> First, this impact of restraint is, in principle, more consistent with Habermas's critical and possibly grounded standard of procedural reason than with Parsons's standard of social influence.

> Second, this impact of restraint may be sustained over time *without the individuals involved internalizing shared normative motivations qua properly socialized individuals.* This is another way of saying that this impact of restraint may remain strictly cognitive rather than becoming either affective or habitual. It may be, and is, institutionalized by individual professionals' and deliberators' *behavior* within the larger social order qua members of collegial formations, and not by their personal beliefs and commitments qua properly socialized individuals. Thus, they may behave in this way driven by any number of competing or even inconsistent normative motivations.

> Third, because this cognitive impact may well remain detached from any formal support by governmental or corporate power holders, i

may remain strictly informational rather than becoming strategically compelling. Indeed, this is the case today within all nonauthoritarian social orders. The alternative is for actors to institutionalize a public realm proper within a civil society by supporting the integrity of collegial formations as a matter of public or corporate policy.

11.2.2. From the limiting case of social authoritarianism to a nonauthoritarian direction of social change

Before proceeding, consider how the situation differs within authoritarian social orders as well as sites of actors' demonstrable social control within any sector of a civil society. When collegial formations are absent from institutionalized environments, power holders and social influentials are not vulnerable to the contingency of scrutiny and criticism. As such, their sole concern is to mobilize the support – or, at minimum, to neutralize the opposition – of competing power holders and social influentials. The latter may well include journalists and others who purport to "represent" and "inform" public opinion.

Ironically, these strictly strategic calculations regarding how to mobilize support and neutralize opposition within social orders marked by the complete *absence* of collegial formations are consistent in every respect with Parsons's relativist approach to "reason" as social influence (as are Laumann and Knoke's and Abbott's accounts of interest competition). In this limiting case, power holders and social influentials indeed fail to anticipate normative restraints of any kind, let alone those that possibly contribute to reasoned social action. This vacuum of voluntaristic orientations within their institutionalized environments can be filled, in practice, in two ways, however: one that remains consistent with an authoritarian social order and another that distinguishes a nonauthoritarian *direction* of social change.

This vacuum is filled in the first way when "moral authorities" surface – by whatever route – who begin to compete *strategically* for social influence within civil society, along the lines consistent with Parsons's concepts (see chapter 9, pages 206–8). Unlike the power holders and social influentials already competing strategically in the limiting case, however, the social influence of emerging "moral authorities" hinges on whether they can challenge all competitors to honor normative restraints on the scope of their immediate pursuit of self-interest. Their social influence hinges, ultimately, on whether they can induce power holders and social influentials to remain aware of normative considerations beyond their calculations of instrumental and strategic rationality. Such awareness is a prerequisite to their keeping their behavior consistent with the substantive core of national traditions or lived social fabrics.

To the extent that "moral authorities' " challenges are institutionalized, an authoritarian social order can be said to be moving away from the limiting case. What this means, in more positive terms, is that "protected spheres" of substantive normative restraints are being maintained *artificially* within a civil society. The problem is that within authoritarian social orders, such spheres are either tied to transcendental concerns or to voluntaristic but strictly substantive worldly qualities. The latter is the case, for instance, with Lockean liberalism's public/private distinction, and with any legal protections of private property. Numerous authoritarian social orders in the Third World (and now in the former Eastern bloc) protect private property in both of its modern senses: as an inalienable location of individuals' citizenship or "natural rights" vis-à-vis government, and as alienable capital (Arendt 1951 revolves around this distinction). Other substantively voluntaristic "protected spheres" that can be kept consistent with an *authoritarian* social order include: (a) networks of environmental groups and activists and (b) networks of museums, preservationist groups, and other organizations bearing fiduciary responsibilities for a nation-state's cultural and architectural patrimony. The addition of more and more protected spheres dedicated to substantive worldly qualities remains consistent with Parsons's reduction of "reason" to social influence and also can be kept consistent with an authoritarian direction of social change and actors' demonstrable social control.

By contrast, the vacuum of the limiting case is filled in a quite different way when collegial formations emerge and institutionalize distinctively *procedural* voluntaristic orientations within a civil society. Unlike the emergence of substantively voluntaristic "protected spheres," this development fundamentally challenges the sovereignty of actors' subjective interests rather than merely restraining the scope of economic and political marketplaces. It moves the competition for social influence and political power beyond Parsons's relativist treatment of substantive "reason" toward Habermas's critical standard of procedural reason. It moves this competition toward the voluntaristic orientation distinctive to a nonauthoritarian direction of a social change and to expanding heterogeneous actors' and competing groups' prospects for social integration.

This transition is not accomplished, however, when interest competition takes place in the presence of prominent journalists, elected officials, private property holders, and others who purportedly "represent" and "inform" amorphous public opinion. After all, this context for interest competition, this institutionalized environment, may be found both historically and today within social orders that rest rather exclusively on social control. Both historically and today, power holders and social influentials within such social orders hold elections and maintain parliaments, tolerate relatively free print and electronic media, and legally protect private property in both senses noted above (e.g. Mexico in particular, but Latin America generally). Thus, what distinguishes a sustained nonauthoritarian and integrative direction of social change is not the extent to which increasing numbers of "protected spheres" of any kind are institutionalized within a civil society. What distinguishes it is rather the extent to which distinctively procedural voluntaristic "protected spheres" become functionally differentiated, in practice, from substantive voluntaristic "protected spheres."

11.2.3. From subtle restraint to a lived sense of anticipation

The voluntaristic orientations institutionalized within *all* nonauthoritarian social orders and sites of heterogeneous actors' and competing groups' possible social integration are, ultimately, *sets of decidedly nonrational and yet intersubjective norms.* These are distinctively procedural voluntaristic orientations that are artificially, and always only contingently, suspended from interest competition within economic and political marketplaces as well as from power holders' "negotiations of meaning" within local social arenas. The *only* modern social orders – national or local – in which all voluntaristic orientations continue to be negotiated, as symbolic interactionists and pluralists contend, are social orders that rest exclusively on social control.[21] After all, it is within these social orders that members of the artificially "protected spheres" that institutionalize substantive voluntaristic orientations indeed find that *these* orientations are *never* suspended from interest competition and local negotiations.

By contrast, within nonauthoritarian and integrative social orders, the professionals and deliberators who are members of collegial formations operate within and through procedural voluntaristic orientations that literally become and remain suspended in this way. Within these social orders, *both* sets of social influentials – "moral authorities" who are members of protected spheres and professionals and deliberators who are members of collegial formations – comprise an enormous network of hundreds of thousands of individuals. The only quality that they share in common, qua individuals, is that they are all permanently "available" to scrutinize and criticize social influentials' and power holders' actions and proposals *anywhere within a civil society.* They are not somehow confined to their respective protected spheres. Yet, their "availability" in the sense above is ultimately contingent on whether these spheres continue to be *artificially* (or nonrationally) protected.

By contrast to Parsons's approach to the professions, professionals' and deliberators' "availability" qua individuals is certainly not based ultimately on their socialization and whatever norms they have happened to internalize. After all, professionals within *authoritarian* social orders may well have internalized more "moral" norms than professionals within nonauthoritarian social orders. Similarly, by contrast to Lockean and Smithean liberals' approaches to property, and to constitutional theorists' views of the constituent force, professionals' and deliberators' "availability" in the late twentieth century is by no means based exclusively or even primarily on their wealth, power, or influence as private citizens who happen to own or control property in either of the senses noted above. Wealthy professionals and other wealthy private citizens may be found in all *authoritarian* social orders.

Within nonauthoritarian social orders, where, when, or even whether particular individuals within this vast network of those "available" ever actually criticize power holders" actions and proposals is a matter of secondary importance to the matter of the sheer size of this *network* itself. Its size may be reduced quite dramatically, however, and within very brief periods of time. It is reduced as professionals and deliberators either purposefully or inadvertently encroach against the integrity of collegial formations, *even as they continue to act rationally (and legally) in their own subjective interests.* By contrast, to sustain an ongoing nonauthoritarian direction of social change is to maintain the integrity of collegial formations. It is to keep the network of "available" individuals at a size sufficient to institutionalize a lived *sense of anticipation* among power holders and social influentials *even as the latter continue to compete rationally (and legally) within economic and political marketplaces.*[22]

11.2.4. Institutionalized anticipation: infrastructure of nonauthoritarian social orders

Power holders within nonauthoritarian social orders anticipate that their actions and proposals might be challenged at some point along the line (a) by "moral authorities" within protected spheres, and, more importantly, (b) by professionals and deliberators within first one and then another set of collegial formations.

> The first set of professionals and deliberators is comprised of the members of collegial formations found within these particular power holders' institutionalized environments. These formations may be thought of as *sectoral collegial formations.*
>
> The second set of professionals and deliberators is comprised of the members of collegial formations found within the very corporations or enterprises that these particular power holders own or control. These formations may be thought of as *divisional collegial formations.*

The presence of sectoral collegial formations renders power holders vulnerable in the sense noted above, and the presence of divisional collegial formations magnifies their sense of vulnerability. Depending on the vigiance of individual professionals and deliberators within sectoral collegial formations, *a lived sense of anticipation* can be institutionalized that spans entire industries and sectors of a civil society. The wax and wane of this lived sense of anticipation is precisely how power holders actually *experience* shifts between drift and direction within any modern nation-state. They experience these shifts in their everyday lives, and, clearly, their lived experiences of directionality might very well strike them (as well as their questioners and other actors) as more stressful personally than their lived experiences of unmediated drift.[23]

Given the presence of peak associations within the civil societies of the Continent, and the concomitant decline of the division of powers in favor of neocorporatist "intermediation," it cannot be that civil law courts in themselves restrain power holders from control and arbitrariness within civil society.[24] Given the presence of the mass media within many unambiguously authoritarian social orders, it also cannot be that a "free press" or "public opinion" in itself restrains them. For the same reason, it cannot be that power holders are restrained by the strictly strategic restraints that their competitors pose within economic and political marketplaces. Similarly, it cannot be that power holders within nonauthoritarian social orders are restrained by the separation of church and state, the public/private distinction, or the presence of any other substantively voluntaristic protected spheres in themselves. It is certainly not the case that the surveillance of "private" enterprises by governmental (or internal corporate) regulatory agencies in themselves restrains power holders from control and arbitrariness within civil society. And, finally, the hypostatization of actors' "natural rights," or of their internalized substantive beliefs and motivations as properly socialized individuals, cannot, in themselves, account for a sustained nonauthoritarian direction of social change under modern conditions.

What subtly yet significantly restrains power holders within all existing (and historical) nonauthoritarian social orders is the institutionalization of a lived sense of anticipation that, at some point along the line, individuals within the network of those "available" might methodically scrutinize and criticize their actions and proposals. This institutionalized sense of anticipation is itself a strictly voluntaristic orientation. Its appearance and continued presence within any sector of a modern civil society remains forever a contingent possibility. Its presence is never overdetermined by modernity itself. Yet, it is a voluntaristic orientation that even the most heterogeneous, competitive, and conflictual sets of power holders and social influentials in fact recognize and understand *in common* when a nonauthoritarian direction of social change is being sustained. This can and does occur *without these power holders and social influentials, internalizing any particular sets of normative motivations in common and without them sharing very many subjective interests, if any.* It can and does occur *without them having to negotiate any particularly restricted set of substantive meanings within their local interactions.* In short, this institutionalized sense of anticipation is the irreducible *social infrastructure* that sustains a nonauthoritarian direction of social change under modern conditions, and it is not established by the presence of bureaucratic, democratic, or patron-client formations within a civil society.

Going beyond the presupposition of exhausted possibilities, this social infrastructure may well be found, in practice, within particular sectors of civil societies of modern nation-states that fail to recapitulate most of the particular political institutions and economic practices of existing Western democracies. Indeed, this social infrastructure is what augments *these* institutions and practices in such a way that *they* may at times contribute, in practice, to a nonauthoritarian direction of social change. It is precisely because these institutions and practices are not always augmented by this social infrastructure that they may be found in various combinations within any number of *authoritarian* social orders.

It must be kept in mind that *actions* taken by individual professionals and deliberators qua members of collegial formations, and not the sheer presence of collegial formations itself, institutionalize power holders' lived sense of anticipation. By their sheer presence, collegial formations institutionalize only (a) an acknowledged range of expectations regarding what is acceptable behavior *within and immediately around these formations in particular,* and, with this, (b) a set of external procedural restraints on drift or on *inadvertently* arbitrary exercises of collective power. This range of acknowledged expectations can only be extended across an entire civil society, however, and thereby sustain a nonauthoritarian direction of social change when individual members of collegial formations act in such a way that power holders anticipate scrutiny and methodical criticisms *even when their actions and proposals are not encroaching against the integrity of existing collegial formations.* But how can this be demonstrated empirically?

The subtle impact of this procedural voluntaristic orientation can be demonstrated empirically by asking why do power holders *ever* bother to *prepare* rationales for their actions and proposals in the first place? After all, preparing rationales is essentially a private act. It is also not sanctioned by law in any modern nation-state. Nor is it something that journalists or amorphous public opinion "sanction" more informally. And yet within all nonauthoritarian social orders without exception the leaders of any "responsible" social movement, network, organization, or institution prepare such rationales, even as they are rarely called on to present them. They do so because, after all is said and done, they acknowledge that their *failure* to do so leaves them unprepared for *individual professionals' and deliberators'* queries. This renders them vulnerable, in principle; whenever this failure is discovered, moreover, it is as likely initially to draw as much attention to an action or proposal as the latter's substance itself.

Putting all of this differently, by preparing rationales, power holders are not anticipating direct queries from government officials or journalists, or even adverse public opinion. They readily sidestep all such queries, and amorphous public opinion rarely affects their interests for very long. How long did consumers' reaction to the Alaskan oil spill affect Exxon's sales? Power holders instead anticipate that individuals within the network of those "available" might pursue some of these queries if rationales are not forthcoming, and then initiate queries of their own.[25] The question that haunts Exxon executives today, and that drives them to prepare many more rationales than they will ever be called on to present is: What new findings by researchers or commission members are likely to bring the Alaska oil spill again into the public eye in the future, spawning yet other queries?

In short, power holders do not prepare rationales because they anticipate methodical or sustained examination by government regulators, "public opinion," or an "investigative press," independently of a sizable network of professionals and deliberators who are "available" as members of sectoral collegial formations.[26] The significance, pervasiveness, and yet subtlety of impact of the latter voluntaristic procedural orientation is not vitiated, moreover, when it turns out that power holders' privately prepared rationales are patently weak as arguments. This impact is not vitiated if the rationales could not possibly qualify as reasoned in the grand sense that Habermas envisions. Indeed, it is not likely that any of them ever could. This impact also is not vitiated, moreover, if the rationales prepared in private are in most instances never presented publicly. This is typically the case, in practice.

11.2.5. The uncertain foundation of nonauthoritarian social order today

As noted at various points in this volume, a public policy of maintaining the integrity of collegial formations cannot be found anywhere in the modern world. What can be found within nation-states that sustain a nonauthoritarian direction of social change, however, is the institutionalization of power holders' lived sense of anticipation of scrutiny and criticism. There are many sectors, industries, and organizations within contemporary Western civil societies where this sense of anticipation is not institutionalized. These are the sectors of Western civil societies wherein actors' demonstrable social control rather than their possible social integration accounts for social order. These sectors also can be said to contribute, however inadvertently so, to social nonauthoritarianism *within Western democracies*.

Conversely, there are also selected sectors, industries, and organizations of civil societies in the East and Third World where this sense of anticipation has been institutionalized. These are the sectors of these civil societies wherein actors' possible social integration accounts *in some part* for social order. They also can be said to contribute, however inadvertently so, to a nonauthoritarian direction of social change within nation-states that currently lack most political institutions and economic practices of Western democracy.

In both cases, these are empirical issues. These are issues amenable to detailed, falsifiable comparative and historical research. To pose these as empirical issues, however, is to jettison the presupposition of exhausted possibilities.

Still, the absence of a public policy of maintaining the integrity of collegial formations means that two crucial bases of a nonauthoritarian direction of social change have not yet been institutionalized anywhere in the modern world, including within existing Western democracies:

> First, individual professionals' *own* behavioral fidelity to the collegial form's procedural threshold has not yet been firmly institutionalized. Such behavior is not sanctioned by law, nor mandated as a matter of public or corporate policy.

> Second, power holders who encroach against the threshold of interpretability of shared social duties are not sanctioned by law. This remains the case even when their actions and proposals are revealed to have this effect.

Institutionalizing these two bases of a nonauthoritarian direction of social change is the very centerpiece of a *public realm* proper. When individual professionals and deliberators, or power holders, encroach against the threshold of interpretability, they simultaneously contribute to drift in two ways. First, they close off any possibility of contributing to reasoned social action in the larger social order. Second, and more importantly, they encroach against the integrity of the threshold of the collegial form, and thereby against the external procedural restraints on drift that this formation alone institutionalizes. To institutionalize these two bases is, by contrast, to sanction all such encroachments by law. It is to establish and then maintain civil "meaning" regarding what drift and direction are, despite: actors' (including professionals') increasing heterogeneity, social units' increasing complexity and functional differentiation, and tendencies toward increasingly rigid levels and types of social stratification.[27]

Today, with neither social base institutionalized, individual professionals and deliberators within universities, corporations, associations, and networks of Western democracies seldom refuse to entertain the rationales provided by elected officials, corporate executives, or other power holders within civil society. They seldom refuse even as these rationales often feign claims of consistency with the "public interest" of a "democratic society." Within nonauthoritarian social orders, such *feigning* is nonetheless an acknowledgement of sorts of the ranges of expectations regarding acceptable behavior institutionalized by collegial formations. As such, feigning is not really as serious a problem for a nonauthoritarian social order as it might initially seem. It certainly does not, in itself, presage a "legitimation crisis" of Western institutions and practices (Habermas 1973a). The real world, after all, is not a courtroom, a graduate seminar, or an ideal speech situation.

What is a serious problem, however, is that power holders are not sanctioned by law when it turns out that their efforts to maximize efficient production or effective administration within private enterprises do indeed threaten the integrity of sectoral or divisional collegial formations. *Unmediated rational action is intrinsically inconsistent with the procedural voluntaristic orientation institutionalized by the collegial form. Yet, it may remain consistent with the substantive voluntaristic orientations institutionalized by other "protected spheres."* This is the case in the illustration presented in chapter 1: Scott's demand that William submit tampered data may well be consistent with the company's (and its employees') immediate material interests as well as with the substantive norms of environmental, cultural, and religious protected spheres. Yet this same demand is inconsistent with professionals' integrity, with the research division's collegial form, and with this formation's contribution to external procedural restraints on drift. Scott's conduct is an indication that: power holders' lived sense of anticipation of scrutiny and criticism has not been institutionalized within this industry, the industry's professionals are being controlled, and the industry is contributing to drift rather than to direction.[28]

Even in the absence of a public mandate to sanction instrumental and strategic actions that encroach against the collegial form, the institutionalization of a sense of anticipation among power holders that characterizes existing nonauthoritarian social orders carries its own subtle restraint. First, it at least slows the pace of drift. Second, it simultaneously exposes the importance of establishing a public realm proper within a civil society. It begins to reveal that the latter is the social infrastructure upon which a nonauthoritarian direction of social change can be sustained in the late twentieth century. Third, it keeps open the possibility at least that selected power holders and social influentials are capable of contributing to reasoned social action in the larger social order.

Whenever individual professionals and deliberators question power holders, and find that their actions and proposals threaten the procedural voluntaristic orientation institutionalized by the collegial form, they are *simultaneously* elevating a broader standard of reason above the narrow norm of rational action. This is the case irrespective of whether they are aware of this or not. They are demonstrating, however implicitly or unknowingly, that even if power holders' actions and proposals are indeed instrumentally or strategically rational, they are nonetheless encroaching against the threshold of interpretability of shared social duties. They are simultaneously demonstrating, again however implicitly or unknowingly, that this disqualifies these actions and proposals as possibly reasoned, possibly integrative, or possibly contributing in any way to a nonauthoritarian direction of social change.

Still, individual professionals and deliberators today lack direct, institutionalized linkages to social or political power even within Western democracies. This is the case particularly when they question power holders outside of the divisions and sectors within which they are employed. *This* is why power holders may ultimately ignore them even as they continue to anticipate the possibility of their questioning: Power holders are ultimately not compelled or impelled to bring their actions and proposals into line with the threshold of interpretability of shared duties and the integrity of either sectoral or divisional collegial formations.

11.3. Unwitting beneficiaries of the collegial form

What does it mean, on the one hand, for there to be a vast network of individuals employed within formations that institutionalize external procedural restraints, and who are thereby "available" to institutionalize a lived sense of anticipation among power holders? What does it mean, on the other, for these same individuals to operate without any direct linkage to political or social power that could result in power holders, being sanctioned to comply with the threshold restraints that ultimately maintain their formations and thereby keep them "available"?

11.3.1. Positivists' apologetic politics

This state of affairs means, in the first place, that there are students of society (that is, sociologists, anthropologists, political scientists, historians, economists, philosophers) holding positions in the academy and government, and also natural scientists holding public and private research affiliations, who do not aspire to institutionalize a public realm *even at the sites of their own professional practice.*[29] To the extent that they are not driven exclusively by the subjective interests of *Homo economicus,* these social and natural scientists are otherwise dedicated rather one-sidedly to keeping the *findings* of their research *scientific,* a seemingly laudable substantive aspiration. However, at the moment that they elevate this aspiration to the status of an ultimate end, the literal end-in-itself of the research *enterprise,* they are simultaneously assuming that this end may be attained *within any* social order and also *within any form of organization*. They may share this unargued assumption during periods of domestic tranquillity. During these periods, they may casually overlook the scientific enterprise's interrelationship with a quite different aspiration: This is the voluntaristic aspiration to keep research *enterprises* consistent with the form of organization distinctive to deliberate bodies, including those of the natural and social sciences themselves. Under modern conditions, this same form of organization also happens to contribute to the social infrastructure capable of sustaining a nonauthoritarian direction of change.

Thus, individual researchers' one-sided aspiration to render their findings scientific, as an end-in-itself, literally obscures from their recognition and understanding the procedural *voluntaristic* orientation that universities, research divisions, and other sites of professional practice contribute *simultaneously* (a) to any research enterprise itself and (b) to the larger direction of social change.[30] This procedural voluntaristic orientation is as much an empirical "fact" in the social world as any demographic trend or pattern, as any index of stratification, as any pattern of group competition. Yet, scientists (and philosophers of science) continue to emphasize the scientific qualities of research *findings* without simultaneously accounting for the impact that this procedural voluntaristic orientation has on research *enterprises*. They fail to account for the impact that different *forms* of organization have on the scholarly context in which research findings are developed, and then, even more certainly, on the scholarly context in which they are presented, debated, and then either accepted or rejected. They thereby obscure the collegial form's *empirical* contribution to researchers' communication communities and to the scientific enterprise as such. Yet, this form contributes to the social infrastructure that underlies the very possibility of their maintaining their own integrity as scientists under modern conditions.[31]

Positivists' characterizations of what qualifies research findings as scientific are in themselves relatively benign in their impact on the direction of social change. They are benign as long as these characterizations affect only the self-understandings of natural scientists. Natural scientists' object domain of study, after all, is ultimately the movement of matter in space (see Habermas 1968a on object domains). But the very same characterizations become pernicious once they affect the self-understandings of social scientists, and then practicing professionals and deliberators, because the object domain here is very different. They become pernicious when they convince social scientists that (a) the integrity of the enterprise of science is unaffected by the type of social order or form of organization in which it is embedded, and that (b) *any* standard of social change purporting to distinguish authoritarian from nonauthoritarian shifts in direction is intrinsically particular and normative rather than possibly generalizable and reasoned.[32] At the moment that positivists' characterizations of the research enterprise affect social scientists in this way, these characterizations begin to jeopardize the integrity of the scientific enterprise itself. Moreover, through social scientists' treatments of *modern institutions, organizations, social movements, and networks*, these characterizations ultimately affect the institutionalized environment within which *professionals, power holders, and social influentials* approach the research enterprise and professional practice generally.

The irony is that social scientists' assumption that standards of social change are intrinsically normative and particular is itself unscientific. It is itself a strictly normative belief. It is a nonrational prejudice that they happen to share with natural scientists and positivist philosophers of science who are addressing a very different object domain. This normative belief is a reflection of what happens when social scientists characterize the research enterprise using concepts that remain consistent with a copy theory of truth: Individual researchers are seen as monads capable of independently establishing the certainty of their (and others') descriptions and explanations. They are not seen as uncertain describers and explainers *who either operate within collegial formations or some other organizational form*, but never operate independently.[33]

By contrast, the moment that social scientists view the research enterprise in terms that remain consistent with a consensus theory of truth, they characterize individual researchers and the research enterprise quite differently. Here, each researcher's "independent" descriptions and explanations are conjectures (to use Popper's 1962 apt term). They are conjectures regarding what "really happened" in the natural or social world. Any researcher's claim that his or her own conjectures are "true" (more "factual") secures credibility only within and through ceaseless peer review. The theory of societal constitutionalism adds to this characterization that under modern conditions uncertain researchers may or may not orient themselves within and around a distinct organizational form that, in turn, secures the credibility of peer review itself. The threshold restraints of the collegial form maintain the integrity of peer review, despite systemic pressures of drift that fragment meaning among researchers and drive them toward patron-client relationships.[34]

11.3.2. Intellectuals' ready cooptation and marginalization

The presence of collegial formations whose members lack any connection to the political or social power that can result in sanctioning power holders' compliance with procedural voluntaristic orientations also carries a second meaning. It means that there are intellectuals, artists, and practicing professionals within modern nation-states who are relatively detached, in practice, from *any* identifiable organizational base. Intellectuals, after all, "do not constitute a corporate body" (Parsons and Platt 1973: 274). To the extent that they also do not become linked to, or supported by, a network of collegial formations within their institutionalized environments, they are, like journalists, mere commentators on the contemporary political and social scene. For all of their eloquence, they are handily controlled by power holders and social influentials in one or more of the following three ways at least:

> First, intellectuals may be ignored altogether. If a network of collegial formations is not already present within a civil society, power holders may repress intellectuals outright. Yet, if they are wiser, they permit them to write or say whatever they wish, because, after all, they are already detached from any organizational base. As a result of this, they are already incapable of resiliently restraining power holders' exercises of collective power.

> Second, intellectuals may be sought out by power holders, as one quite minor set of contributors to a lived social fabric of symbols and cultural "information" that provide upper and middle classes with diversion, refinement, and entertainment. If a network of collegial formations is not already present within a civil society, then intellectuals' prospects of influencing power holders may be *less* promising than those of movie stars, sports stars, or stand-up comedians.

> Third, intellectuals may be readily coopted. After all, political and economic elites directly or indirectly control the purse strings of intellectuals' career networks. If a network of collegial formations is not already present within a civil society, then recruitment into intellectual "circles" may be largely restricted to the patron-client networks of an already compromised intellectual elite. Occasional working-class or lower-class recruits are easily isolated or coopted. Patron-client networks have already been substituted for collegial formations in intellectuals' "institutionalized environment."

Still, the issues that typically concern intellectuals tend to be broader than the issues addressed by social scientists within universities. Intellectuals debate "meaning," "ideology," and actors' "definition of the situation." They cannot be said to be dedicated exclusively or even primarily to maximizing "cognitive rationality" or empirical explanation (Parsons and Platt 1973: 275, 283).[35] Because they often lack an organizational base which is itself dedicated to enhancing actors' recognition and understanding of "meaning" beyond cognitive rationality, intellectuals bring their talk of "meaning" into universities. But university departments are not organized today to deal with issues posed in this way (Alexander 1986). As a result, intellectuals may be quite isolated even within major universities.

There does not now exist any specific organizational framework within the university structure for meeting this ideological need, and so far there has not been a strong demand for it [to be placed within the university]. This structural vacuum may have been a factor in the vulnerability of the universities in situations of pressure to which they have recently been subjected (Parsons and Platt 1973: 292).

One of the ways in which intellectuals may nonetheless prove useful to universities (and other collegial formations) is for them ceaselessly to remind professionals of the importance of maintaining the integrity of collegial formations. The problem with this is that intellectuals ignore the latter's importance as well. They prefer to turn more immediately to the "heat" of substantive matters of "meaning" rather than to bother with issues as "cold" as that of collegial formations' procedural threshold. Ironically, the latter is precisely the standard by which they and social scientists alike may fathom the shifts in the direction of social change that most immediately affect their own integrity.

Notes

Chapter 1. Introduction: societal constitutionalism as critical theory

1 Henrique Cardoso (1977) documents Latin American researchers' early contributions to the *dependencia* debate.

2 Pluralism has been subjected to intense criticisms by a symposium of legal scholars in the *Yale Law Journal* (1988).

3 Included among the institutions and practices of Western liberal-democracy are: a mass franchise and regular elections for major public offices; competing, mass political parties; relatively autonomous interest associations; relatively autonomous print (if not electronic) news media within a relatively "free" market of ideas; recognition by state agencies of actors' formal rights or civil liberties of speech, assembly, and equal opportunity, including a relatively "free" labor market; and, of course, guaranteed rights to own, control, accumulate, and exchange capital. Brennan and Buchanan (1985: 16) add systematic accounting for expenditures of public funds. See Sartori (1962) for a standard discussion of these institutions and practices, Przeworski (1985) for their historical impact on social democracy in Scandinavia, and Bobbio (1987) for an effort to radicalize them.

   Social democracies modify these institutions and practices. Most essentially, they restrict individuals' property rights in an effort to distribute material resources more equitably and, simultaneously, to maintain or even extend actors' civil liberties. In practice, however, social democracies often modify liberal-democracy further by subordinating the autonomy of decentralized interest groups to rather centralized "peak associations." A single interest association stands literally at the "peak" of each functional sector of civil society, straddling the boundary between civil society and state. From its peak it "intermediates" all actions and proposals from either side: Its leaders monopolize the political representation of all interests articulated within its sector, and they greatly influence, if not draft or initiate outright, all state policies affecting these interests (see chapter 4; Schmitter's [1974] seminal statement; and Fulcher's 1987 review of neocorporatism's relationship to social democracy).

4 The only postwar "bourgeois" or non-Marxist social theorist who was convinced of the opposite – that concepts may be grounded against normative relativism and simultaneously inform empirical research – was Talcott Parsons. To consider the works of two other prominent "bourgeois" social theorists, Robert Merton never attempted to ground concepts against normative relativism, and Niklas Luhmann today does not attempt to do so. The three distinct phases of Parsons's theory construction all revolve around frameworks of *analytical concepts*. The only reason that he moved to such a fundamental level, that of analytical distinctions, rather than remaining (with Merton, and then Luhmann) at a more "surface" level of ideal types and both empirical and normative generalizations, was precisely that he was interested in grounding empirical research conceptually. He was convinced that only in this way could research findings be rendered cumulative instead of

remaining incommensurable (see Bershady 1973 for the best treatment of this quality of Parsons's works). Luhmann is explicit in rejecting this project (1982: 365, notes 5–6).

5 The mainstream at one time included modernization theory, and even today it continues to revolve in one way or another around pluralist theory (Skocpol 1980; Laumann and Knoke 1987), despite the many criticisms lodged against the latter.

6 This assertion by Tilly is challenged directly in chapter 6 (page 126).

In presenting "eight Pernicious Postulates of twentieth century social thought," Tilly embraces the lacuna of integrative possibilities and thereby fails to question the presupposition of exhausted possibilities. Indeed, he explicitly collapses social integration into social control in his fifth and eighth postulates (1984: 11, 44–9, 56–7). He also advances two propositions. First, functional differentiation is not a terribly significant systemic force within modern nation-states, as Talcott Parsons believed, because dedifferentiation occurs as well. Second, the analytical distinction between legitimate and illegitimate uses of force cannot be made in comparative study (1985: 169–91). By dismissing the significance of functional differentiation, however, Tilly ends up with a vision of social order that is more conservative and complacent than Parsons' own, including that contained in his indefensible works of the early 1950s (Sciulli in preparation, a). Tilly's abandonment of any effort to distinguish legitimate from illegitimate uses of force is by no means an implicit critique of the collective prejudice regarding Western democracy. It is rather the sort of relativist position that contributes to the latter's elevation by default above significant criticism.

7 The argument here is clearly not that liberal-democratic or social-democratic institutions and practices are immoral or, for that matter, amoral. The argument is decidedly less grand: It cannot be said by anyone that these institutions and practices alone are in some sense "moral," or superordinate to actors' and groups' narrow calculations of their own immediate material interests. These institutions and practices cannot be said by anyone to exhaust all "moral" responses to Olson's (1965) free rider problem (also e.g. Hechter 1987), what Parsons (1937a) called the utilitarian dilemma, and what Weber (1914–20) treated as the entropic drift of rationalization.

8 Jürgen Habermas's works are a rarity today because they continue the Frankfurt school's outright rejection of the presupposition of exhausted possibilities. Yet, his works perpetuate this school's longstanding inability to present critical concepts capable of informing detailed empirical research in the social sciences.

9 See Hall (1987) for a decidedly moralistic endorsement of Western democracy. Instead of endeavoring to explore the limits of the presupposition of exhausted possibilities with grounded concepts, Hall opens the way to a grand, unhesitant apologia for whatever direction of change Western civil societies happen to take in the future. Bloom (1988) is the great antidote to this, as moralistic (and polemical) in its own way. Bloom decries not merely relativism but what he calls "American nihilism."

10 This same definition of social integration is repeated at the end of chapter 2, in the context of a review of the literature of social control. It is specified somewhat further in chapter 4 when the importance of the collegial form of organization is introduced. In chapter 8 the definition of social integration is used again, but by this point within the context (and terminology) of the theory of societal constitutionalism.

11 Michael Hechter (1987) proposes that "solidarity" be reduced to two factors within the framework of concepts of rational choice theory: actors' degree of material dependence on a particular group, and the degree to which the group's leadership can monitor (or "meter," as Hechter puts it) actors' conformity to the groups' shared social duties. In this way he rightly eliminates all concern with actors' *feelings* of moral obligation to conform to group life, since actors' subjective beliefs can just as well be manipulated as genuine (whereas Etzioni 1988, for instance, wishes to bring such feelings into the very center of

economists' studies of aggregate economic behavior). But feelings aside, Hechter then follows comparativists and other researchers in failing to consider a further distinction, one that has a great deal to do with both the presence of group solidarity in itself and then with the quality of that solidarity: What does "solidarity" mean if the shared social duties that the groups' leaders enforce can be demonstrated to be controlling and intrinsically particular in substance? Conversely, what does "solidarity" mean if these shared social duties can be demonstrated to escape reduction to control and particularism? Put differently, Hechter's theory reduces "solidarity" to successful social control, just as Durkheim's theory and then Parsons's reduced "integration" to successful social control. Hechter's reductionism merely substitutes surveillance and material sanctions for Durkheim's and Parsons's hypostatization of actors' purported internalization of shared norms and moral beliefs. One of the purposes of the present volume is to provide theorists and researchers with the analytical distinctions necessary to examine critically both materialist and idealist frameworks of concepts, and thereby to avoid both tendencies toward reductionism.

12 These ideal types can generally be traced to Juan Linz's (1964) seminal essay. For uses of the latter, see, for example, Oberschall (1973) in sociology and McDonough (1981) in political science.

13 What is exciting about network analysis is that it indeed offers a new conceptual framework for comparative study, one not directly traceable to derivations of the classics' theories (S.F. Nadel notwithstanding). See Berkowitz (1982) for a proponent's appraisal of network analysis, Burt (1980) for a review of the literature, and Wellman (1983, updated 1988) for an influential commentary. See David Knoke (1989) for an effort to bring network analysis to comparative study (based on principles from Laumann and Knoke 1987).

14 Lieberson is concerned that researchers too often pose problems because they meet statistical criteria rather than because they are informed by theoretical issues (1985: 89). As opposed to seeking data sets that incorporate variation, and then endeavoring to explain the variation (1985: 88), Leiberson thinks that "the simple case study could be of considerably greater value than presently appreciated if it is possible to mount such studies with a very clear appreciation of some crucial issue and if the data are of very high quality such that the results can be taken seriously" (1985: 105). And he sees this as most useful in comparative study because statistics (such as international crime data) taken out of their social contexts are distortions from the outset (1985: 110–13) or succumb to "the fallacy of nonequivalence" (1985: 114).

15 Durkheim, Parsons, and Giddens are probably the worst offenders (to span generations), and yet, ironically, Parsons' analytical framework of concepts provides an important basis for distinguishing social integration from social control and thereby for filling the lacuna (Sciulli in preparation, a). Both Diana Crane (1982) and Margaret Archer (1987) are highly critical of Durkheim, Parsons, and functionalism generally for positing that a society likely has a single, dominant culture. Each of them argues effectively for the greater likelihood of cultural diversity within any social setting, and in particular within any modern social setting. And yet, ironically, they are very similar to Durkheim in the way that they collapse the concept of social integration into the broader concept of social control. As a distinct concept, social integration is controversial because it hinges on whether parts of a social order that are not based on actors' manipulation, control, or coercion can be isolated. To fail to distinguish this concept, however, is to concede implicitly that instances of very successful social control – when mechanisms of coercion and control are most effective, and thereby manipulative – are instances of "social integration." Crane and Archer are as guilty of this Durkheimian tendency as Parsons and Giddens.

16 The central concern of societal constitutionalism as stated to this point is to address social change, and in particular to fathom its direction. Yet, the situation presented below, for purposes of illustration, is static; a hypothetical situation described at a single point in time. Even worse, it seems to focus on particular individuals rather than on collective actions. Illustrations of how the direction of social change contradicts the presupposition of exhausted possibilities cannot be provided, however, until the theory of societal constitutionalism has been presented, at the end of chapter 8. To present them now would reduce them to assertions. Detailed empirical research has yet to be oriented conceptually to take static situations, like the one discussed in this section, and trace either how they evolved historically or how they are shifting today. In short, there is no available comparative study or case study in the literature that demonstrates that static situations like this one are indeed either increasing or decreasing in frequency within Western democracies or, for that matter, within Eastern or Third World nation-states. Consider, for instance, that there is not a single study that compares how corporations that engage in corporate crimes organize their research divisions and how research divisions are organized within corporations that have reputations for lawful practices (see Braithwaite 1985 for a literature review). The theory of societal constitutionalism is designed to encourage researchers to draw such comparisons, and to monitor particular changes within and across private enterprises.

17 Upon reading this hypothetical illustration, William Lofquist, a graduate student at the University of Delaware, was reminded of a report he had read of an incident that took place in 1967 at a B.F. Goodrich Co. installation in Troy, Ohio, purportedly resulting in the Department of Defense changing its procurement policies. Reported by Kermit Vandivier, a married, then forty-two year-old, data analyst and technical writer at Goodrich with seven children, it was first published in 1972 and is reprinted in a 1987 anthology on corporate crime edited by my former colleague David Ermann and Richard Lundman at Ohio State University. The Troy installation was in 1967 "one of the three largest manufacturers of aircraft wheels and brakes," even as it employed only 600 people (Vandivier 1972: 103). The incident in question revolved initially around the relationship between a new, twenty-six year-old engineer, Searle Lawson, and his immediate supervisor, John Warren, a man who would not tolerate criticism and, as a result, had, over time, insulated himself from peer review (1972: 104–5):

Warren assigns Lawson his first major project. In testing aircraft brakes for an important new customer, LTV Corp., Lawson finds, however, that they cannot meet specifications due to faulty design (1972: 106). Warren rejects Lawson's suggestions for redesign because he wishes to meet the contract's deadline. Lawson responds by moving one step up the corporate ladder. He shows his findings to projects manager Robert Sink, a hard-working man who held his present position without engineering credentials but with an ear to company politics (1972: 107–8). Sink promptly tells the young engineer to follow the orders of his more experienced supervisor, Warren.

At this point Vandivier enters the picture. He notices irregularities in the data from Lawson's tests, and also the subsequent efforts to cover up the unwanted results. By this point, too, the cover-up had expanded considerably. After speaking to Sink, Lawson went dutifully to Ralph Gretzinger, a test lab supervisor, and requested that he miscalibrate the instrument that records brake pressure (1972: 110–11). Ironically, Gretzinger, a man noted for integrity, readily complied, but only because he thought at the time that this was part of an experiment for internal use only, something which is not unusual. For his part, Sink had by this time informed his boss, Russell Van Horn, manager of the design engineering section, of the situation as well (1972: 112). And Gretzinger, soon enraged to learn that the miscalibrated results might well leave the laboratory and be included in the final reports describes the whole incident to Russell Line, manager of Goodrich's entire technical services section (1972: 113).

Line tells all of the subordinates in the cover-up that each of them is working only on one part of the puzzle. Because none of them is apprised of the complete picture, he assures them they are not doing anything wrong. Vandivier cannot believe that this is Line's position, so he discusses it with him personally (1972: 114). Line is indeed adamant (1972: 115). With a family to support and bills to pay, Vandivier goes along by doctoring-up his qualification report, the report to be issued to LTV Corp. and the United States Air Force. Out of conscience, he perfunctorily adds a negative conclusion, one readily dropped by others from the issued report (1972: 118).

Once the aircraft brake comes on line for the Air Force, the young engineer Lawson personally witnesses planes skidding and near fatal accidents. Upon hearing Lawson's personal accounts, Vandivier goes to an attorney who advises him to see the FBI in Dayton. In time, Goodrich officials panic as the Air Force demands to see the raw data from their tests. Individuals seek attorneys. But even now those involved deny that they had lied.

Lawson and Vandivier eventually resign, and a year after that they each testify before a Senate hearing chaired by William Proxmire. Sink testifies for Goodrich's Troy plant. The Senate committee reaches no firm conclusion after four hours of testimony, but the Department of Defense purportedly changes its procedures with this incident in mind. Lawson is now an engineer for LTV Corp., and Vandivier is a newspaper reporter. The Troy plant redesigned its aircraft brake along the lines originally proposed by Lawson, secured new contracts with LTV Corp. and others, and increased its profitability. Both Line and Sink were promoted.

8 On the one hand, charges by sociologists and political scientists of elite authoritarianism or increasing official repression within Western democracies and the United States in particular are generally dismissed as unfounded or polemical, and correctly so (Wolfe 1973, 1977; Isaac Balbus 1973; and, for that matter, Horkheimer and Adorno 1944; and Marcuse 1964b). Such charges tend to be ad hoc or impressionistic (e.g. Wolfe 1974), tied to particular events and left unrelated to any systemic or structural pattern. Or, alternatively, they are based on unrealizable ideals of "democracy" that contemporary practices understandably fail to meet (Wolfe 1977 and the Frankfurt school, including Habermas 1962, 1973a; also Bloom 1987 on the right). Put differently, such charges are not based on a conceptual apparatus that allows researchers to isolate patterns of increasing social authoritarianism in comparative perspective; even Franz Neumann (1936) and Otto Kirchheimer (1961) fail to escape this weakness. On the other hand, charges of "working class authoritarianism" within Western liberal-democracies are usually better received, even if controversial. Yet, these charges are typically based on surveys of workers' attitudes (e.g. toward ethnic minorities) rather than on studies that establish systemic or structural patterns in workers' actions (Lipset 1960; Lipset and Raab 1970). Moreover, it is never made clear how authoritarian *attitudes* among workers, or among any other segment of the population for that matter, contribute to a social order becoming authoritarian in practice. It is simply assumed that this connection is self-evident, but it is not at all.

9 I have not hesitated to incorporate into this volume parts of previously published articles (especially Sciulli 1986, 1988a, 1989a). Nor have I hesitated to both rearrange these parts and substantially rewrite them as they were placed into this more elaborate presentation of the theory of societal constitutionalism. However, there should not be any instance in which rearranging or rewriting has altered the substance of the earlier articles. Changes in the theory of societal constitutionalism might come in time, I suppose, but for now readers should find consistency across these publications. Should readers find inconsistencies of

substance, these can only be mistakes, changes in my thinking of which I am unaware and for which I cannot account.

Chapter 2. Social integration and social control: the importance of procedural normative restraints

1 Consider F. James Davis's definition of social control (Davis et al. 1962: 39): "Social control is the process by which subgroups and persons are influenced to conduct themselves in conformity to group expectations." And then Niklas Luhmann's definition of the political system (1982: 145): "The specific function of politics is fulfilled at the level of concrete interaction because [its] decisions are made binding. A decision is binding whenever, and for whatever reason, it succeeds in effectively restructuring the expectations of those affected and thus becomes the premise for the future behavior. It is a matter, then, of actual learning, and not just formal validity."

2 Conversely, when actors no longer typically meet acknowledged ranges of expectations regarding acceptable behavior, then the social unit is "disordered" even if, ironically, competition over scarce resources decreases in intensity and coercion increases in intensity.

3 This calls to mind Niklas Luhmann's concept of autopoiesis, which he defines as system self-monitoring or reflexivity. He uses this concept to illuminate any social system's tendency to restrict actors' behavior within roles already given by the system. Like other theorists discussed momentarily, he fails to distinguish analytically between instances when autopoiesis is possibly integrative and when it is demonstrably controlling. Habermas insists that the reasoned/nonreasoned or communicative/noncommunicative distinction can be made, but Luhmann counters that any such distinction remains patently normative rather than possibly being grounded conceptually against normative relativism.

4 Some of the best work on informal mechanisms of social control is by Thomas Scheff (1984: 17–35; 1988; 1990).

5 The Frankfurt school long focused on systemic and institutional forms of social control. Habermas, for instance, emphasizes the importance not only of "manipulation," which is purposeful, but also of "systematically distorted communication," which is inadvertent or systemic. Luhmann (1982: 124, 1972) defines law "as a way of constraining behavioral expectations [that] is found in every society."

6 Cognitive self-restrictions are being focused on here precisely because they are not reducible to actors' internalization of norms during primary or secondary socialization (see John F. Scott 1971 on the latter). They are not reducible to blockages *within* an actor's "personality," whether asocial neuroses or cultivated manners. Put differently, because the self-restrictions being focused on here are strictly *cognitive*, they cannot be *reduced* to actors' normative motivations and beliefs, whatever these might be and however they might have been acquired. See R. Stephen Warner (1978) for an impressive statement of Parsons's tendency to collapse these, a statement to which Parsons responded weakly (Parsons 1978a).

7 Brennan and Buchanan (1985: 72) use the term "precommitment," citing both John Elster and Thomas Schelling. Luhmann (1990: 235) puts the matter more abstractly, referring to the "self-despontaneification" of any "autopoietic system," including a personality system. Habermas's communication theory revolves around actors' "manipulation" and "distorted communication."

8 That survey research is also expensive, and appeals generally to researchers who most casually dismiss the possibility that social order may be based on manipulation or latent coercion is not surprising. Who could make better use of the data of successful manipulation?

9 Zald (1978) is more difficult to label. See Sciulli (in preparation, b) for an expanded discussion of these works.
10 By contrast, Luhmann (1990) discusses the welfare state in terms of polar concepts distinctive to each of his systems (including politics, economics, law, science, education, and others). The result is that many of his criticisms are much sharper. Far more than Janowitz, Luhmann reveals internal contradictions of the welfare state, or how its very successes are preparing the way for future structural crises. At the same time, what would actually constitute a "crisis" in terms of Luhmann's systems theory is by no means self-evident.
11 It should be kept in mind, however, that once the social control/social integration distinction is brought to Janowitz's seemingly more basic distinction, the former distinction proves to be more basic. It cannot be demonstrated empirically whether particular instances of social control are possibly integrative merely by demonstrating that physical coercion is not being applied or threatened. But it can be demonstrated empirically that particular instances of physical coercion might well be integrative rather than demonstrably controlling (see chapter 6, note 32).
12 Chapters 4 and 8 contain related wordings. These wordings are altered slightly in each chapter as the conceptual framework of societal constitutionalism is presented.
13 James Buchanan, the public choice economist and Nobel laureate at George Mason University, makes much of the need for students of comparative institutions to address the "model" of *Homo economicus*, the strictly self-interested actor, rather than to operate on the assumption that human behavior is typically more altruistic or moral (Brennan and Buchanan 1985: 46–66; Buchanan 1989: 12–14, 28–321). As he correctly puts the problem: "The objective should be that of designing institutions such that, if participants do seek economic interest above all else, the damages to the social fabric are minimized" (1989: 34). Several fundamental differences between what Buchanan now calls "constitutional economics" and the theory of societal constitutionalism will be noted in this volume. But his point of departure, the need for any sociological study of institutions to deal *conceptually* with the self-interested actor rather than to search *empirically* for counterexamples of more altruistic behavior, in practice, is right on the mark. That societal constitutionalism has the same actor in view will become apparent in the discussion of the Weberian Dilemma in chapter 3. It must be kept in mind that along with the Hobbesian problem of order, this dilemma was Talcott Parsons' very point of departure in the 1930s.
14 Anthony Giddens's view of actors' efforts to create, maintain, and change social structures – "structuration" – recapitulates this failure in a different terminology (1976, 1979, 1984; Cohen 1987, 1989). He then makes a virtue of relativism by ignoring epistemological issues entirely and instead moving to what he calls actors' "ontology of flexibility," an oxymoron. For his part, Niklas Luhmann emphasizes *systems'* flexibility in adapting autopoietically to each other's actions and to "noise" in the larger social system's environment. He sees actors, then, as both constrained and confused by the complexity and rapidity of social changes taking place all around them, literally outside of their individual and collective control (1982, 1986, 1990).
15 Like Habermas (1981a,b), Archer (1987), and many others, Giddens (1979: 75–81; 1981: 66–67, 157–63; 1984: 24, 64) follows Lockwood (1956) in distinguishing between social integration and system integration. The former refers to dense face-to-face interactions and the latter to relations between collectivities. Whether "integration" in either sense is manipulated or latently coerced is something that Lockwood, and then the others, fails to address methodically (see Giddens's confusing discussions of "exploitation," 1981: 58–61, 239–47; and "domination," 1984: 31–4, 1985: 7–11). Luhmann, of course, concentrates exclusively on system integration and does not bother to distinguish this from systemic control (e.g. 1986, 1990).

16 For instance, Jack Gibbs (1981) in particular ties social control to the participation or intervention of third parties. In many instances of his five types of social control, third parties are expected to provide authoritative judgments of one kind or another. Similarly, Donald Black (1984) and John Griffiths (1984) at certain points in their discussions focus on the importance of actors accepting authorities' legitimacy within situations of social control.

17 Skocpol (1980) points this out in reference to certain programs of the New Deal in the United States. Stephens (1980) and Korpi (1983) do the same in reference to the even greater extension of transfer payments in Sweden.

18 Habermas's work is explored at some length in chapter 5. This same emphasis on systemic distortion is what led Karl Marx earlier to examine the "commodity form," and how surplus value is routinely extracted from labor irrespective of capitalists' skills, knowledge, or planning. It is also what led Max Weber to explore the more general relationship between "rationalization" and "bureaucratization" (see chapter 3).

19 See, as examples, Skocpol (1980), Skocpol and Amenta (1986: 136), plus Stephens (1980), Korpi (1983) and Esping-Anderson (1985); also Block (1977), Przeworski (1985), and Therborn (1987).

20 The same distinction also is missing from more specific discussions of interlocking director-ates and "institutional capitalism," and from discussions of "crises" in the welfare state (not only Janowitz 1976; but Wolfe 1977; Cawson 1982; Therborn 1987; and Luhmann 1990).

21 Robert Dahl (1982) explores the tension between autonomy and control as the overriding "dilemma" of pluralist democracy. But there are two great limitations with his study. First, he refers to "autonomy" only in terms of organizations' independence from government. He must then concede that autonomous organizations may "do harm" (1982: 1–3). Sec-ond, he concedes (1982: 4) that he cannot demonstrate which organizations are indepen-dent or autonomous even in this limited sense. By contrast, the theory of societal constitu-tionalism revolves around an operationalizable definition of social integration. It then extends this definition to organizations and institutions across a civil society rather than concentrating exclusively on their relationships vis-à-vis governmental agencies. Social integration replaces Dahl's notion of autonomy, and the former is demonstrated to have more to do with increasing freedom and reducing harm than the latter. Heinz and Laumann (1982: chapter 10) explore problems with the notion of autonomy as applied to the professions.

22 Anthony Giddens (1984, 1987) also wishes to be critical or radical, and lacks a suitable conceptual grounding for critique or radicalism. To his credit, Luhmann methodically addresses why critique is incapable of being grounded theoretically, and incapable of informing actors in practice (1982, 1986, 1990). The theory of societal constitutionalism ultimately rejects both of these conclusions, and yet Luhmann's systems theory is more formidable than Giddens's structuration theory precisely because Luhmann consistently dismisses the possibility of critique under modern conditions. He does not turn inconsis-tently to ungrounded concepts to support criticisms of existing conditions.

23 See Przeworski (1985) on social democrats' steady accommodation of the restrictions and opportunities of electoral democracy, and Przeworski and Sprague (1986) for a historical review.

24 It should be kept in mind that the coup d'etat remains today the most typical way in which governmental leaders are transferred from office, and by no means elections (Luttwak 1968/1984). In the real world, coups are normal, and elections (to say nothing of revolu-tions, civil wars, and putsches) exceptional. Coups and elections aside, questioning beyond the presupposition of exhausted possibilities is taking place in practice today within many modern nation-states. One of the purposes of the theory of societal constitutionalism is to provide a conceptual framework that exposes this to empirical study.

25 See Sewell (1985) and Skocpol (1985) for a fascinating debate over these issues as they apply to the French Revolution, and Laumann and Knoke 1987: 346–72 for an application to the contemporary United States.

26 Alexander (1983b: 62, 75, 77–80, 94–5, 133–4) collapses integration into "voluntary authority" or voluntary social control (which, in turn, collapses informal, systemic, and self-restrictive mechanisms of social control). Like other theorists influenced by Parsons, he appreciates the richness and variety of mechanisms of purposeful social control. But, with this, he addresses the first question only, and only in part, and he fails to move to the next two. This is why he reduces the question of "freedom" to an empirical issue (1978). He fails to see that its institutional and organizational foundations are so distinctive that they are amenable to conceptual specification.

Chapter 3. Liberalism and the Weberian Dilemma: from restraints on government to restraints on civil society

1 It is not coincidental that Sheldon Wolin's influential 1960 survey of *political theories* since Aristotle ends with Weber's social theory.

2 Liberal theorists often acceded to complacent optimism after Adam Smith's *The Wealth of Nations* appeared in 1776. That is, they assumed that the impact of the market on social and institutional change is ultimately benign, for all of the market's fluctuations and uncertainties, including economic depressions. This complacency was a major obstacle to these theorists methodically addressing the concerns raised later by either Marx or Weber (Friedman 1962 remains an exemplar, and rational-choice theory has brought liberal complacency into the center of sociology). As pre-Smith liberals, the American founders were in many respects more pessimistic, and more sophisticated conceptually. Yet, Locke's writings greatly influenced them, and his central concepts (written 1679–80) were far more amenable to later complacency than Hobbes's (written 1651). Locke ultimately accounted for limited government by positing that actors within an allegorical state of nature – a normatively unmediated social arena – are likely to operate on a "natural identity of interests" in limiting government whereas Hobbes would have none of this. Locke's position became one of the bases for constitutional theorists' positing that a "constituent force" in civil society is ever-vigilant in restraining arbitrary government (see chapter 10), and the American founders and framers were greatly influenced by this allegory. There have been exceptions to liberal complacency in the twentieth century, of course, most notably Joseph Schumpeter (1942), Karl Polanyi (1944), Friedrich Hayek (1944, 1973–9), Hannah Arendt (1951), and Theodore Lowi (1969); Brennan and Buchanan (1985) continue the Hobbesian tradition today (see Sciulli 1990 on the contributions of Arendt, Hayek, and Lowi). For all of his insights, even Tocqueville failed as late as the 1820s and 1830s to explore the implications for democratic government of systemic pressures of social change, other than to address the problem of democratization which Michels and Weber would later see as a "leveling" of the governed in the face of oligarchy and bureaucratization (Ortega 1930 and many others developed this argument, including Kornhauser in the United States). Schmitter relied on Tocqueville's "art of association" in his early study of Brazil (1971) before developing his own view of neocorporatism in 1974.

3 Wolfgang Schluchter argues (1981: 86) that Weber's work as a whole may be read as "a socio-historical constitutional theory of a new type, quite different from traditional constitutional theories" (also 1981: 109–14). It is not clear, however, what Schluchter has in mind in saying this. Weber is deservedly remembered for a great many contributions, but, Schluchter notwithstanding, one of them cannot said to be a major (or even minor) contribution to democratic theory, constitutional theory, or categories related even vaguely to the problem of a nonauthoritarian direction of social change.

4 "[I]t is justified to see the question of rationality as Weber's central issue" (Schluchter 1981: 10, note 11). See Polanyi (1944) and Arendt (1951) for what remain most impressive updatings of the sense of drift. By the 1950s, pressures of rationalization were reified by comparativists into the notion of "modernization" (see Huntington 1971 for an account), and Weber's pathos was by then overlaid by Americans' Lockean and Smithean complacency and optimism.

5 Luhmann (1990) captures this well today, but without Weber's sense of pathos regarding the imminence of authoritarianism. Habermas (1989) seems to have resigned himself to drift.

6 Parsons initially characterized this as a "law of entropy" (1937a: 752), and then later (with Smelser 1956) converted it into the systemic process of "functional differentiation." Luhmann has since developed the implications of the latter more than anyone else within the Parsonian tradition (eg. 1982, 1986, 1990).

7 The statement of the Weberian Dilemma that follows is my best effort to carry out the logic of Weber's *conceptual apparatus,* irrespective of what his personal political beliefs happened to be as articulated in his correspondence and speeches (Mommsen 1959/1974; Beetham 1974). My statement also accounts for Weber's pathos, as opposed to Lockean liberals' complacency and optimism. Clearly, Weber on occasion expressed hope in the future of parliamentary democracy, but can his personal statements be rendered consistent with his own conceptual apparatus? Any Weber specialist who wishes to rebut my statement of the Weberian Dilemma, or otherwise to demonstrate that it is faulty, must do more than string together quotations from Weber's personal views regarding parliamentary democracy. The Weber specialist must demonstrate that such personal beliefs by Weber (or anyone else) are consistent with the conceptual apparatus that Weber developed. I do not think this can be done.

8 Aside from its consistency with Michels's iron law of oligarchy, the Weberian Dilemma is also consistent with Kenneth Arrow's (1951) impossibility theorem, and Brennan and Buchanan's (1985: 76) extension of this to what they call the "attenuation of individual control over collective-choice options." Arrow's point was that even if individuals within any social unit express their preferences consistently, the unit's collective decisions will not be internally consistent even if decision-makers follow rules designed simply to combine these preferences. Brennan and Buchanan's point, in turn, is that even if one person is certain that others will not change their preferences over time, it is impossible for this person to predict whether the sequence of actions taken by any social unit will be consistent with his or her own ordering of preferences. What is being emphasized by both points is that even if all actors operate consistently in their own subjective interests within any complex social unit, they cannot be expected to control, or even to predict, how the social unit will react collectively. One result of *conceding* Brennan and Buchanan's argument, however, is to come to a conclusion that they would oppose unhesitatingly: If predictability is to be brought to exercises of collective power within civil society, this can only be accomplished on the basis of a social infrastructure that in turn challenges, or subordinates, the sovereignty of actors' subjective interests.

9 Why would two conceptually sophisticated economists, wedded so firmly to *Homo economicus* as their "model," conclude their book with a call for a civil religion? They do so because, to their credit, they recognize the outer limits of economically motivated behavior for institutional design: "[Economists confuse] the robustness of economically motivated behavior within given constraints and the possible robustness of economically motivated behavior in modifying the constraints themselves" (Brennan and Buchanan 1985: 14). Presumably, only a shared understanding of noneconomic qualities in life, that is of nonrational norms, can modify the constraints on economic behavior themselves. Thus, they advocate a civil religion to this end.

10 For valiant efforts to bring consistency and clarity to Weber's three concepts, see Mommsen (1959/1974), Jean Cohen (1972), Beetham (1974), Burger (1976), Jacobson (1976), Factor and Turner (1979), Kalberg (1980), Zaret (1980), Levine (1981), Habermas (1981a: chapters 2–3), Schluchter (1981: 58, 88–9, 108–10, 128–32), Alexander (1983a), Kronman (1983: chapter 4). Earlier, now "standard" accounts fare no better (Shils 1948, Hughes 1958, Bendix 1960, Freund 1966, and Guenther Roth's 1968 introduction to Weber's major mature work).

11 Weber fails to acknowledge that rationalization or purposive-rational action hinges on whether ends are quantifiable. Habermas perpetuates this failure in his own work (1968b, 1973a, 1979, 1981a) whereas Marcuse (1964a), surprisingly, is more consistent in appreciating this interrelationship. Etzioni (1988: chapters 8–9) recently defined instrumental rationality in terms of the qualities of decision-making processes itself rather than in terms of the quantifiable results of efficient production or effective administration (see chapters 7–8 for additional remarks on the importance of the latter). His reasoning is that unanticipated events beyond decision-makers' control (e.g. a dramatic jump in energy prices) may turn an essentially rational decision into a result which, in retrospect, appears to be "irrational." But surely Etzioni is mistaken to define instrumental rationality in this way. Aside from running contrary to Weber's usage, it leaves Etzioni with the problem of neutrally observing which decision-making processes are more or less rational than others. This is a far more hermeneutically complex undertaking than economists (whom Etzioni is addressing) can be expected to undertake. Consider the following counterexample: Let us say a new technology suddenly rendered the automobile obsolete. Nevertheless, a neutral observer can still look at automobile manufacturing companies and specify which ones manufacture automobiles most efficiently by pointing to various quantitative indices of the production process. That the automobiles manufactured are no longer purchased does not somehow reduce the instrumental rationality with which they were produced. Hechter also fails to see that action can only be called rational on the basis of its quantifiable results. This leaves him in the nether world of fathoming actors' subjective interests: "[Rational choice] theory treats individual preferences as sovereign, but if it is to yield testable implications about group behavior, these preferences must be specified in advance. Otherwise the theory is empty, for any behavior can be viewed as rational with the advantage of hindsight" (1987: 31). He goes on to note (1987: 31–2, note 22) that "the preferences – which provide the motivation for all behavior – are exogenous to the theory, and therefore unexplained." Regardless, literally all of Hechter's examples of rational-choice behavior revolve around enterprises whose ends are clearly quantifiable, from legislative voting and patronage (1987: chapter 5), to credit associations and insurance groups (1987: chapter 6), to capitalist firms (1987: chapter 7). And yet, he fails to work this into the very definition of his most central concept. One other point may be made about Hechter's view of actors' preferences above: to treat actors' subjective interests literally as sovereign is to treat them as either given or random, rather than as possibly principled or otherwise warranted (see chapter 4).

12 Alan Sica pursues an alternative tack, tracing Weber's efforts to sublimate his anxiety over the persistence of the "irrational" in everyday life. The problem pervading Sica's account is his failure to distinguish the nonrational (literally, the nonpurposive-rational) from the irrational. This is a distinction that Parsons made, and most methodically so, across his career (e.g. 1969b for Parsons's best later statement). Indeed, the handiest summary of Parsons's entire body of work is to say that he was a theorist preoccupied with nonrational social action. The same failure on Sica's part prevents him from appreciating the importance of Parsons' (1936; 1937a: 185–95) reformulation of Pareto's concept of the "nonlogical" into the more generally applicable concept of the "nonrational." This accounts, too, for Sica's rough-and-ready slighting of the relationship in

Weber's work between "substantive rationality" and the irrational as Sica defines it (1988: 209–13).

13 Brennan and Buchanan (1985: 17–18, 22, 27–32, 98–107) substitute "unanimity" over meta-rules for a natural identity of interests, and Luhmann substitutes "autopoiesis" for the hidden hand. For Luhmann: "Totally absorbed in its own object, sociology did not even notice that a reorientation had already started among the natural sciences, begun by the law of entropy. If this law that declares the tendency to the loss of heat and organization is valid then it becomes even more important to explain why the natural order does not seem to obey it and evolves in opposition to it. The answer lies in the capacity of thermodynamically open systems . . . to enter into relations of exchange, i.e. environmental dependency, and nevertheless to guarantee their autonomy through structural regulation" (Luhmann 1986: 4). By suspending the law of entropy and then employing the concept of autopoiesis, Luhmann brackets the issue of authoritarianism from his concerns. He accounts for social order as such rather than for nonauthoritarian social order in particular. In this regard, he is as much a follower of Parsons (Sciulli 1988b) as Alexander and Münch.

14 The Frankfurt school in general, and Herbert Marcuse in particular, has been roundly criticized for so categorizing contemporary nation-states, although one cannot say that they were particularly casual about it. The Frankfurt school is nothing if not methodical.

15 Failing to provide answers to either question in the face of considerable empirical evidence to the contrary, contemporary Weberians obfuscate the dilemma itself. They accede to Lockean liberals' complacency by dismissing the entire issue of directionality out of hand as "normative" or "ideological." By default, therefore, liberals' hypostatization of a "hidden hand" or of actors' "natural identity of interests" is left standing unchallenged conceptually. It is startling, actually, how many theorists and researchers who label themselves Weberians, or conflict theorists and radical researchers, operate with concepts indistinguishable from those underlying Lockean liberalism. Indeed, is there a single Weberian theorist or researcher who answers either question by accounting *conceptually* for the presence of nonauthoritarian social orders in the late twentieth century?

16 Brennan and Buchanan (1985) also fail to examine external normative restraints methodically, of course. Yet, they end up appealing to a civil religion as the only alternative to drift. The reason for their rejection of the external, on the one hand, and yet their appeal to a civil religion, on the other, may be traced to their failure to distinguish between norms that are voluntaristic and those that are nonrational. In turn, they fail to see that certain voluntaristic norms are procedural rather than substantive, and thus capable of being institutionalized independently of any civil religion. The importance of these two distinctions is demonstrated in chapter 7.

17 After all, the other view of modern social change supported by Weber's conceptual framework is just as readily supported by the presuppositions of Lockean liberalism. *Any* resilient normative restraint on rational social change invariably fosters authoritarianism.

18 Brennan and Buchanan's constitutional economics revolves around the possibility of successful self-restriction. But they see this as immutable, tied to actors' inability to tailor macrosociological institutions and "meta-rules" to their own subjective interests (1985: 17, 55, 72, 75–81). Thus, they ultimately recapitulate the classic liberal argument in favor of the "hidden hand" of the market even as they initially raise Hobbesian criticisms.

19 Theories of "social closure" (Collins 1979; Parkin 1979; Murphy 1988; Waters 1989) take precisely this tack: Any and all obstacles that actors face in securing access to resources are treated as manifestations of social closure. One combs these writers' works looking for a single exception. In the face of existing institutional obstacles, actors' failure to rebel can only be attributed to their successful manipulation.

Chapter 4. Conceptual foundations of societal constitutionalism: from internal restraints on government to external restraints on drift

1 Procedural internal and external restraints have substantive effects, of course. But their effects are indirect in the following sense. Whatever else they may entail in practice, their effects, too, must remain consistent with, rather than compromise or jeopardize, the integrity of the procedural mediation itself. If the latter is compromised, procedural restraints are no longer being maintained, and only substantive restraints can be said to account for whatever limitations on exercises of collective power happen to persist. Pluralist theory and neocorporatist theory, as examples, are theories of the *substantive* restraints that influentials in civil society bring to bear on state officials. Friedrich Hayek, Hannah Arendt, and Theodore Lowi, among others, including the contributors to *Yale Law Journal's* symposium on the republican civic tradition (1988), roundly criticized such theories precisely because they overlooked the importance of the integrity of *procedural* restraints (Sciulli 1990).

2 Dworkin (1977) hypostatizes rights, but more recently (1985) acknowledges that "principles of legal interpretation" are more fundamental. More surprising, Luhmann hypostatizes rights as well – as a nonnegotiable context framing the legal system's otherwise unrestrained "reflexivity" and amenability to change (1982: 96–7). This is surprising in that Luhmann otherwise criticizes all substantive and procedural normative restraints as anachronistic holdovers within contemporary "autopoietic systems" (1990). Brennan and Buchanan part company on this matter. Buchanan insists that the positing of values purportedly external to individuals' subjective interests is "not consistent with . . . the 'contractarian vision' " (Brennan and Buchanan 1985: 37). If Buchanan ever conceded that there were such external values, he would have to concede that they may restrain *Homo economicus,* or individuals' strictly self-interested competition within economic and political marketplaces. By contrast, Brennan "express[es] misgivings about relating the contractarian position so closely to the denial that objective values exists. It is suggested that there may be an argument to the effect that objective values exist and that these include the value of individual liberty" (Brennan and Buchanan 1985: 37, note 2). It will become clear later in this chapter and then certainly after the discussion in chapter 8 that neither of these positions can account for the possibility of nonauthoritarian social order under modern conditions of drift. In terms of the theory of societal constitutionalism, Buchanan's "contractarian vision" is an accomplice in drift. Brennan's hypostatization of individuals' liberties or rights as "objective values," in turn, cannot remain external to actors' fragmentation of meaning and groups' functional differentiation, and thereby to the drift of social change.

3 Brennan and Buchanan add another: "systematic accounting for expenditure of public funds" (1985: 16). They also insist on the importance of geographic electoral arrangements, but it is unclear why elections as well as representation in parliament cannot be structured by functional rather than geographic location. In many nation-states, and by no means exclusively the plural or communal systems of sub-Saharan Africa, the Middle East, and South Asia, elections are structured for all intents and purposes in terms of actors' ethnic or religious affiliations. Lijphart (1977) presented "consociational democracy" as one way of addressing such situations. It essentially updates John C. Calhoun's "concurrent majority," a proposal originally designed to keep the Antebellum South in the Union. It concedes to an ethnic, religious, or regional minority a veto power over all national policies affecting its vital interests. Such arrangements often are negotiated in one way or another within ethnically, religiously, or regionally divided nation-states; Lebanon is experiencing the limiting case of what happens when they are not, and both Quebec and Lithuania are testing their respective nation-state's capacity to negotiate a settlement.

4 Habermas (1979: 194–5) introduces the concept of strategic action by drawing a distinction *within* Weber's concept of purposive-rational action, depending on whether the latter is directed to things in nature or to actors in society:

(a) Instrumental action follows technical rules and is evaluated by "the degree of efficacy of the intervention into a physical state of affairs."

(b) *Strategic action* also follows rules of rational choice but is evaluated by "the degree of efficacy in influencing the decisions of rational opponents."

Together, these two types of action comprise the "model of purposive-rational action." Every *social* relationship, in turn, is either rational, that is strategic, or nonrational, that is normative. A social relationship is strategic *when each actor or group consciously seeks its own particular advantage* in its own subjective interest. It is normative when they endeavor to secure a mutual understanding of their situation. Habermas (1979: 195–5) uses his own concept of communicative action to specify when the latter social relationships are reasoned rather than merely normative. For him, communicative action and strategic action are both "complex cases" or ideal types. They are closer to empirical social action than analytical concepts or what Habermas calls "pure cases." In analyzing the ideal type of communicative action, he turns to "pure cases," including actors' cognitive utterances, their expressive self-representations, and their normatively regulated actions. It is not necessary to discuss this further in this volume.

5 All of this can get very complicated in practice, of course. For instance, there is little separation of church and state in Sweden. The Lutheran clergy are civil servants whose salaries are paid by the state treasury (Popenoe 1988: 138–9). Yet, Sweden may well be the most secularized nation-state, those of the former Eastern bloc included.

6 Anderson (1964/1982) clearly conveys the strictly strategic nature of elections in his discussion of Latin American regime changes between civilian and military rule. Still, it cannot be denied that in a few modern nation-states – still very few indeed – elections have clearly gained normative status, all evidence of their failure to express any "national will" or "national mandate" notwithstanding. Put differently, within these few nation-states, electoral results may well carry a normative mandate that is popularly considered to be loftier than that of maintaining the integrity of the procedural threshold of interpretability of law. It will become clear in chapter 6 why this is a strictly normative belief rather than a contribution to reasoned social action.

7 Interest group pluralism is quite distinctive to the United States (see Garson 1978 for a review, and Lowi 1969 for a critique). More generalizable types of group competition include "neocorporatism," which involves peak associations (since Schmitter 1974), and "consociational democracy," which involves ethnic sections (see Lijphart 1977; but also Connor 1972, 1973; and Enloe 1973 for early, influential statements regarding the resilience of ethnic sections despite "modernization").

8 This issue is formulated more consistently with the theory of societal constitutionalism in chapter 11. Friedrich (1963) remains a valuable account of the importance of power holders' "anticipated reactions." Hechter's "theory of group solidarity" literally revolves around the institutionalization of anticipated reactions, which he calls "metering" or monitoring (1987: chapter 4). The rare totalitarian regimes (Nazi Germany, Stalinist Soviet Union, and Pol Pot's Cambodia) are distinctive in that methodical steps were taken to reduce dramatically even internal substantive restraints on state officials' exercises of collective power. Leaders of "totalitarian" nation-states radically reduced and realigned the groups permitted to compete, and yet even they could not escape all such strategic restraints (see Hagopian 1978: chapters 4–5 for a useful overview of this enormous literature).

9 Yet, this was precisely the grandest proposal of postwar pluralist theory, and it remains

implicitly at the center of Philippe Schmitter's distinction between societal and state neocorporatism.

10 One of the most significant contributions of Laumann and Knoke's discussion of energy and health policy domains within the United States is that they treat patterns of events as "scenarios" (1987: 17, 249–70), and examine the "joint space" occupied by actors and events (1987: 26–42). They find an "absence of any direct effects of resource possession on event participation" (1987: 284) such that "any organization with a modicum of interest in the policy issues could easily enter into the debates" (1987: 283). Their point is that the scenarios within which events are patterned have a certain life of their own. Each set of policy issues has only some particular moment in the sun, and, presumably, state officials have great control over these moments. It is during these rare moments that participation in debates is particularly significant. In this way, Laumann and Knoke portray state officials as far more active than pluralist theory's portrayals of them as mere referees, enforcers, or vector sums. Indeed, they are more specific in characterizing the state's role than researchers who have insisted that the state's relative autonomy be taken more seriously (Evans, Rueschemeyer, and Skocpol 1985).

11 It can already be seen how this procedural threshold challenges the faith that Buchanan has in his "contractarian vision," and in what he calls "constitutional economics" more generally. Buchanan focuses exclusively on actors' *subjective* interests and beliefs, and he adamantly rejects the idea that organizational forms or procedural thresholds can be used to resiliently restrain actors' self-interested competition within economic and political marketplaces. In terms of "institutional forms," Buchanan sees only two types: monopolies and markets. It is then an easy matter for him to favor markets and the subjective interests filling them (Buchanan 1989: 5, 13–17, 26–7, 32, 41–2; Brennan and Buchanan 1985: 7, 21–4, 27–8, 37–45, 49).

12 With this third assumption, Niklas Luhmann is as much a pluralist as any American political scientist. He sees a "dual sovereignty" operating within the "legal system": actors' sovereignty in invoking the law, and thereby the frequency with which the law is invoked in ongoing social situations; and the sovereignty of lawmakers to change the law, *including the premises on which they make such changes* (1972; 1982: chapters 5–6; 1990: chapter 6). Thus, law is rendered positive (or relativistic) when "we claim an inalienable sovereignty to decide what the law is to be and even to vary the premises according to which such legislative decisions are made" (1982: 125–6). The only conditions that Luhmann sees are that the changes not rattle public opinion sufficiently to change its subjective expectations, and that both political and legal systems continue to function. The problem of arbitrariness, or drift, drops from sight. Indeed, Luhmann advocates that pluralist theory, the theory of the sovereignty of competing subjective interests, be generalized beyond groups and interests into a general principle of system complexity and reflexivity, independently of all external restraints (1982: 383, note 45; also 1990: 27).

13 Hayek and Buchanan reject this assumption, and thereby remain Hobbesian, whereas Hechter and Coleman remain more complacent Lockeans. Hechter in particular is explicit about this (1987: 62–9, 183–6).

14 This allegory of the constituent force may sound farfetched, but it underlies the Western constitutional tradition from the Glorious Revolution to this day. It is discussed more methodically in chapter 10. What is remarkable about Brennan and Buchanan's continuing confidence in such a constituent force is that they simultaneously accept Arrow's impossibility theorem and then update it with their own "theorem" of the "attenuation of individuals' control over collectivities" (Brennan and Buchanan 1985: 73–81; Buchanan 1989: 39; chapter 3, note 8). It never dawns on them that heterogeneous actors and competing groups, operating in their own immediate interests, may never recognize in common what arbitrary government *is* – until it is far too late.

15 David Truman (1951) had insisted that robust interest competition contributes to democracy *only as long as it is kept confined within resilient "rules of the game," * rules which are *independent of this competition or tied to some principle superordinate to the sovereignty of actors' subjective interests.* Moreover, he followed constitutional tradition in positing that a mythical "constituent force" within civil society ultimately upholds these rules, and this principle, in the face of flagrant encroachments. Later pluralists correctly ridiculed such naïveté about a constituent force, and symbolic interactionists have always had none of this. They bracket the entire issue of shifts in the direction of social change from their concerns. The same may be said of Luhmann (1990), but not of Parsons. Pluralists jettisoned the vague notion of rules of the game and principle as unnecessary to their (and interactionists') basic argument. They were certain that the latter can rest securely on the sovereignty of actors' subjective interests, without appealing to any purportedly independent principle. Today, Brennan and Buchanan resuscitate *both* of Truman's ideas, but without seeing how the latter hinge on an independent principle: They refer vaguely to rules of the game (or "meta-rules"), and they evince faith in the workings of an amorphous constituent force or consensual will within civil society. The conjunction of these two ideas is literally what they see as the contribution of what they call "constitutional economics" (1985: 22, 26–8, 51, 98–111).

16 Norms of due process refer to procedural guarantees that actors are accorded, particularly within common-law countries, during criminal arrests, trials, and other formal proceedings (Fellman 1976; McClosky and Brill 1983: chapter 4). The theory of societal constitutionalism by no means contends that any particular set of such guarantees is irreducible either to a nonauthoritarian social order or to actors' prospects for social integration, and thereby capable of informing comparative research. Quite to the contrary, it concedes (chapter 10) that both the historical and contemporary record of common-law countries in this regard is as intrinsically particular as that of civil law countries (e.g. Merryman 1969/1985; Meador 1986; Damaska 1986).

17 Consider the reviews of Marxists' treatments of law by Hugh Collins (1982) and Spitzer (1983), and also the review of Marxists' treatments of morality by Lukes (1985). Weberians' views of law have already been alluded to, and they are addressed in chapters 5–6. For feminism, consider the works of Catharine MacKinnon (1983). Her critique of the "objectivist epistemology" of law embraces all procedural norms, and it is nothing if not absolutist. Her view of how rape laws should be rewritten, for instance, is a case in point. By her own accounting, 80–90% *or more* of the male population could be expected to qualify immediately as rapists for continuing their present behavior. MacKinnon is not calling for violent sexual acts to be prosecuted fully. She is calling for each women's subjective judgment of personal uncomfortableness to be placed beyond question in defining what rape means for her – irrespective of what a man's actions happen to be, and irrespective of what his subjective impressions are. The first call would be eminently reasonable, but MacKinnon's call to reduce legality to a "subjectivist epistemology" is chilling (to say nothing of being oxymoronic). Regarding sociology of law, finally, it is fair to say that the most mainstream position today treats norms of due process as formalities or empty shells, e.g., Hawkins (1984) and Braithwaite (1989). The integrity of these formalities is routinely demonstrated to be jeopardized today by current practices of criminal and civil courts, e.g., Silberman (1978), Abel (1981), Braithwaite (1982, 1984), and Clinard and Yeager (1980).

18 Lowi (1969) presents the most methodical critique of this argument. He proposes a resuscitation of what are here called internal procedural restraints on government, and what he calls "juridical democracy." The problem is that Lowi speaks repeatedly of "principle" as opposed to group competition but he never specifies what he means (Sciulli 1990). Does "principle" not mediate "democracy"?

19 See Vile (1967) for the best discussion of the rise and then fall of the division of powers, the latter even prior to comparativists' recognition of neocorporatism within Western Europe.

20 Aside from providing a rationale for possessive individualism, Locke's (then) innovative view of private property in the seventeenth century (Arendt 1958) was linked to the problem of restraining arbitrary government. This is a linkage that Macpherson (1962) acknowledges but then brackets from his critical discussion of possessive individualism.

21 See Robert Nagel (1989) for a recent assessment, and a call for the courts to show renewed respect for internal substantive restraints of popular opinion and group consensus. Because he fails to see the possibility of institutionalizing resilient external procedural restraints on drift, Nagel has no alternative other than to call for a return to substantive consensus – all evidence to the contrary notwithstanding. This is also why Brennan and Buchanan (1985: 146–50) call for a civil religion – all evidence to the contrary, and all conceptual gaps notwithstanding. The Law and Economics movement at the University of Chicago law school is at least more consistent conceptually by treating drift as immutable and then, like Lockean liberals before them, elevating the sovereignty of actors' subjective interests to a virtue.

22 On this crisis in the postwar era, consider works from Arendt (1951) to Lowi (1969), then Sennett (1978), Hayek (1973–79), MacIntyre (1981), *Pennsylvania Law Review* (1982), and both Michelman (1988) and Sunstein (1988). The European and Marxist literature here is enormous.

23 It will become clear in chapter 6 that the effort on the part of American courts to extend desegregation decisions to more and more juridically defined minorities, and to more and more activities within civil society (Horowitz 1977; Ely 1980), is typically unrelated to the effort to extend internal restraints from the state to civil society.

24 Not only radicals (Habermas 1973a) await a crisis in the West. Hayek (1973–9) proposes "a basic alteration of the structure of democratic government" as "an intellectual stand-by for when the breakdown of existing institutions becomes unmistakable" (see the remarkable preface to his third volume). Brennan and Buchanan (1985: ix) do not sound much different: "The wisdom and understanding of the Founders have been seriously eroded in our time. The deterioration of the social-intellectual-philosophical capital of Western civil order is now widely, if only intuitively, sensed." They go on (1985: 150): "We must come to agree that democratic societies, as they now operate, will self-destruct . . . unless the rules of the political game are changed."

25 Informal processes of social control such as shaming (Braithwaite 1989) and gossiping (Merry 1984) are not of equivalent importance to a nonauthoritarian social order nor to actors' possibilities for social integration. Still, these social controls are also eventually addressed conceptually in this volume.

26 As noted on page 56, under modern conditions there are no institutions of external restraint that are strategic rather than normative. Robust, strategic competition for material resources or political influence recapitulates the marketplace and the pluralist arena and are manifestations of drift rather than restraints on it.

27 Consider West Germany's difficulties in granting citizenship to second and third generation Turkish "guest workers." Similar difficulties may be found across Western and Eastern Europe, to say nothing of the Caribbean, sub-Saharan Africa, and Asia generally (Young 1976, Horowitz 1985).

28 In chapter 7 it is shown why this must be further specified. The external restraints are both procedural *and distinctively voluntaristic* rather than simply normative.

29 Sciulli (in preparation, b) explores implications of its presence within research divisions of corporations, and implications of the courts' legal recognition of the integrity of collegial formations.

30 It is important to keep in mind that Clinard and Yeager (1980) found that sixty percent of
    600 major American corporations were under indictment or federal action of some kind
    in a twenty-four month period. Moreover, thirty-eight corporations accounted for half of
    all of the federal actions during this period. It is not a stretch of imagination, then, to
    propose that William's company may routinely treat its researchers in the manner de-
    picted in the illustration. Consider also Goldner and Ritti's (1967) impressive argument
    that the "professional ladder" within corporations is, in top management's eyes, a mark
    of failure and of second-class citizenship. Unlike the "management ladder," it closes
    employees off from ever being considered for managerial openings. Due to this, profes-
    sionals within corporations lack the status that they are otherwise accorded elsewhere in
    the larger society.
31 It should be kept in mind that Weber did not see systemic pressures of drift causally
    determining the *detailed* results of social changes within any particular modern nation-
    state. He saw these pressures broadly orienting actors and groups, and thereby the
    direction of social change. Similarly, to the extent that actors and groups maintain the
    integrity of collegial formations, and thereby the integrity of external procedural re-
    straints, then this too broadly orients actors and groups, and the direction of social
    change.
32 After formulating this definition and then reading Jack Gibbs's excellent discussion of
    social control, two definitions of social control in particular that Gibbs listed (with about a
    dozen others) could be rendered consistent with the definition of social integration pre-
    sented here, if they are reformulated: those by Jerome Dowd (1936) and August
    Hollingshead (1941) (Gibbs 1981: 51). Their definitions of social control are distinctive in
    that they at least allude to *restraints* on social forces (which they respectively call "momen-
    tum" and "mechanisms of society"). Dowd (1936: 6) uses the term control literally, "as
    contra, against, or contrary to, any momentum, as 'guidance,' 'direction'. . . ." Unfortu-
    nately, he also treats paternal control as a synonym for social control, and this may be
    dropped outright as needlessly confusing his discussion. Dowd goes on to say (1936: 11):
    "The . . . controlling agency in any society consists of one or more individuals who, on
    account of some kind of prestige, are able to bring people together for some common
    purpose, and to induce or compel them to conform to the group interest." This under-
    mines the importance of his discussion of direction by reducing it to purposeful actions
    taken by individuals rather than appreciating the importance of the presence of a particu-
    lar form of organization. Hollingshead comes closer to an appreciation of organizational
    forms, but without seeing the importance of any particular form. For him (1941: 220):
    "[S]ocial control lies not so much in the mechanisms society has developed to manipulate
    behavior in crisis or in the subtle influences so important in the formation of personality, as
    it does in a society's organization. . . . [S]ocial control inheres in the more or less common
    obligatory usages and values which define the relations of one person to another, to things,
    to ideas, to groups, to classes, and to the society in general. In short, the essence of social
    control is to be sought in the organization of a people."

**Chapter 5. Societal constitutionalism's grounding against relativism: from
Weber's legal positivism to Habermas's communication theory**

 1 As evidence of this failure, Parsons never saw that two of his most suggestive but tenta-
    tively developed proposals could have been developed conceptually and brought to empiri-
    cal research if he had interrelated them methodically with Fuller's principles of "proce-
    dural legality." One of these proposals was Parsons's longstanding position, dating from a
    famous article of 1939, that the professions are somehow distinct from other expert
    occupations (Abbott 1988 continues to collapse these). Aside from referring vaguely to

the norms that he was convinced individual professionals internalize during the secondary socialization of their formal training, Parsons otherwise never suggested what it is, if anything, that distinguishes professions. The other proposal, dating from his books of 1951 and 1953, was presented even more tentatively and inconsistently. This was Parsons's occasional distinction between organizations' institutionalized "normative orientations" and actors' internalized "normative motivations" (see chapter 8, notes 5–6). Aside from never developing explicitly what he had in mind, he failed to keep his references to *either* concept consistent across his mature writings. One looks in vain in the literature today for exegetes who have developed this distinction or for critics who have pointed out that it was left undeveloped. Yet, this distinction is one of the ways out of the "normativist perspective" that Hechter (and others) otherwise dismisses out of hand (1987: 20–3). One fails to find the distinction in Scott's (1971) discussion of the notion of the internalization of norms, or in Jonathan Turner's (1988) more recent survey of theories of motivation, interaction, and interpersonal structuring. The same may be said of Alexander's (1983b) volume devoted to Parsons, and of Habermas's long essay and chapter devoted to Parsons (1980; 1981b: chapter 7).

2 It is curious that despite his masterful critique of neopositivism (1968a; 1973b), Habermas has never noted the debate in the late 1950s between Fuller and Ernest Nagel on the fact-value distinction in science and in law: Fuller (1956; 1958b); Nagel (1958); Fuller (1958c); Nagel (1959). It is even more curious that despite his critique of Weber for succumbing to legal positivism, Habermas has never referred either directly or in footnotes to Lon Fuller. Habermas refers indirectly to H.L.A. Hart (1974: 234, note 54) and he has discussed or referred to contract theorists from Hobbes and Locke to Rawls (1963b: 84ff; 1974: 184, 205; 1981a: 230, 263–5). But he failed to discuss the legacy of common law jurists such as Sir Edward Coke in his early study of the bourgeois public sphere (1962). Niklas Luhmann, who studied both sociology and law at Harvard, and attended one course of Parsons's but not any of Fuller's, cites Fuller as well as the Hart-Fuller debate (e.g. 1972: 20, 290, 345, 348, 363, 370). Luhmann was trained as a lawyer–civil servant in the civil law tradition. This does not assist him in seeing how fundamentally Fuller's normative proce-dures of legal interpretability differ from rational procedures of legal enforcement, and thereby how incompatible the former is with his own legal positivism (eg. 1972; 1982: 90–137) and central concept of autopoiesis (e.g. 1986, 1990).

3 This possibility of credibly claiming grounding remains open even if Habermas's communi-cation theory is replaced in time by another that is less idealized but consistent with a *procedural* standard of reason. After all, whether Habermas's critique of positivism and copy theories of truth holds up against positivists' counterarguments is an issue indepen-dent of whether his communication theory holds up against alternative communication theories that *also* reject positivism and copy theories.

4 Again (chapter 1, note 4), the only postwar "bourgeois" or non-Marxist *social* theorist with whom I am familiar who sustained a credible claim to grounding was Talcott Parsons. He turned to analytical concepts precisely because he wanted to ground the social sciences against normative relativism. That Parsons himself never characterized his social theory as critical or radical does not mean that it fails to qualify as such. This point is developed in chapter 10, and it is elaborated at length in a separate volume (Sciulli in preparation, a).

5 Kronman concedes (1983: 72–3) that Weber used the concept rational-legal in a confusing way. Indeed, he finds (1983: 73–5) that Weber used the term "rational" in reference to law in four ways, as: rule-governed, systematic, based on a logical interpretation of meaning, and controlled by the intellect. For Kronman (1983: 78–9, 89–90, 92–3), formally rational law refers in Weber's work to a legal order that is separated from ethical concerns, or to a legal order that is self-contained, comprehensive, and both clearly and self-consciously applied by specialized enforcers.

6 Habermas has expressed reservations about his formulation of motivation crisis (1982: 279–83), but he stands by his thesis of legitimation crisis. Yet, his most recent reflections (1989) do not convey that the latter is imminent.

7 "If you want to know the law and nothing else, you must look at it as a bad man, who cares only for material consequences which such knowledge enables him to predict, not as a good man, one who finds his reasons for conduct, whether inside the law or outside of it, in the vaguer sanctions of conscience" (Holmes 1897: 459).

8 Alexander (1983a: 113–17, 204, note 90) and Kronman (1983:94–5) see Weber's concept of formal-rational law resting on a particular ethical ideal or a substantive postulate, that of "utilitarian individual freedom." Schluchter (1981: 57–8) sees the "idea of freedom of conscience" as central to Weber, beyond economic individualism. Yet, Schluchter acknowledges that Weber failed to develop the implications of this beyond economic individualism, and Schluchter himself relies on Martin L. Hoffman's work to do so (1981: 59–61).

9 Also see Macpherson (1962) on "possessive individualism" in seventeenth-century British political theory, and Summers (1982) on "pragmatic instrumentalism" in early twentieth-century American legal theory. Habermas's object of study is precisely the same as Parsons's: the "nonrational realm," or literally those aspects of social action that are nonpurposive-rational (chapter 7). Like Parsons, too, Habermas fails to distinguish the concept of voluntaristic action within the larger categories of the nonrational and the normative. Because of this, Habermas cannot appreciate that what he calls "procedural reason" is voluntaristic, and invariably restrains the drift of purposive-rational social change rather than broadening and complementing it, as he insists.

10 Schluchter (1981: 88) notes that Weber distinguished the procedural (*formell*) from the formal (*formal*). But Schluchter does not do much with the distinction other than to point it out. He also places Weber's sociology of law in the context of Weber's treatment of rationalization (1981: 82–138). But, as Fuller insisted, a law may be formally rational and effectively enforced and yet not be procedurally reasoned or procedurally warranted. Kalberg (1980) and Levine (1981) offer helpful discussions of Weber's uses of the term "rationality" (also Habermas 1977; 1981a: chapters 2–3; and Alexander 1983a: 25–28). Kronman (1983) offers one of the most detailed discussions of Weber's sociology of law in English.

11 Habermas has been exploring (1984) how law's formalization in this narrow sense, as rational procedures of consistent enforcement, undermines the integrity or robustness of actors' social relations (also 1989 more generally). He refers to this as "juridification."

12 Oliver Wendell Holmes (1897) saw *jurists'* predictable behavior as critical to the practice of law and also to advances in legal training and scholarship (see Grey 1989 on the latter). Yet, he also saw this behavior being directed to citizens rather than to enforcers alone.

13 "Hence the law is not, as Austin formulates it, a rule 'enforced' by a specific authority, but rather a norm which provides a specific measure of coercion as sanction. The nature of the law will not be grasped if one characterizes it as does Austin, as a command to conduct oneself lawfully. The law is a decree of a measure of coercion, a sanction, for that conduct called 'illegal,' a delict; and this conduct has the character of 'delict' because and only because it is a condition of the sanction" (Kelsen 1941: 275). "When the delict is defined simply as unlawful behavior, law is regarded as a system of secondary norms. But this is not tenable if we realize law's character of a coercive order which stipulates sanctions. Law is the primary norm, which stipulates the sanction, and this norm is not contradicted by the delict of the subject, which, on the contrary, is the specific condition of the sanction. Only the organ [of enforcement] can counteract law itself, the primary norm, by not executing the sanction in spite of its conditions being fulfilled. But when speaking of the delict of the subject as unlawful, one does not have in mind the unlawful behavior of the organ" (Kelsen 1945: 61).

14 The Harvard political scientist Carl Friedrich (1963, 1969, 1972, 1974) developed the distinction between *Autorität,* a Latin term, and *Herrschaft,* a German term, into the very basis of his distinction between reasoned authority and (unreasoned) authoritarianism. In many respects, Friedrich's works remain among the very best historical, theoretical, and comparative treatments of governmental constitutionalism. Still, he left his concept of reasoned authority relativistic rather than attempting to ground it, and for this reason his works fail to move beyond the presupposition of exhausted possibilities.

15 This is a major theme for Habermas by 1981. Yet, it was his very point of departure even in 1965 and then in 1967 and 1968 as he elaborated his critique of neopositivism.

16 Habermas's insistence on this point also indicates that his procedural standard of reason is *analytical:* At best, only *parts or aspects* of a complex social action or particular way of life can be reasoned. Yet, Habermas insists explicitly that his social theory, and its standard of reason, is *not* analytical. This is most confusing: Habermas wishes to overcome relativism in order to ground critique. But he does not see the need to bring analytical distinctions into the very core of his social theory. Luhmann, by contrast, has no interest in overcoming relativism since he is not interested in critique. He rejects Habermas's position that there is any generalizable standard of reason, procedural or otherwise. Luhmann readily acknowledges that this is why his concepts need not be analytical (personal conversation in Atlanta, Georgia, August 1988, at the Annual Meeting of the American Sociological Association). Habermas's reluctance to acknowledge the need for analytical distinctions in his project of escaping relativism may be due to his seeing one other implication of basing a social theory on analytical distinctions: Even if a grounding against relativism is secured, analytical distinctions move the critique of existing social arrangements away from the Frankfurt school's absolutism. Put differently, analytical distinctions can support critique, and even quite radical critique, but they cannot support the Frankfurt school's absolutist rejection of entire institutional complexes. Quite to the contrary, analytical distinctions support more specific criticisms, ones more amenable to falsification and operationalization. Because the Frankfurt school seldom appreciated such qualities of research, its members never felt particularly constrained to bring specificity to critique (Jay 1973).

17 This question essentially rephrases Lowi's (1969) central concern in his analysis of American interest group pluralism, and this question also informs the reassessment of the republican civic tradition in the *Yale Law Journal* (1988).

18 Jay (1974) puts these issues well in exploring the Frankfurt school's reactions to Mannheim's (1929) relational view of "truth." Luhmann has been putting these questions quite forcefully to Marxists for three decades, but then he goes further by dismissing Habermas's procedural turn as well. The irony is that Luhmann cites Fuller; Habermas does not (note 2); and yet Fuller would surely side with Habermas on this matter rather than with Luhmann.

19 Brennan and Buchanan (1985: 27) treat subjective interests as sovereign, and as a result treat actors as monads – whose interests are given or random – rather than as members of communication communities whose interests may either be warranted or unwarranted in these contexts. What is ironic is that they anticipate a subjective consensus among such monads over basic rules of the game or "meta-rules." They thereby end up closer to Habermas's ideal speech situation than to Fuller's more practicable threshold of interpretability, but without the support provided by a communication theory.

20 Habermas does not use the term normative orientations. I use this concept in this context because eventually I will demonstrate that what Habermas calls communication communities are themselves mediated by the normative orientations institutionalized by forms of organization (chapter 8, especially note 6). For his part, Collins (1979: 58) refers to professions as "consciousness communities," no different in this respect, says he, than

ethnic groups. In terms of the theory of societal constitutionalism, however, the issue is not whether an occupational group and an ascriptive group happen to revolve around their respective members' shared symbols rather than around their instrumental or strategic calculations of success. Clearly, professions, ethnic groups, and many other social units (religious, cultural, and affective) rely on their members' "consciousness." The issue is that ethnic groups typically are organized in patron-client networks whereas professions proper, unlike other expert occupations, are organized in the collegial form (chapter 8). To bring this distinction to Collins's *The Credential Society* is to call into question his argument from beginning to end: from his conceptual distinctions, to his research findings, to his prescriptions for change.

21 See Karl-Otto Apel (1972) for an excellent essay criticizing neopositivists' "methodological solipsism"; Habermas (1967b, 1968a, 1973c, 1982) for criticisms of neopositivism and substantive standards of scientific truth; Radnitzky (1968) for a masterful overview of this vast literature; and Bernstein (1978, 1983) and Apel (1980) for updates and commentaries.

22 What Habermas fails to see, however, is that qualities of "discourse" are distinctively voluntaristic (see chapter 7). They are qualities in social life that cannot be reduced to the quantifiable outcomes of instrumental actions or scientific experiments. (Nor can they be elevated to the ultimate meanings of symbolic or nonrational actions.) Habermas also fails to acknowledge that positivism may well be warranted as long as it is kept restricted to those areas where reductions to such outcomes go unchallenged. These areas may expand quite considerably over time, moreover, without this threatening or challenging Habermas's procedural turn and communication theory. This point cannot be developed further here, except to say that Habermas's early discussion of "object domains" (1968a) would provide a point of departure.

23 This suggests why Habermas fails to see that qualities of discourse are voluntaristic: At the level of interpersonal communication, he treats these qualities as "universal pragmatics," or as qualities that may be found in every instance of mutual understanding between actors under ideal conditions. At this microsociological level of analysis, these qualities appear to be structurally overdetermined by the very nature of ordinary speech itself, rather than voluntaristic or contingent. But as soon as Habermas attempts to explore how these qualities may be *institutionalized,* beyond this level of analysis, their voluntaristic status comes to the fore. Again, the significance of saying that these qualities are voluntaristic is explored in chapter 7.

24 Habermas's major discussions of his communication theory may be found in 1973c; 1976a; 1977; 1981a,b; and 1982. In addition, see several statements by Karl-Otto Apel (1972, 1979, 1980). Fine commentaries and elaborations include those by McCarthy (1978: especially chapter 4), Dallmayr (1974, 1976, 1977), Bernstein (1978), Wellmer (1976), plus collections by Thompson and Held (1982), Geraets (1979), and O'Neill (1976). Radnitzky (1968) places both Habermas and Apel within the philosophy of science, and Bernstein (1983) provides an update. See Alexander (1985) for a pointed critique of Habermas's use of J.L. Austin's concepts, and Antonio (1989) for the charge that Habermas has not adopted central tenets of pragmatism. Sabia and Wallulis (1983) contains several essays summarizing Habermas's works. For overviews of Habermas's relationship to the Frankfurt school and Marxism, see Schroyer (1973), Held (1980), and Bottomore (1984).

25 Here is a link between Habermas's communication theory and both American pragmatism (Antonio 1989; Rochberg-Halton 1986) and the symbolic interactionism of both Anselm Strauss ("negotiated order") and Ralph Turner ("emergent norms").

26 Thus, Habermas's limiting case standard of ideal speech provides one basis for specifying when ranges of expectations of acceptable behavior are "unduly restricted," as noted in the discussion of social order in chapter 2. But, as will become clear in chapter 6, Fuller

provides a more practicable standard for locating such restrictions, a standard much richer in its implications for research.

27 Habermas does not use the term "artificially protected arenas," but it will become clear in later chapters why this term applies in this context.

28 See Fuller (1969: 23–26) on the ideal of reciprocity; Habermas (1976b) on reciprocity as a grounding; Gouldner (1960) on reciprocity as a norm. Brennan and Buchanan (1985: 22, 27–32, 98–100), surprisingly, have the same outlook on consensus and unrestrained participation as Habermas. Ackerman (1980) attempts to apply it in legal theory.

29 Habermas draws rare exception for Anabaptists. Wuthnow (1987: 230–47), however, places this in sounder perspective.

30 By 1971, Habermas clearly and unhesitatingly acknowledged that he could not bring his communication theory to political practice (1973a: 130–43; 1974: 186–8; 1981: 43; 1982: 220, 232–3, 251–4, 261–3). He conceded that he had to restrict himself to interpersonal relations and "therapeutic critique" (1968a: chapters 10–12; 1971: 28–32, 37–40; 1981: 20–1, 41–2). Habermas has never argued, suggested, or intimated that his earlier works, including his study of the bourgeois public realm (1962), offer him any assistance in making the linkage to political practice. Commentators, exegetes, and critics have yet to offer Habermas a viable proposal for the linkage.

31 See Randall Collins (1986) for an exercise in "Weberian sociological theory" that sidesteps the problem by acceding too readily to conceptual relativism. Alan Sica (1988) also refuses to touch the issue of what distinguishes substantive rationality and substantive irrationality within the Weberian conceptual framework.

Chapter 6. Societal constitutionalism's threshold in practice: from Fuller's legal theory to societal constitutionalism

1 Hart likely remains the most widely read and influential contemporary legal theorist. He and Fuller debated the relationship between positivist (enforcement) and normative (interpretative) aspects of law. The chronology of the Fuller-Hart debate is as follows: Hart (1958); Fuller (1958); Hart (1961); Fuller (1964/1969); Hart (1965); Fuller (1964/1969: chap. 5). Summers's (1984) discussion of Fuller's legal theory and this debate is instructive and yet uneven; MacCormick (1981) and Martin (1987) trace Hart's evolving views.

2 There have been many provocative works in legal theory since Fuller's major debates and works first appeared, of course, including Dworkin (1977, 1986), Ely (1980), Calabresi (1982), Ackerman (1977, 1980) and Unger (1986). Still, the continuing importance of Fuller's threshold of procedural legality hinges on two points. First, he remains the only legal theorist to codify desiderata *of interpretability* that can credibly claim to ground the lawful/lawless distinction under modern conditions. With this, he jettisoned any and all traditional (that is, substantive) natural law standards. Second, Fuller alone opened the way for social scientists to explore whether the comparative study of law can indeed be rendered generalizable rather than left to the particularism of each nation-state's "reflexive" positive laws (Luhmann 1982: 90–121; Nonet and Selznick 1978). Unlike the civil law tradition of the Continent and Latin America (Merryman 1969/1985: 48–55), which revolves around an explicit standard of legal certainty, rather than one of flexibility or equity, the common-law tradition revolves around an implicit standard of legal interpretability. Fuller was the first legal scholar to codify this standard and render it explicit. As noted in chapters 1 and 4, the question is: Can such a standard credibly claim grounding and generalizability, and thereby orient comparative research that encompasses civil law (and, for that matter, Islamic law) countries? The interrelationship between Fuller's legal theory and Habermas's communication theory (chapter 8) establishes, at the least, that this *claim* is credible – rather than unwarranted a priori.

3 Fuller is also remembered for his allegory of the complexities involved in interpreting complex social events: "The Case of the Speluncean Explorers" (1949).

4 Gibbs (1982: 93–4) offers a rare and yet still limited appreciation by a sociologist of the research potential of Fuller's legal theory, and Elkin (1987: 9–12, 103–9) one by a political scientist. Black (1984) dismisses "normative" theory out of hand, and yet his work exhibits a strictly normative, altogether unargued, fealty to the presupposition of exhausted possibilities.

5 The question broadens when converted into the terms of the theory of societal constitutionalism: How can social scientists distinguish in comparative perspective when a *stable* social order is becoming either more controlling or (possibly) more integrative?

6 Brennan and Buchanan (1985: 4–5) also emphasize the importance of enforcement rather than the importance of interpretability.

7 Brennan and Buchanan (1985: 100–4) follow this second path. They reduce law's legitimacy to the ranges of expectations regarding acceptable behavior that actors happen to acknowledge at any given point in time. This is why they end up accepting that actors may agree to "meta-rules" that permit "legitimate lawmaking bodies" to make unannounced or secret changes in the law – as long as the changes do not challenge actors' existing expectations (1985: 107–8). Luhmann offers the same argument (1972; 1982: 90–137; 1990: 187–202).

8 Because Fuller's standard of lawfulness rests on *qualities* of interpretability rather than on quantitative indices of effective enforcement, the former may be called voluntaristic social integration and the latter rational social control. The reasons for saying this are explored in chapter 7. This would eliminate many of the endless disputes over the normative and scientific status of "law" as such. Rational social controls (and the effectiveness of enforcement) close off any possibility of social integration whenever they are institutionalized in and of themselves. As Weber's social theory indicates, they are consistent with any social order rather than being intrinsically consistent with a nonauthoritarian social order in particular.

9 Actually, Fuller wavers in characterizing what these eight qualities establish. At times (1964/1969: 41–9, 101–3), he insists that they are ideals that existing legal orders cannot fully realize, in practice. At other times (e.g. 1964/1969: 17, 27–8, 39–40, 64–5, 204, 215–16; 1969b: 220, 234), he insists, and just as forcefully, that they are irreducible criteria of the lawful/lawless distinction. The reasons why the latter position is emphasized in this volume are presented in the text. The former position, ironically, is not consistent with Fuller's own distinction between a morality of duty and a morality of aspiration; this is discussed momentarily.

10 This is the restraint against which Brennan and Buchanan are prepared to encroach (see note 7).

11 Again, only when the threshold of interpretability is interrelated with the collegial form of organization does its capacity to restrain or mediate *inadvertent* mechanisms of social control and the drift of social change come into view.

12 See Hugh Collins (1982), Spitzer (1983), and Lukes (1985) for recent reviews of this literature, each failing to move beyond Marxism's unsophisticated treatment of law. The latter is exemplified by Lukacs's 1920 essay "Legality and Illegality." The best treatment of law by a Marxist, in my view, remains a very early essay written by Marx himself, in 1842: "Comments on the Latest Prussian Censorship Instruction." Marx's reasons for ridiculing state censorship are completely consistent with the common-law tradition and Fuller's work. Yet, these same reasons are utterly inconsistent with Marx's later references to law, and certainly to references to law by major Marxist theorists since.

13 See Habermas (1963a,b,c) for methodical criticisms of this understanding of the theory and practice of revolutions in the West, both by liberals and Marxists.

14 See Selznick (1961) for an influential statement, and (1987) for an explicit statement of a substantive moral theory. Yet, his other works cannot be said to update a natural law theory, nor, for that matter, to remain consistent with Fuller's strictly procedural approach to due process. Instead, Selznick has, over the years, increasingly treated "due process" as the successful balancing of interested parties' legal claims (Selznick 1969, 1978; Nonet and Selznick 1978). See Dallmayr (1974) for an excellent review and categorization of moral and ethical theories. Unfortunately, he fails to include Fuller's contribution.

15 For Donald Black (1972 1096; 1976; 1984: 2), law is "governmental social control." All other mechanisms of social control, and all unofficial ways of expressing grievances, fall within "normative sociology" (1984: 4). Habermas tailored his communication theory to escape the same two shoals, of course, even as he concentrated on Weber's legal positivism in particular. This too suggests that Fuller's procedural threshold and Habermas's more idealized standard of procedural reason may be read in retrospect today as interrelated. Yet, the former reveals how the latter might be brought to detailed comparative study (and to practice).

16 If anything, one cannot escape the conclusion that the legal systems of Great Britain and the United States are *less* rational-legal than those of the Soviet Union and South Africa. Kronman (1983: 87–92) discusses why this is the case, albeit in more general terms.

17 As shown in chapter 7, Parsons took the same tack in developing his earliest social theory, the "voluntaristic schema of action." Aside from passing references to Locke's view of actors' "natural identity of interests," he largely ignored moral theories. Instead, he concentrated on methodically examining positivists' and utilitarians' unexamined residual category, the "nonrational." Within this residual category, he (albeit unsuccessfully) proposed that "voluntaristic action" is a distinct concept.

18 Kant distinguished duties of virtue and duties of law. Schluchter (1981: 103ff) brings this distinction (and others from Kant) to Weber's sociology of domination, and Münch (1981a, 1982) discusses a "Kantian core" within Parsons's social theory. Brennan and Buchanan (1985: 100) pin their constitutional economics on Kantian notions of keeping promises. Given Weber's legal positivism, Schluchter's use of Kantian concepts fails to yield the critical potential of Fuller's legal theory. Parsons's mature view of law (by the early 1960s) is more sophisticated. He arrived independently at a position consistent with Fuller's. Münch's Kantian reading of Parsons's social theory leads him to emphasize the "interpenetration" of Parsons's concepts as opposed to their analytical distinctiveness. As such, the significance of Parsons's eventual "procedural turn," and the latter's consistency with Fuller's legal theory, is not appreciated.

19 Fuller never stated explicitly that his legal theory is dedicated exclusively to the non-authoritarian/authoritarian distinction. Parsons is guilty of the same oversight (Sciulli 1988b). In both cases, this renders literal interpretations of their works needlessly contradictory and confusing. For instance, Fuller referred to points of interrelationship between positive law and the two moralities as the "internal morality of law" (1969: 5–9). But this phrase misleads readers in their efforts to appreciate the critical potential of his legal theory. His point may be stated more generally, and more accurately, by labeling these points of interrelationship a *normative orientation*. The latter hinges on the interpretability of shared social duties, irrespective of whether the latter are positive laws or more informal expectations regarding acceptable behavior. The term normative orientation is preferred to Fuller's term morality because the latter suggests that actors internalize norms in common whereas the former does not (chapter 8, note 6). Irrespective of whether the procedural norms comprising Fuller's threshold are internalized by actors or not (or even acknowledged by them at all), they nonetheless constitute an irreducible threshold that begins to separate authoritarian from nonauthoritarian social orders, in practice.

20 Fuller also never stated explicitly that he was talking about aspirations that are openly or publicly pursued. Yet, his duty/aspiration distinction runs into enormous problems unless this is added. After all, Nazi death camps were tied to an aspiration of sorts. The same may be said of the strenuous endeavors by the Marquis de Sade, or by Lucky Luciano, Meyer Lansky, and other organized crime figures. In all such cases, aspirations were pursued privately rather than publicly; as such, they could be pursued in the absence of the social infrastructure of shared social duties.

21 Also see Gibbs (1981: 7–21) on the "consensus problem" regarding norms (and earlier Scott 1971). Here is where Braithwaite's (1989) theory of reintegrative shaming suffers problems, as does Brennan and Buchanan's constitutional economics (1985: 29). Braithwaite acknowledges that his theory is less applicable when laws are ambiguous. But he operates on the assumption that basic criminal law typically escapes ambiguity. If so, then why is a generalizable morality of duty not available to comparative research other than Fuller's procedural threshold?

22 All modern nation-states that revolve around a tapestry of patron-client networks, rather than around some combination of public administrations and collegial formations within civil society, have indeed institutionalized a culture of evasion. The former, moreover, likely characterizes the vast majority of *modern* nation-states today (to say nothing of the situation historically). Just as importantly, all modern nation-states without exception are vulnerable to this development under modern conditions (see chapter 8 on patron-client networks as a form of organization, chapter 9 on Brazil and Latin America generally, and chapter 11 for alternatives).

23 This poses the duality represented today by rational-choice theory and symbolic interactionism, on one side, and traditional applications of Parsonian functionalism and Durkheimian social theory, on the other. The latter includes Randall Collins's interaction ritual chain theory (1988: chapters 6, 10). A culture of evasion is a logical product of extending principles of either rational choice or symbolic interaction across any population. Coleman's (1988) examples of "social capital," including actors' shared *feelings* of security in allowing their children to travel alone in familiar (and, by his examples, always ethnically or religiously homogeneous) neighborhoods, rest on decidedly nonrational, internalized normative *restraints* on individuals' rational decision-making. If harassing children brings pleasure and possible material reward to an assailant, with low likelihood of pain or cost, on what rational grounds is an actor discouraged from this practice? Coleman turns to the idea of "social capital" precisely because the institutionalization of rational choice principles is so unappealing that it brings him to reappraise anachronistic alternatives. He concedes implicitly that once a culture of evasion has been institutionalized, there is nothing in rational-choice theory that can help resuscitate prior cultures of shared feeling.

24 As the University of Wisconsin political scientist Herman Goldstein points out (1977: chapter 5), this problem moves beyond that of police discretion or selective enforcement. It moves to the problem of legislators being unwilling, as active politicians, to publicly decriminalize activities that they know full well the police routinely fail to enforce. The police purposefully decide not to enforce certain activities (often "victimless crimes") precisely because full enforcement in these areas would, in their view, reduce the effectiveness of social control at their street level of operation.

25 Put into terminology adopted in chapter 8, this is the rule-making body's normative orientation. Whether these actors happen to internalize shared subjective interests or normative motivations qua well-socialized individuals is a secondary issue.

26 This may well explain why Coleman's (1988) "social capital" withers with modernity (see note 23). That children may no longer walk alone safely in urban America is unfortunate. But this supports Coleman's point about social capital only when considered in isolation. Is it not possible that a great many social contexts within which children remain safe also

happen to be hazardous to *adults?* Is it not possible that it is precisely in these social contexts that adults are not treated as reasoning and responsible beings (see chapter 9, page 209 and chapter 11, note 20)? Why is it not an example of "social capital" to treat adults in the latter way, even if one unfortunate consequence of this is a reduction in children's safety? Coleman can only locate enclaves of "social capital" in his sense within anachronistic situations, such as neighborhoods or schools wherein actors are relatively homogeneous in class, ethnicity, and religion. The rational-choice framework of concepts with which he operates does not permit him to assess such situations more analytically, and critically. Rational-choice theory cannot be used to specify when any direction of social change within any social context is nonauthoritarian in principle and when it is demonstrably authoritarian, other than to recapitulate liberalism's fondness for those social changes that usher in and maintain capital and labor markets and interest competition within government. The safety of children is not a self-evidently critical standard by which to describe or evaluate the direction of social change (as Popenoe 1988, too, might consider).

27 This indicates the superiority of Fuller's procedural approach to law over Kelsen's more immediate concentration on the camaraderie and effectiveness of enforcers.

28 Of course, there are human "needs" so basic, e.g. food, shelter, and clothing, that providing them is clearly a "direct," substantive advance, one that sidesteps Fuller's procedural threshold altogether. Even as this is readily granted, it still leaves unchallenged the central thrust of Fuller's argument: At the moment that any set of power holders moves in even the slightest way *beyond* satisfying such basic "needs" of life itself, the problem of the recognition and understanding of shared social duties immediately comes into play.

29 Again, this would confirm the proposition that Habermas's communication theory rests on analytical distinctions, his objections to the contrary notwithstanding.

30 On Hobbes and the arbitrariness inherent in liberal contract theory, see Arendt (1951: chapter 5); Habermas (1963a: 62–76); and Macpherson (1962). When Weber pointed out that British (and American) common law in particular represents a combination, in his words, of two "nonrational" types of legal practice – which he labeled Khadi justice and empirical law – he told comparative researchers literally nothing at all about this tradition of law, either about its theoretical tradition or about its applications in practice. It is not that Weber was wrong or one-sided in his wording; it is rather that his wording is unhelpful. It conveys nothing at all of significance about his object of study. Moreover, Weber's vision of strictly "formal legal rationality" is neither clear nor compelling (Kronman 1983: 72–95).

31 Useem (1984) documents this in Great Britain and the United States, even as his conceptual apparatus veils this from his direct attention.

32 This directly challenges Tilly's assertion, noted in chapter 1, that the distinction between legitimate and illegitimate uses of force is normative or ideological rather than possibly generalizable and critical. It also throws into doubt Janowitz's most basic distinction, noted in chapter 2, between social control and coercive control. See Giddens (1985) for an absolutist critique of "surveillance"; Hechter (1987) for an uncritical treatment of surveillance, or what he calls "metering"; and Wiley (1987) for a call for greater balance in response to Giddens.

33 See Bollen and Jackman (1985) for some empirical support for the point in the text, even as their definition of "democracy" rests on the presupposition of exhausted possibilities. The latter holds as well for their more recent study (1989).

34 Fuller (1964/1969: 243–4) lists reviews of *The Morality of Law* to that date, reviews that include not only American and international law journals but also American and international social science journals. Summers (1984) reviews these and other criticisms, to which he himself contributed beginning in 1965 in the *Journal of Legal Education* and continuing into the 1970s. In the course of his study of Fuller's work in 1984, Summers acknowledges

that he now considers his criticisms and others' to have been mistaken. He explores the ability of Fuller's work, as it stands, to rebut the major criticisms to which it was subjected, and particularly those from Hart. Imagine how formidable Fuller's work would appear to Summers were its consistency with a grounded concept of procedural reason, and then with a distinctive organizational form, brought into his reassessment.

35 Again, consider the term employed by Richard Stewart (1983), a professor of administrative law at Harvard Law School: "noncommodity values." He resorts to a residual category in an effort to describe those norms capable of restraining or mediating the drift of administrative and regulatory law. Left as a residual category, he fails to locate agents of change (whether power holders or social influentials) capable of institutionalizing such values against interest-group opposition. He also fails to demonstrate any relationship between these values and organizational forms. One result is that even though the residual category implies that Stewart by no means sees the drift of administrative and regulatory law as intrinsically benign, the only reforms he suggests involve substituting market forces for current law – a direct contradiction of his own residual category (Sciulli in preparation, b: chapter 4).

Chapter 7. Societal constitutionalism's organizational manifestation, I: voluntaristic action as a distinct concept

1 The journal, founded in October 1890, was by 1935 still called *International Journal of Ethics*. By April 1938 it was renamed, and it bears this title today: *Ethics*. Its contemporary subtitle recalls its earlier title: *An International Journal of Social, Political, and Legal Philosophy*.

2 Parsons's thesis in *The Structure of Social Action* was that Marshall, Pareto, Durkheim, and Weber independently "converged" in exposing "voluntaristic action" in modern social life even as none of them employed this term. As demonstrated in this chapter, however, Parsons tended to collapse what he meant by voluntaristic action into the more general concept of normative action. Regardless, from his initial isolation of normative concepts within each of the four writer's works, all of Parsons's subsequent work may be read as an elaborate effort to survey all concepts "external" to the norm of formal rationality.

3 Rather than the metaphor "standing on the shoulders of giants," which Merton traced so meticulously (1965), an allegory that better captures Parsons's boldness as a young theorist is that of Nietzsche's tightrope walker in the early pages of *Thus Spake Zarathustra* (1892). A stranger climbs to the highwire, somersaults over the head of the "master" performer who is carefully making his way across, and alights on the tightrope ahead of him. His landing disturbs the line only slightly, and yet enough to undo the "master's" balance and cause him to fall to his death. The master is undone, that is, more by the stranger's breathtaking deftness than by the master's own missteps.

4 Jonathan Turner argued in 1974 that Parsons could be read as a symbolic interactionist (to Herbert Blumer's 1975 consternation), and yet by 1988 he devoted his new "theory of social interaction" explicitly to correcting Parsons's oversight of interaction. Turner's book turns out, curiously, to provide one of the best arguments in years for undertaking a fresh reading of Parsons's social theory. It ends with so many tables, and so many unrelated categories, that even Turner throws his hands in the air and confesses that he cannot possibly provide a synthesis. He can only summarize other theorists' approaches to motivation, interaction, and structure, repeating points made earlier in the book. What is necessary for synthesis, of course, is greater conceptual abstraction and a new terminology. But Turner fails to make this move, in part because all along the way he criticizes Parsons for having done so. Far worse, Turner fails to see that Parsons turned to abstraction precisely

in order not to have to write the kind of concluding chapter that Turner explicitly excuses himself for publishing.

5 Alan Sica (1988) misreads Parsons's works in this respect. First, he contends that Parsons followed Weber in overemphasizing the norm of rational action and drift of rationalization. Then, he fails to follow Parsons's lead in sharply distinguishing analytically between the "irrational" and the "nonrational." The former concept is insignificant for purposes of methodical social theory whereas the latter concept opens up an enormous vista for ongoing theorizing, even though it is a residual category.

6 Parsons's social theory exhibits its own variation of conceptual closure, and this is explored in chapter 10: It is closed to accommodating any concept of reasoned social action.

7 Throughout this discussion, the term "actor" refers not only to individuals but also to either bounded or unbounded collectivities, including social movements, organizations, and institutions, which at times act as a unit.

8 At least three meanings for the concept may be found in Alexander's four volumes (as well as his 1978 article): (a) actors' internalized "normative control" (1982a: 81, 84, 96–112; 1983a: 28–9, 58–9, 102–113; 1983b: 24–5, 35–44, 119–50); (b) actors' "voluntary" responsibility or choice (1982a: 87, 96–8; 1983a: 98–9, 107–8, 112–114; 1983b: 25–6, 120–27, 214); and (c) actors' "motivation" (1982a: 23–4; 1983a: 39–40, 96, 107, 116; 1983b: 31). For Alexander (1978), "formal voluntarism" is actors' inherent capacity to volunteer to act in common, and "substantive voluntarism" is the empirical realization of this capacity.

9 Camic (1989) manages both simultaneously, to render the concept commonplace and redundant. In this way he indirectly supports the thesis of this chapter. After all, if one is going to distinguish a concept from normative action or action in general, then one must specify the analytical aspects that indeed distinguish it. Parsons failed to do this. Camic brings his considerable exegetical skills to bear in demonstrating that, indeed, Parsons's usage results in a "concept" that is commonplace, and thereby unnecessary. The question remains, however: Can voluntaristic action be distinguished analytically, or is it indeed reducible to normative action as such? It is interesting to note the many commentators who ignore the problem of defining or systematically discussing voluntarism, eg. Faris 1953; Swanson 1953; Bredemeier 1955; Cancian 1960; Wrong 1961; Bershady 1973; Rocher 1975; Mitchell 1967; Barry 1970; O'Neill 1972; Madge 1964: chapter 4; Kaplan 1968; Burger 1977. Compare Warner's approach to the problem by 1978, and Wiley's expression of frustration by 1979.

10 Parsons had several opportunities to do so, especially when responding to critics (1974a; 1975a,b; 1976a, 1977a; 1978a) and when offering retrospective summaries of his evolving conceptual schemas (e.g. 1968b, 1970a). Yet, Parsons perpetuated the pattern to which Louis Wirth had called attention as far back as 1939: He remained vague in his later brief, direct references to the concept. On two separate occasions Parsons endorsed Gerstein's (1975: 12) view of voluntaristic action: "By a fortunate circumstance, since the appearance of the last of the Cohen, Hazelrigg and Pope articles, there has appeared a highly relevant interpretative article by Dean R. Gerstein (1975). Gerstein gives a clear and accurate summary of this conceptual scheme as it was presented in *The Structure of Social Action*, of the uses to which it was put in that book and of its continuity with the later theoretical developments involved in the 'four-function paradigm' . . . [which] has been much used ever since" (Parsons 1976a: 362, note 2; also 362, 364). Parsons's second endorsement came in 1977 (1977b: 2) in his "General Introduction" to *Social Systems and the Evolution of Action Theory*. But Gerstein's definition falls into the third set of definitions above, and it fails to bring any greater specificity to the concept than Parsons's own references.

11 See chapter 11 on "moral authorities" and their "protected spheres." Consider also Habermas's treatment of Peter Winch's studies of Azande magic (Habermas 1981a: 43–75; 1982: 270). McCarthy is critical of Habermas's earlier response to Winch (1978: 317–33).

12 By 1938 Robert Merton set up the "polar types" of "instrumental" societies and "ritualistic" societies, and then discussed anomie and deviance within the middle type of "mores and institutions" of modern societies. But this is less distinctive and innovative than Parsons's vague references to voluntaristic action.

13 Another example is the transition from the relatively unemotional preindustrial family to the more emotionally charged nuclear family, one hinging on the primary socialization of children as well as companionship and emotional support among adults. "Most scholars have concluded that in the modern, nuclear family these functions have been conducted at a far higher level of quality (and equality) than ever before" (Popenoe 1988: 69). But, again, this quality is strictly worldly. It cannot be attributed to any sacred or transcendental mandate. Similarly, when Swedes came to fetishize hygiene – mental, bodily, sexual, dietary – in place of earlier religiously based moralities (Popenoe 1988: 119–20), this was a quintessential move from the nonrational to the voluntaristic.

14 To refer to these aspects of a people's lived social fabric as "sacred" is to miss the point of *distinguishing* the voluntaristic from the symbolic or nonrational. It is also to lose any possibility of eventually distinguishing social integration from social control, and nonauthoritarian social order from authoritarian or manipulative social order. This overextension of the category "sacred" is one of the most important differences within the neofunctionalist "school" between the theory of societal constitutionalism and both Alexander's emphasis on multidimensionality and Münch's emphasis on interpenetration. Considering again Popenoe's discussion of the Swedes (note 13), why bother to label a collective fetishization of hygiene, or of any other qualities in social life, "sacred" or "moral"?

15 Menzies (1977), Habermas (1980, 1981b), and many others fail to see Parsons's theses of entropy and authoritarianism in 1937. German theorists, including Habermas, generally read Parsons after an initial reading of the quite different concepts and theories of Niklas Luhmann, the German systems theorist. This gives German commentators a particularly skewed reading of Parsons, given Parsons's own cultural and intellectual roots in American pragmatism and the common-law tradition. To be sure, Parsons was heavily influenced by Continental theories and approaches to social theory – but his work, unlike Luhmann's, cannot be reduced to this influence.

16 Olson (1965) and Hechter (1987) discount this effort more by how they define the groups they choose to study than by direct argument. Each concentrates on groups that are dedicated to attaining quantitative ends of one kind or another rather than addressing methodically those groups that are dedicated to describing and explaining (or creating and maintaining) qualities in social life. Each dismisses the latter groups out of hand by saying simply that their membership size is not as large as that of the former groups. What they fail to consider is that the form of organization of voluntaristic groups differs from the form of organization of rational groups (see chapter 8), and that this is far more important than the size of their respective memberships.

17 Parsons ultimately saw the professions' integrity being supported by systemic pressures themselves, and this position misdirects his entire mature social theory (see chapter 11). The most significant problem riddling Luhmann's systems theory, like so many parts of Parsons's functionalism, is that autopoiesis, or a system's self-monitoring capacities, can just as readily institutionalize an authoritarian as a nonauthoritarian social order. There is no rationale in the social sciences, or in the long and impressive tradition of social theory, for any theorist to dismiss this problem out of hand simply by referring to "social order" as such. The theorist must rather take note at some point of the type of social order being implied.

18 Parsons's footnote (1937b: 251 note 2) clarifies the passage somewhat: "To anticipate: the first of these possibilities is, so long as the norm is a genuine independent variable and not dependent, that taken in general by idealistic theories, the second by positivistic and the

third by the voluntaristic theory of action. . . ." But the trichotomy, respectively, of the symbolic, the intrinsic, and the voluntaristic as discussed above better captures the latter's distinctiveness.

Chapter 8. Societal constitutionalism's organizational manifestation, II: from voluntaristic action to collegial formations

1 Parsons focused less directly on procedural norms and institutions than did Fuller and Habermas, and even his indirect references to them came late in his career (from the mid–1960s at the earliest). Still, his residual references to collegial formations, and his evolution from accepting Weber's legal theory to independently developing a legal theory consistent with Fuller's, are in many respects as suggestive as Fuller's and Habermas's more direct discussions of procedural norms and institutions.

2 It is shown in chapter 10 that constitutional and liberal traditions hinge on the capacity of the "constituent force" of private citizens to recognize arbitrary government. This expectation was idealized from the start, and it is clearly anachronistic in the late twentieth century. Yet, constitutional and liberal theories continue even today to hinge on the presence of an ever-vigilant "constituent force" in civil society. At the moment that this is questioned, these theories can no longer account either for limited government or nonauthoritarian social order under modern conditions.

3 Still, even as this behavior is irreducibly necessary to nonauthoritarian social order and social integration, it is not sufficient: This behavior *alone* does *not* realize either possibility, in practice. This is discussed momentarily.

4 Falsification is the single most important requirement of empirical research in the social sciences (Popper 1934; Merton 1949/1957; Radnitzky 1968). Habermas (1968a, 1973c, 1979) and Apel (1972, 1980) pose weak counterarguments to this standard, even as they effectively attack positivism more generally.

5 This is precisely how the theory of societal constitutionalism escapes Habermas's most central criticism of Parsons's functionalism. For Habermas (1967b: 86): "In the theoretical framework of [Parsons's] action theory, motives for action are harmonized with institutional values, thus with the intersubjectively prevailing meaning of normatively binding behavioral expectations. . . . But we may presume that . . . repressed needs that have not been reabsorbed by social roles, transformed into motivations, and sanctioned have their interpretations nevertheless" (also see the introduction, viii, for a different translation). The theory of societal constitutionalism disrupts the "harmonizing" to which Habermas correctly objects in two ways. First, it emphasizes the distinction between (a) institutionalized normative orientations that are both voluntaristic and procedural and (b) internalized normative motivations that are nonrational or else voluntaristic but more directly substantive (see note 6). Second, it provides a standard by which to recognize whether institutionalized normative orientations possibly are contributing to reasoned social action. This standard is voluntaristic, and thereby practicable; yet, it is also irreducible, and thereby generalizable and possibly grounded.

6 The distinction between normative orientations and normative motivations dates to Parsons's early works: (1935, 1937a), and it remains an important conceptual advance for all of his inconsistency in presenting it across his career. In his well-known article of 1938, "Science and the Social Order," Robert Merton also referred tentatively to the same distinction. To refer to shared normative motivations is to identify a set of actors who have *internalized* (or negotiated) the same sets of substantive norms in common. This already presupposes, of course, that these actors have undergone very similar processes of either primary or secondary socialization. Or else it presupposes that they have been very similarly affected by their symbolic interactions or by their structural positions.

Wrong (1961), Stryker (1980: 64), and others rightly call for the notion of socialization to be extended by an interactionist variant, and network analysts emphasize positions of "structural equivalence." In any event, it is being presupposed that these actors are, in certain important respects, more or less homogeneous. By contrast, to refer to normative orientations is to refer to an *institutionalization* of norms within a complex social unit. Institutionalized norms may broadly orient actors in common, irrespective of how heterogeneous these actors might otherwise be. That is, if these orientations are indeed firmly institutionalized, actors who otherwise operate on the basis of quite diverse subjective interests and normative motivations may nonetheless be able to recognize and understand in common when the integrity of these norms is being maintained or encroached against. Whether they then accept these norms, or prefer to be oriented by them, is a matter quite different from whether they are at least capable of recognizing and understanding them in common. The theory of societal constitutionalism builds on this distinction by distinguishing, in turn, between the possibility of social integration and demonstrable social control, and between procedural voluntaristic restraints and substantive voluntaristic restraints. In both instances the former concepts rest on actors' shared normative orientations, whereas the latter can rest exclusively on actors' shared normative motivations. Again, it must be emphasized that to say that actors recognize encroachments against institutionalized normative orientations is not to suggest at all that they thereby agree in common that such encroachments are to be prevented or punished. Quite to the contrary, some actors (e.g. rebels, disbelievers, iconoclasts, etc.) may believe that encroachments are virtuous and are to be promoted and rewarded. The point is rather that they nonetheless recognize in common when normative orientations are being encroached against.

7 Is it possible that the current wave of "democratization" across the East, and earlier across Latin America, is a product of the recognition by power holders that Western democratic institutions contribute to actors' demonstrable social control? Is it possible, therefore, that this current wave has little to do with power holders' appreciation of the supposed "moral superiority" of these institutions as such? Put differently, when the evidence clearly demonstrates that other mechanisms of social control are far more costly to institutionalize, even Eastern and Latin American power holders may arrive in time at the following conclusion, on the basis of strictly rational-choice calculations: Western institutions of social control are more likely to preserve their privileges *as individuals* than their membership in a party or peak association that attempts to place external substantive restraints on rationalization itself.

8 They are also not consensual (see chapter 9). Parsons saw only four distinct *forms* of organization, the first being what he called the "competitive" (in economics) and the other three being the bureaucratic (in politics), the democratic (in societal community), and the associational or collegial (in pattern maintenance). He never provided definitions for this typology. Moreover, for present purposes the "competitive" form is dropped entirely in favor of the patron-client form. Competition is not a form of organization. It either refers to an economic marketplace, an institutionalized environment within which organizations of any form may or may not be found, or else it refers to a political marketplace, an institutionalized environment that is pervasive and immutable (chapter 4). The patron-client form, by contrast, revolves around actors' networks of personal loyalties, and it may be found across the Third World, the East, and the West. Young people in Western liberal- and social-democracies, for instance, typically find their first jobs through parents' or relatives' personal networks rather than through any "competitive" search. The development of networks of personal loyalties also remains a major goal in any professional career, and yet these networks are a constant source of threats to professionals' maintaining the integrity of the collegial form.

9 This is why Habermas insists, for instance, that when majority rule is detached from the

conditions of ideal speech, it remains procedurally rational but cannot be procedurally reasoned. This is also why both liberal and pluralist theorists operate on the assumption that actors' subjective interests are given or random: They are to be treated equally, irrespective of how actors arrived at them. To ask actors to warrant their subjective interests in terms of any principle is to challenge the sovereignty of subjective interests. Liberals and pluralists alike cannot permit this without exposing the outcomes of economic and political marketplaces to normative or nonrational restraints of one kind or another (chapters 4, 9).

10 The patron-client form is also nondemocratic and nonrational, but it is a substantively voluntaristic organizational form. At times it may rigidify into a more strictly nonrational organizational form (see note 13 below).

11 When arbitrary exercises of collective power are popularly acclaimed, this may be thought of as a one-sided development of democratization. It is helpful to recall that the "republican civic" tradition of the American founders was always seen, for better or worse, as fundamentally distinct from either formal democracy or formal equality. It was seen bringing reason and prudence into the political arena. Yet, it was never seen restraining even the most grievous excesses of possessive individualism within the marketplace or any other manifestations of the sovereignty of actors' subjective interests within civil society. The relationship between republicanism, democratization, and capitalism is currently under debate by legal scholars (*Yale Law Journal* 1988). Bellah et al. (1986) make much of republicanism as well, along with the biblical tradition, but they fail to specify what they have in mind. They fail to do so because they fail to distinguish external substantive restraints, such as those posed by religion and a sense of calling, from the external procedural restraints institutionalized by a multiplicity of collegial formations across a civil society. The republican civic tradition may indeed be resuscitated on the latter basis, but not on the former. Bloom's hyperbole (1987) is a product of his failure to draw this distinction. He begrudgingly recognizes that external substantive restraints once provided by classical music, classical theory, and biblical teaching cannot be resuscitated today, and this realization drives him to distraction. Luhmann (1990) also fails to draw this distinction, but then he substitutes autopoiesis and other systems concepts for external procedural restraints – and thereby defines away the Weberian Dilemma altogether. His might very well be the first Lockean systems theory: Instead of positing that actors have a natural identity of interests in maintaining limited government, he sees subsystems working autopoietically to this end.

12 A consideration in the background of the theory of societal constitutionalism that cannot be brought into the foreground in this volume is that comparativists must begin to come to grips today with a state of affairs in the late twentieth century that differs substantially from that found in the immediate postwar era: the end of the thrust of liberal democratization, or of emphases on *individuals'* rather than groups' political inclusion. Even within Western democracies, many national political cultures no longer revolve unambiguously around the unquestioned value of ensuring individuals' inclusion; instead, groups mobilize for collective "representation." This applies as much to labor unions and other class organizations as it does to ethnic and religious sections or peak associations. It is difficult to assert that the thrust of individual democratization remains unquestioned in the late twentieth century, once one coldly considers: (a) ethnic and religious communalism across the Caribbean, sub-Saharan Africa, and South Asia; (b) the persistence and, if anything, the increasing extent of ethnic mobilization across the West and the former Eastern bloc; (c) the rigid exclusion of the bottom forty percent of the population from Brazil's (and other Latin American countries') arrangements of neocorporatism and patron-client relationships; (d) the strident disinclination of West European nation-states to consider the eligibility of their "guest workers" for citizenship (even as many of these "guests" have

resided in their respective countries for over a generation, and many of their children have known no other country); or even (e) the increasingly rigid exclusion of an estimated twenty or twenty-five percent of the American population from any *effective* role in the pluralist arrangements distinctive to American politics. What comparative researchers must come to grips with is the following question: How are advanced and modern nation-states to be studied which have for all intents and purposes accepted in the late twentieth century that anywhere from twenty to forty percent of their populations are permanently excluded from any and all prospects of effective representation within their major agencies of government and major social units of civil society, and also from any and all prospects of upward social mobility? Gans (1988) is one of the rare contemporary American sociologists to pose this issue. One of the major themes of early status attainment research (Blau and Duncan 1967; Featherman and Hauser 1978) was that with the end of migration from farm to town, upward mobility across generations flattens out, except for people who were otherwise excluded ascriptively from earlier opportunities for upward mobility (e.g. blacks, women, and others). Aside from operating on the basis of the presupposition of exhausted possibilities, comparativists also have operated on another presupposition: That the thrust of individual democratization became an irreversible foundation of modern political cultures during the postwar era, not simply in the West but worldwide. Both presuppositions fail today to account for an already enormous and ever-growing amount of evidence to the contrary. To their credit, Offe (1983) and Laumann and Knoke (1987) call into question this and other "normative" democratic theories.

13 The following three definitions of patron-client relations or clientelism, from John Duncan Powell, James C. Scott, and Ernest Gellner, are as representative as any in the literature:

"At the core of the patron-client relationship lie three basic factors which at once define and differentiate it from other power relationships which occur between individuals or groups. First, the patron-client tie develops between two parties unequal in status, wealth and influence. . . . Second, the formation and maintenance of the relationship depends on reciprocity in the exchange of goods and services. Such mutual exchanges involve non-comparable goods and services, however. In a typical transaction, the low-status actor (client) will receive material goods and services intended to reduce or ameliorate his environmental threats; while the high-status actor (patron) receives less tangible rewards, such as personal services, indications of esteem, deference or loyalty, or services of a directly political nature such as voting. Third, the development and maintenance of a patron-client relationship rests heavily on face-to-face contact between the two parties; the exchanges encompassed in the relationship, being somewhat intimate and highly particularistic, depend upon such proximity" (Powell 1970: 147–8).

"The patron-client relationship – an exchange relationship between roles – may be defined as a special case of dyadic ties involving a largely instrumental friendship in which an individual of higher socioeconomic status (patron) uses his own influence and resources to provide protection or benefits, or both, for a person of lower status (client) who, for his part, reciprocates by offering general support and assistance, including personal services, to the patron" (Scott 1972: 124–5).

"Patronage is unsymmetrical, involving inequality of power; it tends to form an extended system; to be long-term, or at least not restricted to a single isolated transaction; to possess a distinctive ethos; and, whilst not always illegal or immoral, to stand outside the officially proclaimed formal morality of the society in question" (Gellner 1977: 4).

14 They are restrained, of course, by their strictly practical and strategic anticipation of what might happen should they ignore this normative orientation and instead operate more immediately on the basis of material interest alone. See chapter 11 on a "public realm" or the implications of maintaining the integrity of collegial formations within a civil society as a matter of public policy.

15 It is argued in section 8.4 that societal constitutionalism's emphasis on the significance of the presence (or absence) of collegial formations brings greater specificity to John Meyer's (and others') references to organizations' "institutionalized environments."

16 Because Parsons defined professionals' *form of organization* as a residual category, he persisted across his career in stressing the importance of *individual professionals'* "secondary socialization," their coming to *share* internalized value-commitments (Parsons 1937b, 1939, 1952a; Parsons and Platt 1973). His emphasis on *individuals'* shared qualities rather than on the qualities distinctive to a *form* of organization continues to run through references to the professions by social theorists indebted to Parsons's ideas, even as they have since dropped even residual references to the collegial form (Alexander 1978, 1983b, 1986, 1987, 1988; Münch 1981a, 1982, 1987; Barber 1983; Colomy and Rhoades 1988). One of the reasons the theory of societal constitutionalism was developed was to account for professionals' integrity *despite* systemic pressures of drift to the contrary, including professionals' own heterogeneity, their *failure*, really, to internalize shared value-commitments (see chapter 9, pages 194–6 and chapter 10, pages 228–31). At the moment that the threshold of interpretability is demonstrated to be interrelated with the collegial form exclusively (chapter 6), Parsons's emphasis on *individual professionals'* qualities may be jettisoned. It may be replaced by an emphasis on the voluntaristic orientation that collegial formations institutionalize by their sheer presence within a civil society. Moreover, individual professionals' *loss* of integrity can then be specified empirically. It can be specified by exploring whether their *behavior* maintains or encroaches against the integrity of the collegial form *at their own particular work sites*. The norms which professionals may (or may not) have internalized during their training have very little to do with whether they maintain their formation's integrity or their own integrity as professionals, in practice (see Sciulli and Jenkins 1990 on the professions literature).

17 The legal realist Michael Moore (1989: 935ff) concedes this for what he calls the "modest interpretive claims" of certain types of legal practice: the interpretation of statutes and constitutional law rather than the common law.

18 Weber saw "collegiate bodies" in irreversible decline, under pressures of rationalization. Andrew Abbott (1988) fails to see the distinctiveness of this form of organization in his impressive study of the professions. The best effort to bring the Weberian conceptual framework into some harmony with the evidence of collegial formations in advanced societies is by Malcolm Waters. He (1989: 956) defines "collegial structures" as "those in which there is a dominant orientation to a consensus achieved between the members of a body of experts who are theoretically equal in their levels of expertise but who are specialized by area of expertise." The problem here, however, is that references to "dominant orientation to a consensus" and "theoretically equal" but "specialized" are not only vague but open the door to all sorts of organizations feigning collegiality for purposes of manipulation (either of their own membership or of clients). Waters himself is much concerned about professionals' "privileges" and their contribution to "social closure," to upholding unnecessary or unjustifiable status divisions across a civil society. Given his vague definition of collegiality, such concerns are as warranted as the opposite concern: that collegial structures might allow just about anyone into the professions and that equality might be pursued at the expense of expertise. The theory of societal constitutionalism emphasizes, by contrast, that as long as this form's integrity is being maintained, in practice, then actions taken by professionals within collegial formations cannot be reduced to mechanisms of social control or manipulation. Moreover, their actions are not likely to be consensual at all (see chapter 11, pp. 243–9 of this book). Their actions nonetheless remain consistent with possibilities for social integration, not only within collegial formations themselves but across other parts of the larger civil society (see chapter 11). That not all actors across a civil society have utterly equal access to what is indeed a rare possibility,

social integration, is not a sign of social closure. Even more, by no means does the charge of social closure establish a ground on which to criticize the external procedural restraints that collegial formations indeed contribute to a civil society. The latter is a public good or social capital even if they rest firmly on social closure in Waters's sense.

19 Indeed, Collins sees the professions revolving around normative social controls (1979: 48, 58–72, 171–2), political power plays against competitors (1979: 50–3, 71), and patron-client networks or personal cliques (1979: 55–8, 91, 200). Because he fails to notice the form of organization distinctive to professions proper as opposed to expert occupations that secure monopolies over their services by way of a power play alone, he calls for the abolition of credentials (1979: 179–204) – much as Milton Friedman did now nearly a quarter century ago (1962: chapter 9). Collins and Friedman alike fail to acknowledge two important bits of information in their rough-and-ready prescription: First, the abolition of credentials is utter utopianism, and they both know it. Unlike Friedman's early call for education vouchers, which had a variety of intrinsic merits that even opponents were compelled to acknowledge, this prescription will never be proposed as policy, let alone ever acted on, within any modern nation-state (see Freidson 1984b for a methodical discussion of this issue). Neither Collins nor Friedman specifies social influentials or power holders who could reasonably be expected to initiate a public dialogue put in these terms. Second, were it acted on, it would expose a modern nation-state to the Weberian Dilemma shorn of its most resilient institutional mediation against authoritarian drift. The result would be far different from the egalitarianism that Collins imagines (1979: 69–71, 199), and yet far closer to Friedman's vision. He blithely advocates extending the "principle" of caveat emptor from competitive retail stores and automobile mechanics to competitive (and self-selected) physicians and surgeons, lawyers, and therapists.

20 Thus, collegial formations may well decline inadvertently, without Collins having to prescribe an end to credentialling (see note 19). They may decline as professionals encroach against the integrity of this form's threshold, possibly with the assurance from conflict theory and laissez-faire economics that professions are indeed reducible to personal cliques, power plays, and unwarranted monopolies. Encroachments then appear to be either insignificant or liberating. Waters (1989) is similarly concerned that collegial formations are responsible for, or contribute to, social closure. He too misses the point: The integrity of collegial formations is voluntaristic, and thereby always and everywhere only contingently institutionalized. Being voluntaristic, their continued presence in civil society is clearly not compatible with any effort to maximize strictly quantitative indices, including those supporting egalitarian distributions of material resources as an end in itself. To criticize collegial formations for resisting unmediated egalitarianism is to ignore why any truly deliberative body is ultimately inegalitarian. If Waters believes that any nation-state would experience less social closure and greater egalitarianism if the integrity of deliberative bodies were not maintained by the procedural threshold of interpretability of shared social duties, then why not defend such a proposition directly? Similarly, would Collins hold to his call for the abolition of credentials when the issue is posed in this way, in terms of forms of organization and the problem of drift, rather than in terms of what he calls a "sinecure society" and the problem of monopoly?

21 Meyer's work was mentioned in Chapter 1. See Meyer and Rowan (1977); Meyer, Scott, and Deal (1981); and Meyer and Scott (1983). See Zucker (1988) for a collection devoted to the "institutional approach."

22 This provides a good example of how epistemological issues exceed the scope of application of methodological techniques, despite positivists' position to the contrary. The positivist is committed to the view that any empirical study in the social sciences whose methodology escapes criticism cannot possibly "distort" the "meaning" of the events under study.

By contrast, the discussion of Meyer's work in the text provides an example of postpositivists' counterargument: Only a social theory or a framework of concepts can address the matter of whether empirical findings, taken as they stand, distort the meaning of social events.

23 In fairness to Meyer, the same criticism may be lodged against Hannan and Freeman's population ecology approach to organizations as well as Habermas's communication theory and Luhmann's systems theory. What is ironic is that Parsons's AGIL schema, of all things, can be used to draw such distinctions, even though his social theory has long been criticized for being too abstract (Craib 1984). It should be kept in mind that the origins of the institutional approach to organizations may be traced to Parsons's social theory of the 1950s (e.g. Scott 1981/1987), prior to his formulation of the AGIL schema.

24 Early on in the professions literature, Lewis and Maude (1952), for instance, refused to consider the first possibility for the professions.

25 It may now be seen how the theory of societal constitutionalism may be related to network analysts' emphasis on how actors' and groups' behavior is affected by their "structural equivalence." The theory of societal constitutionalism instructs researchers to explore whether structural equivalence itself is substantively immediate or mediated by voluntaristic procedures. If the former, then the behavior in question is reducible to the workings of mechanisms of social control; if the latter, then the behavior in question is possibly integrative. To date, network analysts tie their work exclusively to immediate manifestations of structural equivalence, and they accede to the presupposition of exhausted possibilities. The theory of societal constitutionalism begins to reveal that once this is balanced by taking note of when actors' structural equivalence is mediated by voluntaristic procedures, network analysis may jettison the presupposition of exhausted possibilities. It may thereby inform detailed studies that distinguish sharply between actors' structural equivalence within authoritarian and nonauthoritarian social orders.

26 Jack Gibbs (1981: 129) correctly notes that operationalization rests on findings that are intersubjectively understandable or "concordant" rather than resting on the "reliability of measure." For him, the "criterion of concordance" involves: "The amount of agreement among independent observers in the observations they report about the same events or things, whether those observations pertain to the application of a definition, a formula, or an instrument." This position is consistent with Habermas's consensus theory of truth rather than with any copy theory of truth.

27 One alternative, that of abandoning quantitative indices of egalitarianism as the standard of comparison in favor of one or another substantive standard of the quality of life, is guaranteed today to be even less fruitful. Consider Popenoe's (1988) standard of the quality of child care within the family or, worse, Bloom's (1987) standard of the quality of undergraduate education. Why can't the prospects for social integration within a civil society steadily increase even as children's quality of family life declines and even as the undergraduate curriculum becomes less rigorous? On what basis can it be claimed that the lived experience of children or of undergraduates is a credible standard by which to gauge the direction of social change in comparative perspective?

28 Michael Kennedy (1987), for instance, focuses on the extent to which engineers in Poland had supported the Solidarity movement before the latter came to power. He does not consider whether engineers' nascent collegial formations and those of other professionals in Poland provided Solidarity with the possibility of *institutionalizing* restraints on the government's or the party's actions, once workers invariably demobilize. But Kennedy's work is clearly suggestive in this respect. Openings for social integration may be well be *initiated* by workers' movements within the Eastern bloc that attempt to restrain the governments' and the party's excesses. But these openings can only be *institutionalized,* ironically,

by a formation that is distinctive to middle-class professionals. The collegial form is not likely to remain in place either within labor unions or most manufacturing work sites.

Chapter 9. Procedural institutionalization beyond the Western democracies: three bases of voluntaristic restraint

1 To say nothing of the utopianism that pervades the social sciences. Without saying a word about neo-Marxism, the Frankfurt school, and then Habermas's standard of the ideal speech situation, consider the standard by which Daniel Bell (1976) and Robert Bellah (1975; Bellah et al. 1986) criticize modernity: substantive values. Consider, too, Brennan and Buchanan's (1985) related call for a "civil religion" to normatively frame *Homo economicus.* Consider the standard underlying Frank Parkin's (1979), Randall Collins's (1979), and Raymond Murphy's (1988) critiques of social closure: actors' unmediated access to resources, or else unmediated competition in the marketplace. Consider, finally, the utopianism of any free-market theory, including its various sociological restatements.
2 Scott (1981/1987: 136–7) notes the problems involved in specifying whether any organization is responsive or not.
3 A more recent example is the savings and loan scandal in the United States, the most costly in American history. By all current accounts in the *New York Times,* the leaders (and staffs) of both the relevant congressional committees and executive agencies were quite aware that this scandal was building steadily for well over a decade. With the Bush Administration not wishing to take the blame for Reagan policies of deregulation, and with committee and agency leaders not seeing any reason to initiate the coming public debate, the scandal was literally permitted to build. It is a product of "politics as usual," and not of unusual or exceptional government malfeasance.
4 Such prejudices include: traditionalism; communalism or regionalism; class, ethnic, or gender particularism; or religious fundamentalism. Habermas may legitimately be read taking this position in his debate with Gadamer. Bloom (1987) rails against this position, without clarifying what his alternative is.
5 First National Bank of Boston v. Bellotti, 435 U.S. 765 (1978), rehearing denied 438 U.S. 907 (1978).
6 I am not asserting at the moment that any one of these policies is either reasoned or unreasoned. I am at the moment provoking the reader to attempt to articulate what qualifies any of these policies, or opposition to them, as reasoned.
7 This paragraph rephrases a longstanding concern of constitutional theorists (articulated by Ely 1980, Aleinikoff 1987, and Sunstein 1987). Consider also how this captures what Luhmann is driving at with his term autopoiesis. Officials' actions are essentially self-monitoring and self-regulating, within government agencies' own decision-making processes. Luhmann would be the first to admit, moreover, that the notion of autopoiesis reveals nothing at all about whether the direction of social change is nonauthoritarian or authoritarian.
8 Alexander's (1983b) account of multidimensionality in Parsons's social theory hinges on Alexander's acceptance of Parsons's position regarding the significance of internalized norms. Alexander repeatedly and consistently labels internalized mechanisms of social control "voluntaristic" and "integrative." He never distinguishes the concept of voluntaristic action from normative action in general or from actors' free will in particular (also Alexander 1987). Münch's (1981a, 1982) connecting of Parsons's social theory to Kantian imperatives, and his emphasis on "interpenetration" of roles, results in the same sort of labeling. In these instances, as in Parsons's works originally, the lacuna of integrative possibilities is perpetuated. The presupposition of exhausted possibilities is then removed from possible discussion and questioning.

9 McClosky and Brill (1983: 9–11) point out that the American colonies were riddled by "petty despotisms" and "competing orthodoxies" rather than marked by "tolerance and mutual respect." Prior to 1789, nearly every colony had an established religion, for instance. But consider in comparative perspective the relationship today between first amendment freedoms and the electronic media. The American founders clearly believed in an unbridled press in their day, and they indeed experienced their share of scurrilous political reporting (as did President Lincoln later). But this was reporting by an essentially local press to a readership embedded within a far larger population of illiterates and semiliterates (and religious tolerance remained more a matter of local preference than becoming a matter of principle). This did not change until well into the twentieth century, and in particular until the mass production of the radio dramatically expanded the audience for news and entertainment. In engaging in comparative research today, one wonders whether citizens in any and all modern nation-states without exception can only be "free" if television and radio is as unregulated as it is today within the United States. Many Western democracies subject their electronic media to much more direct governmental regulation, including Great Britain. Would citizens of a modern nation-state really suffer if its electronic media were more controlled even as, say, the quantity and quality of its print media and public library holdings were superior to that in the United States or Great Britain, and, to go one step further, even as many more average citizens actually read the print media and used the libraries on a routine basis than is the case within the United States or Great Britain? Again, an empirical criterion for determining whether actors are integrated or controlled within any modern nation-state is by no means provided by whether its electronic media is relatively unregulated. It is rather whether collegial formations may be found across sectors, industries, and organizations of its civil society. If such formations are found, in practice, then greater national control over electronic media is a matter of secondary importance. By contrast, a nation-state that contains a relatively unregulated electronic media, and that adopts more and more Western institutions and practices even as it continues to lack collegial formations, may well be a contemporary exemplar of successful control under modern conditions (Mexico and Brazil may well qualify here, along with an increasing number of nation-states in the Third World). The exemplar may no longer be a nation-state that strictly controls its electronic media, or that prohibits free elections; these controls are costly and they are no longer necessary in order to manage a population effectively today.

10 Rather than continuing to emphasize the importance of extending actors' "natural rights" in civil society, Selznick (1987) now joins Bellah, Bell, and Brennan and Buchanan in prescribing a civil religion or what he calls a "communitarian morality" (see Etzioni 1989 for a review of this literature).

11 But not as far beyond the common-law tradition. As Haar and Fessler (1986: chap. 2) remind us, the latter indeed addressed instances of purposeful arbitrariness within civil society, particularly when it affected commerce. For example, English courts prohibited common carriers from refusing to accommodate any and all customers by the mid-fourteenth century.

12 Evan misleadingly labels this extension "organizational constitutionalism," Selznick calls it "industrial justice," and Stewart calls it "organizational jurisprudence." Evan is actually interested in extending interest competition, American pluralism, from government to organizations within civil society. A better term for his proposal, and those by Selznick and Stewart as well, is "organizational interest representation" or "organizational pluralism."

13 These questions recapitulate Habermas's longstanding distinction between observers' perspectives of society as systems of behavior and actors' perspectives of society as lifeworlds of action (1981a,b). For him, any social theory that remains tied exclusively to the former perspective, such as Luhmann's systems theory and much of Parsons's functionalism,

cannot possibly be critical or radical. Any critical theory proper ultimately informs actors from their perspectives.

14 Giddens often raises the issue of what happens when actors' routines or daily lives are radically disrupted, say by being interned in a concentration camp (1979: 123–6; 1984: 51–64). I cannot find any instance in which he presents a standard for recognizing in comparative perspective when, apart from such extreme situations, actors' senses of "ontological security" are either increasing or decreasing. Presumably, this is reducible in Giddens's work to actors' subjective opinions, as Buchanan and other liberals would insist.

15 It must be kept in mind that as much as forty percent of Brazil's population currently lives in poverty and is largely divorced from patron-client networks. I cannot find Brazilian specialists who point to internal processes that are likely to lower this percentage. Moreover, Brazilian police even today continue to torture criminal suspects, and otherwise operate outside of internal procedural (and substantive) restraints. It is likely that local and regional *patrons,* and the clients that they protect, are not treated as capriciously by the police.

16 The unraveling of the newly elected Brazilian president's radical economic reform, within only three weeks of Fernando Collor de Mello's first day in office on 15 March 1990, is not surprising (Brooke 1990).

17 Barrington Moore (1966) is less convincing in asserting the opposite proposition than many readers may recall. His thoughts on India in particular reveal his commitment to the presupposition of exhausted possibilities. Liberal democracy is a voluntaristic possibility within the systemic rise of capitalism; neither it nor any other alternative form of government is as systemically overdetermined as is capitalism itself.

18 Consider Hawkins (1984) on vicissitudes of British water pollution enforcement and Braithwaite (1982) on problems of enforcing government regulations and his (1989) proposal that local "shaming" take some precedence over generalizable enforcement. Silberman (1978) discusses the sorry state of formal restraints and protections in American criminal courts. Lowi's (1969) critique of American pluralism revolves around numerous examples of encroachments within distinct policy arenas (whereas Laumann and Knoke 1987 ignore this).

19 It is well to keep in mind that the "bourgeois public" first emerged as discussion groups dedicated to the arts. Only later did these deliberative bodies turn to politics (Habermas 1962). The poets and playwrights involved in Eastern European politics today therefore continue a long tradition (Goldfarb 1989).

20 Studies of the Eastern bloc prior to the fall of 1989 might well reveal unambiguous evidence of collegial formations within certain sectors of selected civil societies. It may also be the case that the leaders of the various reform movements emerged from these very sectors. I have not seen works by Soviet specialists or specialists on Eastern Europe which monitor movements of internal procedural restraints from civil society to government. Yet, Poland, Hungary, and Yugoslavia, and other East European nation-states are likely experiencing such movement (and, of course, reversals and setbacks, too), each in its own way. Burawoy and Lukacs (1985) are suggestive. Yet, they look at machine shops in comparative perspective rather than at sites where either deliberative bodies or professionals may be found, and because of this their work is not directly of use to the theory of societal constitutionalism. Turning to the West, Christopher Stone (1982) considers only the reverse movement of internal procedural restraints, from government to civil society. Then again, he does not consider the possibility of an Eastern country becoming nonauthoritarian even as it fails to institutionalize most liberal-democratic practices. Selznick (1969) sees much more of an interrelationship between developments in civil society and those in the state.

21 In the most methodical interviewing of Soviet émigrés to the West prior to the fall of 1989,

Millar and his associates found that thirty percent favored state ownership of heavy industry, and forty-eight percent favored state-provided medical care (1987: 27–8). Given these views among those that had left the Soviet Union, is it a stretch of the imagination to wonder whether the percentage may well be much higher across the Soviet Union and former Eastern bloc?

22 Here again, as in other respects, the cynicism (or realism) of social influentials outside of the West is, if anything, consistent with current Western social, political, and legal *theories and research*. There are no influential natural-law theories today. The two most prominent legal theories today, other than Fuller's, are those by H.L.A. Hart and Hans Kelsen, and they are remarkably congenial to Charles Anderson's account of how social influentials in Latin America operate as they assess power contenders' claims. No one in the West has proposed any credible or practicable way of revitalizing the division of powers (but see Stewart 1985 for an effort in administrative law). If anything, Western sociologists, political scientists, and even legal scholars would agree much more readily that this is insignificant. The notion of "natural rights" has long been ridiculed in social theory and legal scholarship alike. The controversy surrounding Dworkin's (1977) emphasis on rights is a manifestation of how far the theoretical and research literatures even in legal scholarship have moved away from supporting substantive restraints on purposeful exercises of collective power.

23 Anyone who has ever rejected a friend's manuscript – whether for a refereed session of a professional association's annual meeting or for a grant – and who did so because the paper was not as instructive or compelling as other submissions, has in essence upheld the integrity of a collegial formation rather than subordinated this to a personal network. Not simply scholarly activity but nearly all professional practice in one way or another involves institutionalizing collegial formations so sufficiently that participants' personal networks are kept subordinate to the integrity of deliberation. Indeed, the quality of any academic department may be described and evaluated rather quickly by exploring whether its hiring and promotion practices rest routinely on their senior professors' personal networks or on some set of relatively generalizable standards that typically subordinate the impact of these influences. Unfortunately, a great many academic departments might be more accurately described as patron-client networks than as collegial formations (see note 26). Can it be that the educated public's increasing recognition of this has something to do with the declining prestige and "moral authority" of universities and colleges across the West?

24 This later period also saw the slow, uneven rise of the modern professions, and thereby the rise of new collegial formations in civil society. All five of the accounts noted above ignore this development. They instead look for collegial formations elsewhere in civil society and fail to find them. The professions literature, in turn, revolves around the issue of expert occupations' competition for "jurisdictions" (Abbott 1988) rather than around professions' distinctive form of organization regardless of whatever jurisdiction they happen to carve out.

25 See the discussions of the "constituent force" later in this chapter and in chapter 10 for examples of the sorts of burdens involved, and how constitutional theory once hinged on the expectation that actors are indeed capable of bearing this literally impossible burden immediately.

26 There is an opportunity to apply principles of societal constitutionalism to the United States that might be of particular interest to sociologists (see note 23). Recall that one of the most controversial propositions of pluralist theory was that as long as there are no de jure blockages to any *group's* access to compete for political influence, then one cannot say that any *interest* in society is being discriminated against, distorted, or otherwise ignored. Thus, the blockages of Jim Crow laws in the South were indeed discriminatory because they prevented *interests* from coalescing into *group formations*. But beyond this, pluralists

continue, one would be hard-pressed since the mid-1960s to find comparable blockages today. Instead, the issue at hand becomes whether gays or other sexual minorities are to be classified in the same way as racial or ethnic minorities, or whether affirmative action is reverse discrimination, based on de jure blockages of its own. Pluralists conclude that one of the ways in which Americans' low turnout in both presidential and local elections may be explained, as compared to much higher turnouts in all other liberal- and social-democracies, is that Americans are more pleased with their current political arrangements than are other electorates with theirs. Americans' apathy is a sign of confidence in the system rather than a sign of disaffection or coming delegitimation. Now a comparison to other levels of organization comes into play.

William V. D'Antonio and Steven A. Tuch (1989) have offered essentially the same explanation for low voter turnout in American Sociological Association elections: Members are pleased with the organization and do not bother to vote. The point of societal constitutionalism is that D'Antonio and Tuch might well be right, even as pluralists may well be wrong, or vice versa. This whole controversy may be converted into an empirical issue rather than left to speculation. D'Antonio and Tuch would be confirmed in their view to the extent that researchers demonstrate that more and more collegial formations have been extended not only across the association but also across the academic departments and other work sites of the profession's membership. This may not be the case at all and clearly a methodical case study is in order. Similarly, are researchers likely to find that the integrity of collegial formations has been increasingly secured across sectors of American civil society? If, instead, encroachments have been increasing, then researchers may point with specificity to increasing instances of manipulation and latent coercion within particular sectors, industries, and organizations of American civil society. They may point to such instances even as groups' access to policymakers is not formally blocked and even as open elections continue to be held.

27 This way of putting the issue may be converted into a direct response to Lowi's pathos regarding the drift of American interest-group pluralism: Interest groups in the United States may continue to compete for influence in a more unstructured way than in any other modern nation-state. But at the point that their competition subordinates the significance of either internal or external procedural restraints, Lowi and other researchers may specify when pluralism is becoming increasingly manipulative, controlling, and susceptible to social authoritarianism. Lowi's account is compelling because he indeed demonstrated that this point was already being reached by the mid-1960s. The law journals today team with indictments of "pluralism" for undermining the integrity of the courts, and of legal interpretation generally. This is precisely why the *Yale Law Journal* (1988) devoted a special issue to the civic republican tradition: Legal scholars are searching for a practicable alternative to the drift of what Hurst called pluralism's bastard pragmatism. Too often, however, they merely end up calling for expanding the scope of the economic marketplace instead of pluralism's political marketplace (see Stewart 1985, but the University of Chicago's law and economics movement generally).

28 In the United States today, twenty percent of all children are raised in poverty; among Hispanic and black children, the figure is forty percent. The life expectancy of black males in America's inner cities is actually lower than that of males in Bangladesh. A quarter of the American population lives in substandard housing (to say nothing of the homeless), and each year a quarter of all eighteen-year-olds fail to graduate from high school. Medical care, certainty of employment, unemployment insurance, and social security benefits are among the most uneven in the advanced world. The infant mortality rate and rate of illiteracy in the United States are both higher than in some Third World countries. See Gans (1988) for an account of the way of life and outlook for lower middle income groups in the United States, a group insulated somewhat from the poor. Their disillusionment and

disaffection with institutions is pervasive, and yet in survey research these actors express general satisfaction with their personal lives. Is this only because alternatives have not been available in practice?

29 Nietzsche's and Freud's critiques of religion were not phrased much differently, even as the latter were directed to religion's impact on individuals rather than to its impact on forms of organization.

30 This is exactly what Evan (1976) and Selznick (1969) propose, respectively, as "organizational constitutionalism" and "industrial justice." Neither defines "rule of law" in terms of the threshold of interpretability (see pages 189–91 above). Each instead defines it in terms of the extent to which organized interests are represented and "balanced" in legal proceedings (also see Dobbin et al. 1988). Evan does this explicitly and consistently. Selznick cites Fuller in his opening chapter and thereby alludes to a more critical definition of "rule of law." But thereafter his examples of "industrial justice" as well as his own conceptual apparatus recapitulate the reductionism just noted. Aleinikoff (1987) explores how "balancing" undermines the courts' integrity. Louis Siedman (1987) wonders whether "principle" might again be used to "maintain" some "boundary" against the floodgate of interested parties seeking recognition by the courts. Finally, Michelman's (1988) and Sunstein's (1988) opening contributions to the *Yale Law Journal*'s Symposium on the Civic Republican Tradition revolves around critiques of pluralism, and the need, however vaguely presented, to return to the integrity of deliberation.

31 See chapter 6, notes 23,26 and chapter 11, notes 6,20. Also see Brennan and Buchanan (1985) for an explicit statement of the social contract theorist's reification of actors' subjective interests at the expense not only of objective interests but also of any and all possible intersubjective interests. Richard Stewart (1983) tries to get at the notion of intersubjective interests with his term "noncommodity values," as does Philip Selznick (1987) with his "idea of a communitarian morality." In each instance, however, they fail to distinguish voluntaristic qualities that are procedural from those that are substantive. This moves them too far in the direction of objective interests, and traditional notions of natural law (Selznick 1961). Hechter (1987: 125–45) illustrates the inability of rational-choice theory to distinguish intersubjective interests from strictly subjective ones. As he explores the "limits of compensation in capitalist firms," he notes corporate managers' difficulties in monitoring how much effort each worker contributes to production. Whether corporate managers employ outside contractors or dedicate their own personnel to monitor work sites, this raises a "second-order monitoring problem" (1987: 131–3). How can corporate managers know that enforcers are being vigilant? What Hechter cannot address with the concepts of rational-choice theory is whether *the rules* being enforced are themselves warranted, such that enforcers' (and workers') subjective senses of their legitimacy *might* be established and maintained over time *even in the absence of effective monitoring in his sense*. Instead, Hechter talks vaguely of "trust" within "obligatory groups" as opposed to sanctions within compensatory groups (1987: 140). He acknowledges, however, that his conceptual framework leads him to hinge the survival of obligatory groups not on whether trust is established *within* the group but rather on whether its members lack any viable option *of leaving* the group. His discussion of "internal labor markets" within corporations revolves around the issue of restriction alone (1987: 141–3).

32 Wolin (1960) remains a major study of changing senses of time and space in classical political theory, from Aristotle to Weber.

33 It is well to keep in mind that public-choice theory in political science and economics emerged in the 1950s, in the works of Downs, Buchanan and Tullock, Niskanen, and others, with the proposition that elected and appointed officials are literal political entrepreneurs. They can be expected to act in their own interests exclusively, unless restrained

institutionally from doing so. For instance, William Niskanen proposed in 1971 that bureaucrats will seek to maximize the size of their bureau's budget, unless otherwise restrained (Buchanan 1989: 14–16). Buchanan is quite blunt about the point of departure of public-choice theory (1989: 12): "[T]he assumption that political agents will use any discretionary power that they possess to further their particular private interests can, we believe, be justified even where there seems to be ample empirical evidence to the contrary, on grounds essentially analogous to those for using *Homo economicus* in the monopoly context." Given this point of departure, when it comes to institutional design (1989: 34): "The objective should be that of designing institutions such that, if participants do seek economic interest above all else, the damages to the social fabric are minimized."

34 It is neither unwise nor rhetorical to recall that Hitler was fairly elected, and that a fairly elected (albeit intimidated) parliament retroactively absolved him of fault in the Röhm purge (to say nothing of later events). This retroactive decision clearly encroached against the integrity of threshold restraints, and it just as clearly undermined the integrity of parliament's own collegial form. Yet, all of this remained quite consistent with maintaining the integrity (openness and fairness) of elections. If the Nazis had wished to continue (or even to extend) elections, this consistency would have been demonstrated, in practice (Juan Perón provided some evidence of this later). It is indeed a truism that the plebiscite is the tool of the clever dictator.

35 This notion of "wasted time" is closer to Arendt's distinction between private property as place for citizenship and private property as alienable capital (1951, 1958) than to Luhmann's discussion of why, "in order to be autonomous, a system must first of all 'have time' " (1982: 143). Luhmann explores how distinct subsystems (such as politics, law, and education) become differentiated as the ongoing drift of social change unfolds, whereas Arendt addresses the importance of mediating this drift itself.

36 Laumann and Knoke (1987: 377) demonstrate that something of an informal neocorporatism is emerging within the United States, which they call "elite interest group pluralism."

Chapter 10. External restraints: prospects for reason and "tradition"

1 This opening section explores implications of the discussion of Habermas's social theory in chapter 5, particularly on pages 96–9. For his part, Luhmann relativizes the concept of rational action, with the result that it, too, cannot claim grounding in comparative research: "The sort of rationality I have in mind no longer allows itself to be fastened rigidly to any fixed point nor to be directed toward preset goals. To reduce it to a formula, [system] rationality must now be able to combine a high degree of randomness with a high degree of specification" (1982: 268).

2 Parsons' AGIL schema, which is tied to the notion of functional differentiation, also provides a basis for understanding the direction of social change. This is the case, however, within the context of six reformulations of Parsons's concepts (Sciulli in preparation, a).

3 Today in the United States, David Duke, a former Grand Dragon of the Ku Klux Klan, has essentially updated this local slogan in winning election to Louisiana's state legislature, promoting his National Association for the Advancement of White People (to each his own), and now running for the United State Senate seat currently held by Bennett Johnston. Leo Strauss (1953) demonstrated impressively how Weber's ideal types and perspectivism lead to nihilism, even as Strauss's natural law alternative is not defensible. The most compelling part of Bloom's (1987) otherwise surprisingly sketchy diatribe against contemporary "American nihilism" is how the various faculties responded to the demands of armed students at Cornell. Is it incorrect to say that this response was merely one manifestation of the Cornell faculty's functional differentiation, fragmentation of meaning, and willingness to negotiate even the integrity of the university's collegial formations? Does the Cornell

faculty (or any other) uphold the latter in the face of *any* interested party's concerted demands – whether those of trustees, alumni, administrators, or mobilized students?

4 Moving beyond the focus of this volume, at the moment that Parsons's framework of analytical concepts is thrown open conceptually to the *possibility* of accommodating a concept of reasoned social action *of any kind*, his "functionalism" literally metamorphoses into a critical social theory. It metamorphoses into a social theory that is as *intrinsically* critical as any variant of neo-Marxism. Yet, this new critical theory is ironically far more amenable to informing detailed empirical research than any variant of neo-Marxism (Sciulli in preparation, a). Luhmann sees that Parsons's social theory is available for such a move because of its claim to translate all other theories: "Commensurability, incidentally, is equivalent to the translatability of a theory language. Whoever pursues this translatability in Parsons' sense, must eventually renounce the knowledge of contingent truths [in favor of necessary truths] and must also abjure a theory of evolution" (1982: 395, note 6). Luhmann warns against any move to convert Parsons's social theory into a critical theory, based on any grounding. He advocates instead that systems theories be developed that distance themselves from all previous social theories, including Parsons's: "Renouncing [Parsons's] generalizing techniques, however, means giving up the automatic translatability of all other theory languages into one's own. This renunciation, in fact, can be justified by the distinction between ordinary language and the various media of communication. Translatability is a structural requirement of language but not a requirement of the communication medium 'truth' " (1982: 395, note 5).

5 Postwar writers who have come closest to seeing this are a diverse lot, including: Arendt 1951, 1963; Loewenstein 1957; Habermas 1962; Friedrich 1963; Vile 1967; Fuller 1964/ 1969; Lowi 1969; Selznick 1969; Parsons and Platt 1973; Bell 1976; Evan 1976; Sennett 1978; Hayek 1973–9; Gouldner 1979; Ackerman 1980; Apel 1980; MacIntrye 1981; Schluchter 1981; Unger 1986; Hall 1987; *Yale Law Journal* 1988; Braithwaite 1989; and Waters 1989.

6 See Klockars (1985: chapter 5) for a review of the question of police discretion. See Muir (1977) for an influential statement on which Klockars draws.

7 Gadamer (1960, 1966, 1967) sees this, and then, like Parsons, interprets "prejudice" as the benign, unavoidable prejudging in which actors engage within any particular lived social fabric.

8 Bendix (1960), for instance, does not include the term in his index, nor does Parsons (1937). Schluchter (1981: 108) insists that "substantive rationalization" is a "counter principle" to that of legality; the former involves "the intrusion of ethical imperatives, utilitarian pragmatism or political maxims" into the autonomy of law and administration, resulting in a lack of calculability. It is, therefore a "regression." Levine (1981: 12–13) is similar, adding that substantive rationality "reflects the desire to achieve motivational integrity," whereas formal rationality refers to action "within a calculable order." Sica (1988: 209–10) is more blunt, noting that when Weber relates substantive rationality to irrationality he is more interesting than when he treats them as conceptual opposites. But examples of substantive *rationality* are scarce everywhere.

9 The critical theorists of the Frankfurt school attempted this as well, from the 1950s to the early 1970s. Parsons's writings offer no evidence that he ever understood how dramatically Habermas's early works in general, and his critique of neopositivism in particular, were simultaneously "turning" critical theory away from this effort. Habermas clearly devoted much more time to studying Parsons's writings than Parsons ever devoted to his (Habermas 1967b: 74–88; 1980; 1984). Still, Habermas fails to appreciate how far Parsons's framework of analytical concepts advances beyond Weber's ideal types and normative relativism, irrespective of Parsons's decision to close his social theory to the concept of reasoned social action. Habermas takes no notice at all of Parsons's residual category of

collegial formations, for instance, nor does he note Parsons's increasing (albeit vague) references to procedural institutions. Habermas (and others, including Max Horkheimer) engaged Parsons in colloquy in 1964 on the occasion of the Fifteenth German Sociological Congress in Heidelberg in commemoration of the centenary of Weber's birth (Stammer 1965/1972). But Parsons's thinking about procedural institutions and law was relatively undeveloped in 1964 and, regardless, he was called on to respond directly to Weber's methodological positions regarding value-relevance and value-neutrality.

10 Indeed, such a shift is what institutionalized external procedural restraints restrain. Within an institutionalized environment containing these restraints, policing may simultaneously become more accountable. It need not remain localized and thereby susceptible to personal favoritism, prejudice, and other manifestations of arbitrariness.

11 Donald Black (1984) stresses implications of heterogeneity, functional differentiation, and diverse styles of life in his study of mechanisms of social control (but see note 15).

12 This is the logical fallacy of any sociology of knowledge. Since Mannheim (1929) this has been the approach to the competition of ideas, social arrangements, and institutions preferred by social scientists who accede most immediately, most unreflectively, to normative relativism. The fallacy is that *any* new idea, social arrangement, or institution likely originated in one particular place, or at best one particular region. This is as true of ideas, arrangements, or institutions that are indeed intrinsically particular as those that turn out credibly to claim consistency with a generalizable standard of reason. Thus, to trace any idea, arrangement, or institution to its site of historical origin is a worthy project in and of itself. But this does not establish a priori that the former is intrinsically particular rather than possibly consistent with a generalizable standard of reason. For instance, Fuller's legal theory is readily traceable to the historical experiences of Anglo-American countries. This in and of itself does not somehow establish that his concepts are intrinsically particular rather than possibly contribute to reasoned social action.

13 There is no good reason for the world's peoples to learn English as a preferred second language, as opposed to French, Spanish, German, or for that matter, Japanese or Russian, other than as a strategic response to America's postwar geopolitical hegemony and, until recently, dominant position in the world economy. There is nothing intrinsically generalizable about English or about any other language.

14 Sets of substantive aspects of "tradition" readily transferred to new sites short of being imposed on outsiders include cuisine, popular music, and popular culture generally. *How* they are recognized and understood by "outsiders" is another matter entirely, of course. Are American movies ever recognized and understood similarly by Hindus and Sikhs in Punjab?

15 Luhmann draws the distinction between "genetic and functional methods of inquiry," pointing out that "the original genesis of institutions demands special structural preconditions" but then, later, the "maintenance of an autonomous legal system, for example, does not require the continued existence of its initial preconditions" (1982: 126–7). What Luhmann sees as generalizable across autonomous legal systems is the dynamic interrelationship between what he calls the "dual sovereignty" of (a) the contingency of whether the law is invoked or not in particular social situations and (b) the contingency of which premises are drawn upon in coming to legal decisions. For him, as more and more social situations are "juridified" or defined as legal situations, and as legal decision-making adapts legal premises over time in an effort to accommodate social complexity, the legal system becomes more and more detached from any and all "external" normative justifications. Luhmann's view of law is, thus, far less rigidly "positivist" than Habermas (chapter 5) would lead one to believe. Yet, it lacks any threshold of legality other than the dedifferentiation of the legal system into other systems, whether religious, political, or some other.

16 The "impact" of successful efforts to block the transfer of voluntaristic and procedural aspects of national traditions also is invariant and equally generalizable: unmediated social control and susceptibility to social authoritarianism.

17 Nor, of course, can they treat all analytical aspects of all traditions as if they were ultimately or even primarily based on actors' shared material interests or their positions of "structural equivalence" within a social structure. The literature on structural equivalence spawned by Lorrain and White (1971), along with the literature on network analysis more generally (see Burt 1980 and Berkowitz 1982 for reviews), is impressive precisely because contributors to these literatures attempt to explain actors' solidarity and collective action *by resisting as long as possible* an appeal to their supposed internalization of shared substantive norms. This is also the strength of exchange theory and rational-choice theory. Yet, the notion of structural equivalence seems to offer a potentially richer account of solidarity and *collective* action than does exchange theory's and rational-choice theory's hypostatization of actors' individual calculations of immediate strategic interests. The single greatest defect of the Parsonian tradition is that Parsonians continue to appeal much too readily to actors' supposed internalization of shared substantive norms, rather than resisting such appeals as long as possible in an effort to exhaust *all other* explanations for actors' solidarity and collective action. At the same time, this point may be reversed to indicate the greatest strength of the Parsonian tradition: To the extent that theorists (and researchers) indeed resist appealing immediately to internalization, and instead endeavor to exhaust all other explanations for *heterogeneous* actors' and *competing* groups' solidarity and collective action, the Parsonian tradition remains the richest reservoir of analytical distinctions available to sociologists for accounting for the great diversity of solidary units to be found within modern nation-states.

18 It is difficult to read Rousseau's *Social Contract* (1762), for instance, as contributing to discussions of strategic let alone resilient normative restraints on arbitrary exercises of collective power. Montesquieu and then Tocqueville were in many respects the first theorists to introduce such ideas in France in a methodical way. Sieyes and others raised such issues at times, of course, both during and after the revolution. But a debate among influentials in France along these particular lines cannot be found that compares to that which occurred first in England and then in the American colonies. See Arendt (1963) and Habermas (1963a,b,c) for reflections, respectively, on the authoritarian and radical implications of theoretical discourse in eighteenth-century France, and Masters (1970) for an influential treatment of Rousseau in English.

19 Consider the American framers. Their mandate in going to Philadelphia was at best to amend the Articles of Confederation. When Madison presented the Virginia Plan, and it became the focus of discussion, this exemplified the unlimited power of the constituent group. Consider, too, that only fifty-five people attended these meetings, and only forty really participated. Moreover, their proceedings were held entirely in private, the public being barred from observing and the participants being prohibited from discussing the proceedings outside Constitution Hall. The Federalist Papers, published in the New York press, were among the first efforts to inform the public of what the constituent group had accomplished (for an excellent discussion of the framing, see Diamond, Fisk, and Garfinkel 1966: chapter 2).

20 Luhmann correctly emphasizes that this overloads the personality system (1990: 204): "[N]ot until . . . the last third of [the eighteenth] century did the modern concept of public opinion arise as the 'secret' sovereign and as the invisible authority of political society. Public opinion was stylized as a paradox, as the invisible power of the visible. And in this semantic form it became the culminating idea of the political system. For the first time the result of communication itself was taken as substantive, and thereby became the medium of further communication. This . . . was purchased at the cost of a severe overloading of

the concept which was accompanied with an equally strong idealized concept of the individual. For those who advocated this new idea, public opinion itself now assumed the task of censorship and exercised it objectively and impartially. While more conservative authors looked upon this impartiality with skepticism because it appeared to them one-sidedly directed towards critique and change."

21 Indeed, consider what happened after the American Revolution (Diamond, Fisk, and Garfinkel 1966: 16). It is estimated that over 60,000 Loyalists, and possibly as many as 100,000, fled to Canada or England – out of a total nonslave population in the American republic of only three million! Nearly as much property was confiscated in the new American republic as in the later French Revolution, and, actually, a proportionally greater number of people fled the American republic than fled the Jacobin repression. Of course, far fewer were executed outright in the American republic.

22 It is well to keep in mind that these early theorists could still assume the resilience of external *substantive* restraints of tradition and religious fundamentalism. Part of the reason that they failed to anticipate the mass-based authoritarian regimes and occasional totalitarian regimes of the twentieth century is that they never anticipated even the most zealous absolute monarch going that far. They never anticipated that a monarch would flagrantly violate norms that proscribe mass dislocations and exterminations of one's own citizens.

23 Laumann and Knoke find that policy domains within the United States are "substantially balkanized" rather than centralized (1987: 376–7), and yet: "[M]utual recognition creates and sustains the legitimacy of core actors' involvement in domain issues and events. . . . [T]hese results are comparable to those reported by studies of communication density within far more homogeneous or functionally interdependent sets of organizations than the group interviewed for this project" (1987: 375). The question that the theory of societal constitutionalism brings to this finding is whether these activists' mutual recognition and seeming consensus is procedurally mediated or really substantively immediate. Is elite consensus within the United States really the product of some substantive alternative to Brazilian elites' patron-client networks – as traditional Parsonian analysis would lead one to believe? Or is it instead a product of, and ultimately reliant on, the mediation provided by procedural voluntaristic norms and institutions? These are empirical issues that fall outside the pluralist-elitist and pluralist-neocorporatist debates.

24 Unlike the case with "elite pacts" within those nation-states of the Third World that are attempting the transition from military rule to civilian rule and "liberalization," e.g. O'Donnell, Schmitter, and Whitehead (1986).

Chapter 11. Collegial formations as external procedural restraints: prospects for a public realm

1 Their effect on labor markets is more complicated and cannot be explored in this volume.

2 It should be pointed out that Olson himself used this term once, in quotation marks (1965: 76).

3 Similarly, even if one accepts the logic of much of the Marxian argument regarding the alienation of labor, one cannot conclude that the issue of arbitrary power has been raised or addressed (Sciulli 1984).

4 Works by Pamela Oliver and Gerald Marwell on the "critical mass" lay a foundation on which this argument may be based, e.g. Oliver, Marwell, and Teixeira (1985); Oliver and Marwell (1988); Marwell, Oliver, and Prahl (1988).

5 "A sense of obligation will arise when a stabilization of interactional expectancies has occurred" (Fuller 1969b: 219–20).

6 Hechter (1987: chapter 7) can only account for actors' behavior within such a division when they are "captured," when they cannot leave the division for employment elsewhere

(see chapter 9, note 31). The problem Hechter faces is that millions of professionals and deliberators within scores of modern nation-states are by no means immobilized in this way, even as a great many may be.

7 Recent strikes by health-care professionals in major cities such as San Francisco and New York, for instance, have this flavor to them, and this example is used elsewhere in this chapter (see pages 250–1, 255). Overloaded with clients in emergency wards and strapped for resources and personnel, those who are most professionally committed to providing quality health care are often the leaders of these strikes. One suggestion beyond the scope of this volume, however, is that the success of such strikes likely hinges on the extent to which the integrity of collegial formations in other fields is being maintained locally, regionally, and nationally. To the same extent that professionals in other fields already have learned through experience that they cannot maintain these formations' integrity in the face of social and governmental units' instrumental responses to systemic pressures of drift, health-care professionals' strikes are not likely to "influence" either policymakers or "the public" greatly.

8 This is Luhmann's strongest counterargument to Habermas's communication theory. At the same time, Luhmann fails to address a significant problem. Weber's work demonstrated that if external normative restraints of *some* kind are not resiliently maintained, then there is no good reason to believe that these units can sustain the integrity even of *internal* procedural restraints on purposefully arbitrary exercises of collective power, including those by arbitrary government. Luhmann's systems theory dismisses this whole matter.

9 Baylis (1980) and Waters (1989) see consensus as basic to collegiality. They do so because they assume the latter rests on substantive norms rather than on a procedural threshold. As a result, they also assume that members of collegial formations are homogeneous and consensual rather than increasingly heterogeneous and competitive. Even in passing, Laumann and Knoke (1987: 160–1) operate on the same two assumptions.

10 The same may be said of other forms of organization, of course: As long as conflicts or disruptions do not threaten the integrity of the bureaucratic, democratic, or patron-client forms, interested parties may be said, respectively, to be competing bureaucratically, democratically, or clientelistically. The point being made in the text about actors' competing collegially, however, is that their continued fidelity to the collegial form's procedural voluntaristic orientation distinguishes this competition from that taking place within and around any other formation. Brennan and Buchanan (1985: 98) offer an expression of faith, nothing more, in *Homo economicus*'s consensus over "meta-rules." Laumann and Knoke (1987: 185) argue that elite decision-makers in energy and health policy domains in the United States operate on a "consensus" only in regard to "a common perception of the key players and nonplayers [in their domain] – not consensus about particular policy options." They hastily add, however, that these elites are caught by surprise whenever the issues in their domain are posed in any way other than strategically or instrumentally (1987: 383–6). This is precisely what happens, of course, whenever the rules of the game are brought into question.

11 This brings into view one of the arguments in favor of recruiting individuals into collegial formations from as many classes as possible and from as many subcultural groupings and lived social fabrics as possible: The integrity of the collegial formation must never be confused, in practice, with middle-class sensibilities, nor with the substantive sensibilities of any other class or group. This is not an argument consistent with affirmative action as it is currently designed in the United States. Instead, it is an argument in favor of keeping the integrity of the procedural threshold of interpretability superordinate to any and all substantive standards of performance. In this way, Bloom's (1987) polemic against gender and racial groups may be demonstrated to miss the mark. He launches his polemic against the backdrop of a *substantive* normative ideal that is unrealizable today, and he fails to explore

either the importance of, or the limits to, the university's collegial form. The central problem with affirmative action is not its intent but rather that it codifies a competition between groups (increasingly between African- and Asian-Americans) that is defined not merely substantively but ascriptively, and crudely so at that. A multicultural society intent on integration tends toward intermarriage, but affirmative action raises greatly the symbolic and material obstacles to such choices. A greater irony is that much more could be accomplished to assist the lower and working classes, and accomplished much more quickly, if the integrity of procedural norms were kept superordinate to the middle class's substantive sensibilities. In this way many more of the obstacles to mobility facing members of lower and working classes as well as members of ascriptive groups could be removed.

12 Laumann and Knoke (1987: 348–72) point out that the health-policy domain in the United States differs from the energy-policy domain in that the former revolves around "resource deployment" or a "resource dependence" system whereas energy revolves around a "resource mobilization" system. Their point is that subordinates or consumers in the health-policy domain have greater influence with superordinates or producers in determining policy outcomes. This point may be rephrased in the following way in terms of the theory of societal constitutionalism: What is meant by an adequate or acceptable level of health care for the money spent is less subject to strict quantification than what is meant by an adequate or acceptable level of energy supplied for the money spent. Since adequacy or acceptability is subject to greater symbolization in the health-policy domain, subordinates or consumers invariably have greater influence. Rather than simply mobilizing resources as they compete within economic and political marketplaces, elites in the health-policy domain also must consult with their "dependents" regarding issues of "deployment."

13 One value-commitment that Parsons saw researchers bearing within universities, research centers, and elsewhere is to maximize what he called "cognitive rationality" (Parsons and Platt 1973).

14 See Braithwaite (1982) on "enforced self-regulation;" Stewart (1983) on "noncommodity values" in regulatory law; Sciulli (in preparation, b) on implications for societal constitutionalism.

15 The next three paragraphs address not only Parsons's treatment of the professions but also the related treatments by the other three theorists just noted.

16 Collins (1979) does the same, of course, explicitly treating professions as nothing more than "consciousness communities," equivalent in every respect to ethnic groups.

17 Niklas Luhmann (1988) is very similar, stressing the importance of the relationship between differentiation and "autopoiesis." Social systems' self-regulation as distinct social units replaces all references (a) to collegial formations, (b) to voluntaristic action more generally, and (c) to normative restraints on the drift of rationalization. In many respects, then, Luhmann reifies autopoiesis in precisely the way that Stinchcombe (1986) reifies "reason:" Both are strictly systemic qualities quite independent not only of actors' motivations but also of organizations' orientations.

18 Also consider Habermas's critique of Nietzsche for failing to address adequately actors' cognitive interests (1968a: chapter 12). Despite numerous suggestions to the contrary, Nietzsche ultimately reduces reason to a mere perspective backed up by power. This is very evident, for instance, in the closing pages of *The Genealogy of Morals* (1887).

19 Laumann and Knoke (1987: 347, note 2) and other network analysts continue to employ this reductionist concept as their very definition of power, as does Abbott (1988) in his pathbreaking study of professions. This ensures that they cannot distinguish actors' demonstrable social control from their possible social integration, irrespective of what the evidence happens to be.

20 Recall that Coleman (1988) referred to social capital in reference to whether *children* can

walk the streets safely (see chapter 9, page 209; chapter 6, notes 23, 26). By contrast, the social capital being discussed in the text rests on the relationship between the threshold of interpretability and whether *adults* are treated as reasoning and responsible actors. Whenever power holders prepare (or later present) rationales for their actions and proposals that move at all beyond their strictly instrumental and strategic rationality, they are implicitly treating the actors that they are addressing in this way. This treatment is social capital or a public good, in and of itself.

21 Lauman and Knoke find (1987: 381) that "the boundaries between public and private sectors are blurred, and irrelevant, even in noncorporatist societies" like the United States. Because the public/private distinction is blurred in every modern nation-state, however, it can no longer inform detailed comparative study. What needs to be addressed instead is whether and where voluntaristic procedural orientations persist, and whether and where they collapse.

22 Przeworski (1986: 57–8) wrongly emphasizes the importance of the uncertainty of electoral outcomes and of other governmental actions as the key factor in the transition to "democracy." It was explained in the opening chapter why this obscures more than it reveals about whether actors are controlled or possibly integrated. As examples, as the results of elections and the actions of government in Mexico, or in Chicago, become more uncertain, will this tell social scientists anything at all about whether politics has become more democratic? Moreover, will this tell them anything about whether heterogeneous actors' and competing groups' possibilities for integration are increasing or decreasing within either social order? Przeworski himself acknowledges that it does not, concluding his essay by noting: "Yet what we need, and do not have, is a more comprehensive, integral, ideological project of antiauthoritarianism that would encompass the totality of social life" (1986: 63). The theory of societal constitutionalism is designed to contribute to such a project, provided that the word "ideological" is dropped from Przeworski's call.

23 Thus, the theory of societal constitutionalism can at a certain point charge laissez-faire liberals within complicity in authoritarian drift, much as Arendt accused them of this in 1951. Hayek is a more sophisticated liberal than Milton Friedman, for instance, because he sees that the "rule of law" is both superordinate to the liberal market and something of a restraint on it. Moreover, the theory of societal constitutionalism can radically question actors' subjective impressions of their own interactions whereas researchers employing concepts of symbolic interactionism or structuration theory must ultimately treat these impressions as a fixed datum.

24 Formal lawsuits or other formal judicial proceedings are excluded from consideration in this discussion. If the integrity of sectoral and divisional collegial formations is being encroached against, and in particular within a civil-law country, there is no reason to believe that the courts can maintain their integrity. Not only Nazi Germany and Fascist Italy but also military and civilian dictatorships of Latin America and the former Eastern bloc have amply demonstrated this.

25 This approach to the social infrastructure of nonauthoritarian social order is consistent with how "public opinion" is characterized by social scientists who study it methodically, rather than with how it is hypostatized by those who think a constituent force protects Western democracies from malevolent drift. In political science, since V.O. Key (1942, 1961), public opinion has been seen by specialists as mediated by and through "issue publics" or what sociologists call significant others or opinion leaders. In sociology, Turner and Killian (1957: chapters 9–11) point out that "keynoters" even mediate crowd behavior, and they review the various filters through which public opinion is expressed.

26 Newspapers and electronic news media which remain "free" but operate within nation-states that lack a network of collegial formations (e.g. Mexico) do indeed become altogether latent in their social energy. They become strictly informational, like service

libraries or entertainment centers. See Joshua Meyrowitz (1986) for an illuminating discussion of the respects in which electronic media differ from print media in their social impact. See Anthony Leeds (1964) for a now classic discussion of how "information" within Brazilian newspapers and media supports the entire system of stratification even as it simultaneously publicizes some "circulation of elites," or advances by talented children of the working classes into the elite.

27 Parsons's later references to professions, universities, and intellectual networks may be read as a weak substitute for a public realm proper – one posed within a conceptual framework already closed to the concept of reasoned social action (Parsons 1969a; Parsons and Platt 1973). It is also useful to compare the practicability of instituting a public realm in civil society with the utopianism of Collins's call (1979) to abolish credentials.

28 The theory of societal constitutionalism directs social scientists to explore, for instance, whether such *behavior* by middle-class professionals within private enterprises is a more serious challenge to a nonauthoritarian direction of social change than the working class's *subjective attitudes,* whatever they might be, toward ethnic or religious minorities (see Lipset 1960; Lipset and Raab 1970 on the latter).

29 The strongest point in Bloom's (1987) assessment of university education is by no means his characterization of undergraduate students but instead his characterization of his former colleagues at Cornell. Again, he assesses a faculty in terms of an ultimately un-articulated substantive ideal of the university's mission and of the undergraduate curriculum. With this, he is as intrigued by the situation on the Continent as he is depressed by that in the United States. By contrast, the theory of societal constitutionalism assesses a faculty (or any other body of professionals or deliberators) in terms of the presence or absence of collegial formations, irrespective of whether the individuals involved agree in substance regarding the university's mission or the undergraduate curriculum. With this in mind, let us assume that faculties on the Continent indeed uphold an undergraduate curriculum and express a sense of the university's mission that come closer to Bloom's substantive ideal. What needs to be addressed by Bloom and others, however, is whether collegial formations are really to be found anywhere within French, German, or Italian universities, either historically or today. Or, alternatively, are patron-client networks or hierarchical decrees more likely to characterize their hiring, promotion, and reviewing decisions? Is Bloom prepared to defend this *because* it results in outcomes that come closer to his unarticulated substantive ideal? If so, then Bloom's position regarding the university is not noticeably different, in principle, from Catherine MacKinnon's position regarding rape: Both positions hypostatize some particular group's unmediated subjective judgments of what the university or rape is, at the expense of the threshold of interpretability.

30 See Merton (1938b, 1942) and Hall (1987) for very different accounts of how science supports a democratic society. See Brennan and Buchanan (1985) for a very different account of how the hypostatization of science *threatens* a democratic society. See note 31 on Merton and note 34 on Brennan and Buchanan.

31 Merton (1938b, 1942) argued some time ago that there is a relationship between "democ-racy" and the integrity of scientific research. His way of putting the issue then, as well as later in his career, suffers from three limitations: First, his view of democracy fails to escape the presupposition of exhausted possibilities. Second, and relatedly, his view of democracy is also relativist or quite American-centered in value-commitment rather than generalizable (and then either favorable to American institutions or not). Third, Merton fails to distin-guish encroachments against science from those against "all other institutions" of moral authority (1938b: 258), including religious institutions. His criticisms of Nazism in 1938, for instance, were for this reason and others surprisingly weak: "It would be misleading to suggest that the Nazi government has completely repudiated science and intellect. The official attitudes toward science are clearly ambivalent and unstable. (For this reason, any

statements concerning science in Nazi Germany are made under correction.)" His often-cited four "institutional imperatives [which] comprise the ethos of modern science" (1942: 607–15) – universalism, "communism" of substantive findings, disinterestedness, and organized skepticism – begin to distinguish science from other institutions of moral authority. But they still lack clear thresholds that could enable researchers (or observers) to specify when the integrity of scientific enterprises in particular is being encroached against. Thus, Merton's weak statements regarding science within Nazi Germany.

32 Donald Black's (1984) approach to social control is an exemplar not only of the relativism of contemporary social science but of its increasing nihilism. He proposes to "predict and explain" why different mechanisms of social control appear "in different quantities" within different social settings *regardless of their purpose or consequences*. This is merely relativistic as long as he restricts himself to ignoring their consequences for particular individuals or substantive interests. It becomes nihilistic, however, once he ignores the consequences for organizational forms, and thereby for both internal and external procedural restraints. Black is indeed indifferent to these empirical issues (1984: 6). His thesis is that increased variation in the mechanisms of social control within a society "is a direct function [in the mathematical sense of this term] of social diversity" (1984: 17), and that social diversity also increases variations in judges' rulings (1984: 18). Since it has "become increasingly difficult to predict the disposition of cases with the written law alone," Black concludes (1984: 18–19): "[T]he rules have been losing their importance. The widely held view that law is essentially an affect of rules [and Black cites Hart 1961 and Fuller 1964/1969] may thus be an historically grounded notion that is becoming obsolete." The rules lose their importance, however, only within the purview of Black's positivist social science. The latter revolves around characterizing students of society as monads dedicated to copying objective states of affairs. But this does not mean that the rules are losing importance for citizens who happen to be living within any particular modern nation-state, or for social scientists who happen to be working within any particular form of organization. Black's positivist social science cannot address the distinction between authoritarian and non-authoritarian directions of social change, nor the distinction between social scientists' possible social integration and demonstrable social control. Yet, he has not somehow demonstrated scientifically that these distinctions are merely subjective, or beyond conceptual grounding and empirical operationalization. Black's proposed "general theory of social control" thereby ignores the institutional and organizational preconditions which account for the possibility of Black's own research being undertaken within and around collegial formations. Jack Gibbs (1981: 75) is troubled by the relativism and nihilism of the scientific study of social control. But he, too, does not know what to do about it. He points out, for instance, that a Gestapo agent and a British bobby "cannot be treated as equivalent." But he fails to provide a single conceptual distinction in terms of which they might be treated differently. He instead concedes that this distinction, as well as any defense of due process, for instance, is strictly a value judgment.

33 Ironically, Habermas's consensus theory as well as liberal social contract theories, including Brennan and Buchanan's constitutional economics, share this weakness with positivists' accounts of science. They, too, fail to discuss forms of organization standing between consensual individuals and the legitimate state. Recall, too, that the civil-law tradition is oriented to the certainty of enforcement, and framed by bureaucratic formations of law-making and law enforcement. The common-law tradition is oriented by the interpretability of the rules, and framed by collegial formations that, for instance, permit lower courts to call into question the decisions of national lawmaking bodies and the actions of law enforcement agencies (Merryman 1969/1985).

34 Brennan and Buchanan (1985: 37–45) are opposed to defining democracy by analogy to science and the pursuit of truth rather than by analogy to an economic marketplace and

the sovereignty of actors' subjective interests. They are opposed to this precisely because the former subordinates majority rule to some standard or principle of truth, and thereby challenges their "contractarian vision." But what they fail to appreciate, even though Buchanan is a Hobbesian rather than a Lockean, is that this elevates actors' subjective interests, and the concomitant drift of interest competition within economic and political marketplaces, *to the only standard of reason in individuals' relationship to the state (or to any other powerful enterprise).* They fail to see that there is an *intersubjective* standard of reason that is indeed superordinate to actors' subjective interests. This standard is procedural and voluntaristic rather than substantive or "objective." Brennan and Buchanan adamantly oppose treating democracy by analogy to science, therefore, only because they wrongly accept positivists' accounts of the scientific enterprise (1985: 40–1). Given this questionable point of departure, their opposition to bringing any objective standard or copy theory of truth to politics follows quite logically. The problem is that this prevents them from considering how the voluntaristic orientation and social duties shared by all scientists who maintain their professional integrity are indeed related to the nonauthoritarian/authoritarian distinction.

35 Compare Parsons's references to intellectuals to Arendt's distinction between "hommes de lettres" and "intellectuals" (1963: 115–22). Her distinction rests on her vision of a public realm that directs social change rather than leaving it to drift.

Bibliography

Abbott, Andrew. 1988. *The System of Professions: An Essay on the Division of Expert Labor.* Chicago: University of Chicago Press.

Abel, Richard L. 1981. "Toward a Political Economy of Lawyers." *Wisconsin Law Review:* 1117–87.

Ackerman, Bruce A. 1977. *Private Property and the Constitution.* New Haven: Yale University Press.

—— 1980. *Social Justice in the Liberal State.* New Haven: Yale University Press.

Adriaansens, Hans P.M. 1980. *Talcott Parsons and the Conceptual Dilemma.* London: Routledge, Kegan & Paul.

Alapuro, Risto. 1988. *State and Revolution in Finland.* Berkeley: University of California Press.

Albrow, Martin. 1970. *Bureaucracy.* New York: Praeger.

Aleinikoff, T. Alexander. 1987. "Constitutional Law in the Age of Balancing." *Yale Law Journal* 96: 943–1005.

Alexander, Jeffrey C. 1978. "Formal and Substantive Voluntarism in the Work of Talcott Parsons: A Theoretical and Ideological Interpretation." *American Sociological Review* 43: 177–98.

—— 1980. "Core Solidarity, Ethnic Outgroup, and Social Differentiation: A Multidimensional Model of Inclusion in Modern Societies." Pp. 5–28 in Jacques Dofny and Akinsola Akiwowo (Eds.). *National and Ethnic Movements.* Beverly Hills: Sage [reprinted in *Action and Its Environments*].

—— 1982a. *Positivism, Presuppositions, and Current Controversies. Theoretical Logic in Sociology,* v. I. Berkeley: University of California Press.

—— 1982b. *The Antinomies of Classical Thought: Marx and Durkheim. Theoretical Logic in Sociology,* v. II. Berkeley: University of California Press.

—— 1983a. *The Classical Attempt at Theoretical Synthesis: Max Weber. Theoretical Logic in Sociology,* v. III. Berkeley: University of California Press.

—— 1983b. *The Modern Reconstruction of Classical Thought: Talcott Parsons. Theoretical Logic in Sociology,* v. IV. Berkeley: University of California Press.

—— 1984. "Action and Its Environment." Paper presented at the first German-American Theory Conference, Giessen, Federal Republic of Germany (June) [printed in *Action and Its Environments*].

—— 1985. Review Essay. "Habermas' New Critical Theory: Its Promise and Problems." *American Journal of Sociology* 91: 400–24.

—— 1986. "The University and Morality: A Revised Approach to University Autonomy and Its Limits." *Journal of Higher Education* 57: 463–76.

—— 1987. *Twenty Lectures: Sociological Theory Since World War II.* New York: Columbia University Press.

—— 1988. *Action and Its Environments: Toward a New Synthesis.* New York: Columbia University Press.

325

Allen, William Sheridan. 1965. *The Nazi Seizure of Power: The Experience of a Single German Town, 1930–1935*. Chicago: Quadrangle.

Anderson, Charles W. (1964) 1982. "Toward a Theory of Latin American Politics." Pp. 309–25 in Howard J. Wiarda (Ed.). *Politics and Social Change in Latin America: The Distinct Tradition*. 2d, rev. ed. Amherst: University of Massachussetts Press.

Antonio, Robert J. 1989. "The Normative Foundations of Emancipatory Theory: Evolutionary versus Pragmatic Perspectives." *American Journal of Sociology* 94: 721–48.

Apel, Karl-Otto. 1972. "Communication and the Foundations of the Humanities." *Acta Sociologica* 15: 7–26.

1979. "Types of Rationality Today: The Continuum of Reason Between Science and Ethics." Pp. 307–40 in Theodore F. Geraets (Ed). *Rationality To-day*. Ottawa: University of Ottawa Press.

1980. *Towards a Transformation of Philosophy*. London: Routledge, Kegan & Paul.

Archer, Margaret S. 1987. "The Myth of Cultural Integration." *British Journal of Sociology* 36: 333–53.

Arendt, Hannah. (1951) 1969. *The Origins of Totalitarianism*. Cleveland: Meridian.

(1958) 1971. *The Human Condition*. Chicago: University of Chicago Press.

(1963) 1970. *On Revolution*. New York: Viking.

Arrow, Kenneth J. 1951. *Social Choice and Individual Values*. New York: Wiley.

Balbus, Isaac. 1973. *The Dialectics of Legal Repression: Black Rebels before American Criminal Courts*. New York: Russell Sage Foundation.

1977. "Commodity Form and Legal Form: An Essay on the 'Relative Autonomy' of Law." *Law and Society Review* 2: 571–85.

Barber, Bernard. 1963. "Some Problems in the Sociology of the Professions. *Daedalus* 92: 669–88.

1983. *The Logic and Limits of Trust*. New Brunswick, N.J.: Rutgers University Press.

Barry, Brian M. 1970. *Sociologists, Economists and Democracy*. London: Collier-Macmillan.

Battle, John M. 1988. "Uskorenie, Glasnost, and Perestroika: The Pattern of Reform Under Gorbachev." *Soviet Studies* 40: 367–84.

Bayley, D.H. 1976. *Forces of Order: Police Behavior in Japan and the United States*. Berkeley: University of California Press.

Baylis, Thomas A. 1980. "Collegial Leadership in Advanced Industrial Societies: The Relevance of the Swiss Experience." *Polity* 13: 33–56.

Beetham, David. 1974. *Max Weber and the Theory of Modern Politics*. London: Allen & Unwin.

Bell, Daniel. 1976. *The Cultural Contradictions of Capitalism*. New York: Basic.

Bellah, Robert N. 1975. *The Broken Covenant*. New York: Seabury.

Bellah, Robert N., Richard Madsen, William M. Sullivan, Ann Swidler, and Steven M. Tipton. (1986) 1985. *Habits of the Heart: Individualism and Commitment in American Life*. New York: Harper and Row.

Bendix, Reinhard. (1960) 1962. *Max Weber: An Intellectual Portrait*. Garden City: Anchor.

1978. *Kings or People: Power and the Mandate to Rule*. Berkeley: University of California Press.

Bentley, Arthur F. (1908) 1967. *The Process of Government*. Cambridge: Harvard University Press.

Berkowitz, S.D. 1982. *An Introduction to Structural Analysis: The Network Approach to Social Research*. Toronto: Butterworth.

Berman, Harold J. (1972) 1977. "The Use of Law to Guide People to Virtue: A Comparison of Soviet and U.S. Perspectives." Pp. 75–84 in June Louin Tapp and Felice J. Levine (Eds.). *Law, Justice, and the Individual in Society: Psychological and Legal Issues*. New York: Holt, Rinehart and Winston.

Bernstein, Richard J. 1978. *The Restructuring of Social and Political Theory.* Philadelphia: University of Pennsylvania Press.

1983. *Beyond Objectivism and Relativism: Science, Hermeneutics and Praxis.* Philadelphia: University of Pennsylvania Press.

Bershady, Harold J. 1973. *Ideology and Social Knowledge.* New York: John Wiley.

Bierstedt, Robert. (1938) 1975. "The Means-End Schema in Sociological Theory." Pp. 31–40 in Robert Bierstedt. *Power and Progress: Essays in Sociological Theory.* New York: McGraw-Hill.

Birman, Igor. 1988. "The Imbalance of the Soviet Economy." *Soviet Studies* 40: 210–21.

Black, D. 1972. "The Boundaries of Legal Sociology." Pp. 41–56 in Black and M. Mileski (Eds.). *The Social Organization of Law.* New York: Seminar.

1976. *The Behavior of Law.* New York: Academic Press.

1984. "Social Control as a Dependent Variable." Pp. 1–36 in Black (Ed.). *Toward a General Theory of Social Control, vol. I: Fundamentals.* Orlando, Fla. Academic Press.

Blau, Peter M., and Otis Dudley Duncan. 1967. *The American Occupational Structure.* New York: John Wiley.

Block, Fred. 1977. "The Ruling Class Does Not Rule: Notes on the Marxist Theory of the State." *Socialist Revolution* 33: 6–28.

1987. *Revising State Theory: Essays in Politics and Postindustrialism.* Philadelphia: Temple University Press.

Bloom, Allan. (1987) 1988. *The Closing of the American Mind.* New York: Simon & Schuster.

Blumer, Herbert. 1969. *Symbolic Interactionism.* Englewood Cliffs, N.J.: Prentice-Hall.

1975. "Exchange on Turner, 'Parsons as a Symbolic Interactionist' [with comments by Parsons and Turner]." *Sociological Inquiry* 45: 59–68.

Bobbio, Norberto. (1984) 1987. *The Future of Democracy: A Defence of the Rules of the Game.* Cambridge, U.K.: Polity Press.

Bollen, Kenneth A., and Robert W. Jackman. 1985. "Political Democracy and the Size Distribution of Income." *American Sociological Review* 50: 438–57.

1989. "Democracy, Stability, and Dichotomies." *American Sociological Review* 54: 612–21.

Bottomore, T. 1984. *The Frankfurt School.* New York: Tavistock and Ellis Horwood.

Bourricaud, Francois. (1977) 1981. *The Sociology of Talcott Parsons.* Chicago: University of Chicago Press.

Braithwaite, John. 1982. "Enforced Self-Regulation: A New Strategy for Corporate Crime Control." *Michigan Law Review* 80.: 1466–1507.

1984. *Corporate Crime in the Pharmaceutical Industry.* London: Routledge, Kegan & Paul.

1985. "White Collar Crime." *Annual Review of Sociology* 11: 1–25.

1989. *Crime, Shame and Reintegration.* Cambridge, U.K.: Cambridge University Press.

Bredemeier, Harry C. 1955. "The Methodology of Functionalism." *American Sociological Review* 20: 173–9.

Brennan, Geoffrey, and James M. Buchanan. 1985. *The Reason of Rules: Constitutional Political Economy.* Cambridge, U.K.: Cambridge University Press.

Brooke, James. 1990. "A Swift and Hard Fall for Brazil." *New York Times,* 4 April, pp. D1, D18.

Buchanan, James M. 1989. *Explorations into Constitutional Economics.* College Station, Tex.: Texas A&M Press.

Bucher, Roe, and Anselm Strauss. 1961. "Professions in Process." *American Journal of Sociology* 66: 325–34.

Burawoy, Michael. 1979. *Manufacturing Consent.* Chicago: University of Chicago Press.

Burawoy, Michael, and Janos Lukacs. 1985. "Mythologies of Work: A Comparison of Firms in State Socialism and Advanced Capitalism." *American Sociological Review* 50: 723–37.

Burger, Thomas. 1976. *Max Weber's Theory of Concept Formation: History, Laws, and Ideal Types.* Durham, N.C.: Duke University Press.

1977. "Talcott Parsons, the Problem of Order in Society, and the Program of an Analytical Sociology." *American Journal of Sociology* 83: 320–34.

Burin, F.S., and K.L. Shell (Eds.). 1969. *Otto Kirchheimer: Politics, Law and Social Change.* New York: Columbia University Press.

Burnham, Walter Dean. 1970. *Critical Elections and the Mainsprings of American Politics.* New York: Norton.

Burt, Ronald S. 1980. "Models of Network Structures." *Annual Review of Sociology* 6: 79–141.

1983. *Corporate Profits and Cooptation.* New York: Academic Press.

Buxton, William. 1985. *Talcott Parsons and the Capitalist Nation-State: Political Sociology as a Strategic Vocation.* Toronto: University of Toronto Press.

Calabresi, Guido. 1982. *A Common Law for the Age of Statutes.* Cambridge: Harvard University Press.

Camic, Charles. 1987. "The Making of a Method: A Historical Reinterpretation of the Early Parsons." *American Sociological Review* 52: 421–39.

1989. "*Structure* After 50 Years: The Anatomy of a Charter." *American Journal of Sociology* 95: 38–107.

Cancian, Francesca. 1960. "Functional Analysis of Change." *American Sociological Review* 25: 818–27.

Cardoso, Fernando Henrique. 1977. "The Consumption of Dependency Theory in the U.S." *Latin American Research Review* 12: 7–24.

Cawson, Alan. 1982. *Corporatism and Welfare: Social Policy and State Intervention in Britain.* London: Heinemann.

1986. *Corporatism and Political Theory.* Oxford, U.K.: Basil Blackwell.

Chambers, William, and Walter Dean Burnham (Eds.). 1969. *The American Party System: Stages of Political Development.* New York: Oxford University Press.

Clinard, Marshall, and Peter C. Yeager. 1980. *Corporate Crime.* New York: Free Press.

Cohen, Ira. 1987. "Structuration Theory and Social Praxis." Pp. 273–308 in Anthony Giddens and Jonathan Turner (Eds.). *Social Theory Today.* Cambridge, U.K.: Polity.

1989. *Structuration Theory: Anthony Giddens and the Constitution of Social Life.* New York: St. Martin's.

Cohen, Jean. 1972. "Max Weber and the Dynamics of Rationalized Domination." *Telos* 14: 63–86.

Cohen, Jere. 1975. "Moral Freedom Through Understanding in Durkheim (Comment on Pope 1973)." *American Sociological Review* 40: 104–6.

Cohen, Jere., Lawrence E. Hazelrigg, and Whitney Pope. 1975. "De-Parsonizing Weber: A Critique of Parsons' Interpretation of Weber's Sociology." *American Sociological Review* 40: 229–44.

Coleman, James S. 1986. *Individual Interests and Collective Action: Selected Essays.* Cambridge, U.K.: Cambridge University Press.

1988. "Social Capital in the Creation of Human Capital." *American Journal of Sociology* 94. (Supplement): S95–120.

1990. *Foundations of Social Theory.* Cambridge, MA: Harvard University Press.

Collins, Hugh. 1982. *Marxism and Law.* Oxford, U.K.: Clarendon.

Collins, Randall. 1975. *Conflict Sociology.* New York: Academic Press.

1979. *The Credential Society: An Historical Sociology of Education and Stratification.* New York: Academic Press.

1981a. "On the Micro-foundations of Macro-sociology." *American Journal of Sociology* 86: 984–1014.

1981b. "Micro-translation as a Theory-building Strategy." Pp. 81–109 in Karin Knorr-Cetina and Aaron V. Cicourel (Eds.). *Advances in Social Theory and Methodology: Towards an Integration of Micro- and Macro-sociology.* London: Routledge and Kegan Paul.

1986. *Weberian Sociological Theory.* Cambridge: Cambridge University Press.

1988. *Theoretical Sociology.* San Diego: Harcourt Brace Jovanovich.

Colomy, Paul, and Gary Rhoades. 1988. "Specifying the Micro-Macro Link: An Application of General Theory of the Study of Structural Differentiation and Educational Change." Paper presented at American Sociological Association Annual Meeting, Atlanta, Ga.

Connor, Walker. 1972. "Nation-Building or Nation-Destroying?" *World Politics* 24: 319–55.

1973. "The Politics of Ethnonationalism." *Journal of International Affairs* 27: 1–21.

Connor, Walter D. 1988. *Socialism's Dilemmas: State and Society in the Soviet Bloc.* New York: Columbia University Press.

Coser, Lewis A. 1956. *The Functions of Social Conflict.* New York: Free Press.

1982. "The Notion of Social Control in Sociological Theory." Pp. 13–22 in Jack P. Gibbs (Ed.). *Social Control: Views from the Social Sciences.* Beverly Hills: Sage.

Craib, Ian. 1984. *Modern Social Theory: From Parsons to Habermas.* New York: St. Martin's.

Crane, Diana. 1972. *Invisible Colleges: Diffusion of Knowledge in Scientific Communities.* Chicago: University of Chicago Press.

1982. "Cultural Differentiation, Cultural Integration, and Social Control." Pp. 229–44 in Jack P. Gibbs (Ed.). *Social Control: Views from the Social Sciences.* Beverly Hills: Sage.

Dahl, Robert A. 1982. *Dilemmas of Pluralist Democracy: Autonomy vs. Control.* New Haven: Yale University Press.

Damaska, Mirjan R. 1986. *The Faces of Justice and State Authority: A Comparative Approach to the Legal Process.* New Haven: Yale University Press.

D'Antonio, William V., and Steven A. Tuch. 1989. "Professional Association Voting Patterns: A Mirror of Society?" Paper presented at American Sociological Association Annual Meeting, San Francisco, Calif.

Dallmayr, Fred R. 1974. "Toward a Critical Reconstruction of Ethics and Politics." *Journal of Politics* 36: 926–57.

1976. "Beyond Dogma and Despair: Toward a Critical Theory of Politics." *American Political Science Review* 70: 64–79.

1977. "Hermeneutics and Historicism: Reflections on Winch, Apel and Vico." *Review of Politics* 39: 60–81.

Davis, F. James, et al. 1962. *Society and the Law: New Meanings for an Old Profession.* New York: Free Press.

DeMott, Deborah A. 1988. "Beyond Metaphor: An Analysis of Fiduciary Obligation." *Duke Law Journal* 1988: 879–924.

Diamond, Martin, Winston Mills Fisk, and Herbert Garkinkel. (1966) 1969. *The Democratic Republic.* Chicago: Rand McNally.

Dobbin, Frank R., Lauren Edelman, John W. Meyer, W. Richard Scott, and Ann Swidler, 1988. "The Expansion of Due Process in Organizations." Pp. 71–98 in Lynne G. Zucker (Ed.). *Institutional Patterns and Organizations: Culture and Environment.* Cambridge, Mass.: Ballinger.

Domhoff, G. William. 1967. *Who Rules America?* Englewood Cliffs, N.J.: Prentice-Hall.

1974. *The Bohemian Grove and Other Retreats.* New York: Harper.

Dowd, Jerome. 1936. *Control in Human Societies.* New York: D. Appleton-Century.

Dryzek, John S. 1987. "Complexity and Rationality in Public Life." *Political Studies* 35: 424–42.

1988. "The Mismeasure of Political Man." *Journal of Politics* 50: 705–25.

Duverger, Maurice. (1951) 1959. *Political Parties: Their Organization and Activity in the Modern State.* London: Methuen.

Dworkin, Ronald. 1977. *Taking Rights Seriously.* Cambridge: Harvard University Press.

1985. *A Matter of Principle.* Cambridge: Harvard University Press.

1986. *Law's Empire.* Cambridge: Harvard University Press.

Eisenstadt, S.N., and L. Roniger. 1984. *Patrons, Clients and Friends: Interpersonal Relations and the Structure of Trust in Society.* Cambridge: Cambridge University Press.

Elkin, Stephen L. 1987. *City and Regime in the American Republic.* Chicago: University of Chicago Press.

Ely, John Hart. 1980. *Democracy and Distrust: A Theory of Judicial Review.* Cambridge: Harvard University Press.

Enloe, Cynthia H. 1973. *Ethnic Conflict and Political Development: An Analytic Study.* Boston: Little Brown.

Esping-Andersen, Gosta. 1985. *Politics Against Markets: The Social Democratic Road to Power.* Princeton: Princeton University Press.

Etzioni, Amitai. 1961/1975. *A Comparative Analysis of Complex Organizations: On Power, Involvement, and Their Correlates.* Rev. ed. New York: Free Press.

———. 1988. *The Moral Dimension: Toward a New Economics.* New York: Free Press.

———. 1989. "Toward an I & We Paradigm (Book Review)." *Contemporary Sociology* 18: 171–76.

Evan, William M. 1976. "Power, Conflict and Constitutionalism in Organizations." Pp. 83–111 in *Organization Theory: Structure, Systems and Environments.* New York: John Wiley.

Evans, Peter B., Dietrich Rueschemeyer, and Theda Skocpol (Eds.). 1985. *Bringing the State Back In.* Cambridge: Cambridge University Press.

Factor, Regis A., and Stephen P. Turner. 1979. "The Limits of Reason and Some Limitations of Weber's Morality." *Human Studies* 2: 301–34.

Faris, E. 1953. Review of *The Social System. American Sociological Review* 18: 103–6.

Featherman, David L., and Robert M. Hauser. 1978. *Opportunity and Change.* New York: Academic.

Fellman, David. 1976. *The Defendant's Rights Today.* Madison, Wis.: University of Wisconsin Press.

Frankel, Tamar. 1983. "Fiduciary Law." *California Law Review* 71: 795–836.

Freidson, Eliot. 1984a. "The Changing Nature of Professional Control." *Annual Review of Sociology* 10: 1–20.

———. 1984b. "Are Professions Necessary?" Pp. 3–27 in Thomas L. Haskell (Ed.). *The Authority of Experts: Studies in History and Theory.* Bloomington, Ind.: Indiana University Press.

Freund, Julien. (1966) 1968. *The Sociology of Max Weber.* New York: Pantheon.

Friedland, Roger, and Jimy Sanders. 1985. "The Public Economy and Economic Growth in Western Market Economies." *American Sociological Review* 50: 421–37.

Friedman, Milton. (1962) 1982. *Capitalism and Freedom.* Chicago: University of Chicago Press.

Friedrich, Carl J. 1941. *Constitutional Government and Democracy: Theory and Practice in Europe and America.* Boston: Little, Brown.

———. 1963. *Man and His Government.* New York: McGraw-Hill.

———. 1969. "On Rereading Machiavelli and Althusius: Reason, Rationality and Religion," in *Rational Decisions: Nomos VII.*

———. 1972. *Tradition and Authority.* New York: Praeger.

———. 1974. *Limited Government: A Comparison.* Englewood Cliffs, N.J.: Prentice-Hall.

Fulcher, James. 1987. "Labour Movement Theory Versus Corporatism: Social Democracy in Sweden." *Sociology* 21: 231–52.

Fuller, Lon L. 1949. The Case of the Speluncean Explorers." *Harvard Law Review* 62: 616–45.

———. 1956. "Human Purpose and Natural Law." *Journal of Philosophy* 53: 653–705.

———. 1958a. "Positivism and Fidelity to Law – A Reply to Professor Hart." *Harvard Law Review* 71: 630–72.

———. 1958b. "Human Purpose and Natural Law." *Natural Law Forum* 3: 68–76 [reprinted from *Journal of Philosophy*, 1956].

———. 1958c. "A Rejoinder to Professor Nagel." *Natural Law Forum* 3: 83–104.

(1964/1969) 1975. *The Morality of Law.* Rev. ed. New Haven: Yale University Press.

(1966) 1981. "Two Principles of Human Association." Pp. 67–85 in *The Principles of Social Order.* Durham, N.C.: Duke University Press.

(1969a) 1977. "Some Presuppositions Shaping the Concept of 'Socialization'." Pp. 33–40 in June Louin Tapp and Felice J. Levine (Eds.). *Law, Justice and the Individual in Society: Psychological and Legal Issues.* New York: Holt, Rinehart and Winson.

(1969b) 1981. "Human Interaction and the Law." Pp. 209–246 in *The Principles of Social Order,* edited by Kenneth I. Winston. Durham, N.C.: Duke University Press.

1981. *The Principles of Social Order,* edited by Kenneth I. Winston. Durham, N.C.: Duke University Press.

Gadamer, Hans-Georg. (1960) 1975. *Truth and Method.* New York: Seabury.

(1966) 1977. "The Universality of the Hermeneutical Problem." Pp. 3–17 in *Philosophical Hermeneutics.* Berkeley: University of California Press.

(1967) 1977. "On the Scope and Function of Hermeneutical Reflection." Pp. 18–43 in *Philosophical Hermeneutics.* Berkeley: University of California Press.

Galanter, Marc. 1974. "Why the 'Haves' Come Out Ahead: Speculations on the Limits of Legal Change." *Law and Society Review* 9: 95–160.

Gans, Herbert. 1979. *Deciding What's News.* New York: Pantheon.

1988. *Middle American Individualism: The Future of Liberal Democracy.* New York: Free Press.

Garson, G. David. 1978. *Group Theories of Politics.* Beverly Hills: Sage.

Gellner, Ernest. 1977. "Patrons and Clients." Pp. 1–6 in Gellner and John Waterbury (Eds.). *Patrons and Clients in Mediterranean Societies.* London: Duckworth.

Gellner, Ernest, and John Waterbury (Eds.). 1977. *Patrons and Clients in Mediterranean Societies.* London: Duckworth.

Geraets, Theodore F. 1979. *Rationality To-Day.* Ottawa: University of Ottawa Press.

Gerstein, Dean R. 1975. "A Note on the Continuity of Parsonian Action Theory." *Sociological Inquiry* 45: 11–15.

Gibbs, Jack. 1972. *Sociological Theory Construction.* Hinsdale, Ill.: Dryden.

1981. *Norms, Deviance, and Social Control: Conceptual Matters.* New York: Elsevier.

1982. "Law as a Means of Social Control." Pp. 83–113 in Gibbs (Ed.). *Social Control: Views from the Social Sciences.* Beverly Hills: Sage.

Giddens, Anthony. 1968. " 'Power' in the Recent Writings of Talcott Parsons." *Sociology* (September) 257–72.

1971. *Capitalism and Modern Social Theory: An Analysis of the Writings of Marx, Durkheim and Max Weber.* London: Cambridge University Press.

1976. *New Rules of Sociological Method: A Positive Critique of Interpretative Sociologies.* New York: Basic.

1979. *Central Problems in Social Theory: Action, Structure and Contradiction in Social Analysis.* Berkeley: University of California Press.

1981. *A Contemporary Critique of Historical Materialism, v. I: Power, Property and the State.* Berkeley: University of California Press.

1982. "Labour and Interaction." Pp. 149–61 in John B. Thompson and David Held (Eds.). *Habermas: Critical Debates.* Cambridge: MIT Press.

1984. *The Constitution of Society: Outline of the Theory of Structuration.* Cambridge, U.K: Polity.

1985. *The Nation-State and Violence: Volume Two of a Contemporary Critique of Historical Materialism.* Cambridge, U.K.: Polity.

1987. *Social Theory and Modern Sociology.* Stanford: Stanford University Press.

Gold, David, Clarence Lo, and Erik Olin Wright. 1975. "Recent Developments in Marxist Theories of the State." *Monthly Review* 27: 29–43.

Goldfarb, Jeffrey C. 1989. *Beyond Glasnost: The Post-Totalitarian Mind.* Chicago: University of Chicago Press.

Goldner, F.H., and R.R. Ritti. 1967. "Professionalism as Career Immobility." *American Journal of Sociology* 72: 489–503.

Goldstein, Herman. 1977. *Policing a Free Society.* Cambridge, Mass.: Ballinger.

Gould, Mark. 1981. "Parsons Versus Marx: 'An Earnest Warning . . .' " *Sociological Inquiry* 51: 197–218.

Gouldner, Alvin W. 1960. "The Norm of Recriprocity: A Preliminary Statement." *American Sociological Review* 25: 161–78.

———. 1970. *The Coming Crisis of Western Sociology.* New York: Equinox.

———. 1976. *The Dialectic of Ideology and Technology: The Origins, Grammar, and Future of Ideology.* New York: Seabury.

———. 1979. *The Future of Intellectuals and the Rise of the New Class.* New York: Oxford University Press.

Grey, Thomas C. 1989. "Holmes and Legal Pragmatism." *Stanford Law Review* 41: 787–870.

Griffiths, John. 1984. "The Division of Social Control Labor." Pp. 37–70 in Donald Black (Ed.). *Toward a General Theory of Social Control, vol. I: Fundamentals.* Orlando: Academic Press.

Grossman, Joel B., and Richard S. Wells. 1980. *Constitutional Law and Judicial Policy Making.* 2d. ed. New York: Longman.

Haar, Charles M., and Daniel Wm. Fessler. 1986. *The Wrong Side of the Tracks: A Revolutionary Discovery of the Common Law Tradition of Fairness in the Struggle Against Inequality.* New York: Simon & Schuster.

Habermas, Jürgen. (1962) 1989. *The Structural Transformation of the Public Sphere: An Inquiry Into a Category of Bourgeois Society.* Translated by Thomas Burger. Cambridge: MIT Press.

———. (1963a) 1973. "The Classical Doctrine of Politics in Relation to Social Philosophy." Pp. 41–82 in *Theory and Practice.* Boston: Beacon.

———. (1963b) 1973. "Natural Law and Revolution." Pp. 82–120 in *Theory and Practice.* Boston: Beacon.

———. (1963c) 1973. "Hegel's Critique of the French Revolution." Pp. 121–41 in *Theory and Practice.* Boston: Beacon.

———. (1965) 1972. "Knowledge and Human Interests: A General Perspective." Pp. 301–17 in *Knowledge and Human Interests.* Boston: Beacon.

———. (1967a) 1973. "Labor and Interaction: Remarks on Hegel's Jena Philosophy of Mind." Pp. 142–69 in *Theory and Practice.* Boston: Beacon.

———. (1967b) 1988. *On the Logic of the Social Sciences.* Translated by Shierry Weber Nicholsen and Jerry A. Stark. Cambridge: MIT Press.

———. (1968a) 1972. *Knowledge and Human Interests.* Boston: Beacon.

———. (1968b) 1971. "Technology and Science as 'Ideology'." Pp. 81–122 in *Toward a Rational Society.* Boston: Beacon.

———. (1968–69) 1971. *Toward a Rational Society: Student Protest, Science and Politics.* Boston: Beacon. Chapters 1–3.

———. (1971) 1973. "Some Difficulties in the Attempt to Link Theory and Practice." Pp. 1–40 in *Theory and Practice.* Boston: Beacon.

———. (1973a) 1975. *Legitimation Crisis.* Boston: Beacon.

———. 1973b. "Wahrheitstheorien." Pp. 1–68 in *Wirklichkeit und Reflexion: Walter Schutz zum 60. Gebuntsstag.* Pfullingen: Neske.

———. 1973c. "A Postscript to Knowledge and Human Interests." *Philosophy of Social Science* 3: 157–89.

(1974) 1979. "Legitimation Problems in the Modern State." Pp. 178–205 in *Communication and the Evolution of Society*. Boston: Beacon.

(1976a) 1979. "What Is Universal Pragmatics?" Pp. 1–68 in *Communication and the Evolution of Society*. Boston: Beacon.

(1976b) 1979. "Moral Development and Ego Identity." Pp. 69–94 in *Communication and the Evolution of Society*. Boston: Beacon.

1977. "Hannah Arendt's Communications Concept of Power." *Social Research* 44: 3–24.

1979. "Aspects of the Rationality of Action." Pp. 185–212 in Theodore F. Geraets (Ed.). *Rationality To-day*. Ottawa: University of Ottawa Press.

(1980) 1981. "Talcott Parsons: Problems of Theory Construction." *Sociological Inquiry* 51: 173–96.

(1981a) 1984. *The Theory of Communicative Action, v.1: Reason and the Rationalization of Society*. Boston: Beacon.

(1981b) 1987. *The Theory of Communicative Action, v.2: Lifeworld and Systems: A Critique of Functionalist Reason*. Boston: Beacon.

1982. "A Reply to My Critics." Pp. 219–83 in John B. Thompson and David Held (Eds.). *Habermas: Critical Debates*. Cambridge: MIT Press.

1983. "Interpretive Social Science vs. Hermeneuticism." Pp. 251–69 in Norma Haan et al. (Eds.). *Social Science as Moral Inquiry*. New York: Columbia University Press.

1984. "Interaction Between System and Life-World – Exemplified by Phenomena of Juridification." Manuscript presented at the first German-American Theory Conference, Giessen, Federal Republic of Germany (June).

1989. "The Crisis of the Welfare State and the Exhaustion of Utopian Energies." Pp. 284–99 in Steven Seidman (Ed.). *Jürgen Habermas on Society and Politics: A Reader*. Boston: Beacon.

Hagopian, Mark N. 1978. *Regimes, Movements, and Ideologies*. New York: Longman.

Hall, John A. 1987. *Liberalism: Politics, Ideology and the Market*. Chapel Hill, N.C.: University of North Carolina Press.

Hall, John R. 1984. "The Problem of Epistemology in the Social Action Perspective." Pp. 253–89 in Randall Collins (Ed.). *Sociological Theory 1984*. San Francisco: Jossey-Bass.

Hansen, Roger D. 1971. *The Politics of Mexican Development*. Baltimore: Johns Hopkins Press.

Hart, H.L.A. 1958. "Positivism and the Separation of Law and Morals." *Harvard Law Review* 71: 593–629.

1961. *The Concept of Law*. Oxford: Clarendon.

1965. Book review of *The Morality of Law* by Lon L. Fuller. *Harvard Law Review* 78: 1281–96.

Hawkins, Keith. 1984. *Environment and Enforcement: Regulation and the Social Definition of Pollution*. Oxford, U.K.: Clarendon.

Hayek, Friedrich A. (1944) 1969. *The Road to Serfdom*. Chicago: University of Chicago Press.

1973–9. *Law, Legislation and Liberty: A New Statement of the Liberal Principles of Justice and Political Economy*. 3 vols. Chicago: University of Chicago Press.

Hechter, Michael. 1987. *Principles of Group Solidarity*. Berkeley: University of California Press.

Heinz, John P., and Edward O. Laumann. 1982. *Chicago Lawyers*. New York: Russell Sage. Chicago: American Bar Foundation.

Held, David. 1980. *Introduction to Critical Theory: Horkheimer to Habermas*. Berkeley: University of California Press.

Heller, Agnes. 1972. "Towards a Marxist Theory of Value." *Kinesis* (Fall) 5 (1): 7–76.

Higley, John, and Michael G. Burton. 1989. "The Elite Variable in Democratic Transitions and Breakdowns." *American Sociological Review* 54: 17–32.

Hobhouse, L.T. (1911) 1969. *Liberalism*. New York: Oxford University Press.
Hohendahl, Peter U. 1979. "Critical Theory, Public Sphere and Culture: Jürgen Habermas and His Critics." *New German Critique* (Winter) 16: 89–118.
Hollingshead, August B. 1941. "The Concept of Social Control." *American Sociological Review* 6: 217–24.
Holmes, Oliver Wendell. 1897. "The Path of Law." *Harvard Law Review* 10: 457–78.
Horkheimer, Max. 1940. "The Authoritarian State." Pp. 95–117 in Andrew Arato and Eike Gebhardt (Eds.). *The Essential Frankfurt School Reader*. New York: Urizen
    (1947) 1974. *Eclipse of Reason*. New York: Seabury.
Horkheimer, Max, and Theodor W. Adorno. (1944) 1972. *Dialectic of Enlightenment*. New York: Seabury.
Horowitz, Donald L. 1977. *The Courts and Social Policy*. Washington, D.C.: Brookings Institution.
    1985. *Ethnic Groups in Conflict*. Berkeley: University of California Press.
Hughes, H. Stuart. 1958. *Consciousness and Society: The Reorientation of European Social Thought 1890–1930*. New York: Knopf.
Huntington, Samuel P. 1971. "The Change to Change: Modernization, Development and Politics." *Comparative Politics* 3: 283–322.
Husserl, Edmund. 1934–37 (1970). *The Crisis of European Sciences and Transcendental Phenomenology: An Introduction to Phenomenological Philosophy*. Translated by David Carr. Evanston: Northwestern University Press.
Jacobson, David C. 1976. "Rationalization and Emancipation in Weber and Habermas." *Graduate Faculty Journal of Sociology: New School for Social Research* 1: 18–31.
Janowitz, Morris. 1975. "Sociological Theory and Social Control." *American Journal of Sociology* 81: 82–108.
    1976. *Social Control of the Welfare State*. New York: Elsevier.
Jay, Martin. 1973. *The Dialectical Imagination: A History of the Frankfurt School and the Institute of Social Research, 1923–1950*. Boston: Little Brown.
    1974. "The Frankfurt School's Critique of Karl Mannheim and the Sociology of Knowledge." *Telos* 20: 72–89.
Jenkins, J. Craig. 1985. *The Politics of Insurgency: The Farm Worker Movement in the 1960s*. New York: Columbia University Press.
Jessop, Bob. 1979. "Corporatism, Parliamentarism and Social Democracy." Pp. 185–212 in Schmitter and Lehmbruch (Eds.). *Trends Toward Corporatist Intermediation*. Beverly Hills and London: Sage.
Johnson, Harry M. 1981. "Talcott Parsons and the Theory of Action: Editorial Introduction." *Sociological Inquiry* 51: iii–xvii.
Kalberg, Stephen. 1980. "Max Weber's Types of Rationality: Cornerstones for the Analysis of Rationalization Processes in History." *American Journal of Sociology* 85: 1145–79.
Kaplan, Harold. 1968. "The Parsonian Image of Social Structure and Its Relevance for Political Science." *Journal of Politics* 30: 885–909.
Kaplan, Howard B. 1980. *Deviant Behavior in Defense of Self*. New York: Academic Press.
Katznelson, Ira. 1978. "Considerations on Social Democracy in the U.S." *Comparative Politics* 11: 77–99.
Kelman, Mark. 1987. *A Guide to Critical Legal Studies*. Cambridge: Harvard University Press.
Kelsen, Hans. (1941) 1971. "The Pure Theory of Law and Analytical Jurisprudence." Pp. 266–87 in *What Is Justice?: Justice, Law and Politics in the Mirror of Science*. Berkeley: University of California Press.
    (1945) 1961. *General Theory of Law and State*. New York: Russell & Russell.

Kennedy, Michael D. 1987. "Polish Engineers' Participation in the Soldarity Movement." *Social Forces* 65: 641–69.

Kerblay, Basile. (1977) 1983. *Modern Soviet Society.* New York: Pantheon.

Kerbo, Harold R. 1983. *Social Stratification and Inequality: Class Conflict in the United States.* New York: McGraw-Hill.

Key, V.O., Jr. (1942) 1964. *Politics, Parties and Pressure Groups.* New York: Crowell.

1961. *Public Opinion and American Democracy.* New York: Knopf.

Kirchheimer, Otto. 1961. *Political Justice: The Use of Legal Procedure for Political Ends.* Princeton: Princeton University Press.

Klare, Karl. 1979. "Law-Making as Praxis." *Telos* 40: 123–35.

Klockars, Carl B. 1985. *The Idea of Police.* Beverly Hills: Sage.

Knoke, David. 1989. "Fighting Collectively: Action Sets and Opposition Networks in the U.S. and German Labor Policy Domains." Paper presented at American Sociological Association Annual Meeting, San Francisco, Calif.

Knottnerus, J. D. 1987. "Status Attainment Research and Its Image of Society." *American Sociological Review* 52: 113–21.

Konrad, Gyorgy, and Ivan Szelenyi. 1979. *The Intellectuals on the Road to Class Power.* New York: Harcourt, Brace and Jovanovich.

Korpi, Walter. 1983. *The Democratic Class Struggle.* London: Routledge & Kegan Paul.

Kronman, A. 1983. *Max Weber.* Stanford: Stanford University Press.

Ladd, Everett Carll, Jr. 1970. *American Political Parties: Social Change and Political Response.* New York: Norton.

Larson, Magali Sarfatti. 1977. *The Rise of Professionalism.* Berkeley: University of California Press.

Lasch, Christopher. 1978. *The Culture of Narcissism: American Life in an Age of Diminishing Expectations.* New York: Norton.

Laumann, Edward O., and David Knoke. 1987. *The Organizational State.* Madison, Wis.: University of Wisconsin Press.

Law and Contemporary Problems. 1984. Issue on Selective Enforcement, v. 47.

Leeds, Anthony. (1964) 1974. "Brazilian Careers and Social Structure: A Case History and Model." Pp. 379–404 in Dwight B. Heath (Ed.). *Contemporary Cultures and Societies of Latin America.* 2d. ed. New York: Random House.

Lehmbruch, Gerhard, and Philippe C. Schmitter (Eds.). 1982. *Patterns of Corporatist Policy-Making.* Beverly Hills: Sage.

Leifer, Eric M. 1988. "Interaction Preludes to Role Setting: Exploratory Local Action." *American Sociological Review* 53: 865–78.

Levine, Donald N. 1981. "Rationality and Freedom: Weber and Beyond." *Sociological Inquiry* 51: 5–25.

Lewis, Roy, and Angus Maude. 1952. *Professional People.* London: Phoenix House.

Lieberson, Stanley. 1985. *Making It Count: The Improvement of Social Research and Theory.* Berkeley: University of California Press.

Lijphart, Arend. 1977. *Democracy in Plural Societies: A Comparative Perspective.* New Haven: Yale University Press.

Lindblom, Charles E. 1959 (1965). "The Science of 'Muddling Through'." Pp. 339–48 in Polsby, Nelson W., Robert A. Dentler, and Paul A. Smith (Eds.). *Politics and Social Life.* Boston: Houghton Mifflin.

Lindsay, A.D. (1943) 1965. *The Modern Democratic State.* New York: Oxford University Press.

Linz, Juan. (1964) 1970. "An Authoritarian Regime: Spain." Pp. 251–75 in Stein Rokkan and Erik Allardt (Eds.). *Mass Politics: Studies in Political Sociology.* New York: Free Press.

Linz, Juan J., and Alfred Stepan (Eds.). 1978. *The Breakdown of Democratic Regimes.* Baltimore: Johns Hopkins University Press.

Lipset, Seymour Martin. 1960. *Political Man*. New York: Doubleday.
Lipset, Seymour Martin, and Earl Raab. 1970. *The Politics of Unreason*. New York: Harper & Row.
Lockwood, David. (1956) 1968. "Some Remarks on 'The Social System'." Pp. 281–91 in Demerath, N.J., and Richard A. Peterson (Eds.). *System, Change and Conflict*. New York: Free Press.
Loewenstein, Karl. (1957) 1965. *Political Power and the Governmental Process*. Chicago: University of Chicago Press.
Lorrain, Francois, and Harrison C. White. (1971) 1977. "Structural Equivalence of Individuals in Social Networks." Pp. 67–98 in Samuel Leinhardt (Ed.). *Social Networks: A Developing Paradigm*. New York: Academic.
Loubser, Jan. 1976. "General Introduction." Pp. 1–23 in *Explorations in General Theory in Social Science: Essays in Honor of Talcott Parsons*, edited by Jan Loubser et al., 2 vols. New York: Free Press.
Loubser, Jan, Rainer C. Baum, Andrew Effrat, and Victor M. Lidz (Eds.). 1976. *Explorations in General Theory in Social Science: Essays in Honor of Talcott Parsons*. 2 vols. New York: Free Press.
Lowi, Theodore. 1969. *The End of Liberalism: Ideology, Policy and the Crisis of Public Authority*. New York: Norton.
———. 1976. *American Government: Incomplete Conquest*. Hinsdale, Ill.: Dryden Press.
Luhmann, Niklas. (1972) 1985. *A Sociological Theory of Law*. London: Routledge & Kegan Paul.
———. 1976. "Generalized Media and the Problem of Contingency." Pp. 507–32 in *Explorations in General Theory in Social Science: Essays in Honor of Talcott Parsons*, edited by Jan Loubser, et. al. 2 vols. New York: Free Press.
———. 1982. *The Differentiation of Society*. New York: Columbia University Press.
———. (1986) 1989. *Ecological Communication*. Chicago: University of Chicago Press.
———. 1988. "Tautology and Paradox in the Self-Descriptions of Modern Society." *Sociological Theory* 6: 26–37.
———. 1990. *Political Theory in the Welfare State*. Rev. ed. Berlin and New York: Walter de Gruyter.
Lukacs, Georg. (1920) 1972. "Legality and Illegality." Pp. 256–71 in Georg Lukacs. *History and Class Consciousness*. Cambridge: MIT Press.
———. (1920–22) 1972. *History and Class Consciousness*. Cambridge: MIT Press.
Lukes, Steven. 1985. *Marxism and Morality*. Oxford: Clarendon.
Luttwak, Edward. 1968/1984. *Coup d'etat: A Practical Handbook*. London: Allen Lane.
MacCormick, Neil. 1981. *H.L.A. Hart*. Stanford: Stanford University Press.
MacIntyre, Alasdair. 1981. *After Virtue: A Study in Moral Theory*. Notre Dame: University of Notre Dame Press.
MacKinnon, Catharine A. 1983. "Feminism, Marxism, Method, and the State: Toward Feminist Jurisprudence." *Signs* 8: 635–58.
Macpherson, C.B. (1962) 1970. *The Political Theory of Possessive Individualism: Hobbes to Locke*. London: Oxford University Press.
Madge, Charles. 1964. *Society in the Mind: Elements of Social Eidos*. New York: Free Press.
Maines, David R., and Joy C. Charlton. 1985. "The Negotiated Order Approach to the Analysis of Social Organization." Pp. 271–308 in Harvey A. Farberman and R.S. Perinbanayagam (Eds.). *Studies in Symbolic Interaction, Supplement I: Foundations of Interpretative Sociology: Original Essays in Symbolic Interaction*. Greenwich, Conn.: JAI Press.
Mann, Michael. 1987. "Ruling Class Strategies and Citizenship." *Sociology* 21: 339–54.
Mannheim, Karl. (1929) n.d. *Ideology and Utopia*. Translated by Louis Wirth and Edward Shils. New York: Harvest Book.

Marcuse, Herbert. (1955) 1962. *Eros and Civilization: A Philosophical Inquiry Into Freud.* New York: Vintage.

(1964a) 1968. "Industrialization and Capitalism in the Work of Max Weber." Pp. 201–27 in *Negations.* Boston: Beacon.

(1964b) 1970. *One Dimensional Man.* Boston: Beacon.

Martin, Michael. 1987. *The Legal Philosophy of H.L.A. Hart: A Critical Appraisal.* Philadelphia: Temple University Press.

Martins, Luciano. 1986. "The 'Liberalization' of Authoritarian Rule in Brazil." Pp. 72–94 in O'Donnell, Schmitter, and Whitehead (Eds.). *Transitions from Authoritarian Rule, vol. 3: Latin America.* Baltimore: Johns Hopkins University Press.

Marwell, Gerald, Pamela E. Oliver, and Ralph Prahl. 1988. "Social Networks and Collective Action: A Theory of the Critical Mass, III." *American Journal of Sociology* 94: 502–34.

Marx, Karl. (1842) 1967. "Comments on the Latest Prussian Censorship Instruction." Pp. 67–92 in Lloyd D. Easton and K.H. Guddat (Eds.). *Writings of the Young Marx on Philosophy and Society.* Garden City, N.Y.: Anchor.

(1857–8) 1973. *Grundrisse: Foundations of the Critique of Political Economy.* Translated by Martin Nicholas. Middlesex, England: Penguin.

1967. *Writings of the Young Marx on Philosophy and Society.* Edited and translated by Lloyd D. Easton and Kurt H. Guddat. New York: Anchor.

Masters, Roger. 1970. *The Political Philosophy of Rousseau.* Princeton: Princeton University Press.

Mayer, John A. 1983. "Notes Toward a Working Definition of Social Control in Historical Analysis." Pp. 17–38 in Stanley Cohen and Andrew Scull (Eds.). *Social Control and the State.* New York: St. Martin's.

Mayhew, Leon H. 1982. "Introduction." Pp. 1–62 in Leon Mayhew (Ed.). *Talcott Parsons: On Institutions and Social Evolution.* Chicago: University of Chicago Press.

McAdam, Doug. 1982. *Political Process and the Development of Black Insurgency, 1930–1970.* Chicago: University of Chicago Press.

McCarthy, John D., and Mayer N. Zald. 1977. "Resource Mobilization and Social Movements." *American Journal of Sociology* 82: 1212–41.

McCarthy, Thomas. 1978. *The Critical Theory of Jürgen Habermas.* Cambridge: MIT Press.

McClosky, Herbert, and Alida Brill. 1983. *Dimensions of Tolerance: What Americans Believe About Civil Liberties.* New York: Russell Sage Foundation.

McDonough, Peter. 1981. *Power and Ideology in Brazil.* Princeton: Princeton University Press.

Meador, Daniel John. 1986. *Impressions of Law in East Germany: Legal Education and Legal Systems in the German Democratic Republic.* Charlottesville, Va.: University Press of Virginia.

Menzies, Ken. 1977. *Talcott Parsons and the Social Image of Man.* London: Routledge, Kegan & Paul.

Merry, Sally Engle. 1984. "Rethinking Gossip and Scandal." Pp. 271–302 in Donald Black (Ed.). *Toward a General Theory of Social Control, v. I: Fundamentals.* Orlando, Fla.: Academic.

Merryman, John Henry. 1969/1985. *The Civil Law Tradition.* Stanford: Stanford University Press, 2d. ed.

Merton, Robert K. 1938a. "Social Structure and Anomie." *American Sociological Review* 3: 672–82.

(1938b) 1973. "Science and the Social Order." Pp. 254–66 in *The Sociology of Science.* Chicago: University of Chicago Press.

(1942) 1968. "Science and Democratic Social Structure." Pp. 604–15 in *Social Theory and Social Structure.* New York: Free Press.

(1949/1957) 1968. *Social Theory and Social Structure.* New York: Free Press.

1965. *On the Shoulders of Giants.* New York: Free Press.

1976. (with Elinor Barber). "Sociological Ambivalence." Pp. 3–31 in *Sociological Ambivalence and Other Essays.* New York: Free Press.

Meszaros, Istvan. 1972. *Marx's Theory of Alienation.* New York: Harper & Row.

Meyer, John W., and Brian Rowan. 1977. "Institutionalized Organizations: Formal Structure as Myth and Ceremony." *American Journal of Sociology* 83: 340–63.

Meyer, John W., and W. Richard Scott. 1983. *Organizational Environments: Ritual and Rationality.* Beverly Hills: Sage.

Meyer, John W., Richard Scott, and Terence E. Deal. 1981. "Institutional and Technical Sources of Organizational Structure: Explaining the Structure of Educational Organizations." Pp. 151–79 in Herman D. Stein (Ed.). *Organization and the Human Services: Cross-Disciplinary Reflections.* Philadelphia: Temple University Press.

Meyrowitz, Joshua. 1986. "Media as Social Contexts." Pp. 229–50 in Ralph L. Rosnow and Marianthi Georgoudi (Eds.). *Contextualism and Understanding in Behavioral Science.* New York: Praeger.

Michelman, Frank. 1988. "Law's Republic." *Yale Law Journal* 97: 1493–1537.

Michels, Robert. (1911) 1949. *Political Parties.* New York: Free Press.

Miliband, Ralph. 1969. *The State in Capitalist Society.* New York: Basic.

1982. *Capitalist Democracy in Britain.* Oxford, U.K.: Oxford University Press.

Millar, James R. (Ed.). 1987. *Politics, Work and Daily Life in the USSR: A Survey of Former Soviet Citizens.* Cambridge: Cambridge University Press.

Milsom, S.F.C. 1981. *Historical Foundations of the Common Law.* 2d. ed. Toronto: Butterworths.

Mintz, Beth, and Michael Schwartz. 1985. *The Power Structure of American Business.* Chicago: University of Chicago Press.

Mitchell, William C. 1967. *Sociological Analysis and Politics: The Theories of Talcott Parsons.* Englewood Cliffs, N.J.: Prentice-Hall.

Mizruchi, Mark S. 1982. *The American Corporate Network 1904–1974.* Beverly Hills: Sage.

Mommsen, Wolfgang J. (1959/1974) 1984. *Max Weber and German Politics 1890–1920,* trans. Michael S. Steinberg. Chicago: University of Chicago Press.

1974. *The Age of Bureaucracy: Perspective on the Political Sociology of Max Weber.* Oxford: Basil Blackwell.

Moore, Barrington. 1966. *Social Origins of Dictatorship and Democracy.* Boston: Beacon.

Moore, Michael S. 1989. "The Interpretive Turn in Modern Theory: A Turn for the Worse?" *Stanford Law Review* 41: 871–957.

Morris, Aldon D. 1984. *The Origins of the Civil Rights Movement: Black Communities Organizing for Change.* New York: Free Press.

Muir, W.K. 1977. *Police: Streetcorner Politicians.* Chicago: University of Chicago Press.

Münch, Richard. 1981a. "Talcott Parsons and the Theory of Action, I. The Structure of the Kantian Core." *American Journal of Sociology* 86: 709–39.

1981b. "Socialization and Personality Development from the Point of View of Action Theory, the Legacy of Emile Durkheim." *Sociological Inquiry* 51: 311–54.

1982. "Talcott Parsons and the Theory of Action, II. The Continuity of Development." *American Journal of Sociology* 87: 771–826.

1987. "The Interpenetration of Microinteraction and Macrostructures in a Complex and Contingent Institutional Order." Pp. 319–36 in Alexander et al. (Eds.). *The Micro-Macro Link.* Berkeley: University of California Press.

Murphy, Raymond. 1988. *Social Closure: The Theory of Monopolization and Exclusion.* Oxford, U.K.: Clarendon.

Nagel, Ernest. 1958. "On the Fusion of Fact and Value: A Reply to Professor Fuller." *Natural Law Forum* 3: 77–82.

1959. "Fact, Value, and Human Purpose." *Natural Law Forum* 4: 26–43.

Nagel, Robert F. 1989. *Constitutional Cultures: The Mentality and Consequences of Judicial Review.* Berkeley: University of California Press.

Nelson, Benjamin. 1949. *The Idea of Usury.* Princeton: Princeton University Press.

Neumann, Franz. (1938) 1986. *The Rule of Law: Political Theory and the Legal System in Modern Society.* Dover, N.H.: Berg.

Nonet, Philippe, and Philip Selznick. 1978. *Law and Society in Transition: Toward Responsive Law.* New York: Octagon Books.

Note. 1982. "Constitutional Rights of the Corporate Person." *Yale Law Journal* 91: 1641–58.

Oberschall, Anthony. 1973. *Social Conflict and Social Movements.* Englewood Cliffs, N.J.: Prentice-Hall.

O'Connor, James. 1973. *The Fiscal Crisis of the State.* New York: St. Martin's.

O'Donnell, Guillermo A. 1977. "Corporatism and the Question of the State." Pp. 47–87 in Malloy (Ed.). *Authoritarianism and Corporatism in Latin America.* Pittsburgh: University of Pittsburgh Press.

O'Donnell, Guillermo, Philippe C. Schmitter, and Laurence Whitehead (Eds). 1986. *Transitions from Authoritarian Rule.* 5 vols. Baltimore: Johns Hopkins University Press.

Offe, Claus. 1983. "Political Legitimation Through Majority Rule?" *Social Research* 50: 700–56.

Oliver, Pamela E., and Gerald Marwell. 1988. "The Paradox of Group Size in Collective Action: A Theory of the Critical Mass, II." *American Sociological Review* 53: 1–8.

Oliver, Pamela E., Gerald Marwell, and Ruy Teixeira. 1985. "A Theory of the Critical Mass, I. Interdependence, Group Heterogeneity, and the Production of Collective Goods." *American Journal of Sociology* 91: 522–56.

Ollman, Bertell. 1977. "Marx's Vision of Communism: A Reconstruction." *Critique: Journal of Soviet Studies and Socialist Theory* (Summer) No. 8: 7–41.

Olson, Mancur. 1965. *The Logic of Collective Action.* Cambridge: Harvard University Press.

O'Neill, John. 1972. "The Hobbesian Problem in Marx and Parsons." Pp. 177–208 in John O'Neill. *Sociology as a Skin Trade: Essays Towards a Reflexive Sociology.* New York: Harper & Row.

O'Neill, John (Ed.). 1976. *On Critical Theory.* New York: Seabury.

Ortega y Gassett, Jose. (1930) 1932. *The Revolt of the Masses.* New York: Norton.

Paci, Enzo. (1963) 1972. *The Function of the Sciences and the Meaning of Man.* Evanston, Ill.: Northwestern University Press.

Parkin, Frank. 1979. *Marxism and Class Theory: A Bourgeois Critique.* London: Tavistock.

Parsons, Talcott. 1935. "The Place of Ultimate Values in Sociological Theory." *International Journal of Ethics* 45: 282–316.

1936. "Pareto's Central Analytical Scheme." *Journal of Social Philosophy* 1: 244–62.

(1937a) 1968. *The Structure of Social Action.* 2 vols. New York: Free Press.

1937b. "Education and the Professions." *International Journal of Ethics* 47: 365–9.

(1939) 1964. "The Professions and Social Structure." *Social Forces* 17: 457–67, reprinted Pp. 34–49 in *Essays in Sociological Theory.* Rev. ed. New York: Free Press.

1943. "The Kinship System of the Contemporary United States." *American Anthropologist* 45: 22–38.

1945. "Racial and Religious Differences as Factors in Group Tensions." In Louis Finkelstein et al (Eds.). *Unity and Difference in the Modern World.* New York: Conference of Science, Philosophy, and Religion in Their Relation to the Democratic Way of Life.

(1950) 1964. "The Prospects of Sociological Theory." Pp. 348–69 in *Essays in Sociological Theory.* Rev. ed. New York: Free Press.

(1951) 1964. *The Social System.* New York: Free Press.

(1952a) 1964. "A Sociologist Looks at the Legal Profession." Pp. 370–85 in *Essays in Sociological Theory*. Rev. ed. New York: Free Press.

1952b. "Religious Perspectives in College Teaching: Sociology and Social Psychology." Pp. 286–337 in Hoxie N. Fairchild (Ed.). *Religious Perspectives in College Teaching*. New York: Ronald Press.

(1956) 1962a. "Law and Social Control." Pp. 57–72 in W.M. Evan (Ed.). *Law and Sociology: Exploratory Essays*. New York: Free Press.

(1957) 1960. "The Principal Structures of Community." Pp. 250–79 in *Structure and Process in Modern Societies*. New York: Free Press.

1958a. "Authority, Legitimation, and Political Action." Pp. 197–221 in Carl J. Friedrich (Ed.). *Nomos I: Authority*. Cambridge: Harvard University Press.

(1958b) 1960. "Some Comments on the Pattern of Religious Organization in the United States." Pp. 295–321 in *Structure and Process in Modern Societies*. New York: Free Press.

1962. "Review of Law and Social Process by Hurst." *Journal of the History of Ideas* 27: 558–65.

(1963a) 1969. "On the Concept of Political Power." Pp. 352–404 in *Politics and Social Structure*. New York: Free Press.

(1963b) 1969. "On the Concept of Influence." Pp. 405–38 in *Politics and Social Structure*. New York: Free Press.

(1964a) 1967. "Evolutionary Universals in Sociology." Pp. 500–14 in *Sociological Theory and Modern Society*. New York: Free Press.

1965. "Changing Family Patterns in American Society." Pp. 4–10 in *The American Family in Crisis*, vol. 3. Forest Hospital, Des Plaines, Ill.: Forest Hospital Publications.

(1966a) 1969. "The Political Aspect of Social Structure and Process." Pp. 317–51 in *Politics and Social Structure*. New York: Free Press.

1966b. *Societies: Evolutionary and Comparative Perspectives*. Englewood Cliffs, N.J.: Prentice-Hall.

1966c. "Religion in a Modern Pluralistic Society." *Review of Religious Research* 7: 125–46.

1968a. "Law and Sociology: A Promising Courtship?" Pp. 47–54 in A.E. Sutherland (Ed.). *The Path of the Law from 1967*. Cambridge: Harvard Law School.

(1968b) 1969. "On the Concept of Value Commitments." Pp. 439–72 in *Politics and Social Structure*. New York: Free Press.

1968c. "Order as a Sociological Problem." Pp. 373–84 in Paul G. Kuntz (Ed.). *The Concept of Order*. Seattle: University of Washington Press.

1968d. Introduction to Paperback Edition, *The Structure of Social Action*. New York: Free Press.

1969a. "Polity and Society: Some General Considerations." Pp. 473–522 in *Politics and Social Structure*. New York: Free Press.

(1969b) 1978. "Belief, Unbelief and Disbelief." Pp. 233–63 in *Action Theory and the Human Condition*. New York: Free Press.

(1970a) 1977. "On Building Social System Theory: A Personal History." Pp. 22–76 in *Social Systems and the Evolution of Action Theory*. New York: Free Press.

1970b. "The Impact of Technology on Culture and Emerging New Modes of Behavior." *International Social Science Journal* 22: 607–27.

(1970c) 1977. "Equality and Inequality in Modern Society, or Social Stratification Revisited." Pp. 321–80 in *Social Systems and the Evolution of Action Theory*. New York: Free Press.

1971a. *The System of Modern Societies*. Englewood Cliffs, N.J.: Prentice-Hall.

1971b. "Kinship and the Associational Aspects of Social Structure." Pp. 409–38 in Francis L.K. Hsu (Ed.). *Kinship and Culture*. Chicago: Aldine.

1971c. "The Normal American Family." Pp. 53–66 in Bert N. Adams and Thomas Weirath (Eds.). *Readings on the Sociology of the Family*. Chicago: Markham.

(1972) 1973. "Culture and Social System Revisited." Pp. 33–46 in Louis Schneider and Charles Bonjean (Eds.). *The Idea of Culture in the Social Sciences.* Cambridge: Cambridge University Press.

1973a. "Some Reflections on Post-Industrial Society." *Japanese Sociological Review* 24: 109–113.

(1973b) 1978. "Durkheim on Religion Revisited: Another Look at *The Elementary Forms of the Religious Life."* Pp. 213–32 in *Action Theory and the Human Condition.* New York: Free Press.

1974a. "Comment" [on Turner and Beeghley]. *Sociological Inquiry* 44: 55–7.

1974b. "The Institutional Function in Organization Theory." *Organization and Administrative Science* 5: 3–16.

1974c. "Religion in Post-Industrial America: The Problem of Secularization." *Social Research* 41: 193–225.

1975a. "Comment on [Pope's] 'Parsons' Interpretation of Durkheim' and on [Cohen's] 'Moral Freedom Through Understanding in Durkheim.' " *American Sociological Review* 40: 106–11.

1975b. "On [Cohen, Pope, Hazelrigg's] DeParsonizing Weber." *American Sociological Review* 40: 666–70.

(1975c) 1977. "Some Theoretical Considerations on the Nature and Trends of Change of Ethnicity." Pp. 381–404 in *Social Systems and the Evolution of Action Theory.* New York: Free Press.

1976a. "Reply to Cohen, Hazelrigg and Pope." *American Sociological Review* 41: 361–5.

1976b. "A Few Considerations on the Place of Rationality in Modern Culture and Society."*Revue europeene de sciences sociales et cahiers Vilfredo Pareto* 14.

1977a. "Law as an Intellectual Stepchild." *Sociological Inquiry* 47: 11–58.

1977b. "Comment on Burger's Critique." *American Journal of Sociology* 83: 335–9.

1977c. "General Introduction." Pp. 1–13 in *Social Systems and the Evolution of Action Theory.* New York: Free Press.

1978a. "Comment on R. Stephen Warner's 'Toward a Redefinition of Action Theory: Paying the Cognitive Element Its Due.' " *American Journal of Sociology* 83: 1350–8.

1978b. "A Paradigm of the Human Condition." Pp. 352–433 in *Action Theory and the Human Condition.* New York: Free Press.

Parsons, Talcott, Robert F. Bales, and Edward A. Shils. 1953. *Working Papers in the Theory of Action.* New York: Free Press.

Parsons, Talcott, and Dean R. Gerstein. 1977. "Two Cases of Social Deviances: Addiction to Heroin, Addiction to Power." Pp. 19–57 in Edward Sagarin (Ed.). *Deviance and Social Change.* Beverly Hills: Sage.

Parsons, Talcott, and Gerald M. Platt. 1973. *The American University.* Cambridge: Harvard University Press.

Parsons, Talcott, and Edward A. Shils (Eds.). (1951) 1962. *Towards a General Theory of Action.* New York: Free Press.

Parsons, Talcott, and Neil J. Smelser. (1956) 1965. *Economy and Society.* New York: Free Press.

Pennsylvania Law Review. 1982. Symposium on the Public/Private Distinction. Vol. 130.

Perrow, Charles. 1979. *Complex Organizations: A Critical Essay.* 2d. ed. Glenview, Ill.: Scott, Foresman.

Pike, Fredrick B., and Thomas Stritch (Eds.). 1974. *The New Corporatism.* Notre Dame: University of Notre Dame Press.

Platt, Gerald M. 1981. " 'The American University' Collaboration with Talcott Parsons." *Sociological Inquiry* 51: 155–65.

Polanyi, Karl. (1944) 1963. *The Great Transformation: The Political and Economic Origins of Our Time.* Boston: Beacon.

Pope, Whitney. 1973. "Classic on Classic: Parsons' Interpretation of Durkheim." *American Sociological Review* 38: 399–415.

1975a. "Parsons on Durkheim, Revisited" (Reply to Cohen and Parsons). *American Sociological Review* 40: 111–15.

1975b. "Durkheim as a Functionalist." *Sociological Quarterly* 16: 361–79.

Pope, Whitney, and Jere Cohen. 1978. "On R. Stephen Warner's 'Toward a Redefinition of Action Theory: Paying the Cognitive Element Its Due.' " *American Journal of Sociology* 83: 1359–67.

Pope, Whitney, Jere Cohen, and Lawrence E. Hazelrigg. 1975. "On the Divergence of Weber and Durkheim: A Critique of Parsons' Convergence Thesis." *American Sociological Review* 40: 417–27.

1977. "Reply to Parsons." *American Sociological Review* 42: 809–11.

Popenoe, David. 1988. *Disturbing the Nest: Family Change and Decline in Modern Societies.* New York: Aldine de Gruyter.

Popper, Karl. (1934) 1968. *The Logic of Scientific Discovery.* New York: Harper & Row.

(1962) 1968. *Conjectures and Refutations: The Growth of Scientific Knowledge.* New York: Harper.

Poulantzas, Nicos. 1973. *Political Power and Social Classes.* London: New Left Books.

1974. *Classes in Contemporary Capitalism.* London: New Left Books.

Powell, John Duncan. (1970) 1977. "Peasant Society and Clientelist Politics." Pp. 147–61 in Schmidt, Steffen W., et al (Eds.). *Friends, Followers and Factions.* Berkeley: University of California Press.

Proctor, Ian. 1978. "Parsons' Early Voluntarism." *Sociological Inquiry* 48: 37–48.

Przeworski, Adam. 1985. *Capitalism and Social Democracy.* Cambridge, U.K.: Cambridge University Press.

1986. "Some Problems in the Study of the Transition to Democracy." Pp. 47–63 in O'Donnell, Schmitter, and Whitehead (Eds.). *Transitions from Authoritarian Rule, vol. 4: Comparative Perspectives.* Baltimore: Johns Hopkins.

Przeworski, Adam, and John Sprague. 1986. *Paper Stones: A History of Electoral Socialism.* Chicago: University of Chicago Press.

Purcell, Susan Kaufman, and John F. H. Purcell. 1980. "State and Society in Mexico: Must a Stable Polity Be Institutionalized?" *World Politics* 32: 194–227.

Quadagno, Jill. 1988. *The Transformation of Old Age Security: Class and Politics in the American Welfare State.* Chicago: University of Chicago Press.

1990. "Race, Class, and Gender in the U.S. Welfare State: Nixon's Failed Family Assistance Plan." *American Sociological Review* 55: 11–28.

Radnitzky, Gerard. (1968) 1973. *Contemporary Schools of Metascience.* Chicago: Henry Regnery.

Ridgeway, Cecilia L., and Joseph Berger. 1986. "Expectations, Legitimation, and Dominance Behavior in Task Groups." *American Sociological Review* 51: 603–17.

Rieff, Philip. 1968. *The Triumph of the Therapeutic: Uses of Faith After Freud.* New York: Harper & Row.

Rochberg-Halton, Eugene. 1986. *Meaning and Modernity: Social Theory in the Pragmatic Attitude.* Chicago: University of Chicago Press.

Rocher, Guy. 1975. *Talcott Parsons and American Sociology.* New York: Barnes and Noble.

Roth, Guenther. 1968. "Introduction." Pp. xxvii–civ in Max Weber. *Economy and Society.* New York: Bedminster.

Rosefielde, Steven. 1988. "The Soviet Economy in Crisis: Birman's Cumulative Disequilibrium Hypothesis." *Soviet Studies* 40: 222–44.

Rudolph, Lloyd I., and Susanne Hoeber Rudolph. 1979. "Authority and Power in Bureau-

cratic and Patrimonial Administration: A Revisionist Interpretation of Weber on Bureaucracy." *World Politics* (January) 195–227.

Rueschemeyer, Dietrich. 1986. *Power and the Division of Labour.* Stanford: Stanford University Press.

Sabato, Larry J. 1985. *PAC Power: Inside the World of Political Action Committees.* New York:
Norton.

Sabia, D.R., Jr., and J.T. Wallulis (Eds.). 1983. *Changing Social Science: Critical Theory and
Other Critical Perspectives.* Albany: SUNY Press.

Sartori, Giovanni. (1958) 1962. *Democratic Theory.* New York: Praeger.

Scheff, Thomas J. 1984. "Social Control as a System." Pp. 17–35 in *Being Mentally Ill.* 2d. ed.
New York: Aldine.

1988. "Shame and Conformity: The Deference-Emotion System." *American Sociological
Review* 53: 395–406.

1990. *Microsociology: Discourse, Emotion and Social Structure.* Chicago: University of
Chicago Press.

Schluchter, Wolfgang. 1981. *The Rise of Western Rationalism: Max Weber's Developmental
History.* Berkeley: University of California Press.

Schmidt, Steffen W., et al. (Eds.). 1977. *Friends, Followers and Factions.* Berkeley: University of California Press.

Schmitter, Philippe C. 1971. *Interest Conflict and Political Change in Brazil.* Stanford: Stanford University Press.

1974. "Still the Century of Corporatism?" Pp. 85–131 in Fredrick B. Pike and Thomas
Stritch (Eds.). *The New Corporatism.* Notre Dame: University of Notre Dame Press.

1979. "Modes of Interest Intermediation and Models of Societal Change in Western Europe." Pp. 63–94 in Schmitter and Lehmbruch (Eds.). *Trends Toward Corporatist Intermediation.* Beverly Hills and London: Sage.

1981. "Interest Intermediation and Regime Governability in Contemporary Western Eu-
rope and North America." Pp. 285–327 in Suzanne Berger (Ed.). *Organizing Interests in
Western Europe: Pluralism, Corporatism, and the Transformation of Politics.* Cambridge:
Cambridge University Press.

1982. "Reflections on Where the Theory of Neo-Corporatism Has Gone and Where the
Praxis of Neo-Corporatism May Be Going." Pp. 259–79 in Lehmbruch and Schmitter
(Eds.). *Patterns of Corporatist Policy-Making.* Beverly Hills: Sage.

1983. "Democratic Theory and Neocorporatist Practice." *Social Research* 50: 885–928.

1985. "Neo-Corporatism and the State." Pp. 32–62 in Wyn Grant (Ed.). *The Political
Economy of Corporatism.* Hampshire and London: MacMillan.

1986. "An Introduction to Southern European Transitions from Authoritarian Rule: Italy,
Greece, Portugal, Spain and Turkey." Pp. 3–10 in O'Donnell, Schmitter, and Whitehead
(Eds.). *Transitions from Authoritarian Rule: Prospects for Democracy.* Baltimore: Johns
Hopkins University Press.

In Preparation. "Corporative Democracy: Oxymoronic? Just Plain Moronic? Or a Promising Way Out of the Present Impasse?" Sixty-seven-page manuscript.

Schroyer, Trent. 1973. *The Critique of Domination: The Origins and Development of Critical
Theory.* New York: George Braziller.

Schumpeter, Joseph A. (1942) 1947. *Capitalism, Socialism and Democracy.* 2d. ed. New York:
Harper.

Schwartz, Richard D. 1977. "Social Factors in the Development of Legal Controls: A Case
Study of Two Israeli Settlements." Pp. 579–90 in Lawrence M. Friedman and Stewart
Macauley (Eds.). *Law and the Behavioral Sciences.* 2d. ed. Indianapolis: Bobbs-Merrill.

Sciulli, David. 1984. "Talcott Parsons' Analytical Critique of Marxism's Concept of Alienation." *American Journal of Sociology* (November) 90: 514–40.

1986. "Voluntaristic Action as a Distinct Concept: Theoretical Foundations of Societal Constitutionalism." *American Sociological Review* (December) 51: 743–66.

1988a. "Foundations of Societal Constitutionalism: Principles from the Concepts of Communicative Action and Procedural Legality." *British Journal of Sociology* (Fall) 39: 377–407.

1988b. "Reconsidering Blumer's Corrective Against the Excesses of Functionalism." *Symbolic Interaction* (Spring) 11: 69–84.

1989a. "Analytical Limits of Communicative Action: Two Requirements of Communicative Action and Societal Constitutionalism." Pp. 55–90 in John Wilson (Ed.). *Current Perspectives in Social Theory*, vol. 9. Greenwich, Conn.: JAI Press.

1989b. "Neocorporatism and the Limits of Comparative Political Sociology." Paper presented at Institut International de Sociologie, XXIX International Congress, 12–16 June, Rome, Italy.

1990. "Political Differentiation and Collegial Formations: Implications of Societal Constitutionalism." Jeffrey C. Alexander and Paul B. Colomy (Eds.). *Differentiation Theory: Problems and Prospects*. New York: Columbia University Press.

In Preparation (a). *From Parsons' Functionalism to Societal Constitutionalism: Six Reformulations for a Neofunctionalism*. 10 chapters, 420 pages.

In Preparation (b). Studies in Societal Constitutionalism. 8 chapters.

In Preparation (c). Neocorporatism and Societal Constitutionalism: Limits of Authoritarianism and Democracy. 12 chapters.

Sciulli, David, and Sally Bould. In Preparation. "Neocorporatism, Social Integration, and the Limits of Comparative Political Sociology." 40 pages.

Sciulli, David, and Dean Gerstein. 1985. "Social Theory and Talcott Parsons in the 1980s." *Annual Review of Sociology*, Ralph H. Turner (Ed.), 11: 369–87 (Palo Alto: Annual Review).

Sciulli, David, and Patricia Jenkins. 1990. "Professional By Form and Quality: Professions and the Direction of Social Change." Paper presented at the annual meeting of the American Sociological Association, Washington, D.C.

Scott, James C. (1972) 1977. "Patron-Client Politics and Political Change in Southeast Asia." Pp. 123–46 in Schmidt, Steffen W., et al. (Eds.). *Friends, Followers and Factions*. Berkeley: University of California Press.

Scott, John Finley. 1963. "The Changing Foundations of the Parsonian Action Schema." *American Sociological Review* 28: 716–35.

1971. *Internalization of Norms: A Sociological Theory of Moral Commitment*. Englewood Cliffs, N.J.: Prentice-Hall.

1974. "Interpreting Parsons' Works: A Problem in Method." *Sociological Inquiry* 44: 58–60.

Scott, W. Richard. 1981/1987. *Organizations: Rational, Natural and Open Systems*. 2d. ed. Englewood Cliffs, N.J.: Prentice-Hall.

Selznick, Philip. 1961. "Sociology and Natural Law." *Natural Law Forum* 6: 84.

1969. *Law, Society and Industrial Justice*. New York: Russell Sage Foundation.

1987. "The Idea of a Communitarian Morality." *California Law Review* 75: 445–63.

Sennett, Richard. 1978. *The Fall of Public Man: On the Social Psychology of Capitalism*. New York: Vintage.

Sewell, William H., Jr. 1985. "Ideologies and Social Revolutions: Reflections on the French Case." *Journal of Modern History* 57: 57–85.

Sewell, William, and Robert Hauser. 1975. *Education, Occupation, and Earnings: Achievement in the Early Career*. New York: Academic Press.

Sherman, Lawrence. 1978. *Scandal and Reform: Controlling Police Corruption*. Berkeley: University of California Press.

Shils, Edward A. 1948. "Some Remarks on the 'The Theory of Social and Economic Organization.' " *Economica* 15: 36–50.

Sica, Alan. 1988. *Weber, Irrationality, and Social Order*. Berkeley: University of California Press.

Seidman, Louis Michael. 1987. "Public Principle and Private Choice: The Uneasy Case for a Boundary Maintenance Theory of Constitutional Law." *Yale Law Journal* 96: 1006–59.

Silberman, Charles E. 1978. *Criminal Violence, Criminal Justice.* New York: Random House.

Sirianni, Carmen. 1981. "Production and Power in a Classless Society: A Critical Analysis of the Utopian Dimensions of Marxist Theory." *Socialist Review* 59: 32–82.

Sitton, John F. 1987. "Hannah Arendt's Argument for Council Democracy." *Polity* 20: 80–100.

Skocpol, Theda. 1979. *States and Social Revolutions.* New York: Cambridge University Press.

   1980. "Political Response to Capitalist Crisis: Neo-Marxist Theories of the State and the Case of the New Deal." *Politics and Society* 10: 155–210.

   1985. "Cultural Idioms and Political Ideologies in the Revolutionary Reconstruction of State Power: A Rejoinder to Sewell." *Journal of Modern History* 57: 86–96.

Skocpol, Theda, and Edwin Amenta. 1986. "States and Social Revolutions." *Annual Review of Sociology* 12: 131–57.

Smelser, Neil J. 1962. *Theory of Collective Behavior.* New York: Free Press.

Spitzer, Steven. 1983. "Marxist Perspectives in the Sociology of Law." *Annual Review of Sociology* 9: 103–24.

Stammer, Otto (Ed.). 1965/1972. *Max Weber and Sociology Today.* Oxford: Blackwell.

Stelling, Joan, and Ruee Bucher. 1972. "Autonomy and Monitoring on Hospital Wards." *Sociological Quarterly* 13: 431–46.

Stephens, John D. 1980. *The Transition from Capitalism to Socialism.* Atlantic Highlands, N.J.: Humanities Press.

Stewart, Richard B. 1983. "Regulation in a Liberal State: The Role of Non-Commodity Values." *Yale Law Journal* 92: 1537–90.

   1985. "The Discontents of Legalism: Interest Group Relations in Administrative Regulation." *Wisconsin Law Review* 1985: 655–86.

   1987. "Organizational Jurisprudence" [review of Dan-Cohen] *Harvard Law Review* 101: 371–90.

Stinchcombe, Arthur L. 1986. "Reason and Rationality." *Sociological Theory* 4: 151–66.

Stone, Christopher. 1982. "Corporate Vices and Corporate Virtues: Do Public/Private Distinctions Matter?" *Pennsylvania Law Review* 130: 1441–1508.

Strauss, Anselm. 1978. *Negotiations: Varieties, Contexts, Process and Social Order.* San Francisco: Jossey-Bass.

Strauss, Leo. (1953) 1968. *Natural Right and History.* Chicago: University of Chicago Press.

Streeck, Wolfgang, and Philippe C. Schmitter. 1985. "Community, Market, State – and Associations? The Prospective Contribution of Interest Governance to Social Order." Pp. 1–29 in Streeck and Schmitter (Eds.). *Private Interest Government: Beyond Market and State.* London: Sage.

Stryker, Sheldon. 1980. *Symbolic Interactionism: A Social Structural Version.* Menlo Park, Calif.: Benjamin/Cummings.

Summers, Robert S. 1982. *Instrumentalism and American Legal Theory.* Ithaca, N.Y.: Cornell University Press.

   1984. *Lon L. Fuller.* Stanford: Stanford University Press.

Sunstein, Cass R. 1987. "Constitutionalism After the New Deal." *Harvard Law Review* 101: 421–510.

   1988. "Beyond the Republican Revival." *Yale Law Journal* 97: 1539–90.

Swanson, Guy E. 1953. "*The Approach to a General Theory of Action* by Parsons and Shils." *American Sociological Review* 18: 125–34.

Swidler, Ann. 1986. "Culture in Action: Symbols and Strategies." *American Sociological Review* 51: 273–86.

Szelenyi, Ivan. 1986–7. "The Prospects and Limits of the East European New Class Project:

An Auto-critical Reflection on *The Intellectuals on the Road to Power.*" *Politics & Society* 15: 103–44.

Szelenyi, Ivan, and Bill Martin. 1988. "The Three Waves of New Class Theories." *Theory and Society* 17: 645–67.

Therborn, Goran. 1977. "The Rule of Capital and the Rise of Democracy." *New Left Review* 103: 3–41.

1978. *What Does the Ruling Class Do When It Rules?* London: New Left Books.

1987. "Welfare States and Capitalist Markets." *Acta Sociologica* 30: 237–54.

Thompson, James D. 1967. *Organizations in Action.* New York: McGraw Hill.

Thompson, John B., and David Held (Eds.). 1982. *Habermas: Critical Debates.* Cambridge: MIT Press.

Tilly, Charles. 1975. "Revolutions and Collective Violence." Pp. 483–555 in Fred I. Greenstein and Nelson W. Polsby (Eds.). *Macropolitical Theory.* Reading, Mass.: Addison-Wesley.

1984. *Big Structures, Large Processes, Huge Comparisons.* New York: Russell Sage.

1985. "War Making and State Making as Organized Crime." Pp. 169–91 in Evans, Rueschemeyer, and Skocpol (Eds.). *Bringing the State Back In.* Cambridge, U.K.: Cambridge University Press.

Truman, David. (1951) 1958. *The Governmental Process.* New York: Alfred A. Knopf.

Turkel, Gerald. 1980–1. "Rational Law and Boundary Maintenance: Legitimating the 1971 Lockheed Loan Guarantee." *Law and Society Review* 15: 41–77.

In Preparation. *Between Public and Private: Law, Politics and Social Theory.*

Turner, Jonathan H. 1974. "Parsons as a Symbolic Interactionist: A Comparison of Action and Interaction Theory." *Sociological Inquiry* 44: 283–94.

1988. *A Theory of Social Interaction.* Stanford: Stanford University Press.

Turner, Jonathan H., and L. Beeghley. 1974a. "Current Folklore in the Criticisms of Parsonian Action Theory." *Sociological Inquiry* 44: 47–55.

1974b. "Persistent Issues in Parsonian Action Theory." *Sociological Inquiry* 44: 61–64.

Turner, Jonathan H., and Alexandra Maryanski. 1979. *Functionalism.* Menlo Park, Calif.: Benjamin/Cummings.

Turner, Ralph H., and Lewis M. Killian. (1957) 1987. *Collective Behavior.* 3d. ed. Englewood Cliffs, N.J.: Prentice-Hall.

Unger, Roberto Mangabeira. 1986. *The Critical Legal Studies Movement.* Cambridge: Harvard University Press.

Useem, Michael. 1984. *The Inner Circle. Large Corporations and the Rise of Business Political Activity in the U.S. and U.K.* New York: Oxford University Press.

Vandivier, Kermit. (1972) 1987. "Why Should My Conscience Bother Me?" Pp. 103–23 in David Ermann and Richard J. Lundmann (Eds.). *Corporate and Governmental Deviance.* 3d ed. New York: Oxford.

Vidich, Arthur J., and Stanford M. Lyman. 1985. *American Sociology: Worldly Rejections of Religion and Their Directions.* New Haven and London: Yale University Press.

Vile, M.J.C. 1967. *Constitutionalism and the Separation of Powers.* London: Clarendon

Walker, Henry A., and Bernard P. Cohen. 1985. "Scope Statements: Imperatives for Evaluating Theory." *American Sociological Review* 50: 288–301.

Warner, R. Stephen. 1978. "Toward a Redefinition of Action Theory: Paying the Cognitive Element Its Due." *American Journal of Sociology* 83: 1317–49.

Warren, Roland L. (Ed.). 1977. *New Perspectives on the American Community.* 3d. ed. Chicago: Rand McNally.

Waters, Malcolm. 1989. "Collegiality, Bureaucratization, and Professionalization: A Weberian Analysis." *American Journal of Sociology* 94: 945–72.

Weber, Max. (1914–20) 1968. *Economy and Society: An Outline of Interpretive Sociology,* Guenther Roth and Claus Wittich (Eds.). New York: Bedminster Press.

1958. *From Max Weber,* H.H. Gerth and C. Wright Mills (Eds.). New York: Oxford University Press.

Weil, Frederick D. 1987. "Is/Was There a Legitimation Crisis? New Comparative Evidence." Paper presented at American Sociological Association Annual Meeting, Chicago, Ill.

1989. "The Sources and Structure of Legitimization in Western Democracies." *American Sociological Review* 54: 682–706.

Wellman, Barry. 1983. "Network Analysis: Some Basic Principles." *Sociological Theory* 1983 1: 155–200.

1988. "Structural Analysis: From Method and Metaphor to Theory and Substance." Pp. 19–61 in Wellman and S.D. Berkowitz (Eds.). *Social Structures: A Network Approach.* Cambridge, U.K.: Cambridge University Press.

Wellmer, Albrecht. 1976. "Communications and Emancipation: Reflections on the Linguistic Turn in Critical Theory." Pp. 231–63 in John O'Neill (Ed.). *On Critical Theory.* New York: Seabury.

Whitehead, Alfred North. 1925. *Science and the Modern World.* New York: Macmillan.

Wiarda, Howard J. (Ed.). 1974. *Political and Social Change in Latin America: The Distinct Tradition.* Amherst: University of Massachusetts Press.

Wiley, Norbert. 1979. "Recent Journal Sociology: The Substitution of Method for Theory." *Contemporary Sociology* 8: 793–9.

1987. Critic for Session "Author Meets Critics. Violence and the Nation-State." Paper presented at American Sociological Association Annual Meeting, Chicago, Ill.

Williamson, Oliver E. 1985. *The Economic Institutions of Capitalism.* New York: Free Press.

Winch, Peter. 1958. *The Idea of a Social Science and Its Relation to Philosophy.* London: Routledge, Kegan & Paul.

1970. "Understanding a Primitive Society." Pp. 78–111 in Brian R. Wilson, (Ed.). *Rationality.* Oxford: Basil Blackwell.

Wirth, Louis. 1939. Review of *The Structure of Social Action. American Sociological Review* 4: 399–404.

Wolin, Sheldon. 1960. *Politics and Vision: Continuity and Innovation in Western Political Thought.* Boston: Little Brown.

Wolfe, Alan. 1973. *The Seamy Side of Democracy.* New York: D. McKay.

1977. *The Limits of Legitimacy.* New York: Free Press.

1978. "Has Social Democracy a Future?" *Comparative Politics* 11: 100–25.

Wright, Erik Olin. 1985. *Classes.* London: Verso, New Left Books.

Wrong, Dennis H. 1961. "The Oversocialized Conception of Man in Modern Sociology." *American Sociological Review* 26: 183–93.

Wuthnow, Robert. 1987. *Meaning and Moral Order: Explorations in Cultural Analysis.* Berkeley: University of California Press.

Wynia, Gary W. 1978/1984. *The Politics of Latin American Development.* 2d. ed. Cambridge, U.K.: Cambridge University Press.

Yale Law Journal. 1988. Symposium: The Republican Civic Tradition. Vol. 97.

Young, Crawford. 1976. *The Politics of Cultural Pluralism.* Madison, Wis.: University of Wisconsin Press.

Zald, Mayer N. 1969. "The Power and Functions of Boards of Directors: A Theoretical Synthesis." *American Journal of Sociology* 75: 97–111.

1978. "On the Social Control of Industries." *Social Forces* 57: 79–102.

Zaret, David. 1980. "From Weber to Parsons and Schutz: The Eclipse of History in Modern Social Theory." *American Journal of Sociology* 85: 1180–1201.

Zucker, Lynne G. (Ed.). 1988. *Institutional Patterns and Organizations: Culture and Environment.* Cambridge, Mass.: Ballinger.

Name index

Abbott, Andrew, 54, 167–169, 183, 254, 257, 288n, 305n, 311n, 320n
Abel, Richard L., 286n
Ackerman, Bruce A., 40, 293n, 315n
Adler, Frank, 18
Adorno, Theodor W., 145, 275n
Adriaansens, Hans P. M., 134
Alapuro, Risto, 10, 40
Aleinikoff, T. Alexander, 44, 68, 71, 77, 89, 308n, 313n
Alexander, Jeffrey C., 10, 18, 23, 28, 31, 133–134, 145, 147, 220, 250, 253–254, 269, 279n, 281n–282n, 289n–290n, 292n, 299n–300n, 305n, 308n
Allen, William Sheridan, 216
Althusser, Louis, 32
Amenta, Edwin, 31, 35–36, 278n
Anderson, Charles W., 35, 193, 211, 284n, 311n
Antonio, Robert J., 18, 98, 292n
Apel, Karl-Otto, 99, 128, 292n, 301n, 315n
Archer, Margaret S., 273n, 277n
Arendt, Hannah, 57–58, 200, 222, 248, 258, 279n–280n, 283n, 287n, 297n, 314n–315n, 317n, 321n, 324n
Arrow, Kenneth J., 280n, 285n
Austin, J. L., 102, 290n, 292n

Balbus, Isaac, 275n
Bales, Robert F. See Parsons, Talcott
Barber, Bernard, 18, 159, 253–254, 305n
Barber, Elinor. See Merton, Robert K.
Barry, Brian M., 299n
Battle, John M., 222
Baum, Rainer C. See Loubser, Jan
Baylis, Thomas A., 319n
Beeghley, L., 133–134
Beetham, David, 280n–281n
Bell, Daniel, 34–35, 45, 77, 308n–309n, 315n

Bell, Wendell, 19
Bellah, Robert N., 45, 77, 303n, 308n–309n
Bendix, Reinhard, 9, 34–35, 41, 78, 281n, 315n
Bentley, Arthur F., 67
Berger, Joseph, 23
Berkowitz, S. D., 273n, 317n
Berman, Harold J., 206
Bernstein, Richard J., 104, 292n
Bershady, Harold J., 18, 219, 272n, 299n
Birman, Igor, 222
Black, Donald, 3, 27–28, 31, 94, 111, 278n, 294n–295n, 316n, 323n
Blau, Peter M., 41, 304n
Block, Fred, 31–32, 278n
Bloom, Allan, 17, 78, 146, 178, 247, 272n, 275n, 303n, 307n–308n, 314n, 319n–320n, 322n
Blumer, Herbert, 70, 249, 298n
Bobbio, Norberto, 271n
Bollen, Kenneth A., 194, 297n
Bottomore, Tom, 292n
Bould, Sally, 18, 251
Bourricaud, Francois, 134
Braithwaite, John, 5, 13–14, 19, 25, 78, 183, 189, 274n, 286n–287n, 296n, 310n, 315n, 320n
Bredemeier, Harry C., 299n
Brennan, Geoffrey, 23–24, 31, 44–45, 47, 60, 68–69, 71, 77, 98, 112, 215, 249, 271n, 276n–277n, 279n–280n, 282n–283n, 285n–287n, 291n, 293n–296n, 308n–309n, 313n, 319n, 322n, 323n
Brill, Alida, 60, 69, 286n, 309n
Brooke, James, 310n
Buchanan, James M., 23–24, 31, 41, 44–45, 47, 57, 59–60, 68–69, 71, 73, 77, 98, 112, 169, 209, 215, 222, 249, 271n, 276n–277n, 279n–280n, 282n–283n, 285n–287n, 291n, 293n, 294n–296n, 308n–310n, 313n–314n, 319n, 322n–323n

349

Bucher, Roe, 30, 67
Burawoy, Michael, 34, 310n
Burger, Thomas, 281n, 299n
Burin, F. S., 92
Burnham, Walter Dean, 201
Burt, Ronald S., 31, 194, 273n, 317n
Burton, Michael G. *See* Higley, John

Calabresi, Guido, 293n
Calhoun, John C., 283n
Camic, Charles, 134, 299n
Cancian, Francesca, 299n
Cardoso, Fernando Henrique, 5, 271n
Cawson, Allan, 278n
Chambers, William, 201
Charlton, Joy C., 30
Chomsky, Noam, 102
Clinard, Marshall, 13, 286n, 288n
Cohen, Bernard P., 9
Cohen, Ira, 18, 277n
Cohen, Jean, 281n
Cohen, Jere, 134, 299n
Coke, Edward, 289n
Coleman, James S., 6, 24, 41, 48, 133, 138,
    209, 254, 285n, 296n–297n, 320n
Collins, Hugh, 286n, 294n
Collins, Randall, 1, 4, 15, 28, 54, 98–99,
    169–170, 245, 282n, 291n–293n, 296n,
    306n, 308n, 320n, 322n
Colomy, Paul, 19, 252, 305n
Comte, Auguste, 201
Connor, Walker, 61, 284n
Cook, Karen, 133
Coser, Lewis A., 4
Craib, Ian, 307n
Crane, Diana, 170, 183, 273n
Crozier, Michel, 41

Dahl, Robert A., 63, 278n
Dallmayr, Fred R., 104, 292n, 295n
Damaska, Mirjan R., 286n
D'Antonio, William V., 18, 312n
Davis, F. James, 376n
Deal, Terence E., 306n
DeMott, Deborah A., 122, 159, 166
Diamond, Martin, 317n–318n
Dobbin, Frank R., 313n
Domhoff, G. William, 31–32
dos Santos, Theotonio, 5
Dowd, Jerome, 288n
Downs, Anthony, 313n
Dryzek, John S., 26, 43
Duke, David, 314n
Duncan, Otis Dudley, 304n
Durkheim, Emile, 5, 30, 132, 146, 148–149,
    202, 273n, 298n
Duverger, Maurice, 200

Dworkin, Ronald, 40, 60, 77, 283n, 293n,
    311n
Dynes, Russell, 18
Dynes, Wallace, 19

Edelman, Lauren. *See* Dobbin, Frank R.
Effrat, Andrew. *See* Loubser, Jan
Eisenstadt, S. N., 9, 163
Elkin, Stephen L., 294n
Elster, John, 276n
Ely, John Hart, 40, 49, 68, 77, 287n, 293n,
    308n
Enloe, Cynthia H., 61, 284n
Ermann, David, 274n
Esping-Anderson, Gosta, 10, 175, 278n
Etzioni, Amitai, 26, 28, 41, 272n, 281n,
    309n
Evan, William M., 41, 189–190, 309n, 313n,
    315n
Evans, Peter B., 2, 31, 191, 285n

Factor, Regis A., 281n
Faris, E., 299n
Featherman, David L., 304n
Fellman, David, 60, 286n
Fessler, Daniel Wm., 190, 309n
Finsterbusch, Kurt, 19
Fisk, Winston Mills, 317n–318n
Frankel, Tamar, 159, 166
Freeman, Michael, 307n
Freidson, Eliot, 306n
Freud, Sigmund, 30, 202, 313n
Freund, Julien, 281n
Friedland, Roger, 194
Friedman, Milton, 279n, 306n, 321n
Friedrich, Carl J., 40, 75, 78, 222, 233, 284n,
    291n, 315n
Fulcher, James, 33, 61, 271n
Fuller, Lon L., 16–17, 57, 65, 72, 76, 82,
    87–89, 93–94, 97–98, 105–117, 119–120,
    122–123, 128–129, 131, 150–151, 153,
    156, 196, 288n–293n, 294n–298n, 301n,
    313n, 315n, 318n, 323n

Gadamer, Hans-Georg, 308n, 315n
Gans, Herbert, 15, 32, 304n
Garfinkel, Herbert, 317n–318n
Garson, G. David, 72, 284n
Gellner, Ernest, 163, 304n
Geraets, Theodore F., 292n
Gerstein, Dean R., 18, 133–134, 219, 299n
Gibbs, Jack, 27–28, 31, 136, 278n, 288n,
    294n, 296n, 307n, 323n
Giddens, Anthony, 4, 31, 98, 174, 250,
    273n, 277n–278n, 297n, 310n
Gold, David, 31

Goldfarb, Jeffrey C., 310n
Goldner, F. H., 62, 288n
Goldstein, Herman, 63, 120, 296n
Gouldner, Alvin W., 41, 134, 245, 293n, 315n
Gretzinger, Ralph, 274n–275n
Grey, Thomas C., 92, 290n
Griffiths, John, 28, 278n
Grossman, Joel B., 70

Haar, Charles M., 190, 309n
Habermas, Jürgen, 2, 16–17, 32, 36, 41, 45, 57, 63, 72–73, 75, 78, 88–105, 109–110, 113, 121, 123–126, 128–129, 131, 150–151, 153–154, 156, 159, 185, 200, 210, 222, 226, 234, 236–238, 240, 243, 246, 249, 255–256, 258, 263, 265, 267, 272n, 275n–277n, 281n, 284n, 287n, 289n–294n, 297n, 299n–302n, 307n–310n, 314n–317n, 319n, 323n
Hagopian, Mark N., 284n
Halas, Elzbieta, 19
Hall, John A., 6, 69, 272n, 315n, 322n
Hall, John R., 19
Hammond, Michael, 19
Hannan, John, 307n
Hansen, Roger D., 164
Hao, Pan, 19
Hart, H.L.A., 64, 94, 107, 289n, 293n, 298n, 311n, 323n
Hauser, Robert M., 304n
Hawkins, Keith, 97, 112, 286n, 310n
Hayek, Friedrich A., 44, 57, 113, 222, 279n, 283n, 285n, 287n, 315n, 321n
Hazelrigg, Lawrence E., 134, 299n
Hechter, Michael, 6, 24, 36, 43, 45, 48, 68–69, 98, 133, 138, 202, 208, 215, 243, 254, 272n–273n, 281n, 284n–285n, 289n, 297n, 300n, 313n, 318n
Heinz, John P., 278n
Held, David, 292n
Higley, John, 194
Hobbes, Thomas, 43, 124, 138–139, 279n, 289n, 297n
Hobhouse, L. T., 40
Hoffman, Martin L., 290n
Hollingshead, August B., 288n
Holmes, Oliver Wendell, 64, 92, 107, 290n
Homans, George, 133
Horkheimer, Max, 145, 275n, 316n
Horowitz, Donald L., 68, 287n
Hughes, H. Stuart, 281n
Huntington, Samuel P., 4, 280n
Hurst, John Willard, 187–189, 312n

Jackman, Robert W., 194, 297n
Jacobs, David, 19

Jacobson, David C., 281n
Jaguaribe, Helio, 5
Janowitz, Morris, 28–31, 35, 277n–278n, 297n
Jay, Martin, 41, 291n
Jenkins, J. Craig, 36
Jenkins, Patricia, 19, 168, 305n
Johnson, Harry M., 134

Kalberg, Stephen, 45, 281n, 290n
Kant, Immanuel, 295n
Kaplan, Harold, 299n
Kaplan, Howard B., 23
Katznelson, Ira, 35
Kelsen, Hans, 64, 93–94, 290n, 311n
Kennedy, Michael D., 19, 307n
Kerbo, Harold R., 35
Key, V. O., Jr., 321n
Killian, Lewis M., 36, 249, 321n
Kirchheimer, Otto, 275n
Klockars, Carl B., 19, 119, 315n
Knoke, David, 32, 36, 61, 70–71, 74, 76, 185, 187, 257, 272n–273n, 279n, 285n, 304n, 314n, 318n–321n
Kornhauser, William, 279n
Korpi, Walter, 9, 175, 278n
Kronman, A., 91–94, 281n, 289n–290n, 295n, 297n

Ladd, Everett Carll, Jr., 201
Lakatos, Imre, 128
Larson, Magali Sarfatti, 1, 54, 169
Laumann, Edward O., 32, 36, 61, 70–71, 74, 76, 185, 187, 257, 272n, 273n, 278n–279n, 285n, 304n, 310n, 318n–321n
Law and Contemporary Problems, 119
Lawson, Searle, 274n–275n
Lechner, Frank, 19
Leeds, Anthony, 322n
Lehmbruch, Gerhard. *See* Schmitter, Philippe C.
Leifer, Eric M., 249
Levine, Donald N., 19, 281n, 290n, 315n
Lewis, Roy, 307n
Lidz, Victor M. *See* Loubser, Jan
Lieberson, Stanley, 273n
Lijphart, Arend, 283n–284n
Lindblom, Charles E., 42
Lindsay, A. D., 40
Line, Russell, 275n
Linz, Juan J., 179, 273n
Lipset, Seymour Martin, 9, 34–35, 41, 275n, 322n
Llewellyn, Karl, 107
Lo, Clarence, 31
Locke, John, 279n, 287n, 289n, 294n

Lockwood, David, 277n
Loewenstein, Karl, 40, 315n
Lofquist, William, 19, 274n
Lorrain, Francois, 317n
Loubser, Jan, 134, 147
Lowi, Theodore, 59, 61, 63, 67, 72, 113,
    186, 279n, 283n–284n, 286n–287n, 291n,
    310n, 312n, 315n
Luhmann, Niklas, 4, 32, 62–64, 70, 75, 78,
    89, 94–95, 98, 113, 134, 147, 174, 185,
    192, 211, 220, 223, 271n–272n, 276n–
    278n, 280n, 282n–283n, 285n–286n, 289n,
    291n, 293n–294n, 300n, 303n, 307n–309n,
    314n–317n, 319n–320n
Lukacs, Janos, 41, 124, 294n, 310n
Lukes, Steven, 286n, 294n
Lundman, Richard, 274n
Luttwak, Edward, 278n

MacCormick, Neil, 293n
MacIntyre, Alasdair, 78, 287n, 315n
MacKinnon, Catherine A., 71, 118, 286n,
    322n
Macpherson, C. B., 59, 243, 287n, 290n,
    297n
Madge, Charles, 299n
Madsen, Richard. *See* Bellah, Robert N.
Maines, David R., 30, 42
Mann, Michael, 4, 6, 100
Mannheim, Karl, 41, 215, 291n, 316n
Marcuse, Herbert, 275n, 281n–282n
Marsh, Robert, 19
Marshall, Alfred, 132, 149, 298n
Martin, Bill. *See* Szelenyi, Ivan
Martin, Michael, 293n
Martins, Luciano, 194
Marwell, Gerald, 318n
Marx, Karl, 2, 5, 26, 40, 68, 124, 201, 238,
    278n, 279n, 294n
Maryanski, Alexandra. *See* Turner, Jona-
    than H.
Masters, Roger, 317n
Maude, Angus, 307n
Mayer, John A., 28, 250
Mayhew, Leon H., 134
McAdam, Doug, 36
McCarthy, John D., 18, 36
McCarthy, Thomas, 292n, 299n, 301n
McClosky, Herbert, 60, 69, 286n, 309n
McDonough, Peter, 164, 194, 273n
McNall, Scott, 19
Meador, Daniel John, 116, 286n
Menzies, Ken, 134, 300n
Merry, Sally Engle, 287n
Merryman, John Henry, 286n, 293n, 323n

Merton, Robert K., 4, 19, 41, 215, 253–254,
    271n, 298n, 300n–301n, 322n
Meszaros, Istvan, 78
Meyer, John W., 9, 19, 151, 157, 171–173,
    305n–307n
Meyrowitz, Joshua, 322n
Michelman, Frank, 287n, 313n
Michels, Robert, 41, 202, 279n–280n
Miliband, Ralph, 31
Millar, James R., 311n
Milsom, S.F.C., 233
Mintz, Beth, 31
Mitchell, William C., 299n
Mizruchi, Mark S., 19, 31
Mommsen, Wolfgang J., 280n–281n
Moore, Barrington, 9–10, 34–35, 41, 78,
    310n
Moore, Michael S., 305n
Morris, Aldon D., 36
Mosca, Gaetano, 202
Muir, W. K., 315n
Münch, Richard, 134, 220, 282n, 294n–
    295n, 300n, 305n, 308n
Murphy, Raymond, 1, 15, 28, 54, 282n,
    308n

Nadel, S. F., 273n
Nagel, Ernest, 107, 289n
Nagel, Robert F., 287n
Nedelmann, Birgitta, 18–19
Nelson, Benjamin, 78
Nemedi, Denes, 18
Neumann, Franz, 92, 275n
Nietzsche, Friedrich, 202, 298n, 313n, 320n
Niskanen, William, 313n–314n
Nonet, Philippe, 293n, 295n
Note, 70, 183

Oberschall, Anthony, 36, 273n
O'Connor, James, 31
O'Donnell, Guillermo A., 5, 75, 164, 194,
    318n
Offe, Claus, 160, 304n
Oliver, Pamela E., 318n
Ollman, Bertell, 34
Olson, Mancur, 36, 104, 202, 243, 272n,
    300n, 318n
O'Neill, John, 292n, 299n
Ortega y Gasset, Jose, 279n

Panitch, Leo, 10
Pareto, Vilfredo, 47, 132, 138–139, 146–
    147, 149, 202, 281n, 298n
Parkin, Frank, 1, 15, 28, 282n, 308n
Parsons, Talcott, 4, 16–17, 23, 28–30, 41–

43, 87–88, 90, 95, 98, 108–109, 131–135,
138–140, 145–151, 153–154, 160, 174,
183, 187–189, 214, 217–219, 221–232,
243, 251–259, 269–273n, 276n–277n,
279n–280n, 281n–282n, 286n, 288n–290n,
295n, 298n–302n, 305n, 307n, 308n,
314n–316n, 320n–321n, 324n
Pennsylvania Law Review, 40, 60, 77, 287n
Perrow, Charles, 9, 41, 61
Platt, Gerald M., 28, 183, 253, 269–270,
305n, 315n, 320n, 322n
Polanyi, Karl, 279n–280n
Pope, Whitney, 134, 299n
Popenoe, David, 1, 178, 207, 284n, 297n,
300n, 307n
Popper, Karl, 102, 128, 215, 268, 301n
Poulantzas, Nicos, 32, 41
Pound, Roscoe, 107
Powell, John Duncan, 304n
Prahl, Ralph, 318n
Proctor, Ian, 134
Przeworski, Adam, 10, 34, 64, 176, 178,
271n, 278n, 321n
Purcell, John F. H., 164
Purcell, Susan Kaufman, 164

Quadagno, Jill, 35, 185

Raab, Earl, 275n, 322n
Radnitzky, Gerard, 292n, 301n
Rawls, John, 289n
Ressell, Terence, 19
Rex, John, 4
Rhoades, Gary, 252, 305n
Ridgeway, Cecilia L., 23
Ritti, R. R., 62, 288n
Rochberg-Halton, Eugene, 292n
Rocher, Guy, 299n
Roniger, L., 163
Rosefielde, Steven, 222
Ross, Edward A., 27
Roth, Guenther, 281n
Rousseau, Jean-Jacques, 317n
Rowan, Brian, 9, 151, 157, 306n
Rudolph, Lloyd I., 41
Rudolph, Susanne Hoeber, 41
Rueschmeyer, Dietrich, 2, 31, 285n

Sabato, Larry J., 32
Sabia, D. R., Jr., 292n
Samuelson, Paul, 209
Sanders, Jimy, 194
Sartori, Giovanni, 40, 271n
Scheff, Thomas J., 27, 159, 250, 276n
Schelling, Thomas, 276n

Schluchter, Wolfgang, 42, 78, 279n–281n,
290n, 295n, 315n
Schmidt, Steffen W., 163
Schmitter, Philippe C., 5, 9–10, 36, 61, 73,
75, 175, 178n–179n, 194, 208, 271n, 279n,
284n–285n, 318n
Schroyer, Trent, 292n
Schumpeter, Joseph A., 279n
Schwartz, Michael, 31
Sciulli, David, 17, 31, 34, 109, 139, 168, 200,
219, 227, 251, 272n–273n, 275n, 277n,
279n, 282n–283n, 286n–287n, 289n, 294n,
305n, 314n–315n, 318n, 320n
Scott, James C., 304n
Scott, John Finley, 29, 133–134, 276n, 289n,
296n
Scott, W. Richard, 9, 306n–308n
Selznick, Philip, 41, 189–191, 209, 241,
293n, 295n, 309n–310n, 313n, 315n
Sennett, Richard, 287n, 315n
Sewell, William H., Jr., 279n
Shell, K. L., 92
Sherman, Lawrence, 120
Shils, Edward A., 281n
Sica, Alan, 281n–282n, 293n, 299n, 315n
Siedman, Louis Michael, 77, 313n
Sieyès, Abbé, 317n
Silberman, Charles E., 286n, 310n
Sink, Robert, 274n–275n
Sirianni, Carmen, 34
Sitton, John F., 200
Skocpol, Theda, 2, 9–10, 31, 34–36, 272n,
278n–279n, 285n
Smelser, Neil J., 9, 36, 42, 280n
Smith, Adam, 68, 279n
Soltan, Karol, 19
Sorel, Georges, 202
Spitzer, Steven, 286n, 294n
Sprague, John, 64, 278n
Stammer, Otto, 316n
Stelling, Joan, 30
Stepan, Alfred. See Linz, Juan J.
Stephens, John D., 10, 175, 278n
Stewart, Richard B., 41, 189, 209, 298n,
309n–310n, 312n–313n, 320n
Stinchcombe, Arthur L., 214, 320n
Stone, Christopher, 70, 310n
Strauss, Anselm, 30, 67, 249, 292n
Strauss, Leo, 145–146, 314n
Streeck, Wolfgang, 75, 208
Stritch, Thomas. See Schmitter, Philippe C.
Stryker, Sheldon, 19, 250, 302n
Sullivan, Teresa, 19
Sullivan, William N. See Bellah, Robert N.
Summers, Robert S., 64, 107, 290n, 293n,
297n–298n

Sunstein, Cass R., 287n, 308n, 313n
Swanson, Guy E., 299n
Swidler, Ann, 231, 249

Teixeira, Ruy, 318n
Therborn, Goran, 32, 34, 36, 278n
Thompson, James D., 61
Thompson, John B., 292n
Tilly, Charles, 2–3, 6, 9–10, 32, 34–35, 272n, 297n
Tipton, Steven M. *See* Bellah, Robert N.
Tocqueville, Alexis de, 279n, 317n
Truman, David, 61, 69, 286n
Tuch, Steven A., 312n
Tullock, Gordon, 313n
Turkel, Gerald, 18, 91
Turner, Jonathan H., 30, 36, 133–134, 249, 281n, 289n, 298n, 321n
Turner, Ralph H., 292n
Turner, Stephen P. *See* Factor, Regis A.

Unger, Roberto Mangabeira, 70, 293n, 315n
Useem, Michael, 31–32, 183, 297n

Vandivier, Kermit, 274n–275n
Van Horn, Russell, 274n
Vile, M.J.C., 76, 113, 234, 287n, 315n

Walker, Henry A., 9
Wallace, Ruth, 18
Wallulis, J. T., 292n
Warner, R. Stephen, 19, 134, 254, 276n, 299n
Warren, John, 274n
Warren, Roland L., 137
Waterbury, John, 163

Waters, Malcolm, 52, 282n, 305n–306n, 315n, 319n
Weber, Max, 9, 26, 31, 40–48, 60, 64, 67–68, 76, 81, 88, 90–96, 104, 106, 109, 111, 115, 127, 132, 135, 137–139, 145, 149, 154, 200, 202, 209, 215, 222, 224–226, 231, 238, 278n–281n, 288n–290n, 295n, 297n–298n, 301n, 305n
Weil, Frederick D., 126
Wellman, Barry, 41, 273n, 292n
Wellmer, Albrecht, 98–99
Wells, Richard S., 70
Wessely, Anna, 19
White, Harrison C., 317n
Whitehead, Laurence, 75, 194, 318n
Wiarda, Howard J. *See* Schmitter, Philippe C.
Wiley, Norbert, 297n, 299n
Willer, David, 19, 133
Williamson, Oliver E., 191
Winch, Peter, 216, 299n
Wirth, Louis, 299n
Wolfe, Alan, 35, 275n, 278n
Wolin, Sheldon, 279n, 313n
Wright, Erik Olin, 31, 34
Wrong, Dennis H., 299n, 302n
Wuthnow, Robert, 293n

Yale Law Journal, 40, 71, 77, 200, 233, 271n, 283n, 291n, 303n, 312n–313n, 315n
Yeager, Peter C., 13, 286n, 288n
Young, Crawford, 287n

Zald, Mayer N., 18, 31, 36, 277n
Zaret, David, 281n
Zucker, Lynne G., 9, 306n

Subject index

Actor, definition of, 299n
Affirmative action, 319n–320n
AGIL schema, 87, 307n, 314n
Alienation, 99
 Marx's concept of, 2, 6, 16, 318n
Altruism, 277n
American democracy, realist appraisal of, 72–73. *See also* Pluralism
American politics, substantive drift of, 188
Anachronistic nationalism, 58
Analytical concepts, 219
Analytical distinctions, 218
Anglo-American tradition, analytical restatement of, 191–196
Anomie, 146, 300n
Anticipated reactions, 61
 institutionalization of, 260–265, 284n
Arbitrary government, 62–64, 68–69, 75, 285n, 287n. *See also* Collective power, arbitrary exercise of
 restraints on
  codified in Western tradition, 76
  internal, 189
  internal normative, 72
  internal procedural, 71
  internal substantive, 75–76
  voluntaristic, 198
Argentina, 194
Aspirations. *See also* Morality of aspiration
 public, 116–118, 296n
Authoritarianism, 8, 38–39, 43, 179, 282n
 drift toward. *See* Drift
 elite, 275n
 governmental, 69
 in non-Western nation-states, 15
 political (and social), 43–47
 social, 40–41, 57, 114, 257–259
  external procedural restraints on, 82
 in Western democracy, 13–15, 275n
 working-class, 275n

Authoritarian/nonauthoritarian distinction, 8, 139, 217
Autonomy, Dahl's concept of, 278n
Autopoiesis, 113, 276n–277n, 282n–283n, 289n, 300n, 303n, 308n, 320n
Autorität, 94, 291n

Bastard pragmatism, of interest-group politics, 208, 312n. *See also* Interest-group pluralism
 institutionalization of, 208–209
Behavior. *See also* Collegial form(ation), actors' behavior within and around
 acceptable, 244
 acknowledged ranges of expectations of, 23–24, 110, 156, 211–212, 243–244, 292n, 294n
 altruistic, 277n
 deviant, 23
 economically motivated, limits of, 280n
 subjectively unacceptable, 24
B.F. Goodrich Co., 274n–275n
Bourgeois legality, 123–124
Bourgeois public (sphere), 200, 209–210, 222, 234–239, 310n
Brazil, 194–196, 310n
Bribery, 244
Bureaucratization, 42–44, 46, 137, 163, 201
 restraints on, 145–148

Capitalism
 and inadvertent social control, 32–33
 institutional, 278n
 and purposeful social control, 31–32
 reform and, 33
Charismatic leadership, 43
Citizenship, criteria for, 79, 287n
Civil law, 293n, 323n
Civil religion, 44–45, 49, 77, 280n, 282n, 287n, 308n–309n
Clientelism, 163, 201, 304n

Coercion, 23–24, 126, 276n
  latent, 31, 35
  legal, 91
Coercive control, 28–29
Coercive order, law as, 290n
Cognitive contributions, of individual professionals and deliberators, 254–257
Cognitive rationality, 269, 320n
Collective action, 317n
Collective force, legitimate vs. illegitimate
  uses of, 3, 272n, 297n
Collective power
  abuses of, restraints on, 15
  arbitrary exercise of, 239–241, 303n. *See
    also* Arbitrary government
  in civil society, 13
  inadvertant, 110
  by private enterprise, 41, 76
  purposeful, 62–64, 109–110, 187, 189–
    205
  exercise of, 15–16
  predictability of, 280n
  innovative exercise of, 43
  purposeful exercise of, 59, 72, 121
Collectivities, self-regulation of, 29–31
Collegial form(ation), 17, 77, 82, 87, 90,
    114, 121–122, 128–130, 143, 159–
    160, 164–170, 209–210, 220–221,
    228, 232, 259, 292n, 294n
  actors' behavior within and around, 153,
    160–161
  availability for transfer or generalizability,
    233
  characteristics of, 240
  compared to constituent group, 233–241
  contingency of, qualities and, 169–170
  and contingency of qualities, 167
  contribution to scholarly context of re-
    search, 267
  current status and future prospects, 242–
    270
  definition of, 80, 164
    in residual terms, 160–162
  and direction of social change, 8, 153–154
  distinctiveness of, 80–81, 167
  distribution of, 183
  divisional, 157, 260–263
  encroachments against, 165–167, 178, 306n
  and group competition and potential con-
    flict, 244–246
  historical decline of, 197, 199–202
  institutionalization of, 173
    as public policy, 205–213
  as institutionalized restraint beyond left
    and right, 254–266
  integrity of, 170, 178, 183, 260, 306n,
    311n

  and public policy, 178
  interrelationship with threshold of inter-
    pretability, 129
  invariant impact and permanent presence
    of, 239–241
  links to social power, 242–254
  local negotiations of meaning within, 249–
    250
  loss of qualities, implications of, 167–169
  and middle-class sensibilities, 246–249,
    319n
  orienting hypothesis regarding, 175
  and possessive individualism, 242–243
  sectoral, 157, 260–263, 321n
  sites of, 129
  social bases for, 187
  and social order, 243–254
  and social stratification, 243–254
  subtle restraint by, 255–257
  support from public policy, 178, 183–184,
    205–213, 221–222, 257
  unwitting beneficiaries of, 266–270
  voluntaristic orientation of, 166, 205–206,
    242–248, 262
Common-law theory, 16, 65–66
Common-law tradition, 124, 293n–294n,
    297n, 323n
Communication
  nondistorted, 100
  quality of, 102
  systematic distortion of, 32, 276n, 278n
Communication communities, 100–101,
    291n
Communication theory, 125
  Habermas's, 2, 16, 88, 101, 109, 121, 128,
    276n, 289n, 292n–293n, 295n, 297n,
    319n
Communicative action, 2, 6, 96–106, 121,
    124–125, 151–152, 284n
  in courtrooms, 124
Communism, 99
Communitarian morality, 209, 309n, 313n
Comparative research
  beyond left and right, 175–179
  beyond presupposition of exhausted possi-
    bilities, 179–180
  limits of, 1–10
  proposals for, 175–180
  and reasoned social action, 220–221
Comparativism, 9–10
  and collective prejudice of presupposition
    of exhausted possibilities, 14
Competition, 209, 302n
  group, in collegial social order, 244–247,
    319n
Compliance theory, 26
Concordance, Gibbs's criterion of, 307n

Concurrent majority, 283n
Conflict, 209
    in collegial social order, 244–246
Conflict theory, 28, 99
Consciousness communities, 291n–292n,
    320n
Consensus, 246
    and collegiality, 319n
Consensus theory of truth, 101–102, 105,
    159, 268, 307n, 323n
    vs. societal constitutionalism, 243–249
Consociational democracy, 283n–284n
Constituent force, 68–69, 202, 222, 285n–
    286n, 301n, 321n
    vs. constituent group, 233–239
Constituent group, 232–233
    characteristics of, 239
    compared to collegial formations, 233–
    241
    vs. constituent force, 233–239
    restricted impact and temporary presence
    of, 233–239
Constitution (U.S.), framing of, 317n
Constitutional economics, 44, 48, 277n,
    282n, 285n–287n, 295n–296n, 323n
Constitutional theorists, 40–41, 279n
Consumerism, 242–244
Contractarian vision, 283n, 285n
Copy theory of truth, 99, 101–102, 104, 128,
    159, 289n
Corporate crime, 5, 13–14, 274n, 288n
Corporatism, 179
Council system, 200
Coup d'état, 278n
Credentialling, 245, 306n, 322n
Criminal law, 117
Critical Legal Studies movement, 77
Cultural diversity, 273n
Culture of evasion, 119–120, 296n

Decision-making processes, 280n–281n
Deliberative bodies, rise and decline of,
    within civil society, 200
Demagogues, 125
Democracy, 323n–324n. *See also*
    Consociational democracy; Liberal
    democracy; Social democracy; West-
    ern democracy
    and integrity of scientific research, 322n
    nonliberal, 10
    possibilities for, 178
Democracy/authoritarianism distinction, 8
Democratization, 191, 200–201, 205, 209–
    210, 302n–303n
Dependencia, 1, 271n
Depth hermeneutics, 103
Diagnosis, 167

Directionality, 214, 224
    Parsons's concept of, 188–189
Discourse
    artificially protected arenas of, 103, 293n
    symmetry-requirement of, 103
    voluntaristic qualities of, 292n
Division of powers, 59–60, 62, 73, 75, 189,
    261, 287n, 311n
Domestic policy-making, 62–63
Domination, 94, 277n
    legitimacy of, Weber's definition of, 91
    rational-legal, 91, 95–96
Drift, 41–43, 64, 70, 78–79, 90, 96, 98, 109–
    110, 114, 147, 280n, 287n, 314n
    liberal-democratic institutions as accom-
    plices in, 60
    macrosociological, 82
    manifestations of, 42–43
    microsociological, 82
    negative implications of, 57
    problem of, 43–44
    problem of recognizing, 187–189
    restraints on, 43–45, 55, 131, 145–148,
    210–211
        external, 164
        external procedural, 79–81, 287n
        institutionalization of, 151, 153
        as intrinsically unreasoned, 224–228
        voluntaristic action as, 144–145
    theorists' complicity in, 222–224
    unmediated, 45–46
Drift/direction distinction, 187–189, 217–
    218, 221
Due process, 295n
    norms of, 71, 286n
Duties of law, 295n
Duties of virtue, 295n
Duty. *See also* Morality of duty; Social du-
    ties
    vs. aspiration, 117–118

Eastern bloc, 4–5
    civil law systems in, 116
    collegial formations in, 176, 307n–308n,
    310n
    conflict and struggles within, as policy de-
    bates, 35–36
    developments in civil society vs. develop-
    ments in state, 310n
    workers' movements within, 307n
Economic individualism, 290n
Egalitarianism, 38
Elected officials, 211, 314n
Elections, 59–67, 278n, 283n, 321n
    in Latin America, 193
    strategic nature of, 60, 284n

Electoral participation, 312n
  in United States, 201, 312n
Elite consensus, within United States, 318n
Elite interest group pluralism, 314n
Elite pacts, 75, 194, 318n
Elite solidarity, 31–32
Elitism, 61
Empirical research
  conceptual grounding of, 2–3, 271n
  resource mobilization approach to, 36,
    204
Empirical study, in social sciences, 306n–
    307n
Energy-policy domain, 320n
Entropy, 225
  law of, 280n, 282n
Ethics, 298n
Ethnic communalism, resilience of, in Third
    World, 61
Ethnic groups, 292n
Exchange theory, 174, 317n
Expert occupations, 170, 306n
Exploitation, 277n
External normative restraints, on interest
    competition, 46–51, 282n
External procedural restraints, 55, 140, 224,
    226–227
  conceptual grounding, 79–81
  on drift, 287n
    invariant impact of, 79–81
  importance of, 56–59, 151–152
  on inadvertent or systemic exercises of col-
    lective power, 55–56, 187
  indirect effects, 283n
  institutionalization of, 79–83, 90, 122, 221
  institutionalized, threshold of, 153
  institutionalized by collegial formations,
    232–233
  vs. internal procedural restraints, 81–83
  normative or nonrational status of, 79
  qualities of, 79
  on social authoritarianism, 82
  substantive effects, 283n
  voluntaristic status of, 90, 202–205
  and wasted time and space, 211–213
External restraints, 56, 58. *See also* External
    normative restraints; External proce-
    dural restraints; External substantive
    restraints
  on bureaucratization and drift, 145–148
  on drift, 164
  on inadvertent exercises of collective
    power, 55
  institutions and norms of, 55, 77–83
External substantive restraints, 224, 303n
  on inadvertent or systemic exercises of col-
    lective power, 55–56

  institutions of, 77–79
  vs. internal, 224

Factions, 42–43
Falsification, 301n
Feminism, 71, 286n
Fiduciary relations, 159
Force. *See also* Collective force
Formal rationality, 315n
Fragmentation of meaning, in modernity,
    41–43, 45, 51–52, 54, 67, 70, 78, 96,
    98, 109, 147, 283n
Frankfurt school, 5, 41, 92, 272n, 276n,
    282n, 291n, 315n
  rejection of presupposition of exhausted
    possibilities, 272n
Free-rider problem, 243, 272n
Functional differentiation, 55, 67, 70, 98,
    280n, 283n, 314n
Functionalism, 16, 174, 273n, 301n

Good life, 116
Governmental constitutionalism, 75, 291n
  agent of change for, 233
  institutions of, 73
  vs. societal constitutionalism, 57, 232–233
Governmental power, proscriptions on, 59–
    62, 70, 78. *See also* Division of powers
Great Britain, legal system of, 116, 295n
Group competition, 60–64

Health-care professionals, strikes, 250–251,
    255, 319n
Health-policy domain, 250–251, 320n
Herrschaft, 94, 291n
Hobbesian problem of order, 41, 47
Hobbesians, 285n
Homo economicus, 45, 59, 67, 252–253,
    277n, 280n, 283n

Ideal speech situation, 101–105, 246, 291n–
    292n
Ideal types, 218
Impossibility theorem, 280n, 285n
India, 310n
Industrialization, 202
  social implications of, 40
  social theorists' analyses of, 40
Industrial justice, 309n, 313n
Institutional capitalism, 278n
Institutional forms, 285n
Instrumental action, 51, 284n
Instrumental calculation, 42, 281n
Instrumental rationality, 281n
Instrumental theorists, 32
Instrumental versus ritualistic societies, Mer-
    ton's polar types of, 300n

Integration, 223. *See also* Social integration; System integration
Intellectuals, 324n
  cooptation and marginalization of, 268–279
Interactionism, 30–31, 69–70, 286n
Interaction ritual chain theory, 296n
Interest competition, 42, 44–45, 47–48, 59–60, 67, 72, 190, 257, 283n. *See also* Bastard pragmatism, of interest-group politics
  contribution to democracy, 70, 286n
  external normative restraints on, 46–51, 282n
  pluralists' concept of importance of, 68–70
  strategic nature of, 60–64
Interest-group pluralism, 188, 284n
  drift of, 312n
Interest group politics, in United States, criticisms of, 1
Intermediation, neocorporatist, 74–75
Internal labor markets, 208
  within corporations, 313n
Internal normative restraints, 60
  on arbitrary government, 72
  procedural, 58, 64–67
  substantive, 60–64
Internal procedural restraints, 55, 121, 166
  on arbitrary government, 71
  contingency of, on government, 197–199
  extension from government to civil society, 204
  vs. external procedural restraints, 81–83
  on government vs. private enterprise, 189–191
  Habermas's oversight of, 123–126
  indirect effects, 283n
  institutionalization of, 125–126
  institutions of, 64–67
  integrity of, 231–232
  normative, 58, 64–67
  organizational expression of, 159–164
  proliferation of, 199
  and purposeful arbitrariness, 189–205
  on purposeful exercises of collective power, 55–56, 123, 154
    by private enterprise, 189
  strategic, 58, 64–67
  substantive effects, 283n
  threshold of interpretability, 111, 124–126, 154–159
    grounding against normative relativism, 156, 159
    irreducible nature of, 156, 158–159
    voluntaristic nature of, 156–158
  as voluntaristic action, 196–202

Internal restraints, 58. *See also* Internal normative restraints; Internal procedural restraints; Internal substantive restraints; Procedural mediation
  contemporary crisis of, 67–72
  directly substantive, 60
  institutions and norms of, 55, 59–77
  on purposeful exercises of collective power, 55, 59
  strategic, 60
Internal substantive restraints
  on arbitrary government, 75–76
  institutions of, 60–64
  on purposeful exercises of collective power, 55–56
  strategic, 60–64
International Journal of Ethics, 298n
Intersubjective interests, 209, 313n
Intrinsic means-end schema, 134–135
Irrational action, 281n–282n

Japan, internal labor market in, 208
Judicial review, 59
Juridical democracy, 286n
Juridification, 290n

Labor mobilization, 61
Labor-movement theory, 33, 175
Lacuna of integrative possibilities, 2–3, 5, 37, 54, 69, 272n, 308n
Latin America, 1, 193–194
  conflict and struggles within, as policy debates, 35–36
Law, 276n
  as coercive order, 290n
  formalization of, 93, 290n
  formally rational, 93, 290n
  formal-rational, 290n
  internal morality of, 295n
  Luhmann's view of, 316n
  Marxism's treatment of, 71, 115, 286n, 294n
  objectivist epistemology of, 286n
  procedural integrity of, 115
  rational, 92, 289n
  Weberians' views of, 71, 286n
  Weber's definition of, 90–91
Law and Economics movement, 77, 287n
Law enforcement, 64–67, 227, 316n
  effectiveness of, 109, 120, 122
    indices of, 111
  by specialized enforcers, 110–111
Lawfulness, Fuller's standard of, 294n
Law journals, 40
Lawless/lawful distinction, Fuller's, 109, 294n
Law of entropy, 280n, 282n

Laws, positive, 95, 115. *See also* Procedural threshold of interpretability of positive laws
  arbitrary, 110
  enforcement, 109
  rationalization of, 94
Lebenswelt, 229–230
Legal formalism, 107
Legal interpretation, 64–67
Legalism, 92
Legal positivism, 88–96, 107, 117, 289n
  Fuller's alternative to, 115–116
Legal procedures, as secondary traditionalism, 94–95
Legal realism, 107–108
Legal system
  dual sovereignty in, 285n
  social interactions underlying, 107–108
Legal theory, 311n
  Fuller's, 87–89, 105–110, 128, 151, 293n, 295n
  Hart's, 107, 293n
  Parsons's, 295n, 301n
Legitimacy, 95–96
Legitimation, concept of, 91–92
Legitimation crisis, 76, 92, 105, 126, 290n
Liberal democracy, 43, 310n. *See also* Western democracy
  institutions and practices of, 1–2, 271n
Liberal democratization, individuals' vs. groups' political inclusion in, 303n–304n
Liberalism, criticisms of, 114–115
Liberalization, 191, 200, 205, 209
Liberal theorists, 40–41, 279n
Liberal theory, and pluralist theory, 68–69
Lived social fabrics, 229–230
Lockean liberal tradition, 40–41, 43–44, 46–48, 280n, 282n, 285n

Magic, 141
Majority rule, 160–161, 302n–303n, 324n
Manipulation, 31, 35, 50, 276n, 282n
Market, hidden hand of, 46, 282n
Market economy, 115, 222, 242
Market society, 40–41, 43
Marxism, 15–16, 31, 33–34, 36, 41, 71, 92, 104, 133
  criticisms of, 114–115
  structuralist, 5
  as tradition of theory and research, 33–34
  treatment of law, 71, 115, 286n, 294n
  treatment of morality, 71, 286n
Mass society, 41
Media
  in nation-states that lack collegial formations, 321n–322n

regulation of, 309n
Meta-rules, 286n, 291n, 294n, 319n
Metering, 284n, 297n
Methodologists, 17–18
Modernization, 280n
  nonauthoritarian response to, 45. *See also* Social change, nonauthoritarian direction of
Modernization theory, 4, 272n
Monopolist theory, 168–169
Monopoly, 306n
Moral authorities, 140, 257–259
Morality, 115–116
  Fuller's concept of, 117
  Marxists' treatment of, 71, 286n
Morality of aspiration, 116
Morality of duty, 116–117
  vs. morality of aspiration, 294n
Moral theory, substantive, 295n
Motivation crisis, 290n

Nation-states
  ethnically, religiously, or regionally divided, 283n
  modern
    authoritarian vs. nonauthoritarian, 46
    bureaucratized vs. nonbureaucratized, 46
    totalitarian, 284n
Natural law, 115, 295n, 313n
  criticisms of, 114–115
  rational, 123
  substantive norms of, 78
Natural rights, 47, 57, 60–64, 66, 73–74, 123, 189–191, 198, 210, 261, 283n, 309n, 311n
Nazism, Merton's criticisms of, 322n–323n
Negotiated order, 30
Neighborhood, 137–138, 142–143
Neocorporatism, 5, 10, 61, 175, 179, 271n, 279n, 283n–284n
  criticisms of, 1
  European, 73–75
  informal, in United States, 314n
  societal, 179–180
  societal and state, 285n
  state, 179–180
Neo-Marxism, 6, 92, 98–99, 124, 126
Neopositivism, 101, 128, 289n
  criticisms of, 101, 292n
  Habermas's critique of, 291n
Network analysis, 174, 273n
Newspapers, in nation-states that lack collegial formations, 321n–322n
Nihilism, 216, 314n
  of contemporary social science, 323n
Noncommodity values, 209, 298n, 313n, 320n

Nonrational action, 132–133
and transcendental ends, 139–140
Nonrational realm, 140–141
Normative action, 225
vs. voluntaristic action, 144
Normative breakdown, 146
Normative mediation. *See also* Interest-group pluralism
Normative orientations, 213, 295n
encroachments against, 302n
institutionalization of, 301n
vs. normative motivations, 158, 301n–302n
of rule-making body, 120–121, 296n
Normative relativism, 2–3, 6, 108–109, 115, 127, 224
Normative restraints, 186, 220, 223. *See also* External normative restraints; Internal normative restraints
directly substantive, 55–56
external to systemic drift, 131
pluralism's critique of, 67–72
substantive, 55–56, 60–64, 225
Normative sociology, 295n
Normative theory, 108, 294n
Nuclear family, 300n

Organizational constitutionalism, 309n, 313n
Organizational forms, 162–164, 210. *See also* Collegial form(ation); Patron-client networks
bureaucratic, 163, 168, 247, 319n
democratic, 160, 163, 168, 247, 319n
Parsons's typology of, 302n
Organizational interest representation, 309n
Organizational jurisprudence, 309n
Organizational pluralism, 309n
Organizations literature, five empirical issues for, 172–173
Organizations research, 41
proposals for, 171–175

Parent-child relationship, 218
Parliamentary democracy, Weber's views on, 280n
Parsonian Dilemma, 228
Party machines, 201
Patron-client networks, 59, 163, 168, 194, 205, 292n, 296n, 302n–304n, 319n
in Brazil, 194–195
in intellectuals' institutionalized environments, 269
Peak associations, 205, 261, 284n
effects of, on Western democratic institutions, 74
intermediation, 74

leaders of, 73–74
neocorporatist, 5, 59, 73–75, 271n
Peer review, 268
Pluralism, 179, 191, 286n, 312n. *See also* Interest-group pluralism; Organizational pluralism
American, 310n
criticisms of, 271n
critique of normative restraints, 67–72
as critique of Western institutions and traditions, 72–73
Pluralist interest groups, 59
Pluralist theory, 44, 61, 272n, 283n, 285n, 311–312
and liberal theory, 68–69
postwar, 284n–285n
Political machine, 210
Political parties, 59–60
mass, 210
rise of, 200–202
Political sociology
conceptual limitations in, 33–37
critical, 35–36, 278n
postwar concerns of, 41
social control in, 30–33
Political system, definition of, 276n
Political theory, 40, 279n
Positivism, 102, 266–268, 292n, 306n–307n, 323n. *See also* Legal positivism
Habermas's critique of, 88–89, 289n
Possessive individualism, 244, 287n
and collegial form, 242–243
Postmodernism, 98
Power. *See also* Collective power; Governmental power
arbitrary, 13. *See also* Arbitrary government; Collective power, arbitrary exercise of
Power holders, anticipation of challenges to actions and proposals. *See* Anticipated reactions
Pragmatism, 98, 292n
Prayer in public schools, 70
Precommitment, 276n
Prejudice, 225–226, 315n
Press, freedom of, 261, 309n
Presupposition of exhausted possibilities, 2–3, 7, 36, 69, 98, 108, 126–128, 158–159, 175, 204–205, 214–215, 217, 219, 226, 231–232, 272n, 294n, 308n, 310n
as collective prejudice, 3–4
comparative research beyond, 179–180
conceptual alternative to, 2
and conceptual limitations in research, 10
Frankfurt school's rejection of, 272n
institutionalization of, 4

Presupposition of exhausted possibilities (*cont.*)
  as normative generalization, 5
Private property, 258, 314n
Private/public distinction, 57, 62, 68, 70, 74–75, 207, 239, 258, 321n
Procedural aspiration, 129
Procedural duty, 129
Procedural legality, 87, 122–123
  Fuller's principles of, 288n
  as irreducible threshold, 109–121
Procedural mediation, 55–56, 60, 96–97, 99, 283n
Procedural norms and institutions, importance of, 150, 301n
Procedural reason, 16–17, 88–89, 96–106, 123–128, 258
  purposive rationality and, 96–99
Procedural restraints. *See also* External procedural restraints; Internal procedural restraints
  extension of, from government to civil society, 208–211
  in system of shared social duties, 112–113
Procedural threshold of interpretability of positive laws, 60, 64–67, 72, 76, 82, 105–106, 113, 284n, 291n
  Fuller's concept of, 16–17, 110, 151, 293n
  relationship to procedural grounding, 121, 126–128
Professional-client relationship, 218
Professional integrity, 51–53, 66, 252–253
  normative standards of, 54
Professionals. *See also* Health-care professionals
Professions, 288n–289n, 291n–292n
  Alexander's view of, 253–254
  within authoritarian social orders, 259
  Barber's view of, 253–254
  collegial formations in, 311n
  criticisms of, 1
  form of organization distinctive to, 305n–306n
  integrity of, 305n
  Merton's view of, 253–254
  Parsons's treatment of, 227, 253–254, 320n
Protected spheres, 203, 207–210, 212, 223, 241, 258–259
  within civil society, 166, 169–170
Protocol statements, 102
Psychoanalysis, 103
Public choice, 36
Public-choice theory, 174, 204, 313n–314n
Public interest, 234
Public opinion, 238, 258, 261–262, 321n
Public policy, voluntaristic, 207

Public realm, 257, 264, 304n, 322n
  within civil society, 240–241
  institutionalization of, 222
Purposive-rational action, 44–45, 281n, 284n. *See also* Rationalization
  conceptual limitation of, 138–139
  and survey research, 136–137
  Weber's standard of, 91–92

Rape laws, 286n
Rational action, 51, 135, 214, 314n
  quantifiable ends, 136
  standard of, narrowness of, 51
Rational-choice theory, 6, 36, 48, 174, 204, 272n, 279n, 281n, 296n–297n, 313n, 317n
Rationality. *See also* Formal rationality; Substantive rationality
  vs. reason, 214
  Weber's concept of, 93, 290n
Rationalization, 280n. *See also* Purposive-rational action
  drift of, 64. *See also* Drift
  entropic drift of, 272n
  implications of, 41–43
  response to systemic pressures of, 202
  systemic pressures of, 46
  unmediated drift as, 45–46
Rationalized myths, Meyer's concept of, 171–172
Rational-legal, 109, 295n
  Weber's concept of, 289n
Rational means-end schema, 160
Rational realm, 140–141
Realism, 102
Reason
  intersubjective standard of, 324n
  objective or substantive standard of, 96
  Parsons's concept of, 255
  procedural turn to, 99–101
  vs. rationality, 214
  as social influence, 257
Reasoned authority, concept of, 291n
Reasoned social action, 97–98, 214–215, 217, 222, 256
  and comparative research, 220–221
Reciprocity, 293n
Reform politics, rise of, 201
Relativism, of contemporary social science, 323n
Religion, 313n. *See also* Civil religion; Protected spheres; Separation of church and state
  state, 79, 118
  substantive norms of, 78
Republican civic tradition, 200, 312n
Republicanism, 233, 303n

Research. *See also* Comparative research;
  Empirical research; Organizations
  research; Scientific research; Survey
  research
  and collective prejudice, 8–10
  conceptual framework in, 10–11
  context of, and organizational forms, 267
  Marxism and, 33–34
Research enterprise, characterization of,
  267–268
Resource mobilization, approach to empiri-
  cal research, 36, 204
Resources, competition over, 23, 276n, 287n
Revolution, 294n
Ritual behavior, 139–140
Rule-making body, normative orientation
  of, 120–121, 296n
Rule of law, 208, 313n, 321n
  institutionalization of, 208–209
Rules of the game, 68, 286n, 291n

Sacred qualities, 142–143, 300n
Savings and loan scandal, 308n
Scandinavia, 5, 175
  neocorporatism in, 73–75
  social democracy in, 1, 271n
Scientific research, 267
  integrity of, and democracy, 322n
Selective enforcement, 119–120, 296n
Self-despontaneification, 276n
Self-interest, 277n. *See also* Interest competi-
  tion
Self-restriction, 24–25, 50, 282n
  cognitive, 25, 276n
  unnecessary, 25–27, 110
Separation of church and state, 60, 62, 73,
  284n
Shaming, 310n
  reintegrative, Braithwaite's theory of, 296n
Small-town values, 308n
Smithean complacency, 279n–280n
Social action
  irrational, 281n–282n
  nonrational, 281n–282n
  reasoned, 97–98, 214–215, 217, 222, 256
    and comparative research, 220–221
  Weber's concepts of, 9
Social authoritarianism, 40–41
Social capital, 209, 256, 296n–297n, 320n–
  321n
Social change
  direction of, 7–8, 56–57, 105, 187–189,
    274n, 288n. *See also* Drift/direction
    distinction
    and collegial formations, 77
  drift of. *See* Drift
  nonauthoritarian direction of, 122, 140,
    148, 257–259, 261

institutionalization of, 153
  prospects for, 15, 36, 46, 48–51, 72–73
  social infrastructure of, 14–15, 37–39,
    49, 69, 77, 127, 163–164, 207, 236, 262
  systemic pressures of, 40, 279n
Social closure, 54, 305n–306n, 308n
  theories of, 282n
Social control, 8, 216, 272n. *See also* Social
    integration/social control distinction
  American literature of, 27–33, 37
  Black's approach to, 323n
  definition of, 276n, 288n
  excessive, 28
  formal, 42–44
  inadvertent, 27, 37, 294n
    capitalism as mechanism of, 32–33
    influentials' competition as mechanism
      of, 33
  informal, 24–26, 29, 43, 276n, 287n
  institutional or systemic, 25–26, 29, 31, 276n
  internalized mechanisms of, 308n
  Janowitz's concept of, 28–30
  in literature, 27–33
  mechanisms of, 24, 27, 41, 250, 316n
  purposeful, 27, 31, 37–38, 94, 114, 279n
    capitalist state as instrument of, 31–32
  rational, 294n
  restraints on, 37–38
  in social theory and political sociology,
    30–33
  systemic, 69
  third parties in, 278n
  voluntary, 279n, 282n
Social democracy, 34, 61
  criticisms of, 1
  institutions and practices of, 271n
  in Scandinavia, 1, 271n
Social duties, 25
  as optional performances, 117–118
  overextension of, 117–119
  shared, 25, 37, 60, 64–67, 110, 112, 117
    clarity, 112
    congruence, 113
    constancy, 113
    evasion of, 119–120
    generality, 112
    interpretability, 93
    noncontradiction, 112–113
    possibility, 113
    procedural restraints on, 112–113
    promulgation, 112
    prospectivity, 112
    recognition and understanding of, 297n
    retroactive enactments of, 112
    threshold of interpretability, 113, 156,
      243, 266
    threshold restraints, 113
    voluntaristic nature of, 156–159

Social integration, 143, 150–159, 273n
  concept of, 5–8
    definition of, 28–30
    implications of, 37–39
  definition of, 83–84, 272n, 288n
  heterogeneous actors' and competing
    groups', 27–28, 30, 36–39, 140
  nonliberal or nonmarket, 128–129, 298n
  possibilities for, 187, 206–207, 220, 248–
    249, 258
  specifying, 154
  vs. system integration, 277n
  voluntaristic, 294n
Social integration/social control distinction,
    3, 6–7, 10, 27–28, 51–54, 56–57, 67,
    111–114, 124, 139, 158, 189, 252,
    272n, 320n
Social movements, heterogeneous actors'
    and competing groups' integration
    within, 36–39
Social order, 6, 174, 243, 246–247, 254,
    273n, 300n
  authoritarian, 259
    vs. nonauthoritarian, 295n
  and cognitive limitations, 25–26
  and collegial form, 243–254
  within collegial formations, 243–246
  definition of, 23
  legitimacy of, 31, 278n
  Lockean, 132
  nonauthoritarian, 114, 147–148, 259
    foundation of, 263–266
    infrastructure of, 260–263
    power holders in, anticipation of chal-
      lenges. *See* Anticipated reactions
    social infrastructure of, 187, 321n
  problem of, 243
  relativist definition of, 23–24
  spectrum of types of, 177–178
Social sciences, 50
  accession to relativism and subjectivism,
    98
  and critical theory, 219
  Fuller's contribution to, 109–121
  reason in, 100
Social solidarity, 243
Social stratification, 264
  and collegial form, 243–254
Social systems, self-regulation of, 320n
Social theorists, 17–18, 40
Social theory
  critical, 89, 289n
  Habermas's, 291n
  Parsons's, 217–220, 223, 255, 295n, 308n,
    315n
    conceptual limitations and dilemma,
      226–227

radical, 89, 289n
Weber's, 41, 294n
Social unit
  absolutist critique of, 105
  actors' self-restriction within, 24–25. *See
    also* Self-restriction
  disordered, 23–24, 276n
  ordered, 23–24
  subjective interests with, 280n. *See also*
    Interest competition
Societal constitutionalism
  agenda for, 48–51
  agent of change for, 233
  conceptual grounding of, 123–128, 221
  vs. consensus theory, 243–249
  as critical theory, 15–17, 89
  foundations of, 121–130
  four analytical distinctions of, 54–56
  vs. functionalism's accounts of profession-
    als' motivations, 251–254
  vs. governmental constitutionalism, 57,
    232–233
  normative means of, 122–123
  vs. other non-Marxist theories, 221–222
  qualitative ends of, 128–130
  vs. symbolic interactionism, 249–251
  theory of, 7–8, 38, 66, 152–153, 204, 248–
    249, 321n
    comparative research informed by, 175–
      180
    conceptual foundations of, 17
    conceptual openness of, 220
    orienting hypothesis, 175
    presuppositions, 174–175
    and research, 274n
    synthesis of procedural duties and proce-
      dural aspiration, 127
    threshold of interpretability, characteris-
      tics of, 154–159
  vs. tradition, 77–83
Sociology. *See also* Weberian sociology
  postwar concerns of, 41
Sociology of law, Weber's, 71, 87–88, 286n,
    290n
Solidarity, 132, 272n–273n, 317n
  elite, 31–32
Solidarity Movement, 307n
South Africa, legal system of, 116, 295n
Sovereignty, monarch's versus constituent
    force's, 234
Soviet Union, legal system of, 116, 295n
Speech acts, 16, 102
Statistics, as distortions, 273n
Strategic action, 284n
Strict constructionism, 77
Structural equivalence, 307n, 317n
Structuration, 277n

Structuration theory, 174, 250, 278n
Subjective interests. *See also* Interest competition
balance of power between, 68
social contract theorist's reification of, 313n
sovereignty of, 67–68, 79–81, 108–110, 223–224
Substantive norms, shared, actors' supposed internalization of, 317n
Substantive rationality, 45, 225–227, 315n
Weber's concept of, 16–17, 282n
Substantive rationalization, 315n
Substantive reason, 258
Substantive restraints, 283n. *See also* Internal substantive restraints
extension of, 207–208
Surveillance, 297n
Survey research, 276n
and purposive-rational action, 136–137
Sweden, separation of church and state in, 207, 284n
Swedes, fetishization of hygiene, 300n
Symbolic interactionism, 72, 108, 147, 174, 216, 292n, 296n, 298n
vs. societal constitutionalism, 249–251
Symbolic means-end schema, 134–135
Systemic drift. *See* Drift
System integration, 277n
Systems theory, 32, 98
Lockean, 303n
Luhmann's, 89, 174, 278n, 319n

Talking clubs, 237–238. *See also* Bourgeois public (sphere)
Therapeutic critique, 125
Threshold of interpretability. *See also* Procedural threshold of interpretability of positive laws; Societal constitutionalism, threshold of interpretability
of internal procedural restraints, 111, 124–126, 154–159
Totalitarianism, 284n
Tradition, 224–226, 228–232
anachronism of, 77–79
analytical aspects of, available for transfer, 230
prospects for, 232–241
vs. societal constitutionalism, 77–83
substantive aspects of, transferred to new sites, 316n
as transferable, generalizable, and invariant in impact, 230–231
Tribal nationalism, 58
Truth. *See also* Consensus theory of truth; Copy theory of truth
procedural turn to, 99–101

United States
application of societal constitutionalism to, 311–312
authoritarianism in, 14–15, 275n
constitutional crisis in, 76–77
energy and health policy domains within, 285n
internal labor market in, 208
legal system of, 116, 295n
lower middle income groups in, 312n
postwar, 4
poverty in, 312n
Universalization thesis, Habermas's, 103
Universal pragmatics, Habermas's, 102
Universal syntactics, 102
University faculty, 322n
Urbanization, 202
Utilitarian dilemma, 43, 272n
Utilitarianism, 133
Utopianism, 308n, 322n

Value-commitments, 252–253, 320n
Value-neutrality, 216
Value-rational action, 45
Value relativism, social scientists', 214–215, 221, 223
Values, objective, 283n
Voluntaristic action, 17, 151, 220, 225, 298n, 308n
as central to conceptual schema, 148–149
as contingent institutions, 145–148
definition(s) of, 131, 133–134, 299n
differentiation of, in practice, 152–153
distinct concept of, 134–143
external procedural restraints as, 202–205
importance of, 131
institutionalization of, 145–148, 164
internal procedural restraints as, 196–202
in literature today, 133–134
vs. normative action, 144
Parsons's concept of, 90, 295n
and qualitative ends, 140–143
as restraint on drift, 144–145
substantive and procedural, differentiation of, 152
three meanings of, 144–149
Voluntaristic means-end schema, 134–135
Voluntaristic restraints
on arbitrary government, 198
bases of, 187–205
external procedural, 90, 202–205
institutionalization of, 198
internal procedural, 196–202
procedural vs. substantive, 302n
Voluntary authority, 279n

Wasted time and space, and external proce-
    dural restraints, 211–213, 314n
Weberian Dilemma, 79, 110, 114, 140, 145–
    146, 148, 153, 184–187, 222, 249
  Fuller's alternative to, 115–116
  as negative liberalism, 43–45
  resolution of, 46–51
Weberian pathos, vs. liberal complacency,
    43–44
Weberians, 71
  views of law, 71, 87–88, 286n, 290n
Weberian sociology, 293n
  limits of, 51–53
Welfare state, 33
  crises in, 278n
  Janowitz on, 28–29
  Luhmann on, 277n
Western democracy, 206, 221

authoritarianism in, 13–14
comparison to protection rackets, 3
conflict and struggles within, as policy de-
    bates, 35–36
criticisms of, 1, 3
encroachments against internal procedural
    restraints in, 198
institutions and practices of, 1–2, 271n
legitimation crisis of, 76, 92, 105, 126,
    290n
moralistic endorsement of, 272n
moral status of, 4–5
Western Europe, 5
  neocorporatism in, 73–75
Western institutions and traditions
  Habermas's absolutist critique of, 105
  pluralism as critique of, 72–73
  problems for, 75–77

Other books in the series

J. Milton Yinger, Kiyoshi Ikeda, Frank Laycock, and Stephen J. Cutler: *Middle Start: An Experiment in the Educational Enrichment of Young Adolescents*

James A. Geschwender: *Class, Race, and Worker Insurgency: The League of Revolutionary Black Workers*

Paul Ritterband: *Education, Employment, and Migration: Israel in Comparative Perspective*

John Low-Beer: *Protest and Participation: The New Working Class in Italy*

Orrin E. Klapp: *Opening and Closing: Strategies of Information Adaptation in Society*

Rita James Simon: *Continuity and Change: A Study of Two Ethnic Communities in Israel*

Marshall B. Clinard: *Cities with Little Crime: The Case of Switzerland*

Steven T. Bossert: *Tasks and Social Relationships in Classrooms: A Study of Instructional Organization and Its Consequences*

Richard E. Johnson: *Juvenile Delinquency and Its Origins: An Integrated Theoretical Approach*

David R. Heise: *Understanding Events: Affect and the Construction of Social Action*

Ida Harper Simpson: *From Student to Nurse: A Longitudinal Study of Socialization*

Stephen P. Turner: *Sociological Explanation as Translation*

Janet W. Salaff: *Working Daughters of Hong Kong: Filial Piety or Power in the Family?*

Joseph Chamie: *Religion and Fertility: Arab Christian–Muslim Differentials*

William Friedland, Amy Barton, and Robert Thomas: *Manufacturing Green Gold: Capital, Labor, and Technology in the Lettuce Industry*

Richard N. Adams: *Paradoxical Harvest: Energy and Explanation in British History, 1870–1914*

Mary F. Rogers: *Sociology, Ethnomethodology, and Experience: A Phenomenological Critique*

James R. Beniger: *Trafficking in Drug Users: Professional Exchange Networks in the Control of Deviance*

Andrew J. Weigert, J. Smith Teitge, and Dennis W. Teitge: *Society and Identity: Toward a Sociological Psychology*

Jon Miller: *Pathways in the Workplace: The Effects of Gender and Race on Access to Organizational Resources*

Michael A. Fala: *Dynamic Functionalism: Strategy and Tactics*

Joyce Rothschild and J. Allen Whitt: *The Co-operative Workplace: Potentials and Dilemmas of Organizational Democracy*

Russell Thornton: *We Shall Live Again: The 1870 and 1890 Ghost Dance Movements as Demographic Revitalization*

Severyn T. Bruyn: *The Field of Social Investment*

Guy E. Swanson: *Ego Defenses and the Legitimation of Behaviour*
Liah Greenfeld: *Different Worlds: A Sociological Study of Taste, Choice and Success in Art*
Thomas K. Rudel: *Situations and Strategies in American Land-Use Planning*
Percy C. Hintzen: *The Costs of Regime Survival: Racial Mobilization, Elite Domination and Control of the State in Guyana and Trinidad*
John T. Flint: *Historical Role Analysis in the Study of Religious Change: Mass Educational Development in Norway, 1740–1891*
Judith R. Blau: *The Shape of Culture: A Study of Cultural Patterns in the United States*
Fred C. Pampel and John B. Williamson: *Age, Class, Politics and the Welfare State*
Thomas J. Fararo: *The Meaning of General Theoretical Sociology: Tradition and Formalization*
Lewis F. Carter: *Control and Charisma in Rajneeshpuram: The Role of Shared Values in the Creation of a Community*
David M. Heer: *Undocumented Mexicans in the United States*
Kenneth Baugh, Jr.: *The Methodology of Herbert Blumer*